#100913-2

P9-CQI-679

"This truth-telling book brims with wisdom for every woman who sees injustice and asks herself 'What can I do?' Linda Silver Dranoff, a lifelong change agent, is the perfect role model for a new generation of feminists."

—RONA MAYNARD,
former Chatelaine *editor, author of* My Mother's Daughter

"A most extraordinary account of the women's movement in Canada through the last 60-plus years. Linda deserves so much recognition for her tremendous efforts in the evolution of the rights that women enjoy today."

—CLAIRE L'HEUREUX-DUBÉ,
retired justice of the Supreme Court of Canada

"*Fairly Equal* is a wonderful history of the challenges, the advocacy, and the progress that women in Ontario and Canada have made to achieve equality. Linda is an excellent storyteller, an activist, and an advocate. Her story is a must read and her achievements are amazing."

—ELINOR CAPLAN,
*former MPP, MP, and cabinet minister
(Liberal Party of Ontario and Canada)*

"Linda Silver Dranoff has that elusive 'it' factor when it comes to telling stories. They are invariably about the law, women's rights, and about her, and in fact about you. But she strings them all together in memorable, important (sometimes cheeky, sometimes hilarious) anecdotes that leave you smiling and way better informed and somehow bolder and kinder. Like her other books, this one is another Dranoff gem."

—SALLY ARMSTRONG,
journalist and human rights activist

"Women's rights activists beginning in the 1960s reshaped Canadian society—often in ways we now find imperceptible. From her role at centre stage, including in the struggle for family law reform, Linda Silver Dranoff writes a lively account of history in the making. She demonstrates convincingly that one person can indeed make a difference."

—SYLVIA BASHEVKIN,
professor, Department of Political Science, University of Toronto

A FEMINIST HISTORY SOCIETY BOOK

Fairly Equal

LAWYERING THE FEMINIST REVOLUTION

Linda Silver Dranoff

Second Story Press

Library and Archives Canada Cataloguing in Publication

Dranoff, Linda Silver, author
Fairly equal : lawyering the feminist revolution / by Linda Silver Dranoff.

(A feminist history society book)
Includes index.

Issued in print and electronic formats.
ISBN 978-1-77260-039-1 (hardback).–ISBN 978-1-77260-022-3 (paperback).
–ISBN 978-1-77260-023-0 (epub)

1. Dranoff, Linda Silver. 2. Lawyers–Canada–Biography. 3. Women
lawyers–Canada–Biography. 4. Feminists–Canada–Biography. 5. Women
social reformers–Canada–Biography. 6. Women–Legal status, laws, etc.–
Canada. 7. Women–Canada–Social conditions. 8. Women's rights–Canada–
History–20th century. I. Title. II. Series: Feminist History Society book

KE416.D73A3 2017   340.092   C2016-906968-0
KF345.Z9D73 2017   C2016-906969-9

Copyright © 2017 by Linda Silver Dranoff

Editor: Kathryn White
Cover design by Michel Vrana
Cover illustrations from iStockphoto.com
Book design by Melissa Kaita
Original series design by Zab Design & Typography

The author and publisher thank the *Toronto Star* for their kind permission to reproduce the
clippings, copyright © the *Toronto Star*, on pages 76, 126, 160, 217, 222, 248, 269, and 276.

Every effort has been made to secure permission and provide appropriate
credit for photographic material. The publisher deeply regrets any omission
and pledges to correct errors called to its attention in subsequent editions.

Printed and bound in Canada

*Second Story Press gratefully acknowledges the support of the
Ontario Arts Council and the Canada Council for the Arts for our
publishing program. We acknowledge the financial support of the
Government of Canada through the Canada Book Fund.*

ONTARIO ARTS COUNCIL
CONSEIL DES ARTS DE L'ONTARIO
an Ontario government agency
un organisme du gouvernement de l'Ontario

Canada Council   Conseil des Arts
for the Arts   du Canada

Funded by the Government of Canada
Financé par le gouvernement du Canada

Canada

Published by
Second Story Press
20 Maud Street, Suite 401
Toronto, ON M5V 2M5
www.secondstorypress.ca

This book is dedicated to all those who strive for a better world.
The future is in your hands.

CONTENTS

FOREWORD

This is a unique book and surprisingly difficult to introduce. It is an intensely personal memoir set in the era of second-wave feminism in Canada, and it is an historical account spanning many decades. Yet it is even more. It is, in the most profound sense of the word, a witness statement.

And what a witness. My good friend Linda Silver Dranoff is no bystander. She was—and she remains—a conscious participant. I have known her for many years, and we have been having wide-ranging conversations about life, feminism, and public policy since we first met some thirty years ago, when we both served on the Advisory Board of Women in Educational Administration Ontario. I have seen this civically conscious woman, combining her profound personal convictions with uncompromising professional competence, spearhead change that advanced women's lives in crucial ways. In fact, one of the remarkable aspects of Linda's life was the unity between her professional and civic life—she was a lawyer and writer, a mother, a member of a family and community, and an activist, all at once.

The world in which Linda grew up and later decided to enter law school was vastly different from the one in which we live today. In those days of restricted opportunities and expectations, women rarely became lawyers—especially not one who was divorced and a mother. There was almost no publicly available child care, discrimination against women flourished, and job opportunities were limited.

Many of the changes that Linda's work helped enact are now "normal" parts of Canadian life—so much so that students of my students find it difficult to imagine a Canada before laws required equal sharing of assets accumulated during a marriage, or maternity leave, or pension sharing, or pay equity, or the availability of divorce. For those who did not live through these times—and for many of us who did—this book will serve as a vital reminder of the magnitude of social change this country has experienced over the past decades, change that includes enormous and beneficial shifts in family law, an improved attitude toward women's equality, and laws to ensure that positive changes can be maintained.

Even more striking is the way in which many of these changes occurred. As a lawyer and writer, Linda elucidated the inequities facing women and knew what had to be done to resolve them. The fact that she was able to inspire others to join her in the fight—be they members of the legal system, politicians, or like-minded men and women from all walks of life—speaks volumes about her determination, her sense of fairness and justice, and her tenacity. Working on her own and with others, she convinced the "establishment" of the day to recognize and lighten the burdens of unfairness, injustice, and inequality, primarily, but by no means exclusively, on women. By working to improve the lives of women, she chose to be a catalyst for the betterment of all, and she demonstrated what one person can do, even seemingly against all odds.

It is perhaps this unique quality that made others respond to Linda in the way they did. Her influential columns in *Chatelaine* were written from a wish to share her knowledge and perspective. She could imagine herself in the place of the reader who needed to understand the legal realities. Her letters to the editor, written to influence policy-makers and public opinion, not only became treasures for the women's movement but also examples of the competence and thrust that made them publishable and quotable.

Shining through the text like a light behind illuminated pages is Linda's enduring love for Canada and her profound concern with our country's standards of justice and fairness. We owe her a debt of gratitude, not only for the contributions she has made to the well-being of Canadians, women and men alike, but also for the diligent record-keeping that allows all of us to now share some of

her views and accomplishments. The clarity of the record and, through it, its lucid authenticity, is an important aspect of this book.

Ursula Franklin addressing the gathering after receiving the FLAC Award for Commitment to Equality, 2007

Today, in a public environment of modulated and mediated communications, it is important to emphasize that this book is, in the most rigorous sense of the term, an eyewitness statement. Linda was directly involved in all the issues about which she writes, and she takes us behind the scenes in the struggle for change. The praxis of "bearing witness" is the underlying theme—the leitmotif—of the book; for Linda, being an eyewitness means being a participant in word and deed.

The book concludes with an important set of reflections. Under the banner "Over to You," Linda summarizes her legacy, her advice, and the core of her insights. By being resolutely centred in a viable Canadian nationalism—rooted in the history and practices of our country without being intentionally discriminatory or judgmental—the historical roots of Canadian institutions and attitudes are clearly part and parcel of what Linda hands on to the next generation of feminists.

Building on her own unrepentant identification as a feminist, Linda reaffirms her belief in the strength of the community of women, a community that has room for individual forward-looking initiatives, while simultaneously maintaining the fundamental connectedness and sisterhood among all women.

Notwithstanding change and adaptation, the personal remains political, and the political demands personal commitment and active intervention. Linda's words are a reminder of this fact, and an inspiration for all women.

Ursula M. Franklin, CC, FRSC
Ursula M. Franklin, Companion of the Order of Canada, Member of the Royal Society of Canada, University Professor Emerita at the University of Toronto, long-time active Canadian citizen and feminist, and Board member of Voice of Women for Peace.

Introduction
THE WAY IT WAS

I was born into a world where women were still, as they had been through much of human history, defined by their role in the family—as daughter, sister, wife, mother. Find a man, fit into his life, and get your status, satisfaction, and financial support by caring for husband and family. That's what was instilled into us. But the financial security promised to a woman was difficult to enforce, and if a woman did not behave according to societal norms, she could lose her children and become an outcast. In this culture, independence was an alien word for women. The word *equality* was rarely whispered, either in society or in the context of the relationship between a man and a woman. Patriarchy had put women in our place throughout history—it was still that way when I was growing up in Toronto in the 1950s.

The prevailing culture was backed up by tradition and enforced by law. It wasn't just that a woman's reproductive powers were subject to her husband's control; the sale and advertising of contraceptive devices was banned and breach of the law could bring a penalty of up to two years in jail. Most women wouldn't know that only the advertising prohibition was enforced.[1] Abortion was a criminal offence,[2] and women with no other choice endangered their lives and health by having what was termed a "back-alley abortion" using the services of often ill-trained practitioners in unsanitary settings.

A husband and wife were considered "one person" in law— the husband. This concept of the legal unity of husband and wife allowed a man to control his wife in every respect. It also permitted a husband to discipline his wife or even rape her. Wife abuse was ignored, as if it did not exist. Women were expected to be known by their husband's surname.

Divorce was rare and hard to get. There was no divorce available on the simple grounds of separation—matrimonial misconduct such as adultery or cruelty was a prerequisite.[3] Husbands controlled the purse strings, property, any pension, and the children. A woman might lose support rights if she did not remain chaste. Her husband could sue his wife's lover for "criminal conversation"—compensation for injury to his feelings and property. If she tried to leave, there were few shelters, and anyone who took her in could be charged as a criminal for "harbouring" her.

Married women were discouraged by custom and in some cases by law from engaging in outside employment. For example, in 1941 fewer than 4 percent of married women were employed.[4] It was not until 1955 that married women were eligible to be employed in the federal civil service. Once pregnant, a woman almost always left paid employment, partly because of societal assumptions that mothers had to raise their own children and partly because there were few other options. There was almost no publicly supported child care. There were no laws protecting women from discrimination in employment. Women who worked, whether married or single, could *legally* be paid less, never mind be overlooked for promotion or even fired if a man needed the job. Most women who worked were doing "women's work" and weren't helped by the first of the equal pay laws in the early 1950s, which asserted that women should be paid equally for doing the very same work that men did. While there was, however, protective legislation dealing primarily with safety and working conditions for women, it was considered by some to be a mixed blessing. For instance, all women used to be excluded from hazardous occupations such as mining, even if a particular woman was able to do the work.[5]

Few women were in politics, and government policy-makers mostly overlooked issues of concern to women. In 1921, Agnes Macphail was the first woman elected to the House of Commons in the first election held after the right of women to run for office came into existence, and she served there until 1940. She came to see herself as representing and acting for the women of Canada and was criticized for it.[6] Only five women were elected to the federal parliament before 1950.[7] It was not until 1957 that the first woman was appointed to the federal cabinet—Ellen Fairclough as secretary of state in the Progressive Conservative cabinet of John Diefenbaker.

Citizenship rights were inconsistent. On the one hand, women had secured the right to vote, and they hoped that this would allow their interests to be heard by those in power. Starting in 1918, when the government of Canada passed "An Act to Confer the Electoral Franchise upon Women," women across Canada got the right to vote in federal elections. Manitoba was the first province, in 1916, to grant women the right to vote in provincial elections, and in 1940, Quebec was the last.[8] But not every woman was permitted to vote; there were race restrictions on the federal right to vote—on Asian Canadians until 1948, Inuit until 1950, and First Nations until 1960.[9] However, women took their citizenship status from husbands or fathers, and children took it from their fathers.[10] And until the 1950s, women were generally not allowed to sit on juries. There were no human rights protections against discrimination.[11]

A woman lawyer was a rarity.[12] In 1951, there were 197 women lawyers in Canada out of a total of 9,038—about 2 percent. They were not represented on governing bodies, and the few there were had no protection from openly admitted discrimination.[13]

There had been some modest inroads prior to the 1950s. Women were needed during World War II to work the jobs of men who had gone overseas. They were actively encouraged to work outside the home, in jobs where they felt appreciated and independent. Moreover, they were helped with the care of their children—day nurseries were established to free women for employment. When the war ended, returning male veterans were legally entitled to displace women from their jobs. Many women obediently returned to be homemakers, and the wartime day nurseries were closed. Some were not ready to return home and continued to work outside the home. By 1951, 11.2 percent of married women were employed outside the home.[14]

Women benefited from the efforts of the early women activists such as Nellie McClung, Emily Murphy, Irene Parlby, Louise McKinney, and Henrietta Edwards who individually were forces in their communities for the rights of women.[15] Together, they were known as the "Famous Five." In the 1920s, they had contested the fact that women were not defined as "persons" in Canadian law and took their case to the final appellate court for Canada—at that time, the Judicial Committee of the Privy Council of the House of Lords in England, where the battle was won in 1929. That challenge confirmed the interpretation of "person" in Canadian laws to include women, and it opened the path to the appointment of the first woman senator, Cairine Wilson, which in turn paved the way for further advances in the legal treatment of women.

Women were helped by the efforts of the early women's clubs that were sowing the seeds of change.[16] For example, well before the 1950s, unbeknownst to me and many others at the time, the National Council of Women (NCW, founded in 1893) and the Canadian Federation of Business and Professional Women's Clubs (BPW, founded in 1930) were lobbying the federal cabinet annually to advance the political and economic status of women.[17] Lawyer Margaret Hyndman was the national president of BPW from 1946 to 1948, during which time it successfully protested the open discrimination against women by the federal government when it advertised for men only to fill certain jobs. The BPW played a leading role in obtaining the right for women to serve on juries and achieving the first—albeit inadequate—equal pay laws.[18] They lobbied successfully to establish the Women's Bureau of the federal Department of Labour, which gathered and disseminated information and statistics on all facets of women's employment.[19] The founding director in 1954 was Marion Royce. Sylva Gelber, who served as director from 1968 to 1975, was ahead of her time when, in 1969, she stated publicly that perhaps the time had come for housewives to "insist on a value…being placed on the unpaid domestic services they provide."[20]

A significant medical advance was on the horizon to give women greater control over childbirth. During the 1950s, scientists were working on the development of "the pill," which became available on prescription in 1961. Brave doctors like Dr. Marion Powell, following the lead of Dr. Elizabeth Bagshaw, had made birth control available by establishing clinics, notwithstanding the criminal law that still prevented them from doing so.[21] But a pill to manage reproduction was ground-breaking.

Individual activists and the women's organizations had started the drive for women's rights. Even with these efforts, patriarchy still prevailed, and women were not considered equal to men. That's just how it was.

Increasing numbers of women became aware that it did not have to be that way. Constraints on the expression of women's full humanity were not right. By the late 1960s, this was termed "consciousness-raising," and women participated in various ways, both in our own lives and in deciding how to be part of a growing movement.

In 1960 the first of the modern women's groups was founded. The non-partisan Voice of Women (VOW—later called the Voice of Women for Peace) was founded in response to a column in the *Toronto Star* by journalist Lotta Dempsey. She pointed out the failure of the Paris Summit Conference on Disarmament and challenged women to *do something*. She received an enthusiastic response in the formation of VOW, which by the fall of 1961 had five thousand members. VOW was active initially and primarily in peace issues, but evolved to also become active in other women's issues of the day. Ursula Franklin, Kay Macpherson, and Muriel Duckworth— pacifists and feminists all—were some of the founders and leaders of this peace movement.[22] VOW was also active in other women's issues, including the campaign to achieve a Royal Commission on the Status of Women.

It was Laura Sabia, when she was president of the Canadian Federation of University Women, who gathered a number of women's groups together to form the Committee on Equality for Women (CEW) and led the drive for the establishment of the Royal Commission on the Status of Women. In Quebec, Thérèse Casgrain[23] was a leader of the Quebec women's movement for suffrage, achieving the right to vote in 1940. She also founded the Quebec wing of Voice of Women and the Fédération des femmes du Québec (FFQ), which joined forces with the CEW to press for the Royal Commission.[24] All these efforts set the stage and sowed the seeds for the continuing campaign for women's rights. By the late 1960s and throughout the 1970s, many women came on the scene, in hope and sisterhood, in what has been called "the second wave of feminism."

We found there was a great deal of work to be done. Family laws were still stuck in the past—property and pension sharing, spousal and child support, and custody and access to children were in great need of improvement. Reproductive rights were critical—not only the right to have choices over child-bearing but even the opportunity to have a midwife in attendance. Criminal laws were of little help to victims of rape and other crimes, and women who were abused had little recourse to shelters and legal assistance. Employment laws were inadequate to provide equitable pay and work opportunities, protection from sexual harassment, and protection against discrimination in employment.

While women started joining the workforce in greater numbers, they came up against these systemic inequities and discriminatory attitudes. Work was still identified as "women's work" and "men's work," and women did not have many opportunities or rates of pay equivalent to the men's. Even those women who broke into men's fields faced barriers. For example, journalists were confined to the women's sections of newspapers. Some became pioneering editors, columnists, reporters, and feature writers and revealed the scope and systemic nature of the discrimination against women—such as magazine editors Doris Anderson and Sally Armstrong, columnists and reporters Michele Landsberg, June Callwood, Penney Kome, Judith Finlayson, Rosemary Speirs, Margaret Weiers, and others.

Women were enrolling in universities and then becoming leaders in women's education, like Pauline Jewett, the first female president of a co-ed university in Canada, when she became president of Simon Fraser University in 1974, followed by Margaret Fulton as president of Mount Saint Vincent University in 1978. Professors started the first consciousness-raising women's studies programs,[25] among them, Naomi Black at York University. Historians concentrated on telling and writing about women's history, including Veronica Strong-Boag. Political science professors such as Sylvia Bashevkin and Jill Vickers taught and wrote about women and politics. Women became government bureaucrats and brought their focus on the role of women where they could; for example, Elaine Todres and Glenna Carr in Ontario, and Sylva Gelber and Sylvia Ostry in the federal civil service. Women studied medicine, despite quotas in many schools on the number of women accepted, and in the process some focused on health issues specific to women or went into politics, such as Dr. Bette Stephenson and Dr. Carolyn Bennett. Women such as Adrienne Clarkson, Dini Petty, Betty Kennedy, Barbara Frum, and Marilyn Denis took roles in broadcasting, initially limited to daytime shows focused on women's interests. Women artists such as Helen Lucas, Joyce Wieland, Jean Townsend, and Maryon Kantaroff, and authors such as Margaret Atwood brought feminist perspectives to the arts and literature.

Women also ran for public office.[26] By 1979, there were ten women elected to the federal House of Commons—four each from Ontario and Quebec and two from British Columbia—the largest contingent until then. They included Flora MacDonald, Pauline Jewett, Margaret Mitchell, Jeanne Sauvé, and Monique Bégin. Women were entering other fields as well—science, engineering, religion, publishing, the corporate and banking world, and more.

And then there was the law. When women became lawyers, we realized that our skills and training could be used to improve the lives of all women, from all backgrounds and levels of vulnerability. We believed we were in a unique position because the law affected so many areas of society and so many of the issues affecting women—in family law, employment, human rights, criminal law, and more. Discrimination touched everyone—it was systemic. Lawyers could try to reinterpret the law that existed by taking forward precedent-setting cases; they could lobby for changes to improve the situation, or teach, or write books; they could work in clinics to help the less fortunate; or they could become judges. We had the education and the tools and many of us saw it as our duty to contribute in ways that would help to achieve equality for women.

We were everywhere in Canada and in many legal specialties. Some were constitutional lawyers, such as Beverley Baines and Mary Eberts (Ontario), Lynn Smith (British Columbia), Eloise Spitzer (Yukon); some were employment and labour lawyers, for example, Mary Cornish, Elizabeth Shilton, and Beth Symes (Ontario); some worked in human rights, such as Barbara Hall (Ontario), Yvonne Peters (Saskatchewan), and Eve Roberts (Newfoundland and Labrador). Others, like Judith Huddart and me, were family lawyers, including Carole Curtis and Shirley Greenberg (Ontario). Others were academics, such as Constance Backhouse and Mary

Jane Mossman (Ontario) and Kathleen Mahoney (Alberta). Many became judges, including Rosalie Silberman Abella (Ontario), Flora Buchan (Nova Scotia), Sheilah Martin (Alberta), Freda Steel (Manitoba), Juanita Westmoreland-Traoré (Quebec). Mary Lou Fassel was one of those who spent her career helping women who suffered violence.

Lorna Marsden, who had been a Canadian senator, president of Wilfrid Laurier University from 1992 to 1997 and then of York University from 1997 to 2007, and active in the Canadian Women's Movement, aptly summarized our role when she wrote that women lawyers

> led a type of social change different from the others. It is change brought about by a group of experts from a powerful occupational group educating and mobilizing women and men to create a broad social movement.... The women lawyers played a crucial role in these years by educating women about the opportunities and limitations of the laws in Canada. The process of law in the legislatures, both provincial and federal and in the courts, are very complex. The logic of law is not intuitive to the thinking of most citizens.[27]

I have mentioned particular women whom I knew or knew of, but there were so many others as well, those who lived and worked in other parts of Canada, and indeed around the world. Fortunately, others have written valuable accounts of the women and issues of second-wave feminism.[28] You will also meet many of these activists in the course of this book as our paths crossed and as I set my own experiences within the broader context. We were all part of the groundswell that became the feminist movement. We wanted to change the status quo for ourselves and for others. Our goal was to achieve real equality for women within the family, the workplace, and in public policy decisions and bring a feminist perspective to Canadian culture and society.

This book is my contribution to the record of second-wave feminism in Canada. It is my personal account of my own lived experiences that drew me to feminism, and the experiences that raised my awareness of the difficulties that women encountered. To me, feminism means a search for equality, which embodies fairness for everyone. Every legal case I took on, the books and columns I wrote, the public policy issues with which I was involved, taught me about the search for justice, the need for equity, and the ongoing unfortunate gap between reality and equality. I tried to narrow that gap wherever and whenever I could. I am starting this book where I began—growing up in the 1950s—because it is important to understand just how different life for women was back then, and the path that led me—as one example—to surmount the cultural expectations of that era. I figured if I was going to tell you what I did, I had better tell you where I came from. While family law was my main focus in both my professional life and my lobbying efforts, I was involved in many of the feminist and public policy issues of the day as an activist, lawyer, and writer. In the process I learned a great deal from my experiences and from my feminist colleagues about how to build a consensus to transform a society resistant to change.

I am writing this for feminists—egalitarian women and men—of the present and future. Knowing what we faced, what we achieved, and how easily it can be taken away hopefully will encourage vigilance and sisterhood and solidarity in those who follow us. It doesn't have to be the way it was.

PART 1

FINDING MY WAY

Chapter 1
LESSONS FROM CHILDHOOD

There was no way to predict my life's evolution. As a child, I was not even aware that women had a subordinate status in society. I just knew that very little was expected of us beyond fulfilling our roles in the family. Women were not destined to obtain a university education, have a professional career, or seek the opportunity to contribute to social change. Certainly none of this was imaginable for me. In any event, I did not know of any woman lawyer in my community or in public life who might have served as a role model or mentor or inspiration.

My mother once asked me in wonderment, "Where did you come from?" My parents definitely had traditional expectations for me, and they never expected nor took credit for what I did. But I have come to appreciate how much I owe to them, to the circumstances of my youth, and to the people and forces that had such an instrumental role in shaping the person I would become.

Being born in Canada as a third-generation Canadian was my first stroke of good luck. Both sets of grandparents had fled Poland's anti-Semitic pogroms, arriving in Toronto in 1907. They were poor immigrants with large families (we ended up with twenty-four cousins), and their children had to leave school early to help earn income. Both of my parents went to work after completing grade eight, although my dad found a way to finish grade eleven at night school.

After marrying in 1932, during the depths of the Great Depression, my parents had four children, two girls and two boys.

I was the second oldest, but my formative years were spent as the middle child between my two brothers, Marty and Stevie. My sister, Judy, was born later, at a time when I was old enough to help out, and I adored "mothering" my loveable younger sister. I was a classic middle child, mediating disputes between members of the family. It was excellent training for a law career. I remember the times my mother would ask me to "talk to Stevie" or "intervene with Marty" or "help Judy." The environment at our home was benign, and kindness and courtesy were expected. I imagine myself as a seed planted in fertile and healthy soil and left to blossom. My parents never put me down, never questioned the intelligence of my views and thoughts; they only emphasized the positive. This helped me to eventually find my own way.

I attended high school in Toronto in the 1950s, a place and a time when girls—at that time, young women were identified as "girls"—were still discouraged from higher education and full-time employment after marriage. It might be overlooked that she worked part-time for extra money once her children were attending school. If she was single and wanted a career, the best she could aim for was to be a secretary, teacher, or nurse, none of which required a university education. Many young women married right out of high school and presumed they would be financially supported by a husband and behave as dependants, putting husbandly needs ahead of their own. In return, we were encouraged by the prevailing culture to hide our brains, make the man feel that all good ideas came from him, and to value appearance ahead of other virtues and talents. We were to bear and raise children, and if we had the good fortune to go to university, it was primarily for what was jokingly (but in all seriousness) called an "MRS" degree—that is, access to marriageable men.

It is not at all surprising, then, that I felt compelled to marry by the time I was twenty-one or risk being scorned as an "old maid." I also felt bound to be a "good girl" until then. Good girls did not have sex before marriage—a girl's virginity "belonged" to her husband. This message was everywhere. This was part of the legal premise that a woman was her husband's "property," and this was the main reason that sex before marriage was portrayed as wrong. Of course, there was also the significant risk of pregnancy. The birth control pill had not yet been invented, and no one I knew would chance (or admit to) going to a doctor to be fitted for a diaphragm.

How far we were from the coming sexual revolution of the 1960s and 70s! The movies of the day reinforced these messages about the role of women and had a big impact. The 1948 film *The Red Shoes*—in which a ballerina forced to choose between marriage and a career picked suicide instead—told women that we certainly couldn't "have it all," at least not in the way that men did. *The Detective Story*—a 1951 film in which a woman who has undergone a "back alley" abortion is called a tramp and abandoned by her husband—warned that sex before marriage puts a girl in jeopardy either for an unwanted pregnancy or a risky abortion, and makes her unmarriageable. That's how the cultural expectations that developed over centuries were decoded when I was growing up.

Nothing my parents said or did contradicted these messages, but at the same time, they had ideas that did not precisely mirror the culture and expectations of the 1950s. Perhaps it was their immigrant background; perhaps it was their moral and common sense. They expected all their children to learn a skill and acquire an education that would enable us to make a living. The message to me as the eldest female was more limited: in accordance with the times, the expectation was that I would marry and have a family. Even so, I was told that I needed something "to fall back on." My mother assumed I would follow in her footsteps and become a typist, as this had served her well.

I also learned from watching my parents. They had a happy married life. They behaved respectfully toward each other and were true partners—including when it came to sharing the financial rewards of the marriage. I assumed it was this way for everyone. Later, as a family lawyer, I came to learn otherwise.

Despite their many traditional hopes and dreams for me, my parents were quite untraditional in ways that clearly left a mark. Contrary to the prevailing mood of the day, my mother continued to work outside the home after she married—it was the Great Depression and they needed her income because, at that time, my father earned much less than she did. She enjoyed her work and was a world-class typist, with awards from both Underwood and Remington, the leading typewriter manufacturers. She typed 115 words a minute accurately on a manual typewriter, a remarkable accomplishment at a time when fifty words a minute was standard. But when she took salaried jobs, other staff came to resent her because employers would expect everyone to produce work at her speed. She cleverly figured out a better—and more profitable—working arrangement. She asked to be paid by the piece, typing individual envelopes and letters for mass mailings. As a result she earned an entrepreneurial twenty-five dollars a week, much more than a salaried typist could make at that time.

In the 1930s, most employers did not permit women to work after they married, so my mother chose not to announce her new marriage at her workplace. Three years later, she became pregnant. If married women were not permitted to work, they *certainly* were not allowed to work while pregnant. Even so, she kept her job until just before the pregnancy was starting to show, and then asked for a leave of absence due to an unexplained illness. She offered one of her younger sisters as a temporary replacement and assured her employer that she would train her. The employer agreed; my mother was bright and capable, and they wanted her back. My mother resigned only after her sister was an accepted member of the staff. Her sister, who remained single, kept the job for the rest of her working life. Mum would say that the only thing she lost out on was a wedding gift and a goodbye party. (She returned to outside employment once her youngest child was able to walk to and from school alone.)

My father always expressed pride in my mother's abilities. He had no "male ego" to protect. In fact, he had been proud of his own mother's capacity to raise a family by running a rooming house with only a modest contribution from her husband (a house painter). I took it for granted at the time, but later realized how lucky I was in that era to have a father who could accept an accomplished woman. He had a strong, accomplished mother, which enabled him to marry a strong, accomplished wife and raise strong, accomplished daughters.

Dad was a salesman in the garment industry. He worked at home, mostly at the dining room table, when he wasn't visiting customers. He sold buttons, laces, and other fashion accessories, but he would say that he really sold "ideas." He would visit garment manufacturers with concepts and suggestions for how his wares could enhance their designs, and he became a leading salesman in the industry. By choice, he worked on commission rather than salary. He used to tell me about his experiences working for others, instances when he was treated unfairly or taken advantage of, and he would usually comment that "it's better to be your own boss." His message wasn't lost on me.

I also learned from keeping my eyes open and taking in the world around me. In the early 1950s, the Army–McCarthy hearings in the United States were playing out in real time on our radios and (relatively new) television sets. I recall being frightened by the image of Senator Joseph McCarthy challenging people for their alleged ties to communism. (I can still remember the livid expression on his face as he hit a table and yelled, "Point of order!") People lost their jobs because of his often-unproven allegations. I also heard news reports about the Rosenbergs, an American husband and wife who were charged, convicted, and given the death penalty for alleged treason against the United States. I gleaned enough information from the Canadian news reports to suspect that the charges against them may not have been true. Even at the relatively young age of twelve, I could not understand why there was so much unfairness in the world.

My reading selections at the time did nothing to dampen my burgeoning sense of social justice. I was an avid reader, and by age ten I had charged through all the books in the children's section of the nearby Wychwood Public Library. I took my reading life in my own hands and persuaded the children's librarian to allow me access to the adult books; she led me up the winding back stairs to the second-floor adult reading room and tried to find a book that she thought might not be too grown-up for me. She hesitated when I picked up Victor Hugo's *Les Misérables* but reluctantly let me borrow it. I was outraged at the punishment meted out to Jean Valjean for stealing a loaf of bread and shocked that his society thought this acceptable. I could imagine myself there, in that time and place, sharing my bread. I remember reading everything written by Baroness Orczy describing the adventures of the heroic and daredevil Scarlet Pimpernel, who helped people escape the excesses of the French Revolution.

My ideas about fairness—or its absence—were no doubt also fuelled by my parents' strong sense of right and wrong. Following World War II, they rented the two-room suite in our house to a young couple who could not find a place to live because they were of Japanese ancestry. At that time, Japanese Canadians were often treated as enemies, even though they'd had nothing to do with the war overseas in which Japan was involved. The women who had styled my mother's hair and cut and washed my long hair since I was five years old were just Verna and Averil to me for the longest time. When I reached my teens it suddenly occurred to me to ask whether they were Negroes, as Blacks were called then. My mother answered my question with a simple "Yes." I have always been grateful that she accepted differences among people as if she were unaware of them. And the Workmen's Circle—a centre for secular Jewish thinking that worked for the preservation of Yiddish as a living language, for social justice, and for a better world—was a part of our lives. My siblings and I attended their after-school programs and summer camp to learn the language, culture, and history of the Jewish people. We put on plays by Jewish storytellers and sang songs of social protest. I still can recall the tears-invoking power of the Partisan Hymn from the 1943 Warsaw Ghetto Uprising. We learned about the horrors and injustices of the Holocaust from teachers who had survived its evils.

My dad was for many years on the board of the Bureau of Jewish Education and a member of the Canadian Jewish Congress. He would come home and describe what happened at the meetings he attended. He seemed never to be afraid to stand up and challenge the status quo or ask the questions no one else was ready to ask. I think I came to emulate him without even realizing it.

· · · · · · · · ·

And so there was the beginning of my good luck—a peaceful childhood in Canada; a society with low expectations for women but parents with modern ideas of their own; a growing anger at injustice. I had no idea at the time what specific direction my life would take, but I assumed I would live a traditional life, focused on family. It took me quite some time to sort it out and find my way.

Chapter 2
COMING OF AGE

If you'd picked a moment during grade nine or ten and asked me or my parents whether I was university bound, the answer almost surely would have been no. This was not just because I was female. I did not really hit my stride academically until grade eleven.

In elementary school, I was such an indifferent pupil that my parents planned to send me to Central High School of Commerce for secretarial and bookkeeping courses. But I wanted to go to an academic high school—Oakwood Collegiate—like my brother Marty did. I didn't see why his path should not also be mine. My parents agreed, but on two conditions. If I did not succeed within two years, I would transfer to a one-year commercial "crash" course. I also had to learn typing.

At first, I did not thrive at Oakwood. I was stymied by grade ten geometry, low marks in typing, and my inadequate effort overall. In grade ten, the principal summoned my father and me to his office. I pleaded for one more year at Oakwood—and to drop typing, as it was bringing down my average. My father acquiesced, but when we arrived home we felt my mother's wrath. She thought I was reducing my options and insisted that I would still have to teach myself how to type. To encourage this, she refused to type my school assignments, as she was doing for my brothers—*they* weren't expected to become typists. My parents also agreed that I would have only one more year—grade eleven—to show some academic ability. In grade eleven, I stood fourth in my class—to my delight and my parents' astonishment. They allowed me to finish high school (which then ended at grade thirteen) at Oakwood.

Grade eleven was a positive year on other fronts as well. For the first time, I became involved in extra-curricular activities. My friend Jay Waterman did not seem to think like the other boys did; he encouraged me to join him at a discussion group at *Citizens' Forum*.[29] He also emboldened me to be part of the public speaking club and other intellectually oriented activities, all of which interested and challenged me. Without his support, I am not sure I would have had the confidence to do this. Public speaking and debating made me so nervous that I couldn't fathom why I persisted. I do remember that I eventually decided it was good for me, as I vaguely thought I would need the skill "someday." It never occurred to me that I would end up speaking out about women's rights and law reforms, and on behalf of clients.

I was elected to the student council in a year when a school fair was a major item on the agenda. The students wanted to run a certain kind of fair; however, the vice principal (who sat in on our meetings) vetoed our plans. Jay and I were outraged. Jay proposed a motion, which I seconded, to abolish the student council on the basis that it was undemocratic. We lost the vote, with only two in our favour (ours), but I look back fondly on this as an early act of fearless rebellion against unfairness.

There were other signs of my future self in these years. Then, as now, I got involved in everything. By the time I graduated high school, I had worked on the school newspaper, was class representative on the student council, participated in the current events club, and was selected by my classmates to be grade thirteen class president, president of the school's *Citizens' Forum* group, president of the public speaking and debating club, and head of our school's delegation to the student UN Model Assembly. I even joined the drama group and portrayed Mrs. Hardcastle in the school's production of Oliver Goldsmith's *She Stoops to Conquer*. High school was certainly good for me. It provided opportunities to dig deep and develop talents I wouldn't otherwise have known I had.

UNIVERSITY BOUND

Growing confidence and my brother Marty's plan to go on to university started me thinking that it should be possible for me too. My parents went along with me. I had grown and developed far beyond what they or I had anticipated. I completed high school with a 72.3 average—a good B+ mark at that time. When I revealed my marks to my very surprised mother, she asked, "Why don't you go to medical school?" I laughed at the irony, given the pressure she had once put on me to go for secretarial studies, but I demurred by noting I lacked both the science subjects and the talent for medicine. As I look back now, I am awed that she was even open to that possibility in 1957. Given the limited opportunities for her and her sisters and nieces, it was surprising that the thought even entered her mind— yet another example of how my parents were flexible enough to see that there might be so much more waiting for me out in the world.

So despite the lack of expectations and the long time it took for me to show the ability to succeed at school, I went to university after all. When I entered the University of Toronto's University College in September 1957, I *knew* how fortunate I was, not just because I was a late-bloomer, but also because few had the chance. Even our high school teachers had cautioned us that only about 5 percent of the university-eligible population were admitted. Among those, even fewer women than men were accepted, and there were almost no female professors or graduate students. I later came to understand how the demographics worked in my favour—and in favour of my siblings, too. All of us went to university; my brother Marty ended up in law, my brother Steve in dentistry, and my sister Judy in psychology. Universities in the 1950s had room; it was only the later surge of "baby boomer" births after World War II that created more competition for places. And it was financially feasible to attend as long as I could earn enough in part-time jobs to pay the tuition and expenses. My recollection is that it cost about $250 a year, something I could (and did) earn through part-time jobs and summer employment—working in the university library, teaching at a synagogue school, and camp jobs.

I was the first girl in my family to attend university, and I made the most of the opportunity. I lived at home, as most of us did at that time; I stayed at school most days until evening—at classes, in the library, participating in extra-curricular activities, and doing part-time jobs to earn money.

I took a variety of humanities and social science courses in my first year. When it came time to choose a major for second year, I preferred philosophy, but my practical father intervened. He suggested I study something that I could teach in high school. He added that being a teacher would fit into family life, as I could be home after school and in the summers. This made sense to him, and to me—as a skill I could "fall back on" to earn a living.

I made the decision to major in history, which I had enjoyed in high school. The University of Toronto history department featured professors who were the leading historians of the day, including Donald Creighton, Maurice Careless, Ramsay Cook, and John Saywell. The university offered either a three-year BA or a four-year Honours BA; the Honours BA was the prerequisite for a Type A certificate in teaching, which would have allowed me to become a high school department head. And so the decision was made. I received an outstanding education in the relatively small classes and didn't even notice that there were no women professors and no courses in women's history—the absence of women was just part of the fabric of life.

The most challenging project I undertook was a work of original research for John Saywell's fourth-year seminar course in Canadian history. My interest in social justice led me to study Adrien Arcand, the homegrown French-Canadian fascist who had flourished in the Quebec governed by Premier Maurice Duplessis, who was in power between 1936 and 1939 and again from 1944 to 1959. My paper ended up being about a hundred pages. My mother typed the final version for me, sitting at her typewriter in the dining room while I wrote and revised upstairs in my bedroom. This was the only time she typed for me, making an exception to the notice she'd given me that long-ago day in grade ten when I had dropped the typing course against her wishes. I received a good mark, which meant to Professor Saywell that the paper was worthy of publication. Even so, I lacked the confidence and connections to know how to do so, so it languished in my drawer.

While most of the other history students were male, they were usually friendly. I don't recall any particular event or statement that would have made me feel a victim of discrimination as a woman. That is all the more reason I was astounded to discover, almost fifty years later, that there was a "men only" history club—The Historical Club—and that the female students had been excluded. The revelation surfaced on a TV program that I was watching in 2007 featuring Adrienne Clarkson, the former governor general of Canada, who, it turns out, attended the University of Toronto at the same time as I did. Since then, I've learned that the male history students gained the advantage of meeting and being hosted by the business and political elite of the day.[30]

Despite this unnoticed discrimination, my years at university were wonderful. I met many interesting people, had more fun than ever before, and grew intellectually. I learned a great deal from my involvement in extra-curricular activities. I was (and remain) deeply interested in public policy. The process of creating positive change in society was fascinating. Although I never joined the party, I participated in the progressive CCF[31] campus club and was given the opportunity—although only a first-year student and a "girl" to boot—to speak at a campus party convention. I was too inexperienced to realize how unfortunate I was to be placed on the agenda immediately after David Lewis, the leader of the federal party and a brilliant orator. His voice, his phrasing, his ability to simplify the issues was so impressive—the audience was enthralled with him and showed it. They were still basking in the afterglow when I tried valiantly to get their attention. Watching and listening to him taught me some valuable lessons about public speaking, and from then on, I was acutely aware of the order of placement in any program in which I was asked to take part.

I participated in the annual Model Parliament, where the campus political clubs patterned themselves after the regular Parliament, sitting in the seats of the MPPs in the Ontario legislative buildings at Queen's Park, near the university. The event was held in early January when the real legislative house was in recess. Stephen Lewis (David Lewis's son and even then a fine speaker) served as CCF leader for the Model Parliament held in January 1958. Stephen asked me to speak on the education bill as the third of three speakers. I was given a narrow part of the subject to explore and allowed five minutes.

On the day I was to deliver my speech, Stephen found me study-ing in the Wallace Room library, took me aside, and said they had changed the line-up. They decided that the subject I was canvassing should be raised first, and I was asked to expand my presentation from five to fifteen minutes. It never occurred to me to refuse, even though I only had a couple of hours' notice. I always thought I should try to rise to every occasion; I still do. I managed to expand my speech, but was I ever nervous. I spoke for the full fifteen min-utes and when I finished received one of the best compliments of my life when Stephen Lewis, sitting in the row behind me, leaned over and said, "That was superb."

HART HOUSE: EARLY BATTLES

It was during my first year of university that I learned that Senator John F. Kennedy, then being touted as the possible next president of the United States, was coming to Toronto on November 14, 1957, as a guest speaker in a Hart House debate on the topic "Has the United States failed in its responsibilities as a world leader?" He was scheduled to cross swords with Stephen Lewis, by then the university's pre-eminent speaker and debater.[32] Everyone wanted to be present. Women were excluded.

Hart House was, in those days, a men-only facility for athlet-ics, theatre, music, debates, and other student activities. Vincent Massey had given the building to the university in 1919, in memory of his grandfather, Hart Massey—son of the founder of the Massey Ferguson farm equipment manufacturer and heir to its fortune—conditional on its men-only status. This had been modified slightly over the years so that access to the Arbour Room coffee shop after 3 p.m., or for special dances if accompanied by a male, was available to women. Also, just one of the monthly Hart House debates each year was open to women. It was the Hart House "warden" (executive director) in conjunction with the Hart House Debates Committee who chose which debate would accept females in the audience. The Kennedy/Lewis debate was not selected.

In a move that would become a hallmark of my career, I wrote a letter to the editor of the student paper, *The Varsity*, which attempted to persuade the student readers that it was "time for a change" and exhorted women to "get together and FIGHT!!!" Several of us, including Margaret Brewin and Judy Graner (later Sarick) arranged to meet with the warden to try to persuade him to open this particular debate to women. Warden Joseph McCully looked bemused at our great intensity and determination; his expression appeared to me to say, *There, there, girls. What are you making such a fuss about?* We were very polite and not at all confrontational, but we got nowhere. We accepted his rebuff with lady-like grace and were ushered out of his inner sanctum and then out of the building.

When we didn't achieve our desired goal with persuasion and rationality, we banded together to stage a protest. About twenty of us marched back and forth beneath the open window of the Debates Room in the rain under umbrellas and armed with placards emblazoned with the words "Unfair" and "Equal Rights for Women." We knew our chants were heard. Meanwhile, Judy Graner had dressed in male clothes and tried to get into the debate, but her nail polish was spotted and she was ejected; she joined us in our picketing. Sadly, our protest did not end with us being welcomed into the building. It did, however, make the local newspapers (the *Toronto Star* and the *Toronto Telegram* both ran reports).

I am very proud of this; it is my first memory of my own activism on behalf of women's rights and my readiness to stand up and fight for what was right. While most Canadian women had achieved voting rights in 1918—and the activists who had helped push for this came to be known much later as the "first wave" of feminists—in 1957, nobody I knew or had heard of was working for equal rights for women.[33] It wasn't on the agenda anywhere to my knowledge, although the seeds of feminism's "second wave" were not far away.[34] Our little group of student protesters was making a statement by our action: the exclusion of women just wasn't fair.

John F. Kennedy's reaction to our protest highlights the reality for women in those days. He was quoted in the *Toronto Telegram* the next day: "The drive toward female superiority in my land to the south has gone so far that it is a pleasure to come here where males are not afraid to say what they think of the opposite sex." The *Toronto Star* also quoted him as saying: "I personally rather approve of keeping women out of these places." *The Varsity* added this quote to its report: "It is a pleasure to be in a country where the women cannot mix in everywhere." How neatly he illustrated our point.

WHICH STAR
RISES FASTEST?

THE VARSITY

KENNEDY OR
SPUTNIK?

Vol. LXXVII—No. 34   THE UNIVERSITY OF TORONTO   Friday, November 15, 1957

Confidence Vote For U.S. After Kennedy's Defence

By MARK NICHOLS

United States Senator John Kennedy last night heard the foreign policies of his country labelled "fraudulent," "stop-gap," and "a pack of moralistic, legalistic gibberish."

The Senator was Honorary Visitor at last night's Hart House debate.

The resolution, "Has the United States Failed in its Responsibilities As World Leader?" was defeated when a record house divided 204 to 194 against the motion.

Upholding the motion, A. H. Low (I Law), and S. H. Lewis (II U.C.), accused the United States of contravening all "principles of leadership", vacillating "in the face of pressure", and acting poorly as "policeman, baby-sitter and bank of the world."

Low said the United States had misused the possibilities of foreign aid and the fumbling policies of Dulles had succeeded only in creating an impression the U.S. was run by a "bunch of trigger-happy bullies."

Lewis charged the U.S. with "a negative foreign policy" that gave

"too little, too late."

He called the U.S. policy on Suez the "immorality play of the century." He said U.S. foreign policy was "conceived in despair, executed in a mental dither."

Lewis accused the U.S. of mismanaging the handling of crises in the Suez, in Egypt, in Hungary and in China.

In his speech, Senator Kennedy, a Democrat, said the points speakers against the U.S. were v

"Many of the strictu he said, "have been ma

He said, however, t policies of the U.S. mus by the "law of the po

He stressed the str unity among the very U.S. is attempting to such con

woman in pants
breaks barrier

This story is by a girl who, by devious means, spent an hour in the East Common Room of Hart House listening to the debate. She regards her exploit as a triumph for the cause of rights.

Last night I wa

Senator Scorn
Toronto Co-ed

University of Toronto women students paraded outside Hart House carrying placards reading We Want Kennedy.

But U.S. Senator John Kennedy of Massachusetts, an idol of American women, didn't want them.

Speaking during a Hart House debate, from which women are traditionally barred, Sen. Ken-

a "generous standard" applied, because in in al affairs actions are n but merely "less wro they might have been

"To be a leader, have followers," he sa

"American foreign

See KENNEDY, P

demand entry to hart house
women protest with pickets

Groups of angry young women barred from hearing Senator John Kennedy last night formed a picket line in front of Hart House.

Senator Kennedy was honorary speaker at the Hart House debate.

Every available seat in Hart House was taken by 7.45 p.m. Members squeezed into the last

The girls only protest for women, that many were turned they far-si lize that th room for teer.

Two bo from Mb porter th ed off while yelled "Let House terest allow fema

Judy Grand versity colleg women repre lege and facu "We feel w allowed in fu said.

A spokesma committee sai have been fair

one girl moaned "aw, this murder" One girl, dressed as a n managed to get a place in East Common Room.

rt House member to he

Earlier the cr presenting all gan to gather main door of women's reside tacted by S girls.

chairs in the Debates Room at 7.35. By 7.40 the gallery was filled to capacity. Five minutes later the last possible space for standing room in the Com mon Room, to w was being tra taken.

... fill in the shadows as co-eds de...

CAN'T HEAR U.S. KENNEDY
GIRLS PICKET HART HOUSE

While nearly 400 male Varsity students jammed Hart House debates room last night to hear U.S. Senator John F. Kennedy speak, women student pickets paraded outside the building protesting because they were not allowed in, too.

Signs reading "Equal Rights for Women," "nedy" and ried by the v should have the male san ator Kennedy

eds in. "It would not be fair to our members," he said.

Senator Kennedy apparently did not miss his women fans. "I personally rather approve of keeping women out of these places," he said. "It's reassuring to come again to a place that does not fear to express its opinion of the female"

Upstart Co-Ed Upsets
Light-Hearted Debate

A University of Toronto co-ed last night threw the staid Hart House debates room into confusion when she insisted she be recognized by the chair during a Toronto-McMaster debate.

Second-year University College student Linda Silver, earlier warned by Speaker Ken Wyman she and another female were present "on suffrage only," told the house she would remain standing until recognized by the chair.

The house was debating "Now is the time," and the Toronto debaters came out on top nine to seven.

After standing for five minutes, Miss Silver told the house the speaker had been mistaken on a point of order.

Speaking for the motion, Pat Wooten (I Trin.) said "nothing has ever succeeded by doing nothing". He insisted we should take a definite stand in present day affairs. "Today, no man will act, and I ask you, where are we? We are being pursued

It's somewhat astonishing, from the vantage point of the early twenty-first century, to realize that Kennedy did not hesitate to belittle women. It was so much a part of the culture of the time that I wasn't even surprised by it. Women sure did not view this attractive and charming man as an enemy. On the contrary, in 1960 women helped get him elected president of the United States.

The Kennedy/Lewis debate was not to be the end of my rebellion against the exclusion of women at Hart House. A year later, on November 19, 1958, Hart House selected the debate that would welcome women that year. The subject was a boring one: "Resolved: Now Is the Time." I attended on principle and arrived to find that

Readers On HH

Dogmatic Approach: - Time For a Change

Dear Sir:

The dogmatic approach of the Hart House Debates Committee toward allowing women students to the debate at which John Kennedy is the honorary guest, is one belonging more to medieval times than to our present supposedly enlightened age.

Women are as interested and acitve in politics and debating as are the men and should certainly be given the opportunity to hear as distinguished a man as Mr. Kennedy, possibly the next President of the United States.

The Committee has said that there won't be sufficient space even for Hart House members. If this is true, why aren't debates which will attract a large audience held in Convocation Hall? Warden McCulley has said that a debate held in any place other than the Debates Room of

Hart House couldn't be a proper one. I submit that a debate in Convocation Hall would be a real challenge to debaters, a test of their ability to have rapport with a large audience.

It has been brought to my attention that the Massey will forbids women in any Hart House activities. If this were absolute and unchangeable, why were women allowed to hear Pickersgill in Hart House? Why are women allowed in the Arbor Room? Why to Art Exhibits? To the Sunday Concerts?

A precedent has been set and there is no plausible reason for refusing women admittance to further 'special' debates.

It's "TIME FOR A CHANGE." Women, let's get together and FIGHT!!!

Linda Silver,
I UC

Left: Newspaper coverage of Hart House protests. Above: Linda's letter to the editor of *The Varsity*, November 1957.

I was required to sit in a separate, roped-off women's section of the hall. Ken Wyman, the chair of the debate, warned at the outset that "women are present on sufferance only." After the debaters concluded their submissions, the time came for audience participation. I stood up. The chair refused to recognize me. So women were welcome— as long as we were quiet and could be ignored. I stayed on my feet, my heart pounding; I did not want to be defeated. Ken cautioned me to sit down. I continued standing silently; it felt like forever, but I think it must have been about ten minutes before he finally acknowledged me and let me have my say. The story was covered in *The Varsity* the next day with the headline "Upstart Co-Ed Upsets Light-Hearted Debate." The lead paragraph read, "A University of Toronto co-ed last night threw the staid Hart House debates room into confusion when she insisted she be recognized by the chair

The 2014 Hart House Exhibit
"Not Behaving Like Ladies"
commemorating the 40th
Anniversary of the Admission
of Women to Hart House

during a Toronto/McMaster debate." I had defied expectations and
stood up for the right of women to be heard.

In my second year, I tried out for the University Debating Team
(a completely separate entity from Hart House). Even though there
had never been a girl on that team to my knowledge, the first one
was in fact chosen that year—and it wasn't me. This letdown did not
stop me from participating in other ways. I was active on the executive of the University of Toronto Debating Union (UTDU), the
organizational arm of the debating team, as public service debates
director. In that capacity, I organized debates at Toronto-area high
schools to encourage students' interest in debating. I also helped
organize tournaments with other university teams as well as special
occasions. The UTDU gave me considerable organizational experience, which I used in my later activism.

One of the more significant UTDU events I organized was held
on January 4, 1959. I had contacted the Canadian Broadcasting
Corporation (CBC) about getting an upcoming debate between U

of T and McGill University broadcast on *Citizens' Forum*. Norman May and Roy Heenan (then law students and later Toronto and Montreal lawyers respectively) came to Toronto to represent McGill. Malcolm Wallace and Sidney Peck were the Toronto debaters. It was certainly the Toronto team's televised debut; my guess is that the same was true for the McGill team. The debate topic was "Resolved: There Is a New Case for Pacifism." Part of my job was to find an audience of a hundred to fill Victoria College's Alumni Hall. The packed event included about thirty invited students from Toronto high schools who had participated in UTDU's high school debating program. Questions from the floor were encouraged. I knew enough to ensure that someone was primed to ask the first question to get the ball rolling. I asked my father to attend for that purpose, and he did not let me down.

It was not until third year, on my second attempt, that I was selected to be a debater on the U of T team, the second woman ever to be chosen. Debate trials were held to assess the abilities of the candidates. I remember vividly the resentment levelled at me by one losing male candidate who had obviously set his heart on making the team and decided that my selection was the reason he lost. Once the results were announced, he confronted me and snarled his ridicule and consternation at how I could have been chosen over him. I've never forgotten his fiery ire or that he allowed himself to be so open and vocal about his displeasure—nor that he didn't hold it against the guys who had made the team instead of him. He saw only me as the one who had stood in his way. It showed me what male entitlement looked like. It also taught me a lesson in what I would have to face as a woman whenever, just by being myself, I challenged a man's pre-eminence.

As a member of the debating team, I took part in tournaments in Toronto and elsewhere. I remember one trip to Boston University, where most of the participating teams were from the United States. Americans relied on massive card indexes of dry facts, and their debates were filled with numbing and often boring and humourless factual statements. We practised the British/Canadian debating style—using wit and humour and well as facts to persuade. The contrast was apparent to one of the judges, an American professor of debating, who complimented us (both verbally and with winning points) on our style and said he wished the Americans could loosen up a little and emulate us. Another said, memorably, that I was "the best woman debater he had ever heard." I knew there were very few women debaters and that the judges, therefore, had low expectations. The corker, though, was a female judge who made this comment about my debating style: "Sarcasm does not become a lady." What she identified as sarcasm from a lady would likely have been considered dry wit from a male debater. I realized that I would get no special favours from some women, who were ready to judge me with harsher eyes than they used to judge the men.

Although the University Debating Team had given me the opportunity to be a debater, Hart House and its debates remained closed. It was partly the times; few men thought this was unfair, and few women seemed to have any interest in the debates. The prevailing culture accepted as valid the condition set down by the Massey gift, even though it promoted discrimination against women. It was the late 1950s and women were expected to stay in their designated place and not object. Tradition, not fairness, was the salient factor.

Despite the early protests, Hart House remained mostly off limits to women. Later, after Vincent Massey's death in 1967 and increasingly loud objections from a new generation of women students, Hart House's board of stewards consulted legal counsel about whether the deed could be challenged. The university's presidential advisory committee commissioned a report on the future role of Hart House, which recommended the admission of women. The university's student council also supported the admission of women.[35] The Massey Foundation agreed to amend the Deed of Gift.

Hart House was opened to women on the first day of term in 1972. When I heard about it (I was in law school then), I could not resist dropping by and celebrating with lunch at the Arbour Room coffee shop. Years of female exclusion meant there were no washrooms designated for women's use. I decided to "liberate" the men's washroom, while my boyfriend stood watch outside. Hart House had existed only for men for fifty-three years. It had been fifteen years since we had picketed Hart House to attend the Kennedy/ Lewis debate. Some victories take time.

WHAT NEXT?

It was 1961 and my university years were drawing to a close. I had to decide what to do next. Although I had planned to go to the Ontario College of Education to get my teaching credentials, it wasn't really what I wanted to do. In fact, I didn't know what I truly wanted to do, except that my short (and secret) list included law and the diplomatic service.[36] I didn't know any women who had become lawyers, nor had I heard of any. I also knew no women diplomats, and I did not have the languages required for eligibility. If I had been able to complete the Russian language studies[37] I took on in third year as an extra subject, perhaps I could have pursued diplomatic service, but how did one combine that with marriage and motherhood—something I always assumed I would do. I was at a loss.

I missed the year-end dinner put on by the University College Literary and Athletic Society. I was at loose ends and did not look for anyone to go with or something appropriate to wear. I didn't even realize that it was an awards dinner. Surprise! Leaving the library that evening, I ran into a fellow student who had attended and who told me I had won an Honour Award—an engraved pewter cup. I was mortified, both because of my absence and the reasons for it. I more than made up for this lapse about fifty years later when, in November 2012, I was honoured by University College as one of only one hundred in the inaugural group of living and dead "Alumni of Influence" since the founding of the college in 1853. Not only did I attend, but so did eighteen family members and friends. *And* I had something nice to wear!

Chapter 3

THE SCHOOL OF LIFE

Serendipity often makes up our minds for us. As I was finishing my course work (and nearing the magic marriageable age of twenty-one), I found myself courted by a young man who lived in New York and was the son of an old friend of my mother's. Morty pursued me vigorously and romantically until I said yes.

The wedding took place in the summer of 1961. I was twenty-one and had just graduated. I expected to experience the romantic myth I had been taught and had internalized—that we would "live happily ever after." So I moved to New York and adopted the lifestyle and friends that my husband had chosen. The man was the head of the household in those days, and most women did not question it. I tried to fit into the paradigm. From the perspective of the twenty-first century, with what I have learned as a feminist and a lawyer since then, I shake my head ruefully at my foolish innocence.

New York was a very exciting city for me, having come from a sheltered Toronto background. I obtained my first job in New York as a fundraiser for the Federation of Jewish Philanthropies in Manhattan at a salary of $4,000 a year—not bad for those days, I guess.[38] Within a few months, I received a raise to $5,000 a year,[39] an increase of 25 percent. While he never came out and said so directly, my husband seemed troubled; he was an experienced high school teacher with a master's degree who was then earning the same as me, about $5,000 a year. He began to pressure me to quit, ostensibly because of the weekend and evening hours sometimes required when fundraising events were held. Eventually, when I was asked, once again, to cover for someone else one Sunday afternoon (not my job), he persuaded me that it was one time too many. I told my boss that I couldn't, and she was angry—so much so that she told me that if I didn't turn up on that Sunday for the event, I shouldn't bother coming to work on Monday.

This was 1962, and a fledgling white-collar union for office workers was just emerging in New York. I talked to the union steward; she told me that my boss was well-known for her high-handed attitude, but that no aggrieved employee had thus far been willing to stand up to her. I was told that I could not be fired for refusing to do someone else's job and that my work record was exemplary (the raise I had been given didn't hurt), but that I would have to be prepared to stand up for myself. The union was anxious to have someone finally challenge my boss. I nervously agreed to do so. I turned up early at the office on Monday morning and sat at my desk trying to look busy. When my boss arrived, she glared at me and asked what I was doing. I told her I was there to work, as I had been coached to say.

She stormed out of the office to talk to the CEO, who brought the union into the discussion. I was asked to attend a meeting. All I remember now is that I received a substantial severance paycheque, even though I had only worked there for about six months, and the union was pleased that we had been vindicated in our assessment that I had been wrongfully dismissed. And I was proud that I had not been cowed, but had stood up for myself (and other employees) when I was treated unfairly. My husband was not displeased at the outcome. When I eventually found another job, this time at the United Synagogue of America, the national association of Conservative Jewish congregations, I was back to earning $4,000 a year. By the time my salary again approached $5,000, my husband's salary had increased, and he was able to keep ahead of me, which his ego seemed to require.

I worked at the United Synagogue of America between 1962 and 1967. It was located at the Jewish Theological Seminary at Broadway and 122nd Street in Manhattan. I started out as administrative assistant/secretary to the assistant executive director, Jack Mittleman. I remember realizing that my university degree was of no use to me in

New York and did not improve my employment prospects. Despite my long-standing resistance to becoming a typist, I took dictation when I started that job. However, I soon lost patience and offered to compose the letters myself once my boss told me what he wanted. He never again dictated a letter. Once he learned what I could do, he transferred all kinds of responsibilities to me, including managing the administration and registration of the two thousand participants for the 1963 biennial convention of the member synagogues at the Concord Hotel in Kiamesha Lake, New York. Jobs kept being added to my daily tasks. I became assistant director of synagogue administration, assistant director of programs, and advertising manager of the quarterly *United Synagogue Review*. (I sold ads.) By then, I was no longer an assistant and had a secretary of my own.

Unfortunately, life at home wasn't nearly as rewarding. I wasn't happy in my marriage—a consciousness-raising experience in itself—but I stuck with my lot. I didn't know anyone who had divorced, and it didn't seem to be an option. In 1967 I became pregnant, and I had to figure out how to deal with my wish to continue working, given the prevailing customs. Pregnant women were expected to leave work as soon as possible after the pregnancy started to show. There was no such thing as legally mandated maternity leave, and no one even thought about it as a possible option. I arranged to continue working until six weeks before my due date, which was the latest any employer of the day would permit. I offered to continue one of my three jobs from home. The executive director initially expressed surprise and consternation at this radical departure from the norm, but I laid out for him how it could be done. I would continue the job of advertising manager at home, except that I asked to be paid not by salary but by a 15 percent commission (common in the advertising sales industry at the time). He would provide a part-time secretary at the office and pay for my telephone and for the occasional courier service. If I had to go into the office, I would do it on weekends or evenings. And I assured him that if it did not work out from his perspective, he could say so and the deal would be off. We had no written contract, just an understanding, and that was fine with both of us. But it did work out, and I ended up earning the same income from commissions from my part-time, at-home job as I had earned previously working three jobs at the office. This was reminiscent of my mother's entrepreneurial creativity when she opted to be paid by the piece rather than by a weekly salary.

My daughter, Beth, was born in December 1967, and my life changed overnight. I also had another experience of advocacy on a personal level. Beth was born early one Sunday morning at Mount Sinai Hospital in Manhattan. When she was not brought to me for the first feeding, I went looking for her. I was upset to find she had been placed in an isolette unit to help her breathe. Nobody knew what the problem was. When I asked whether a specialist had seen her, I was told that the pediatrician provided by the Health Insurance Plan of Greater New York (HIP) had checked her over. Because Morty was a teacher, we belonged to HIP and were required to use their physicians. I could not get a straight answer, nor were HIP doctors involved or available. I found a hospital medical resident and asked her for the name of the best specialist to assess the situation. She told me she knew a pediatric ear, nose, and throat specialist but that HIP would not pay for his services.

This was my first experience with the limitations and frustrations of insurance-ruled medicine, and I was not going to let an insurance company decide what medical care my daughter needed. I asked the resident to arrange for the specialist to give us an opinion, and I undertook to pay the doctor directly, whatever the cost. I resisted the nurse's pressure to take a sleeping pill for my anxiety, so that I would be awake and alert when the doctor arrived. When he turned up later that evening direct from a formal event, in his tuxedo, he looked like a knight in shining armour. He examined Beth and advised that the issue could either be an infection or a blockage that would require a tracheotomy, which was particularly risky on an infant. He proposed treating the problem as if it were an infection—with medication—and adopting a wait-and-see approach, at least until the next day.

We were lucky, and Beth improved without surgery. The experience, which remains so vivid in my memory, taught me a huge lesson in standing up for myself and mine. I chose not to leave it to the hospital staff to decide what was required, because they weren't acting fast enough for my liking. And I certainly decided not to let money stand in the way of getting the best doctor possible. I paid the doctor's bill on receipt, but then wrote to HIP, chastising them for inadequate care and pressing them to reimburse me for the bill, which they eventually did. Thankfully, I will never know what my advocacy prevented—only that my daughter recovered.

Beth was a pure delight and a joy. I found motherhood completely absorbing and fulfilling. I would work in the afternoons while she slept and go into the office on the occasional Sunday if needed. A courier would bring back and forth the huge galley proofs of the ads—mocked up on hardboards, maybe four-by-four feet in size—for my approval before the magazine was finalized. I clearly remember one particularly hectic day when I was asked to review and approve the galleys on a rush basis. The courier brought them to my door and then waited in the lobby of the apartment building where we lived to take them back. Just after the proofs were handed to me, Beth woke up and needed to be fed; at the same time, the office phoned with questions. I sat at my desk with my baby cradled in my left arm, sucking at my left breast, with my right arm moving these awkward-sized galleys around as needed so I could give instructions to my secretary over the phone, which was wedged between my right jaw and my right shoulder.

My daughter's birth put into startling clarity the difficulties in my marriage. I was forced to face facts and stop playing the societally prescribed game of "let's pretend." A marriage was not automatically successful and, in fact, was usually unsuccessful if the couple themselves were incompatible. I had to replace what my culture had taught me with the evidence of my experience and intelligence. I had to take charge of my own life.

I decided to divorce. This was rare at the time, and it took courage just to make the decision. It was, however, a pivotal moment in my life and my daughter's. I returned to Toronto—and to my family and community—with Beth in the spring of 1969. Fortunately, my husband had acquiesced to this arrangement. We engaged in reasonably peaceful settlement negotiations, followed by an uncontested divorce in New York. I was an active participant in the negotiations, and I recall my lawyer encouraging me to undertake a career in law.

Once again, it seemed, I was being faced with an important question: What next?

PART 2

BECOMING AN ADVOCATE, 1969–79

Chapter 4
AN EDUCATION IN LAW

So here I was, back in Toronto after eight years away, with a Bachelor of Arts degree, but no obvious career path unless I returned to school or took an office job. It was May 1969. I was now a single mother with sole responsibility for the care of a seventeen-month-old child. Daycare facilities were rare in Toronto—in fact, they were rare everywhere in Canada—and society frowned on mothers who were employed and didn't stay at home and raise their children.[40] Even so, statistics reveal that some women resisted this pressure, either out of choice or necessity. By 1967, 21 percent of all mothers in Canada held down jobs—whether full- or part-time—outside their homes.[41]

My original intention had been to go to the Ontario College of Education for a year and get my credentials to teach high school history. It still seemed the practical thing to do. But by 1969, I knew that I really wanted to be a lawyer. I wanted to be an advocate for fairness and use my speaking and writing abilities and my drive for social justice in the public interest. But I certainly had no plan to be a women's rights advocate.

I had thought I would wait one year, until Beth was a little older, before returning to school. My father, however—bless him—encouraged me *not* to wait, saying that life might intervene and prevent me from fulfilling my plans. I agonized over making the impractical choice of a five-year program of study to qualify for law as compared to the one-year program required to get a teaching certificate. I was twenty-nine and worried that I was too old to undertake such a long program; by the time I finished I would be thirty-four. In those days, it was rare to go to law school except in a direct progression from undergraduate education. In the end, though, I grasped the fact that the five years would pass whether I went to law school or not, and I might as well have what I wanted at the end of that period of time. I had some savings from my years in New York and decided to invest them in my own future.

OSGOODE HALL

I was accepted at both Osgoode Hall Law School at York University, in the northern part of the city, and University of Toronto Law School, but Osgoode's dean, Harry Arthurs, arranged for early admission without requiring that I take the still optional Law School Admission Test (LSAT). I had told the dean of my unique situation and that I needed early admission in order to arrange for housing and child care. I found an apartment near Osgoode, and a woman who lived on the same floor with one child already in care was willing to take on another. Elaine Henwood was a godsend.

I entered Osgoode Hall Law School in September 1969. I clearly remember the joy I felt as I strode up the path to the school on that first day. As a woman and a single parent, no less, I felt like a pioneer—as if I were daring the fates and shaking tradition loose from its place of safety by being audacious enough to think that it could be acceptable for me to become a lawyer. I was exhilarated just to be there.

Being a woman in law school at that time was a rarity. I was one of only fourteen women in our first-year class of three hundred. (We made up fewer than 5 percent of the student population, and we were divided among the four sections of seventy-five, each with up to four women.) On top of that, I was the only one with a child. Few of my fellow students even knew I was a mother, let alone that I was a single parent. I don't recall discussing this much as I really wanted to be treated like the other students. Even when I was barely on time to an evening seminar starting at 7:00 p.m., where I was presenting the legal argument, I did not make any excuses or try to justify my lateness. I did not feel that I could or should explain that I had a babysitting problem, solved by my father, who reached my apartment just in time. My unique circumstances did come out gradually as I became friendly with some of the other students and began bringing Beth to the library with me on the weekends, when she became more able to sit still and amuse herself while I was doing research or studying. I was lucky that she was a good child, easy to have around, willing to sit quietly and play or draw while I worked. I was also lucky that she spent time with my parents, siblings, and extended family to allow me some concentrated study time, and this gave Beth some entertaining experiences.

My days were spent at the law school. I was there from nine to five, six at the latest. Many of the guys played bridge in the common room between classes, but there was no bridge for me. When I wasn't in class, I was in the library doing homework. And when I returned home, my time was for my daughter—at least until she fell asleep, at which point I cracked open the books again. Once we were able to choose our own subjects in second year, I did so with half an eye on my ability to carpool to nursery school (Beth went to a Montessori nursery school from the age of two-and-a-half), either taking the children for 9 a.m. or picking them up for 11:30 a.m. I worked at the law school administering student course selections, part-time during the year (in between classes) and full-time in the summer. I also worked part-time for my father. Between these jobs, my savings from my years working in New York, and some child support from my ex-husband, I managed to pay for tuition, books, child care, and everyday expenses. But I had almost no time for a social life either at home or at school.

For the most part, I did not experience discrimination while in law school. The male students were generally friendly, although there was the occasional one who resented women in the profession. They would complain that women were taking up places getting degrees that we would not use, since they expected us to stay home and raise children after graduation. I remember only one professor who specifically picked on the women students, one at a time and without warning. He humiliated and ridiculed the women students in our section and seemed to enjoy doing so. He also called us by our first names, although he treated the men with the respect accorded students at the time by addressing them by their surnames. The class was stressful. I know that at least one of the male students felt uncomfortable about it and spoke privately to the professor

Avvy Go and Linda received the Women's Law Association of Ontario President's Award, 2002.

about the atmosphere he created in the class for female students, trying (unsuccessfully) to discourage his conduct. He appeared oblivious to the effect of his behaviour on the women students. The impact on me was a C in his course, compared to my higher marks in the others. He stopped me in the halls to ask why "a smart girl like you" didn't do better. I did not have the nerve to tell him why; I just wanted to become a lawyer—a complaint would have drawn unwelcome attention to me.

My interest in the position of women in society had not diminished since the day when I picketed Hart House for unfairly excluding women from the Kennedy/Lewis debate—although I had not done anything about it. At the beginning of second-year law school, I wrote a tongue-in-cheek essay that was published in the law school newspaper, *Obiter Dicta*. I proposed that a new field of law—Women's Liberation Law—be developed:

> As a women's lib lawyer, the opportunity for variety and spice is limitless: Marriage counselor; Personnel intervenant; Advocate before a U.N. Commission on the Status of Women; Agent for a just-recently-impregnated woman before hospital abortion

committees; Arranger in artificial sterilization cases; Negotiator for pay increases, maternity leaves and pink paint in ladies' washrooms; Impleaders before legislative committees for day care legislation.... "Vive la femme libre," you should be shouting.[42]

Although the article was intended to be humorous, it concluded with serious encouragement to the students to create this field of law. Little did I realize that this would become one of my areas of interest and activism.

There was no organized women's group at law school at that time; the caucuses formed by the National Association of Women and the Law came after I was called to the Bar. Nor were there women law professors; the only woman on the faculty taught not a substantive law course but the first-year course on legal writing. However, I did join the Women's Law Association of Ontario (WLAO) when I first entered law school and still maintain this membership today. The group had been formed in 1919 by the first (and few) women lawyers in Ontario at that time and continues to this day as a networking, support, and advocacy group. As a student, it was helpful to me to meet the few women in the profession. These pioneers were friendly and helpful to the students, and it was an eye-opener to see how they had actually survived as lawyers. Laura Legge had her own practice with her husband; Rainey Hunter worked for Legal Aid Ontario; Miriam Kelly was a real estate lawyer with a large firm—these are just some of the people I remember from those early days. It was a keen pleasure in 2002 to be honoured by the WLAO with its President's Award for my "exemplary work in the advancement of family law and women's rights."

EARLY DAYS FOR WOMEN'S LIB

While I was in law school, women's issues began taking on major importance, and organizations were starting to form. They were loosely called the "Women's Liberation Movement," and it did not take long for this significant movement to be disparaged with the abbreviation "women's lib." I suspect that people were so shocked by its revolutionary goals of equality for women that they used ridicule to try to suppress its ideas. I remember when the worst scorn one could direct at a woman who expressed non-traditional ideas was to challenge her with the question "What are you, a 'woman's libber'?"[43] I was on the receiving end, and at first, I was embarrassed and did not know what to say, but after a while would answer coolly, "Yes I am." Even so, I felt more comfortable describing myself as a feminist when the label "women's lib" fell into disuse and feminism replaced it.

In Canada, the pivotal event of the era was the creation, in 1967, by Lester B. Pearson's Liberal government of the Royal Commission on the Status of Women (RCSW) to identify what needed to be done to improve women's status. Under the leadership of journalist Florence Bird as chair, sociologist Monique Bégin[44] as executive secretary, and Elsie Gregory MacGill[45] as one of the members, the commission's landmark report was released in 1970. I remember being so surprised that any government was paying attention to women's issues. It was only later that I learned how a group of remarkable women made it happen.

The secretary of state in Pearson's cabinet was lawyer Judy LaMarsh (only the second woman ever to be a federal cabinet minister; the first had been Ellen Fairclough in 1957 in the Diefenbaker Progressive Conservative government), who was gradually forced by circumstances "into the role of acting as spokesman and watchdog for women."[46] Soon after her cabinet appointment in 1963, she broached the subject of a royal commission with Prime Minister Pearson, and kept after him. "Nothing was so hard to accomplish during all the time I was in cabinet as the appointment of a Royal Commission to inquire into the Status of Women."[47]

In 1966, Laura Sabia, president of the Canadian Federation of University Women, called a meeting of twenty leaders of national women's organizations to discuss and champion an improved status for women in Canada.[48] Held in the basement meeting room of the University Women's Club on St. George Street in Toronto, the meeting resulted in a demand for a royal commission on the status of women. A small group, which included lawyer Margaret Hyndman and Dorothy Martin of the Federation of Women Teachers Associations of Ontario (FWTAO), prepared a brief and presented it to the justice minister in November 1966. *Chatelaine* magazine's editor, Doris Anderson, supported the campaign with editorials and articles.[49] The Pearson Liberal government was finally persuaded to act when Laura Sabia was asked by the press what she would do if the government failed to act. She responded that she would ask two million women to march to Ottawa in protest.[50] The threat was enough.

Judy LaMarsh later commented, "I have no doubt in my own mind that I would have been unable to convince the Government to set up the Commission without the remarkable organization of Mrs. Laura Sabia...who, for the first time in history, brought together women's organizations from all over the country to speak with one voice in Ottawa. That was the pressure needed to make Pearson act."[51]

I was just entering my second year of law school when the commission issued its ground-breaking report. The recommendations were broad and substantial and contained a huge number of changes that would be required in order for women in all areas of society to be treated equally with men. I studied it intently (but not for any course in school—there was none), and my copy is underlined and annotated, with numerous pieces of paper stuck in pages to which I wanted to return. What I found encouraging was that the commissioners did not just wring their hands by stating the problems; for each problem they found, they proposed solutions. The report became the game plan for women concerned about achieving change. I found it revealing and empowering.

One of the major proposals was a process for ensuring both the implementation of change and the vigilance required to keep any gains. Knowing that change does not come about on its own, the Royal Commission recommended the establishment of a federal government advisory council that would be directly responsible to Parliament. It also proposed that provinces and territories establish similar councils with sufficient authority and funds to make its work effective. As it turned out, governments established advisory groups that reported not to Parliament but to a minister, and it is questionable whether they gave the councils sufficient authority and funding.

Before any government responded to the report or established any councils, women's volunteer groups formed their own watchdog organizations. In 1972, the National Action Committee on the Status of Women (NAC) was born, supported by most of the major women's volunteer organizations of the day, many of which had participated in that meeting organized by Laura Sabia, which led to the Committee on Equality for Women, then the National Ad Hoc Committee on the Status of Women, and finally the National Action Committee on the Status of Women. With its head office in Toronto, NAC began as an umbrella organization with thirty member groups and ended up with seven hundred major groups, such as the YWCA, Business and Professional Women's Clubs, Canadian Federation of University Women, as well as unions and religious groups. Laura Sabia was the first chair,[52] and NAC's goal was to work toward the implementation of the recommendations of the Royal Commission on the Status of Women.

During the 1971–72 school year—my third year at law school—I became aware of the existence of Women's Place, a centre located in an old home at 25 Dupont Street where women gathered and talked. Toronto's Women's Place was one of the earliest spots where consciousness-raising about women's issues occurred. I was intrigued and nervous about participating in such a radical idea, but I wanted to be part of this adventure. So I offered to create and teach a course there on the history of women's legal issues, structured to canvass the law as it affected women's different roles—as single woman, as wife, as mother, as property owner, as divorced woman, as citizen, and within the economy. Women were eager for information and there were lots of questions, and lots of discussion. I also remember how little available information there was and the huge amount of original research needed to fill in all the gaps. Unlike my many extra-curricular activities as an undergraduate at the University of Toronto when I was single, I did not have the time to get involved in many things outside of law school, my daughter, and part-time work. But I made an exception for Women's Place.

During that same year, one of the courses I chose was a seminar on the legal profession taught by Professor Harry Arthurs, which required me to write a major paper instead of exams. I suggested a survey of women in the legal profession in Toronto. I wanted to find out the extent of discrimination there might be when I graduated and how women already in the profession coped. Professor Arthurs accepted and encouraged my idea.

I created a questionnaire that asked women lawyers about their areas of law, how they came to choose them, and about their income. It also probed any experiences of discrimination they might have had, and questioned who exhibited more discrimination—colleagues or clients. The questionnaire also explored marital status, motherhood, and pregnancy; how child-bearing and rearing was managed; and housekeeping practices. If women were married, it asked whether their husbands helped out.

My goal was to uncover how the legal profession treated women lawyers and how those same female lawyers behaved as professionals. I wanted to address the back-handed allegations that suggested we should not be allowed to take up places in law school, on the assumption that we would either give up on our law degrees for marriage and motherhood or that we would end up treating law as a hobby. I wanted to find out if the allegation made by some women was true—that women lawyers faced discriminatory hiring practices and pay scales, as well as limitations in their choice of specialty. Above all, I wanted to know what to anticipate in this profession I had chosen.

I located lists of lawyers primarily through the Law Society of Upper Canada, the legal profession's governing body, and the Women's Law Association of Ontario. It appeared that there were about 152 women lawyers in Toronto, and they represented about 3 percent of the practising bar. Fifty women responded to the survey.

Seventy-four percent of the women surveyed denied suffering discrimination. In fact, everyone who volunteered a written comment said that if a woman worked hard and did a good job, she would be accepted. However, none of the survey responses showed that this was true. Among the responders, 26 percent found it very difficult to find an articling position and 34 percent found it difficult to land their first job. More women than men tended to work in government, and women were most scarce in the largest firms. Many women congregated in work specialties that were based on where they were permitted entry rather than personal choice. Women were not paid equally with men.

Discrimination was so blatant at that time that a separate survey, conducted by my classmate Felicia Folk, of Toronto law firms that hired articling students revealed that 40 percent of the firms openly and freely admitted to discrimination against women applicants.[53] Because of that result, she reported that an additional survey, this time of 1971 female law school graduates, was undertaken, which revealed discrimination against women students in terms of both law firm attitudes and the ability of the women to find articling jobs.[54] This confirmed my suspicion: it was more often the male lawyers, rather than the clients, who objected to female lawyers.

The survey revealed that the most successful women solved the problem of combining a law career with marriage and motherhood by sharing both home and professional life with a lawyer husband. That made it easier to have and raise children, because it allowed them to control and balance the time needed to do both well. However, this was not because the men helped out with the children and the household to any great extent. Women lawyers were primarily responsible for the household and child-care responsibilities in addition to their professional responsibilities. Not one husband of the women surveyed took sole responsibility for any particular household function, although some did help out. Several women who hired help seemed to feel guilty for doing so. More than half of the women in my sample were childless, which suggested to me that many women still believed (as the movie *The Red Shoes* had taught me long ago) that they had to choose between having children and having a career. The ones who did get pregnant had planned their pregnancies to minimize conflict with their professional lives. Few suspended their practices for any appreciable length of time after their children were born; the average length of time off was fifteen weeks—six weeks before the birth and nine weeks after. Of those who stayed home to rear a child, most took one year off. The survey proved that there was little evidence to support the contention of male lawyers that women would be lost to the profession after childbirth.

I had found the answer to my fundamental question: women themselves were serious about being members of the legal profession, and I wrote up the analysis for the course requirements. The paper concluded with the observation that the traditional excuses for differentiating between female and male lawyers were not valid: "Attitudes which question a woman's temperamental and practical suitability for law are rooted in social mythology. One hopes that the legal profession will come to view femaleness as neither a handicap nor an advantage, but simply a personal attribute unrelated to fitness as a lawyer."

On Professor Arthurs's recommendation, the *Osgoode Hall Law Journal* published my paper "Women as Lawyers in Toronto."[55] As helpful as my survey results were, I did not really know how the legal profession would treat *me*. But I did not have to wait long to find out. Life itself was the most realistic teacher, as I continued to discover.

THE SEARCH FOR AN ARTICLING POSITION

During the third and final year at law school, every student who wanted to go into private practice looked for an articling position. It was mandatory to apprentice to a practising lawyer or lawyers on the completion of law school. The program was called "serving under articles," or "articling," and was managed and supervised by the Law Society of Upper Canada. At that time, the rules were rigid: one had to serve twelve consecutive months between September 1 and August 31. One could start earlier, but this was not counted toward the prerequisites. Articling was followed by a six-month Bar Admission Course.

The search started in the fall of third year. Some of the lawyers on firm hiring committees would call their buddies among the law school professors and ask them to recommend exceptional candidates. I felt fortunate to have been recommended by my professors to three of the largest and most prestigious firms of the day (Blake, Cassels & Graydon; Goodman and Goodman; and McCarthy & McCarthy). Members of their committees wrote me flattering letters and asked me to lunch, where I was interviewed and courted by the young lawyers who were in charge of the first vetting in the hiring process. Since the firms had been the ones to initiate the interviews and the meetings went very well, I assumed I would have my pick of one of these firms. I was mistaken.[56] None of them made me an offer, and I found out later through impeccable sources that some senior lawyers in all three firms had nixed the hiring of any female lawyer.[57] Undaunted, I applied to a huge number of other Toronto firms and from these applications was invited to thirty interviews. By then, it was apparent I was not going to find a job easily, and that being a woman, a single parent, and a mature student with work experience was not going to help. Most of the other women students were in a similar position, given the survey results mentioned earlier. The firms seemed to want fresh, eager, young, and energetic male articling students, prepared to devote their full energy and long hours to the job, which sometimes included stocking the office fridge with beer and picking up a senior lawyer's dry cleaning.

One particular firm had seemed compatible. On my return to class after that interview, a friend said he had also been interviewed by that same firm. He generously commented that if they made the decision on merit alone, I would get the job. I thanked him but told him not to be so sure. In fact, he got the job, not me. Someone else I knew, who had a speaking acquaintance with one of the principals at that firm, asked his contact why I had not been chosen. The candid response was that "the other guys" did not want to be limited in what they could say and how they could behave—and that they swore a lot. How do you fight against that? I also recall the pretty obvious sexism during some of the interviews. One lawyer asked if I actually intended to practise law.

In the end, with time passing and no job in sight, I asked Dean Harry Arthurs for advice. If I did not complete my articles, I would not have the right to enter the Bar Admission Course to be licensed to practise law. He made some calls, and I got two further interviews. I gratefully accepted the first job offer I received, from Bernard Eastman of the seven-man firm Du Vernet, Carruthers, Beard, and Eastman. Bernie taught part-time at Osgoode Hall Law School and interviewed me there. The more eminent firm of Goodman and Carr also indicated interest at a later date, but I had made a commitment and kept it. There came a time when I wondered whether I had made the right decision. But for then, I at least had an articling job to look forward to once I graduated from law school.

GRADUATION

It was 1972, and I had completed the requirements for my LL.B., my Bachelor of Laws degree. I was overjoyed to attend the graduation ceremony—the acknowledgment that I had accomplished the first step toward the practice of law. My daughter, Beth—then almost five years old—was there with my parents, brothers, and sister. When I crossed the stage and accepted my law degree from Dean Gerald LeDain, I remember being taken by surprise at his comment "You have a lot of friends." That was when I became aware of the enthusiastic applause from my classmates. Just then Beth, adorable

Graduating Class
Osgoode Hall Law School
York University

in a starched and embroidered dress with her curled hair in ribbons, broke loose from her seat with my family near the back of the hall. As I came down the stairs and off the stage, Beth was running down the centre aisle of the auditorium and scampered straight into my arms, whispering "Congratulations, Mummy" in my ear. The audience erupted with thunderous and exuberant applause. It was one of the best moments of my life—one that lives on in my mind's eye and can still bring tears of joy.

ARTICLING

Right after graduation in May 1972, I began my work with Du Vernet, Carruthers, Beard, and Eastman. Although the articling year officially started on September 1, the firm wanted us—Terence Gain was the other articling student—to begin in May, and I was happy to earn an additional four months' pay. I was paid $100 a week, which was eventually raised to $115. I was exposed to real estate law, litigation, criminal law, and corporate and commercial law, which taught me a great deal. My work was done between nine and five, and if there were tasks that would have kept me later, I took them home to do once Beth was asleep.

By then, my daughter was attending Hawthorne Bilingual School in mid-town Toronto, and I had moved from the York University environs to a flat near Hawthorne and nearer to the downtown office where I was articling. I had done my research to try to find daycare and education for my daughter. From the provincial government, I secured a list of schools with daycare facilities. In those days, daycare services were few and far between, and I learned first-hand just how tough it was for working women to find child care. I remember that Jesse Ketchum Public School had an affiliated daycare centre at a central location at Bay and Davenport, but to have Beth attend that facility, I would have had to fill out a means test. Only children in families who qualified for welfare could secure a place there. I checked out all of the schools on the provincial government list, and no public schools had after-school care; just a handful of private schools were ahead of the times.

Hawthorne Bilingual School was the only one that had everything I needed: it was affordable and centrally located, and had care from 8 a.m. to 6 p.m.—with a late charge of one dollar for each minute past 6 p.m. that a parent picked up a child. The school had been founded in 1969 by Margaret and Frank Tilbrook, and it was innovative for its time. It was child-centred and the classes were small, each composed of multi-age groupings. The children learned French from an earlier age than was then available in the public schools. Parents were expected to participate in organizational committees and school activities. The Tilbrooks had a farm in the country and ran a summer program, so working parents had full-year coverage for their children. Beth was almost five when she started at Hawthorne in September 1972, and she stayed there for five years until she was almost ten and started grade four. By then, Hawthorne was having financial difficulties and was in danger of closing. I transferred her to Cedarvale Public School, chosen in part for its location less than a block away from my parents' home, where she went at lunchtime and after school.

I learned about the practice of law while articling. However, I also had challenging experiences that helped to form my expectations and my view of the legal profession, as it then was. The fact that I was a woman mattered, and not in a positive sense.

One lawyer in the firm—Michael Gordon—asked me to simply

sit at the counsel table with him at a trial, even though I had played no part in the preparation of the brief for the case. The reason? It was about appearances: he was defending a men-only private club that was being sued for its discriminatory policy. I saw that I would only have been subliminal window-dressing, displayed as a woman who, it might be inferred, thought it not unfair to exclude women from that private club. I told him I felt uncomfortable doing so.

I was asked by another one of my supervising lawyers to set a trial date in a criminal court. The presiding judge, Robert Dnieper, refused to acknowledge my presence and in fact admonished me in a harsh tone to get away from the counsel table. "Secretaries are not permitted to set a date," he said. I tried to tell him I was an articling student but he wouldn't listen. "Go away," he said. Trying not to show my embarrassment and upset, I had to gather up my briefcase, my winter coat, and the rest of my paraphernalia while everyone in court waited and watched. Thankfully, an unknown male lawyer from another firm took pity on me and told me he would do it for me. He represented for me the kind of behaviour shown by the finest lawyers.

There was an expectation that students should be visibly "at work" in the evenings, even if the student's work was completed. I, of course, was unable to play this game. If I had work to do, I took it home and completed it before the next morning. But that did not satisfy every lawyer in the firm. I was aware of the displeased eyes following me as I left the office by 5:30 p.m. each day.

It was toward the end of the articling year, in June 1973, that I ran into real trouble—trouble that put at risk my future in law. I had worked successfully at Du Vernet, Carruthers, Beard, and Eastman for twelve months and three weeks, but had not completed my articles under the Law Society's strict rules—I needed about ten weeks more to take me to the end of August. The problem started with a court motion. At the request of Ernest Du Vernet, I had researched and prepared the argument for submission. I had taken him through it in the office ahead of time and he seemed impressed with what I had done and appeared to understand the issues. However, when he made the argument in court (I was there with him) and the judge asked him questions, it was clear that he lacked a grasp on the legal argument. Du Vernet lost the motion.

When we returned to the office, Du Vernet called me into his office and fired me. When I asked why, he admitted that every time he looked at me, he would have to think about losing the motion and he couldn't face that. I reminded him that he would be preventing me from going into the Bar Admission Course. He just shrugged. I could hardly believe this was happening. This was June of 1973, and I had spent four years so far to get the legal training to entitle me to practise law. I couldn't accept this; I had to do something.

I challenged his decision by talking to every other lawyer in the seven-man firm, one by one, hoping for their intervention and assistance. None of them—Douglas Carruthers, John A. B. MacDonald, Michael Gordon, David Beard, or Richard Winter—would help me. Even Bernie Eastman, the lawyer who had hired me on behalf of the firm, was unable to protect me or get me reinstated. He told me that he himself was leaving the firm. When I asked him where he would go, he said he was looking for a space-sharing arrangement. I put him in touch with my old friend Jay Waterman, who had some space in his law offices, and they came to an understanding.

So there I was: fired, no income, with an incomplete prerequisite to enter the Bar Admission Course. While I could have registered a complaint with the Law Society of Upper Canada, I was afraid it would label me a troublemaker at the start of my career. I also came to realize that I had a way around this setback. While the firm had fired me, it was Bernie Eastman who had signed the Law Society articling documents. Fortunately, only one lawyer could sign a student's articles, no matter what the size of the firm. I had taken the documents that prior September to Bernie. He said it was the managing partner who usually did that, but I said I would really prefer him to sign my articles. He agreed. By then, I had already worked at the firm for four months and had had a chance to assess the people for whom I was working. It turned out to be a shrewd decision.

Bernie helped me figure out how to handle the situation. I was required to article full time until the end of August, but Bernie was no longer in a position to provide me with full-time work. So we came up with a solution: he would continue to give me work, and I would do work for other lawyers as well, whether or not they could pay me. As long as he could assure himself that I was articling full time, he would sign my articles and vouch for my articling experience. I did work for several lawyers in addition to Bernie, including Jay Waterman, my brother Marty, and one of his associates. Bernie signed my articles of clerkship. To my great relief, I ended up being eligible to attend the Bar Admission Course of the Law Society of Upper Canada for the mandatory six-month course from September 1973 to February 1974.

If the other lawyers for whom I articled had had their way, I would never have completed the requirements needed to practise law. Lesson learned: I wasn't going to be under someone's control to that extent ever again. In a way, I was lucky to have been mal-treated so early in my career: it taught me not to count on anyone's hand up the ladder of success. I made my plans accordingly and decided to open my own office for the practice of law. I figured out how much I had to earn and felt I could do it. Being my own boss and doing it my way became an important and sustaining goal for me in my career.

Chapter 5
HANGING OUT MY SHINGLE

I was not yet a full-fledged lawyer as the women's movement continued to gain strength. The first hint that my career and the movement would progress along similar paths occurred when I was invited to attend and speak at the first-ever Conference of Women and the Law in March 1974.

1974 CONFERENCE ON WOMEN AND THE LAW
Just one week before my Call to the Bar, I found myself on the campus of the University of Windsor, joining an enthusiastic group of women who shared the goals of education and consciousness-raising.[58] The organizers were University of Windsor law professors Christine Davies and Gabriella Lang and the staff and female students in the law faculty, including Mary Anne Sanderson,[59] then in her final year of law school, who was my primary contact. I was thrilled to be part of this unprecedented symposium. From all over, women attended—lawyers, law students, even the few female judges there were at that time. Women from other spheres were there too—historians, film-makers, journalists, professors, and more.

The conference focused on the fact that women's secondary status was reflected in and preserved by the laws of Canada. What a challenge this was! The four major panels explored the legal status of women in Canada; family law and married women's rights; the Royal Commission Report on the Status of Women; and Women in the Law School, the Law Firm, and the Legal Profession. The

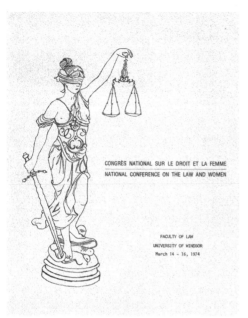

CONGRÈS NATIONAL SUR LE DROIT ET LA FEMME
NATIONAL CONFERENCE ON THE LAW AND WOMEN

FACULTY OF LAW
UNIVERSITY OF WINDSOR
March 14 – 16, 1974

The 1974 Windsor conference drew committed women from many disciplines to discuss the status of women under the law.

speakers included the most notable, informed, and active women of the day.[60] Keynote speakers were Otto Lang, then the federal minister of justice, and Pauline Jewett, political scientist, former member of Parliament, and then president of Simon Fraser University, the first woman to be president of a co-educational university.

It was my research on the experience of women lawyers that had garnered my invitation to be on the panel "Women in the Law School, the Law Firm, and the Legal Profession." The panel included Sydney Robins (then treasurer—head—of the Law Society of Upper Canada), Madam Justice Claire L'Heureux-Dubé (then a Superior Court judge in Québec), Mary Carter (a Saskatoon judge), Jennifer Bankier (a fellow law student), and Joan Sullivan (a legal secretary who had organized a union for Windsor legal secretaries). Justice L'Heureux-Dubé was moderator, participant, and a real dynamo, who welcomed the audience to what she proudly described as "one of the first discussions on the subject that I know of."[61] I had good reason to agree with her, knowing that mine was the only such research done in Ontario about women lawyers. She came laden with statistics on the dearth of women judges and pointed out that there were 485 federally appointed judges in Canada of whom only seven were women; this meant that fewer than 1.5 percent of judges in 1974 were women.

Jennifer Bankier also brought statistics demonstrating how few in number we women lawyers were. In 1969–70, when I was in first-year law school, only 6.3 percent of the total Osgoode student body was female. Statistics like these highlighted how remarkable it was to attract a sufficient number of women to even populate a conference. Jennifer spoke in detail about discrimination and quoted

the biased and outrageous remarks directed to some women students when they were interviewed for articling jobs.

Sydney Robins congratulated Linda when she received the Law Society Medal in 2006.

I had decided that this was a perfect opportunity to point out that women in the legal profession were not protected by our governing body, the Law Society of Upper Canada, from discrimination. The speech I walked in with urged the Law Society to create a new rule of professional conduct prohibiting discrimination against women lawyers. Such a rule would mean that those in the profession who discriminated against women would be dealt with by our governing body, as law is a self-governing profession. But Law Society head Sydney Robins spoke before I did. I was intrigued when he started by describing the history of women in law and how important it was for the profession to be tolerant and welcoming of the forces of social change. But I was nonplussed when he went on to announce that the Law Society had in fact, *just days earlier*, on March 12, 1974, agreed on a rule that discrimination against women by the legal profession amounted to professional misconduct.

Ontario's was the first law society in Canada to prohibit discrimination against women, but not only women. This was the new Rule of Professional Conduct: "There shall be no discrimination by the lawyer on the grounds of race, creed, colour, national origin, or sex in the employment of other lawyers or articling students or in other relations between him and his fellow members of the profession."

I wasn't expecting the announcement, but I knew I had to comment on it. While Mr. Robins finished his speech, I scanned the words of the new rule. When it was my turn to speak, I applauded the new rule as an important first step and an act taken in good faith by the benchers. (*Bencher* is the title given to lawyers elected to represent and govern other lawyers on the Law Society of Upper Canada.) I noted that it was now up to women to use this new tool to deal with discriminatory treatment by registering complaints. My speech went further than either my law school paper or my published law journal article when I asked and answered the question of what we should do more concretely about discrimination. In what was to become a theme of my career, I encouraged women to act together in sisterhood, and I suggested accessible solutions, such as mentorship, active placement committees in women's law organizations, "sickness" benefits for maternity leave included in Bar Association plans, and, if the Law Society rule was inadequate to deal with a problem, to use the means provided in the Human Rights Codes to challenge discrimination.[62] During the question-and-answer session, I commented that there wasn't one female among the elected benchers of the Law Society of Upper Canada. "It would be very valuable to have one, not to say that it also would be more equitable," I said, given that women at that time represented about 4 percent of the lawyers in Ontario. I also urged women to join together and put forward a candidate for bencher. Mr. Robins agreed with me.

It was in the following year that women lawyers joined together to campaign within the legal community to choose one woman to run for bencher of the Law Society of Upper Canada, who would then receive the endorsement of the Women's Law Association of Ontario (WLAO) and Kappa Beta Pi Legal Sorority. The WLAO organizers thought we would not be able to elect more than one. I participated in the campaign that saw Laura Legge become, in 1975, the first woman bencher. As it happened, she had her nominations form signed by ten male colleagues.[63] According to Christopher Moore,[64] Laura Legge felt she had been elected as a voice of solicitors[65] rather than women—she received 1,500 votes of which fewer than 300 were women. She was very successful as a bencher and was the first woman treasurer (head) of the Law Society of Upper Canada in 1983. She never acknowledged the discrimination that women suffered at the hands of the legal profession. She put it this way: "You see, I never thought of myself as a woman lawyer. I always thought of myself as a lawyer.... My experience was you don't become obsessed with discrimination and problems; just work around them and get on with life."[66]

Laura Legge was open about her views. After being chosen treasurer, she commented that men came to realize "that just because you were female, you weren't a monster, and you weren't going to make a lot of waves...."[67] There were always some women lawyers who felt this way, as I had learned when I did my survey of women in the legal profession in 1972. Part of the reason for their success was that they did not threaten men in power but played on their team. Laura Legge's success made her a pioneer and a role model, but this was not her intention. I admired her, even though I saw the world differently than she did.[68]

• • • • • • • • •

The Women in Law Conference was exciting and filled with the promise of things to come. It was exhilarating to experience the momentum sparked by so many great and compatible minds in one place working toward a common goal. I met the two women judges that Ontario could boast of at that time: Mabel Van Camp (appointed in 1971 to the High Court of Ontario as the Superior Court was then called) and Janet Boland (appointed in 1972 to the Ontario County Court, which was later merged with the Superior Court), and I met many of the women—both lawyers and non-lawyers—who I would work with in the women's movement.

At the end of the conference, a number of us crowded into a smoke-filled room to challenge each other to continue the momentum. It was this group that agreed to found the National

Association of Women and the Law (NAWL), which was initially set up as women's caucuses at the law schools. I moved the resolution. This organization of women lawyers and law students made a great contribution to the advancement of women's legal concerns.[69]

A resolution was also passed "that the persons attending this conference advise the federal government that abortion be removed from the Criminal Code"; this was a very early effort to accomplish what later came to be a major goal of the women's movement, at a time when Dr. Henry Morgentaler was beginning his efforts to make safe abortions available to Canadian women. But it wasn't the first effort. In 1970, members of the Vancouver Women's Caucus led the Abortion Caravan to Ottawa to protest the 1969 amendments to the Criminal Code that stated that abortion was prohibited unless the woman's health was threatened and even then, only if a hospital committee of three doctors approved. They wanted the prohibition against abortion removed from the Criminal Code.

Call to the Bar

What an exciting way to start my law career! Just one week after the conference, on Friday, March 22, 1974, I was called to the Bar and licensed to practise law in the province of Ontario. I have always remembered the date; my brother Steve gave me a sterling silver letter opener, which I have used throughout my career, on which is engraved my name and academic degrees and the date of my Call to the Bar. I wore for the first time my new court robes, purchased for my anticipated work in court as a barrister. We were required to wear specially made white shirts featuring white tabs at the neckline, topped by black wool vests and robes. These could be bought custom-made, which was a good thing since the tailoring firm, Harcourt's, did not have much practice yet in fashioning ready-to-wear garments for a woman's shape. My family attended the ceremonies, and I still laugh when I remember my father greeting me after the ceremony with a "report card" from Sydney Robins. As head of the Law Society, he attended the ceremonies for admission of new lawyers to the Bar of Ontario. Afterwards, he happened to be in the men's washroom at the same time as my father, and somehow they started talking. Knowing my dad, I can imagine that he introduced himself, but however it happened, my dad reported back to me, beaming, that Mr. Robins said to him, "You have a very bright daughter." On the following Monday, March 25, 1974, I opened my office for the practice of law.

THE WAY IT WAS IN 1974

So this was 1974: a time when women continued to be treated unequally and inequitably. I experienced first-hand what it was like for most women. There were almost no affordable and accessible public child-care supports. Women workers who became pregnant had no legal protection under human rights codes to be able to return to their jobs. Discrimination against women in pay, promotions, working conditions, and access to non-traditional jobs was systemic. In my own family, my aunt Lil worked for the government as a secretary. My mother used to deplore the fact that one of her sisters was continually passed over for promotions, even though her ability was undisputed—she was the one asked to train the young men who were then promoted instead of her.

All women suffered unfairness, but Indigenous women were uniquely disadvantaged. A prominent issue was that, under the federal Indian Act, an Indian woman who married a non-Indian man was deprived of her "Indian status" under this Act, and her children were also disenfranchised. This meant she could no longer live on the reserve and lost the right to own land or inherit family property; she could not receive treaty benefits or participate in band councils and political or social affairs in the community, and she lost the right to be buried in cemeteries with her ancestors. On the other hand, an Indian man who married a non-Indian woman was not deprived of these statutory rights and, moreover, his wife and children were given Indian status under the Act.[70]

This law was challenged in the early 1970s in two separate cases by two women who had lost their Indian status, Jeannette Corbière Lavell and Yvonne Bédard, and the cases were heard together at the Supreme Court of Canada.[71] One of the early and respected women lawyers, Margaret P. Hyndman, along with recent Osgoode graduate Frances Smookler, represented a number of intervenants.[72] In 1973 in a 5–4 decision, the Court ruled against them, deciding that the Indian Act did not deny them the Canadian Bill of Rights protection to "equality before the law"—as they were treated equally in the enforcement and application of the laws of Canada. This result served as a warning to feminist lawyers that it was essential to use clear and unambiguous wording to ensure women's equality rights in lobbying for the 1982 entrenched Charter of Rights and Freedoms.[73]

The issue remained on the feminist agenda. We had discussed it at the Windsor conference and passed a resolution to urge Jean Chrétien, then minister for Indian Affairs, to provide funding to women who had lost their Status under the Indian Act so they could present their point of view in the negotiations underway with the Indian Brotherhood to review the Indian Act. The response by Chrétien to the resolution was that he looked "to the National Indian Brotherhood (now the Assembly of First Nations) to substantiate clearly that the views of Indian women are reflected in any proposal they make for legislative change."[74] This review did not result in improvements for women who had lost their Status under the Indian Act.[75] The National Action Committee on the Status of Women, among others, kept up the pressure to improve rights for these women—the issue was featured at its 1980 meeting at Toronto's City Hall, "Feminist Visions: The Mothers of Confederation."

· · · · · · · · ·

When I had studied family law in law school, it was impossible to ignore the imbalance between how women and men were treated. I knew that I saw some of the cases from a different perspective than the guys. I remember analyzing a case in which a farm wife named Constance Thompson[76] had contributed to the down payment of the home and worked side-by-side with her husband, but even so was deemed to have no property rights in the family farm. She actually had few rights of any kind after divorce. The Supreme Court of Canada commented that "no case has yet held that, in the absence of some financial contribution, the wife is entitled to a proprietary interest from the mere fact of marriage and cohabitation." I considered this unfair and tucked the story away in the back of my mind.

In 1974, the courts still did not appear to think it unfair that the law limited a woman's rights both during marriage and after separation and divorce. Spousal and child support payments to women were paltry and difficult to enforce. Women (but not men) could be deemed guilty of matrimonial misconduct, like adultery and cruelty, and, as a result, be denied custody of their children. Women had no claim to any share of property owned by their husbands and certainly no right to any part of his business, investments, or pension—not even the matrimonial home. Whoever had title to a property retained its ownership, so it was pointless to enter into a dispute over sharing property.

In 1974, few lawyers practised family law; it was the poor relative of the legal community. In fact, when I joined the Family Law Section of the Canadian Bar Association—Ontario (as it was then called; it is now called the Ontario Bar Association), there were only about fourteen members present at any meeting.

Even divorce was a relatively new entitlement. It had been almost inaccessible until just six years earlier, when the federal government passed the 1968 Divorce Act. This federal law was considered progressive; it was the first time divorce could be sought on the simple grounds of a three-year separation—marital misconduct, such as adultery or cruelty, no longer needed to be proven. Although the opportunity was becoming available, most women couldn't afford to divorce. And so they stayed in even the most wretched marriages. If they left and sought a court order requiring their husband to pay financial support, a judge decided what they needed, and the approach was paternalistic. There was no sense that women were entitled to an equal (or any) share of the financial product of the marriage.

The Murdoch Case

Few people in power thought this state of matrimonial affairs was unjust, if they thought about it at all, until Irene Murdoch's case hit the headlines and focused attention on the issue in 1971. The proceedings unfolded during the years I was studying for my law degree, and they resonated with me, just as they did for many women. I had been shocked by the *Thompson* case, and now here was another patently unjust legal situation involving a farm wife. Mrs. Murdoch was an Alberta farmer's wife whose claim for a share of assets and spousal support was given short shrift by the courts of the day. The trial judge dismissed her claim for an equal share of the farm since he thought she did not do anything special—just what any farm wife does. But when one read her own description of what she actually did, one could not avoid understanding how women's work was diminished and undervalued.

"Haying, raking, swathing, mowing, driving trucks and tractors and teams, quietening horses, taking cattle back and forth to the reserve, dehorning, vaccinating, branding, anything that was to be done…just as a man would…."[77]

Moreover, during the five months of the year when her husband was working off the farm, she ran the ranch herself. Even her husband admitted the extent of her activities over twenty-five years of marriage. When asked what his wife did around the ranch, he responded: "Oh, just about what the ordinary rancher's wife does. Most of them can do most anything."[78]

There was also evidence at trial that she made cash contributions from her non-farm wages toward the down payment on the property and used funds gifted by her mother to buy household furnishings and appliances. Irene Murdoch left her husband after he violently assaulted her, fracturing her jaw in three places and leaving her jaw and lip permanently paralyzed.

None of these facts persuaded the trial judge to order her a share of the property. The judge said that if she got half the ranch, "it would be tantamount to establishing a precedent that would give any farm or ranch wife a claim in partnership"—as if to say that this would be a dangerous precedent. As for financial support, the trial judge ordered that she should receive just $200 a month.

Irene Murdoch's appeal to the Alberta Court of Appeal was dismissed in 1972. At her further appeal to the Supreme Court of Canada in 1973,[79] eight of the nine judges were of one mind in ruling that the appeal should be dismissed—they agreed with the trial judge. While they accepted the fact that she had made a substantial contribution to the building of the ranch enterprise, they considered her financial provision as a loan to her husband, and her labourer role as normal for a rancher's wife. They dismissed her claim on the basis that there wasn't "any common intention" that she would get a share. Believe it or not, on November 27, 1974, Mr. Murdoch was able to transfer the ranch to his son, who then leased it back to him for fifteen years, thus avoiding any chance his wife would benefit from all her hard work. He was not legally prevented from doing so, and he needed no one's consent—certainly not Mrs. Murdoch's.[80]

Like so many, I was outraged and frustrated. How could the law be so unfair to this woman? Were women just expected to be beasts of burden, hired hands without pay or compensation of any kind? It is difficult to overstate the impact this case had—not only on me, but on so many Canadian women. It shook us up and led to a public outcry. It highlighted the inequities facing women in the legal system and in life.

The case hit the headlines at the same time as divorce rates were on the rise. Since the passage of the Divorce Act a few years earlier, more women were choosing to end unsatisfactory marriages and struggling with the consequences of doing so. Women had to ask themselves, How will I survive? How will I manage to raise my children? They read about Irene Murdoch's fate in the newspapers and they watched it on TV, and they were horrified. It was in the headlines for more than two years as each level of court heard arguments and made rulings. Doris Anderson editorialized in *Chatelaine* about it and brought its import close to home for many women when she wrote, "For all women in Canada who work beside their husbands in family stores, motels, small businesses of any kind, this should be a chilling warning. The Supreme Court protects males but not females."[81]

The *Murdoch* case was part of the background when the Ontario Law Reform Commission (OLRC) was reviewing the law of family property on marriage breakdown. In 1974, the commission released a massive report that recommended the establishment of a new matrimonial property regime based on the principle of marriage as an economic partnership, unless the couple agreed to the contrary in a marriage contract. The commission proposed that all assets accumulated during the marriage be shared equally if the marriage was terminated by divorce or death. The commission proposed that the husband and wife be deemed co-owners of the matrimonial home.

Once released, the report was up for public discussion. I was one of four women lawyers asked by the volunteer-run Ontario Committee on the Status of Women[82] to summarize the document for distribution to the public. I can hardly believe it now, but we four (Rosalie Abella, Mary Eberts, Jane Maddaugh, and I) managed to summarize the five-volume report into a twelve-page pamphlet. I remember our meetings, filled with laughter and camaraderie and earnestness. Mary and I went on to become active in the women's movement and at the same time carried on law practices—Mary as a constitutional lawyer and I as a family lawyer. Rosalie became a judge, eventually rising to the Supreme Court of Canada. We lost touch with Jane Maddaugh; she may have left Toronto. The attorney general's policy chief, Karen Weiler—she later became a judge, rising to the Ontario Court of Appeal—distributed more than 50,000 copies of our summary around the province to help focus public attention on the issues. Mary, Rosalie, Karen, and I continued to get together for periodic lunches, and with my proclivity for puns, I named our foursome of women lawyers "The Portian Society."

PARTICIPATING IN THE PUSH

The inequities in family law became a focus of consciousness-raising among women everywhere. One month after I opened my law office, as the burgeoning women's movement flourished, I participated in the first Toronto women's conference, sponsored by the Humber College Centre for Women and guided by Marnie Clarke. The theme was Women and the Law, and it dealt with family law, equal pay, public assistance, abortion, pensions, and legal issues affecting women under the Indian Act. I was a workshop leader in family law and used the opportunity to press for a system in which men and women would be required to share their assets "from day one of the marriage." I had also raised this issue at the Windsor Conference where it received a favourable reception. I participated in the preparation of two resolutions—worked out simultaneously in separate, heavily attended workshops—that approved the concept.

Not wanting to chance this being buried, I wrote to then Ontario attorney general Robert Welch to advise him about the resolution. He responded that his ministry was "studying" the Ontario Law Reform Commission Report on Family Law, making me think that he was likely to ignore our resolution, as it was different from the OLRC one. I also collected a list of the names of forty-two women in my workshops who were interested in becoming involved in activism for better family laws and forwarded the list to the Ontario

Committee on the Status of Women, hoping they would find a way to use these volunteers.

So here I was, in my first year of practice, participating in the push for reform. In October 1974, another family law conference was sponsored by the Ontario Council on the Status of Women. This was the advisory council established by the Ontario government in response to the Royal Commission on the Status of Women. One of its first public events was the "Fair Share Conference on Family Property Law." The chair at the time was Laura Sabia and the organizers included Marie Corbett—who was later appointed a judge and after 1990 sat on the Superior Court of Ontario—who arranged for interested lawyers, including the new wave of women in law, to lead the seminars. In those days, conferences did not provide child care for the attendees, and I had no one to babysit my daughter that Saturday. But having made a commitment to go, I took Beth (and her games and crayons and other play materials) with me. She was the only child there. Fortunately, she was comfortable with adults, and she was able to sit quietly and let me participate. She even sat with me at the luncheon, sharing a table with, as I recall, family lawyers Rodica David and Emile Kruzick (now a Superior Court judge), who continue to ask after her to this day.

A female journalist, Margaret Weiers for the *Toronto Star*, attended the conference and reported how even-handed women were in their thinking. They wanted equal partnerships with men, they wanted equal ownership of the matrimonial home, and they wanted the deferred community of property system recommended by the OLRC. "Above all," she went on to write, "women want any reforms in family property law to be made retroactive—to apply to existing marriages..."[83]

In order to meet the uproar over the unjust *Murdoch* case head-on, the Ontario government decided not to wait until it could determine an overall solution to the law affecting families. Instead, it chose to legislate a stopgap measure, intended to avoid a Murdoch-type case in Ontario. The short 1975 law recognized the importance of a spouse who "contributes work, money, or money's worth in respect of the acquisition, management, maintenance, operation, or improvement of a business, including a farm, in which the other has a property interest" and stated that the spouse would

Women want the law to be fair to them and men, too

By MARGARET WEIERS
Star staff writer

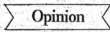

> Opinion

Professor Richard Gosse must surely have gone home to the University of British Columbia less apprehensive than when he came to Toronto.

Gosse, the keynote speaker at last weekend's conference of 500 Ontario women discussing reform of family property law, expressed concern that solutions to the knotty problems of property ownership between married persons weren't being discussed by men and women together.

Surely he wasn't afraid that men wouldn't have their say in what the reforms will be. Or had he forgotten that the members of the Ontario Law Reform Commission, whose report provided the basis for the discussion, are all men?

What's more, whatever new laws Ontario eventually gets will be proposed by a cabinet consisting of 24 men and one woman and debated and voted upon by a legislature of 114 men and three women.

So there's no way men won't have their say.

More likely, Gosse was concerned that women would demand laws stacking the deck against men if for no other reason than that, so far, many of our present property laws have seemed to give men all the trumps and leave women with the jokers.

He needn't have been so worried. For what came through, loud and clear, during the two days of intense discussion and debate in small group sessions and plenary meetings was that women want the law to be fair to them and to men, too.

Reasonable approach

children, the contribution they make be recognized, in economic terms. And they're quite prepared to shoulder the responsibilities that go with equality.

Hence, while they talked about and want to have, as an eventual goal, a community property system in Ontario, they recognize the difficulties inherent in immediate introduction of such a system. The women realized that effects of a community property system on commercial enterprises, on taxation, and on the economy generally need to be carefully assessed, and safeguards against mismanagement need to be devised, before any such law can be made.

Equal division

So women are quite willing to settle, for now, on a system of deferred sharing that provides for assets accumulated during marriage to be divided equally between the spouses when a marriage ends.

Essentially, that's what the Law Reform Commission recommended.

They accepted wholeheartedly enactment of a law that would oblige husbands and wives to support each other, throwing out the present law that obliges only husbands to support their wives. And they approved a resolution that both parents should have equal responsibility to support children of the marriage.

Of course, there was the occasional outburst like the one from a successful young lawyer: "I'm not going to marry a woman who

WOMEN WANT to be treated as equal partners with men in marriage, before the law.

that support payments, on the breakup of a marriage, never be allowed to continue for longer than the marriage lasted; the resolution that carried the plenary session was less frivolous

---

Margaret Weiers wrote this piece for the *Toronto Star*, October 30, 1974, about the conference sponsored by the Ontario Council on the Status of Women on family property law.

not be disentitled to any right to such property "by reasons only of the relationship of husband and wife or that the acts constituting the contribution are those of a reasonable spouse of that sex in the circumstances." This was the first time that Ontario law said that a wife had an independent and separate legal identity from her husband's. In other words, an Ontario husband could not say, "Why should she get a financial benefit when she did what any good wife does?"

Women started pushing to be part of the agenda. In 1971, maternity benefits were added to unemployment insurance. In 1974, Studio D of the National Film Board of Canada was launched to focus on films about women in society. Family laws were a live issue.

It was a start, but there was still a long way to go.

It was amidst this wave of growing awareness of the injustices suffered by women that I hung up my "shingle."

In opening my own office, I was truly taking charge of my life—on my own and as my own boss. I did not want to have to ask permission to take time off if my daughter needed me, nor did I want to work for other lawyers. I chose not to climb a ladder built by others. I imagined I would place my hands and feet on this ladder only to have them stepped on from above. That image was crystal clear in my head. My articling experience had prepared me for the worst, and the results of the survey I had done in law school were not reassuring. I did not need even more experience to teach me that a woman in a man's world would be accepted grudgingly and abandoned speedily if it was in someone else's best interests. I decided, instead, to try to succeed on my own terms; if I failed, so be it. I wasn't going to let being a woman stop me from trying. My definition of failure was not having enough clients to keep me busy, and not being able to make a modest living for my daughter and myself. So I told myself: *If you aren't busy enough, you can go to the movies in the afternoon; if you don't make a living, you can always take a job.* I did not end up doing either.

It was a challenging time to be a woman in law, and many women were trying to find their way in large firms or corporate environments or government. But some had goals similar to mine—to be in our own practices—and we set up the early all-female law firms. In the 1970s, Toronto saw Mary Cornish, Lynn King, Harriet Sachs, and Geraldine Waldman open up shop as Cornish, King, Sachs, and Waldman,[84] and Beth Symes, Frances Kiteley, and Elizabeth McIntyre joined together as Symes, Kiteley, and McIntyre.[85] Shirley Greenberg and Catherine Aitken launched Ottawa's first feminist law firm, Aitken Greenberg.[86] The lawyers in these groups, and maybe others elsewhere in Canada, went on to make great contributions to the law and to women.

As for me, I had arranged to share space with Jay Waterman and Bernie Eastman in an office building at Bay and Richmond Streets in Toronto, where they had offices for three lawyers, three secretarial desks, and a small reception area. I spent $1,000 on modest furniture, including a personal desk and chair and credenza, two client chairs, a filing cabinet, and a small two-seater couch. I did not buy equipment; instead, I paid Bernie for the services of one of his secretaries and her typewriter for two days a week—since he needed one full-time and one half-time secretary. Jay and Bernie assured me of enough agency work helping them with their cases to at least pay my rent on the office space. I was fortunate that Bernie and Jay mentored me, answering questions about law and strategy when I was in doubt, and they were generous with their time.

I went looking for a bank that would give me an operating loan to ensure cash flow while I was getting started. In those days, a law degree was all that was supposed to be needed in order to get a bank loan for set-up costs and even living expenses until the income started—or at least that's what was said at law school. A number of my male classmates borrowed between $75,000 and $100,000 each and set up lavish offices. I wasn't ready to take that kind of gamble. I went to the Bank of Nova Scotia closest to my new office and asked for a small loan—$5,000 to $10,000. The bank loan officer said he would need my father to co-sign. I guess a woman's law degree wasn't a sure thing from their perspective, especially since I was in the unusual position of embarking on my own practice. I refused to ask my father to co-sign (although I am sure he would have). The request was offensive, and I was angry that I was being treated differently from the male graduates. Fortunately, not all bank business loan policies were as unreasonable—the Royal Bank extended me the loan on my own signature. I set up my business banking with them and stayed with Royal for the rest of my career. For a time, I also opened an additional business account at Fidelity Trust, a small company around the corner from my office, and they sent business my way. I looked after foreclosures and powers of sale for them from time to time, which gave me excellent experience in understanding how these issues affected families.

My mother was surprised that I had chosen to set up on my own, and she worried about where I would get clients, especially as Canada was in a period of economic recession in 1974. I really did not have an answer for her, except that I planned to practise any branch of law for which I could get clients. The real answer, however, came soon enough: the clients came from anywhere and everywhere. It actually started on Sunday, March 24, when my home phone rang.

It was the father of the teenager who sometimes babysat for me. He asked, "Are you a lawyer yet?" I confirmed that I was and that my office was opening the very next day. He asked if I would be doing divorces, because he needed one. I had my very first client.

And so, when I went to the office on my first day, I already had some promised agency work from Bernie and Jay and one client who wanted a divorce. At the start, I took in every type of case that offered a fee. I practised litigation of all kinds and was in court often. I did some commercial work for small businesses. I did real estate sales and purchases and some litigation arising from property transactions. I prepared wills and administered estates. I declined criminal law cases; I thought I might be asked to represent alleged rapists and abusers. I reasoned that an accused person would hire someone with my limited trial experience only to parade her as a member of his defence team, as if to say, *How could I have raped that woman if this female lawyer believes in me enough to represent me?* It was a strategy I had encountered during my articling days, and now, as then, I refused to allow myself to be used in that way. I also did not want to be responsible for anyone's incarceration. So, with the exception of criminal law, I took on every type of case that came in and, as a result, learned about almost every branch of law. Family law gradually became my main focus—not only because that was the work that walked in the door but also because that was the work that interested me. I understood it on a personal level, and I felt I could make a difference.

Within three months I had earned enough in fees to cover my modest overhead costs and have something left over for Beth and me. Within a year and a half, I had so many clients that I needed a full-time secretary, and Bernie, Jay, and I required more space. By 1978, just four years after starting out, I shared an articling student with the other lawyers in the group. By 1980, with the space-sharing group splitting up, I sublet an office with room for five lawyers. The name on the door was Linda Silver Dranoff and Associates. By then, I was pleased to have Judith Huddart articled to me, and I was joined by four female lawyers—I always called the group my personal affirmative action program.

As a practitioner in a small office, I had to learn how to do everything that in large firms is handled by more specialized persons. I was the personnel department, the contact with the Law Society for administrative functions, the arranger of insurance, the procurer of equipment, the manager of work flow, the organizer of Christmas parties, and, above all, the rainmaker—the person who brought in the work. I always felt those challenges were worth the effort because I was my own boss. I made a point of seeking out and listening to the opinions and ideas of the staff, to such an extent that I would, with tongue firmly in cheek, call the firm the DDR, short for "Dranoff Democratic Republic."

Only six years had passed since I was called to the Bar. It turns out that my mother needn't have worried.

Chapter 6
THE LEARNING CURVE

As my practice flourished, I was continually challenged to deal with difficult lawyers, demanding clients, disdainful judges, painful learning experiences, the financial rigours of self-employment, and a legal system that focused more on expeditious resolution than on achieving justice. There were many cases that brought home powerful lessons about the practice of law and what the search for justice meant on a practical level. I learned about the vagaries of clients and the emotional reactions that affected their behaviour toward me and others. I had to figure out how to keep my emotional distance while at the same time be sympathetic to their concerns and interests. I attracted both male and female clients, but the preponderance were female in the early years. The men who came to me in those days sometimes wanted to appear to their wives to be fair, or they were ready to accept a female lawyer if they had been referred to her. There were a couple of men who wanted to use the fact that I was female and advocated for them as a sign that their position was reasonable. If they were not, in fact, reasonable, I would suggest they go elsewhere. Later, I attracted both male and female clients just because I was recognized as a good lawyer.

I saw people at their best and their worst. The best put their children's needs first and were realistic and amicable. Others pressed for their "rights." It could be difficult to get people to be rational when the trust inherent in a good marriage had broken down and one or both spouses viewed the other with suspicion. Much depended on which spouse made the decision to end the relationship and whether the reason was love for another person. I tried to get through to those who would listen, to tell them that they had to be sensible and not "stir the pot," that rationality often yielded a better result where the possibility of settlement existed at all. If they couldn't agree and the case had to go to trial to be decided by a judge, that changed everything.

The worst cases could be pretty awful and unfair. One shocker was a wife who lost her closest allies at the same time. After she was diagnosed with cancer, she found out her twin sister (who was also her best friend) was having an affair with her husband. I had to help her sort out both the financial and emotional difficulties. In another memorable case, my client could no longer bear being the sole real parent and breadwinner in a family with three children and a husband who did nothing to help her in any way or even to work. Once she announced that the marriage was over, he refused to move out and instead tried to win over the children. He sued his wife for custody, child support, and spousal support. It took years to resolve the issues in an unsatisfactory way; in the end, she concluded she'd had an easier life before the separation.

Another staple of family law was that men who have affairs often expect there to be no consequences. In one unforgettable instance, my client succumbed to a seductive woman who, it turned out, wanted him to impregnate her because her husband couldn't. He had no idea why she'd arranged to have sex with him periodically and had no clue when she produced three children. It was only years later, when her husband lost his job and left her, that she went after my client for support for "his" three children. A DNA test verified how successful her machinations had been, and he was on the hook for child support. The law was clear: he was the biological father, so he had to pay. In another case, my male client alleged that the woman who claimed child support had raped him. Since the DNA test proved positively that he was the biological father, he, too, was required to pay child support, regardless of how the impregnation had occurred. The emotional wreckage of divorce proved difficult for everyone. I cannot recall a client, male or female, for whom it was a ho-hum experience. Some, however, found it impossible to live with the breakdown of their marriage. I had two women clients during my career who, after the negotiations were concluded and the divorce decree had been issued, took their own lives. Neither one could imagine living a life separate from her husband; in each case, the wife's whole sense of self was bound up with her spouse. I was devastated when I learned about what each of them had done. I knew I had done everything possible to support them emotionally in the legal process, but I could not affect the outcome when a woman's identity was so closely tied to her marriage. Nor was it in my power to maintain a compassionate process when the opposing client and his lawyer focused only on the result they wanted to achieve and did not take the wife's vulnerabilities into consideration.

HARD LESSONS

About three years into my practice, I took on a case for a father who was being unfairly prevented by a determined mother from seeing his children, who had been four and one years of age when they separated. By the time the case came to trial, they were nine and six, and the years in between had been fraught with conflict between the parents.

The mother's lawyer had just been called to the Bar and had not yet learned to distance himself from his client's emotions. He brought motion after motion, to the extent that one day he brought two motions to be heard *at the same time* before two different courts. I received a telephone call from a clerk at the Court of Appeal at 9:30 a.m. on a day when I was preparing to respond to one of the lawyer's interim motions before a master (a master is a court official below the rank of judge, who, at that time, heard interim motions).

He told me that the lawyer was in his office seeking an appointment before an Appeal Court judge on that very case. I told the clerk that I had no notice of the appearance and had no knowledge of what the motion was all about and, in any event, was about to appear in front of the master at 10 a.m. to deal with that very case. The other lawyer was not permitted to have access to an Appeal Court judge without my presence.

The mother was determined to protect her children; in her view that meant keeping them from their father. He had a close and devoted relationship with his boys, particularly the older one, and he had assumed that nothing could interfere with that. He had not considered the impact of their mother's brainwashing. He had not realized that she would be the likely winner in a conflict of loyalties because the children lived with her.

I recall one time prior to trial when the father and I still hoped that the boys would defy their mother for the sake of access to their father. Previously, the father had repeatedly turned up at the door at the time of court-ordered access, and either the mother failed to answer or the children would say they did not want to go. In this instance, the father implemented my idea of hiring a horse and buggy. When the father arrived at the home in the horse and buggy, the children couldn't resist. They raced to him and had a grand time. However, when they returned home, their mother told them they'd been tricked by their father; the next time he came to call, he was greeted by a child saying, "You tricked me."

The case ended up being a long and intensely fought battle. After thirty-nine interim motions and twenty-two days of trial, the judge ordered the parties to go for mediation with a psychiatrist. This was the first time to my knowledge that mediation was ordered in an Ontario family law case. Since mediation required the parties to agree, I was concerned that this would be a futile effort (as we'd already tried valiantly to settle). Before the trial was adjourned, I instinctively asked the judge to order the mother to deposit the children's passports with the court for safekeeping, to prevent her from taking them out of the jurisdiction. The judge refused, stating it was not necessary.

When we returned to court some months later to hear the mediator's report, a different lawyer represented the mother. He reported that she and the children had left Toronto and her whereabouts were unknown. I was so disheartened that the legal system had let this injustice happen to the father and to his children.

I had sensed the judge's anxiety in the mother's presence and wondered if that was a factor in his failure to order the passports kept by the court. Years later, the judge's obituary said he had been threatened and narrowly missed death at the hands of a violent spouse in a family law case. The timing of this unfortunate event? It was several months before my client's case was heard. This case helped me understand just how vulnerable judges can be to the emotions of the parties and how tough-minded a person must be to do the judicial job properly. I also experienced first-hand and early on how complex and fraught with risks custody and access cases are, and how the children are affected.

This case also taught me about the business of law and getting paid for my services. Based on this father's verbal promise to pay, I took his lengthy trial forward, at the end of which he went bankrupt. He acknowledged in a letter to me that I had provided massive legal support for him out of a sense of compassion and that I had trusted his word that he would someday clean up the bill. He promised to pay the monthly sum of $200 without interest, and acknowledged the impact on the rest of my practice, suggesting that I was not "survival-oriented enough to demand payment at the beginning." How true! He thanked me, but he never paid me a cent of the outstanding amount. It taught me a huge lesson, which was not top-of-mind as often as it should have been. I began to be wary of clients who couldn't pay as you go, but sometimes I would rankle at the injustice they were suffering and accept the risk of non-payment anyway.

Another case stands out. I had achieved in court for my client an exceptional result in her divorce, given that we could not prove what her husband earned, but only what lifestyle he lived. Even so, I persuaded a judge to order him to pay her a monthly amount based on his lifestyle and not on his tax return. I assumed that if he failed to meet the monthly payments, my client could garnishee part of the proceeds of an inheritance he expected to receive. She complained to the Law Society that I had secured an award that her husband could not pay. She also refused to pay my bill and agreed to let the husband reduce the amount of the support. Sometimes, you can be too successful. The Law Society dismissed her outrageous claim, and I did not pursue the unpaid balance of my fees.

On occasion, I would lose a client because he or she bought into a promise that another lawyer could achieve more than I could. I remember in the 1970s the two male lawyers who lured vulnerable female clients with the promise that they would receive the sum of $300,000 as a settlement. I knew about it because several clients came back to me and asked why I couldn't promise the same. The reality, as I would explain, was that I could only give a range of possible results; I could not guarantee what would happen in court. Cases that went to trial often were reported in the official law reports, so I learned just how poor the outcome had been for several of my former clients, in one case far less than the offer that had been on the table before she switched lawyers. In other instances, the clients returned to me or wrote me, thanked me, and expressed regret that they had left. I was sorry that they did not realize better results.

In those days, once a judge ordered one party to pay the other's costs, another decision-maker—a designated court official—held a hearing to determine the amount to be paid, after considering whether the amount requested was fair and in keeping with precedents. I always found this a difficult process since the court official had not been at the trial and had no prior knowledge of the case. No matter what precedents from other cases I brought forward as to amount, I never achieved those for myself. I had the feeling that these court officers thought a woman should not earn that much, even if she had put in the work. Eventually, the system changed, and the judge who conducted the trial was given the responsibility to deal with costs orders. But even then, I sometimes felt that there was an unspoken assumption—that even among lawyers, women were not entitled to earn what men did for the same work. As a result of these experiences, I would find a way to settle any such disputes outside court if possible.

NOT FOR THE FAINT OF HEART

I also learned about the vagaries of judges and their ability and occasional willingness to dump all over counsel. It only reinforced the common view that being a litigation lawyer was not for the faint of heart. Two instances stand out in my mind, but there were more.

I was in a judge's chambers to respond to a motion made on behalf of a husband. He wanted the judge to rule that the lawyers had settled the case on behalf of their clients in an exchange of letters. There were only three of us present—the opposing lawyer, the judge, and me. I submitted that the case should be decided at a trial, according to legal process. I argued that the parties themselves had to sign an agreement in front of witnesses in order to have an enforceable settlement.

As I made my pitch, the judge glared at me, deeply emotional and angry, and spoke with vituperation. I remember feeling undeservedly attacked and particularly recall these odd and inappropriate words he spat out: "Do you think I'm your water boy? That I'll just do what you say because you say it?" I was shocked and responded very quietly: "I am only making submissions on behalf of my client, Milord." I was, after all, only doing my job and had not said or done anything disrespectful. That was never my style, in life or in court. I wondered if my being a woman played a part. The judge certainly did not treat the male lawyer who acted for the husband in the same way; he had presented his case no less earnestly than I did and was as shocked as I was by the judge's conduct. Neither of us questioned the judge, for fear of exacerbating an already difficult situation. Afterwards, my opponent commented, "Where the hell did that come from?"

The judge said he would reserve his decision and release it later in writing. I guess since he had to write publicly available reasons for his decision, which could be appealed to a higher court, he had to come to a conclusion that would not reflect badly on him. I won the motion because the facts and the law were on my side. But the judge still found a way to insert a dig at me in the Reasons for Decision he issued, which was included in the published law reports. In the ruling, he included these words directed at me: "In a manner that brooked no other considerations…[counsel] implied that the court was expected to rubber-stamp the order for trial…."

While the judge did not ignore the facts of the case or the law in coming to his conclusion, the case made me realize once again how vulnerable I was. It taught me that I had to stick to my guns, no matter what. It also made me realize that decisions made behind closed doors in arbitration and mediation settings did not have the same safety mechanism built in—the arbitrator did not have to justify his decision by publicly releasing Reasons for Decision. In this case, at least the judge had to make a decision based on the facts and the law, or face reversal on appeal.

Then there was the case that really challenged my confidence in the legal system. I was ready to start a divorce trial in which I was acting for the wife. At 10 a.m., just before the trial was to start, with all witnesses present and all the trial preparations completed, the judge called the opposing lawyer and me into his chambers. He demanded to know why the case had not been settled. We told him we had made every effort but that the parties were adamantly opposed, and the matter needed to be decided by a judge at a trial.

The judge looked at me, not at the more senior male lawyer opposing me, and said, "If you don't settle this, I will order that you pay the legal costs personally for both parties." Nothing I said would persuade him to be reasonable. The opposing lawyer was silent. We went out again and talked settlement. I had to explain to my client what was happening, but could see no solution other than settlement on the best terms we could negotiate. By 2 p.m., the time when the judge had instructed us to return to his chambers, we had come to a resolution that gave my client her dignity but not the result she had hoped for and might have achieved if a proper trial had taken place before a judge who was prepared to listen. The opposing lawyer had taken advantage of the situation. My client was furious that she did not get her day in court, and she refused to pay my fees.

When we returned to the judge's chambers, I could tell that he was inebriated—both his manner and the odour of alcohol gave him away. I figured out afterward that I should have brought the matter to the attention of the chief justice of the court or possibly the Judicial Council that, since 1971, monitors the conduct of judges. But that was early in my career, and I did not have the experience or, as I saw it, the credibility to take that kind of action against a judge. I vowed that the next time anything like that happened I *would* take action. Fortunately, I never had to; no other judge gave me cause to make that kind of complaint. That judge remained on the bench for almost twenty years; I am told that eventually his colleagues became aware of his problem and his later years were spent on desk work and not trial work.

It was my bad luck to come up against these unusual judges in my early years of practising law. Most were not so outrageously memorable. I remember a very civilized and respectful trial conducted by one of the first women judges, Donna Haley. She was not taken in by the opposing male lawyer who ridiculed what I said and then summed up his attitude with a statement directed at me: "A court of law is not a tea party, my dear."

There were many other cases that taught me about the nitty-gritty of the practice of law. I faced reality on a daily basis and learned the ropes as well as I could. I learned from my clients, other lawyers, and officiating judges—all of whom were my unintentional educators in the rough and tumble of litigation and what it meant to be in an adversarial profession. I also recognized that the only way to achieve a truly just and precedent-setting result was to go to court and hope to draw a fair-minded and knowledgeable judge who would see the law my way. This was especially the case when the opposing lawyer would not or could not control his own client. When a lawyer would accept instructions to take the most outrageous positions, only a judge could resolve it. When a lawyer allowed a client to back out of a deal, it made good faith negotiations impossible. I remember one lawyer and his client both blaming *me* for the breakdown of the marriage!

The practice of law also gave me essential tools in my fight for equality for women. Standing up for my clients showed me how to stand up for the rights of women. I also found myself in situations where I had to stand up for myself.

In 1977, there was a threat to my entire legal career. I had been in practice for about three years and had been doing some public speaking, particularly on family law and women's issues. I had received an invitation to address the University Women's Club of North York in late October 1977. I agreed to speak, and when the club asked for my curriculum vitae, I sent it. One of their members introduced me. The wife of one of the lawyers at Du Vernet Carruthers was in the audience.

About a month later I received a letter from the deputy secretary of the Law Society, C. I. Scott, advising me that the flyer to promote that meeting had been brought to his attention. I had not previously seen it, but it apparently included the following wording: "Come hear the news from an expert. Linda Silver Dranoff is the author of the new book *Women in Canadian Law*.... Linda comes to us highly recommended by Judge Rosalie Abella of the family court.... Bring your questions." He added, "It has been alleged that your office address and suite number were given to the audience." The rules were very specific at that time. Rule 30 of the Rules of Professional Conduct of the Law Society of Upper Canada dealt with Public Appearances by Solicitors and included the following:

No solicitor should solicit appearances in his professional capacity as a solicitor, attempt to use appearances as a means of professional advertisement.... Where the reason for a solicitor's appearance is his professional capacity, he may be described by name...the description barrister and solicitor...and a reasonable amount of biographical material, but...no reference may be made by him or any other to indicate that he is a specialist in any branch of law. The overriding principle is...good taste.... Compliance with this ruling shall *prima facie* be the responsibility of the solicitor...

Mr. Scott did not say who had made the complaint, nor did he provide me with a copy of it. He wrote as follows:

The Society's attention has been drawn to a flyer apparently issued by the University Women's Club of North York, a copy of which is enclosed. Also enclosed is a copy of Ruling 30 of the Rules of Professional Conduct. It has been alleged that your office address and suite number were given to the audience. May I have your comments in the light of the provisions of Ruling 30. I am particularly interested in knowing...how you came to be classed as an expert.

It took me several weeks and many drafts to answer the complaint against me. I felt that my career was being threatened. My response to the Law Society was a carefully worded letter in which I responded to the complaint, doing my best to avoid colouring it with the indignation I was feeling.

I was invited by the University Women's Club of North York to speak to them on the subject of women's legal status and I accepted. At the time, I was not aware that Judge Rosalie Abella had suggested my name to them as an appropriate speaker on the subject. The only flyer I ever received from them was a copy of their year's program, in which my presentation was noted. I thought that the printed material which I saw was tasteful. I did not see the flyer that you sent with your letter of November 22 until you sent it. At no time was it discussed with me, nor was I aware that it was being prepared or distributed.

I did not give my office address to the audience, of course.

It may be however, that the member who introduced me did mention it in passing. I do not recall for certain. My memory of the introduction I received that evening was that it was flattering and amusing and that the member got carried away at times by her own enthusiasm. I consider that it would have been in bad taste for me to have asked for the text for my advance approval.

The University Women's Club classed me as an expert; I did not refer to myself in those terms. I imagine they assumed my expertise from knowing of my various publications, and lectures on the subject.

I have always endeavoured to ensure the good taste of my public appearances. If a complaint has been made that any public appearance of mine was not in good taste, warranting that I be noticed by the Law Society, then I believe it to be appropriate and in accordance with Law Society practice to provide me with a copy of the complaint, so that I may know who has complained and the nature of the alleged error on my part.

It appears to me that the complainant made no effort to ascertain the facts but simply, for his own purposes, put the worst possible interpretation on the situation. It is distressing that your office should be used as the means of inquiring into such a simple matter....

While the Law Society at that time had a rule against advertising by lawyers, I couldn't see how an introduction by someone else should affect my licence to practise law. I asked for an indication of how I had contravened Ruling 30, and Mr. Scott replied that compliance with the ruling was my responsibility, that I should not have been referred to as a specialist (they actually said "expert"), and that supplying my office address could be seen as a means of professional advertisement. He then advised that he was forwarding it to a senior member of the discipline committee for consideration. He still did not advise me who had made the complaint.

In early February 1978, I heard again from Deputy Secretary Scott. To my great relief, he advised that the discipline committee senior member was satisfied with my comments and had instructed him to take no further action. Then he felt compelled to add: "The Society trusts that you will continue to appreciate the necessity of trying to ensure that the appearance of soliciting business is avoided." The implication was that I had done something wrong and the Law Society was going to keep an eye on me. Since the Law Society controlled my professional licence, the rebuke gave me cause for concern. It seemed to me that no matter what I did, I was going to be questioned and challenged, and I had better watch my back. I was once again reminded that, like others before and after me, I was not part of the protected establishment, and my presence was accepted reluctantly and "on sufferance only" just as it had been at that debate at Hart House long ago. Just like other women and members of other disadvantaged groups, I was tolerated but not welcomed into the profession.

Even though I became, in due course, no longer young and quite so vulnerable, I did watch my back for the rest of my legal career, knowing that the Law Society had the ability to take away everything that I had worked so hard to achieve.[87]

SEARCHING FOR WORK-LIFE BALANCE

During these early years in practice, I had to come to grips with these threats to my career and to my security within the profession, as well as face the pressures of a law practice. I tried to keep most of my concerns to myself, although I was able to confer with the colleagues with whom I practised. I did not want my daughter to have to deal with my stresses. I wanted her to have her childhood and not be forced to fill the role of confidante to a single parent in a pressure-cooker career. While some of my anxieties inevitably spilled over into my relationship with her, I tried to limit this from happening.

Happily, I also had some good friends and close family to turn to. I had a good friendship with my first husband's Uncle Ben and Aunt Sally, who acted as "surrogate grandparents" to Beth. Sally was like a girlfriend. Like my mother and aunts, she was one of those women who, had they been born in a different time, would have gone on to university and the professions and excelled in that role. I felt so blessed that Beth and I were objects of her loving devotion, and particularly grateful that she seemed to always be available as a sounding board and supportive presence.

Then, in the summer of 1978, serendipity introduced me to Harvey. I had always been interested in finding a strong and enduring relationship with the right man. Over the years, I met many good men and even dated some, but for one reason or another, they did not turn into long-term relationships. As I grew older and busier, finding a committed and permanent relationship became more difficult. The fact that I had a child was an obstacle for some men. And I was more particular because I wanted the right parental figure for my daughter. In some cases, the relationship just did not work out. Just as my first husband had reacted negatively to my earning more than he did, some of the men I met and dated wanted a more traditional woman than I was—and am. It was usually not stated outright, but became obvious in more subtle ways. I found that some men wanted someone to take care of them—including putting dinner on the table and managing the home. This dampened my enthusiasm. While I practised law, I made the choice to employ people to do many of those homemaking duties. I was put off by traditional expectations, and I wanted a partnership with a peer, not a dependant. I preferred to be alone rather than be with a man who did not have similar values. Finding this was not easy.

In 1978, I took a week's holiday in the Bahamas, and it was there that I met an accountant with an MBA who hailed from New Jersey and had a business in Brooklyn, New York. Harvey was a fine man, and by the end of the week, we were making plans to see each other again. Soon we were spending every other weekend together. Usually he came to Toronto, but occasionally I flew to New Jersey. He respected my successes and his ego was not challenged by them. In fact, he was a valued advisor—in our nightly talks, he would give me business advice at a time when my practice was expanding.

We started to plan a life together. I had told him definitively when we first met that there was no way I would move back to the United States. My law degree would not be recognized there, and the fact that I would be giving up the life I had built with Beth in Toronto made even the thought of it intolerable. I had relocated once for a husband, and I wouldn't do it again. He assured me from the outset that he would be the one to move and, in fact, started making plans to open a business in Toronto.

This was a very happy time for me. Harvey and I had an early "commuter relationship," and it worked for us. Well, it certainly worked for me. My career was thriving, and this non-traditional relationship allowed me the time and energy I needed to pursue the opportunities that were coming my way, as well as my work with the feminist movement, about which I was increasingly passionate. I was so busy during the week with my law practice, writing, media work, and activism that a more traditional relationship might not have worked. Everyone figures out their own way to have a balance between a career and a life, and at that time, this was mine.

Chapter 7
CHAMPIONING FAIRNESS

The fight for equality of rights and opportunities was a major thrust of second-wave feminism. It was also a driving force in my life. It overlapped and intersected all the compartments of my life—the law practice, the writing, the public speaking, the activism. I dipped into all those compartments to lobby for law reform, to present my clients' cases, and to educate the public. I tried to do more than bemoan unfair circumstances. Decision-makers might sympathize with those who suffer an injustice, but they needed advice on what to do about it. Those of us on the front lines of the legal struggles to benefit women thought we knew what needed to be done and that it was our personal responsibility to contribute to the discussions. In my case, I also learned about inequities in the law when situations faced by clients tipped me off about them.

WORKING WITH CLIENTS
Lawyers are often the last bastion and bulwark in protecting liberal and humanitarian values and the rule of law. In my law practice, I was an advocate for justice for my clients, and I suspect that my innate impatience and anger about injustice may have drawn them to me, just as it drew me to the law. Of course, everyone has a different idea of what fairness looks like. I have my own ethical norms, and I challenged myself to find ways to persuade legal institutions to improve the situation for women.

Many women could not afford legal counsel, and it was difficult to get a fair shake without the help of a good lawyer. I tried to assist some of these women but learned quite quickly that this was not realistic; I could not afford to work for free, and the needs were extensive. I used to fantasize about winning the lottery and donating funds to set up a legal clinic with free family law services for women. Well-funded legal aid was one systemic way to improve access to justice for those who could get it in no other way, but the availability of legal aid had become more and more limited due to financing cuts by governments. Legal aid gave lawyers so little compensation compared to what clients in private practice were paying. As time went by, fewer lawyers could afford to take on the neediest clients and fewer lower-income people qualified for legal aid—the system has evolved to a point where a legally aided client has to be almost penniless in order to qualify for help. I remember one individual who received only partial legal aid as she had savings of $6,000 and minimum-wage employment. She was expected to spend some of that small $6,000 cushion for legal services. While I took on some legal aid cases in these early years of my practice, I quickly concluded that I could make a more substantial and wide-reaching contribution by working toward more systemic solutions.

My emphasis on fairness was sometimes at odds with the views of those lawyers and judges who only wanted to resolve disputes, to "make a deal." While this was an admirable goal, and I also wanted to and did settle differences, I was not willing to do so at the price of basic fairness. The outcome had to be even-handed. If it wasn't, the parties had little chance of making it work over the long haul, especially if they had children.

Sometimes fair-minded people could be persuaded to come to a reasonable result without a court's ruling. In one such case, in 1979, I convinced the opposing counsel and husband to alter the standard clause terminating spousal support if the wife remarried or lived with another man as if married. It was unreasonable to terminate support if she remarried someone who could not afford to support her, especially if he had his own first family to maintain. The husband was reasonable enough to amend the clause so that support could be varied or ended only if his wife received a financial benefit from her new relationship. As it turned out, this provision continued in effect for at least twenty-five years; my client came back to see me about another matter and reported that she was still getting spousal support from her first husband, although she had remarried. It was an unusual deal in 1979, but by 2004 when she returned to see me, it was a more common expectation because some judges stopped assuming that a remarried wife automatically would be supported financially by her new husband. Once the courts acknowledged this, lawyers made settlements accordingly. I suppose other lawyers might have been doing the same thing, but since settlements are not reported, I never knew about them.

At this time, a trend began to pick up steam: the use of mediators and arbitrators outside the court system to resolve family law disputes. Private dispute resolution was usually no less expensive or time consuming than court, and, more important from my perspective, did not offer the opportunity to set precedents that would help others. When a case is mediated or arbitrated, the reasons for the decision are not publicly available. When a case is tried in a court of law, the judge's reasons for the ruling and analysis of the applicable law are printed in the law journals and sometimes reported on in the media, which helps others in subsequent cases to interpret and change that law. As a result, this privatization was useful only in limited circumstances and was not the best solution for women. If the process was hidden and the result unsupported by written reasons, then women might suffer. The threat of going to court often aided the settlement process. In some cases, a party was forced to go to court because the opposing party refused to compromise. There were times when I would take the battle as far as it needed to go to get my client the best possible result. I was always prepared to take my cases to court and felt that no lawyer could successfully work in family law if he or she was not prepared to go to court and champion a client's cause. I made it known to every lawyer I had a case with that I was prepared to fight to the finish, even if that meant going all the way to the Supreme Court of Canada. Ironically, once I got that reputation, I settled many of my cases. Court was the weapon in my back pocket.

Those of us who were looking to fundamentally change the system looked for systemic solutions. We wanted the legal system to be effective for people and, to that end, kept in mind the help that a precedent-setting case would provide in making new law for the benefit of other litigants. Besides legislation, only a court ruling was able to change the law. I found the opportunity to do this early in my career. In 1976, after just two years in practice, I represented a woman whose husband was seriously behind in his support payments. I had been in provincial family court about the case four times before the judge ordered the husband to make an immediate payment of $150 or go to jail for one month, and then pay thirty-five dollars a week toward the arrears.

Since the husband was found to be in the wrong, I felt he should also pay something toward my client's legal costs. However, there was no rule or precedent on this matter in the provincial family court.[88] That did not seem reasonable to me. Costs could be ordered in the higher courts; why shouldn't the provincial court that ruled on the cases of poorer people also be able to do so?

It seemed to me that it was worth trying to make progress on this front. I researched the law that applied to the provincial family courts and conceived an argument based on a technical interpretation of the interconnection among five pieces of legislation that were central to the topic: the Deserted Wives' and Children's Maintenance Act; the Summary Convictions Act; the Justices of the Peace Act; the Administration of Justice Act; and the Criminal Code. I felt lucky to have drawn Judge James Karswick. Not only did he seem willing to listen to an unusual argument, but I also had the feeling that he was pleased to do so—and to be given the opportunity to make new law that would both benefit many and give judges more tools with which to do their job.

In the end, Judge Karswick agreed that he did have jurisdiction, and he ordered the husband to pay thirty dollars toward my client's legal costs.[89] While the amount was modest, the principle was significant. From that point on, the provincial family court made costs orders in many other cases and, eventually, this was incorporated into the court's rules. This was my first precedent-setting case. It made me recognize that it was up to lawyers to bring new issues to the courts to decide, as the sympathetic judges could not take the initiative. I also realized that the time to do this was when I was already in court acting for a client—as there would be no added cost to speak of. Even so, it all had to come together: the right judge, the right facts, arguable law, and all the right personalities. I suspect the growing awareness of women's issues in society may also have been part of the mix.

During this same period, I dealt with another case that showed how important it was to have the courage of your own convictions. This time, the husband and his lawyer had a very different sense of fairness than his wife and I did. The challenge was to persuade the court that justice was on our side and, therefore, the law should follow. I was consulted by a mother of three whose married life had been spent as a wife, mother, hostess, and social support to her executive husband. She had already signed a separation agreement, thinking it was a temporary resolution dealing only with monthly financial support. She had done so before the 1978 Family Law Reform Act—with its property-sharing provisions—came into being. Her husband thought he was generously taking care of his wife's needs by providing monthly spousal support. The case could not be resolved between the parties even with the help of lawyers, so the matter had to go to court.

I argued that the separation agreement did not preclude a hearing on her property-sharing rights since the law was not in effect when she signed the agreement, and she couldn't give up a non-existent right. As a precaution, I contended in the alternative that a lump-sum support payment, which was available under the Divorce Act, should be ordered if the property-sharing provisions of the Family Law Reform Act were not applicable.

The trial judge ruled that the wife was to get not only monthly support but also a lump-sum support payment of $300,000 plus $100,000 in lieu of her interest in the matrimonial home and cottage. The total amount represented about one-half of the value of the family's assets, which was a very unusual and substantial result for that time. Fortunately, the judge's sense of fairness accorded with ours. I was delighted, and my client was thrilled, but the prominent senior male lawyer acting for the husband was irate, and his anger was directed at me, not the judge. I can remember to this day his indignation and how red his face was. It seemed to me that he was personally piqued that he had been bested by me, a much less experienced lawyer.

This case taught me a valuable lesson, one I've never forgotten: if something is fair and you can find a peg to hang your hat on, you should take it to court and see if you can win it on principle. In this case, I think the judge felt it unfair that the wife had walked away with only the right to monthly support when the laws had in the meantime changed to benefit her with a share of property. I offered him a way to mete out a just result, and he took it.

I worked hard to find new ways to achieve a double objective: obtain a just result for an individual client and create progress in the law, a "precedent," that would help others in the same circumstances. A divorced mother of a son with cerebral palsy came to see me many years after her divorce, at a time when she was terminally ill. Florence Lesser told me that she needed an increase in support from her wealthy ex-husband, then paying $1,500 a month for her and $350 a month for her twenty-three-year-old disabled son. Given her poor health, it seemed to me that any increase in her spousal support would not last long or be a cost-effective exercise. I asked her how her son would manage on $350 a month once she was gone. She was very worried about that, but felt there was no solution; she had been advised by a number of lawyers that her husband would not have any obligation to continue that $350 a month payment after she died. None of those lawyers were prepared to take the case forward. I went to my bookshelf and pulled out a copy of the Divorce Act. Going back to the precise wording in the law often gives me ideas. This case was no exception.

The definition of "child of the marriage," whom a parent is responsible to support, includes a child who is age sixteen or over and is under a parent's charge "but unable by reason of illness, disability, or other cause, to withdraw himself from their charge or to provide himself with necessaries of life." However, the law appeared clear that the parties to the divorce decree, namely the ex-husband and ex-wife, were the only ones who could return to court for a variation of the court order. I advised Mrs. Lesser that the best chance of success would be for her to bring an application to court in her lifetime for a variation in the amount of both her son's and her own support payment, and then, in her will, authorize her estate to continue the proceeding at the estate's expense. If her son was required to sue on his own after her death, he might be perceived to have no legal basis to do so. She was accompanied at the consultation by one of the executors of her will, Dorothy Stossel, who agreed with the plan and understood what must be done to continue the action. I liked both of them, as well as Lesser's son Robert and his brother Brian, whom I later met.

In March 1983, Florence Lesser brought the application to vary spousal and child support, but as anticipated, she died before the application could be heard. I went to court on behalf of the estate and obtained an order authorizing the estate to continue the legal action. Elaine Newman, who then was a lawyer at the Advocacy Resource Centre for the Handicapped, acted for Robert, and we co-operated in pressing the case forward. Mortimer Lesser, the ex-husband, took the position that his obligation to pay child support ended with the death of his wife, and he appealed to set aside the estate's Order to Continue the proceeding. Mr. Justice George Walsh, the head of the Supreme Court of Ontario's Family Law Division—as it was then called—heard the matter and ruled in favour of the estate. He agreed with me that there was nothing in the Divorce Act that, on the death of one of the spouses, prevented the mandatory continuation of payments for a child of the marriage. He concluded that Robert continued to be a "child of the marriage" and therefore continued to be entitled to support even if he was living with neither parent. (In fact, Robert resided with his brother after their mother's death.) Justice Walsh said the child support order could be varied and the estate could continue the lawsuit. The Ontario Court of Appeal, where the father challenged the decision, agreed with Justice Walsh.

The next issue was whether the child support amount should be changed or ended. The issue became the father's ability to pay, and he refused disclosure of the financial information and documents that would help determine how much he could afford. He claimed that he was suffering financial reverses that made him unable to pay, but would not prove them. He submitted that Robert was no longer a child of the marriage and that he could support himself. As a result, we were required by the court to subject Robert to an assessment, which concluded that he would always be a dependant. Then the father took the position that Robert could live in a group home. He alleged that the estate should sell all the mother's assets and use the income to support Robert. In fact, the main asset was a modest home, in which the two brothers continued to reside.

Due to his lack of voluntary financial disclosure, it was complicated to prove at trial the father's ability to pay. A certified appraiser was retained to determine the value of a building we knew he owned in Toronto, and the appraiser attended on the first day of trial to give evidence. The father's insurance company was subpoenaed to bring to court all the appraisals they had as backup to their insurance coverage of his reputedly substantial collection of Canadian art. Evidence was given as to the cost of an annuity that would guarantee to Robert Lesser a specific amount of support for the rest of his life. The father's accountant was subpoenaed. In fact, the courtroom was full of individuals summoned as witnesses. Mr. Lesser and his lawyer, Joel Goldenberg, were surprised to see them. I had called their bluff.

When Justice Walsh arrived at the courtroom and everyone stood up to greet him, as was customary, his first question was "What's all this?" I explained that these were witnesses who were there to give evidence that Mr. Lesser had the financial ability to pay child support to his son for his lifetime, and that we needed their evidence because we had been given so little voluntary or court-ordered disclosure. Justice Walsh leaned over his raised bench and spoke directly to Mr. Lesser's lawyer: "Do I really need to hear from all these witnesses? Are you telling me that Mr. Lesser can't afford to pay whatever amount of child support I order?"

Mr. Goldenberg and Mr. Lesser conferred. Eventually, Mr. Goldenberg stood and admitted on behalf of Mr. Lesser that he could pay whatever was ordered. After all, we had prepared a budget of Robert's expenses, and it was unlikely that Justice Walsh would order that Robert be paid anything above and beyond this. We proceeded without financial evidence; all that had to be proven was that Robert was a child of the marriage and needed support in the amount set out in the budget.

The judge ordered that the father pay $1,700 a month for his son's lifetime, with a review on a specified date and a contribution to costs. In the end, with the trial over, Dorothy Stossel's beaming smile made me feel that Florence Lesser was at peace. I also knew that the results of these proceedings[90] would serve other disabled children of divorce whose lawyers might otherwise have said, "It can't be done." This was a clear example of litigation and a trial being the only means of resolving a case and achieving fairness for a child and peace of mind for a mother. The law had not been clear, even though the morality was.

There were other cases involving children that had to be resolved by a judge in court because they could not be settled any other way. In one such troubling situation, the biological father sought access to his very young daughter, despite the fact that all signs pointed to his having sexually abused her. I acted for the mother of the young child during a long and costly trial. The child was too young to give evidence in court but the Children's Aid Society and police were able to get enough of a story from the child to lay criminal charges. At the same time, a case went forward in family court regarding access. While the criminal charge did not stick, a compassionate family court judge, David Main, had enough evidence, after a lengthy hearing, to find that a relationship with the father was not in the child's best interests. He gave an order preventing the father access to the child. The father was also ordered to pay some of the mother's legal costs. It took a good judge and an effective court system to protect this young girl.

SHARE WHAT YOU KNOW

It's one thing to press a case in court and hope to achieve fairness, or even to change the law. The client gets justice and the judge writes up the decision and, sometimes, the case is reported in the daily press. But this doesn't help people to really *know* the law, or know how to use it for their own advantage. I had always been interested in writing, which served me well in my practice and especially in preparing litigation documents. When the opportunity to write about the law for the public was presented to me, I welcomed it. It gave me the chance to educate people about the law, to enable them to know when to consult a lawyer, and to help them understand the process. I didn't believe—and still don't—that knowledge of the law should be the exclusive purview of lawyers and courts.

Women were in particular need of legal knowledge, and it turned out that I was one of the first among second-wave feminists to write for the public about women's legal issues and share my knowledge.[91] In the early days of my career, women did not have many rights, and what they did have, they did not necessarily know.

The writing projects I undertook were intended to educate, yes, but they were also an effort to create fertile ground in which pressure for law reforms could take root.

Women in Canadian Life: Law (1977)

There was very little information about law in the public arena for anyone but certainly not for women. When *Toronto Star* journalist Margaret Weiers wrote her 1970 five-part series for the newspaper on Women and the Law, she observed that "research was difficult because there was no single source of information." She noted that she had to visit different legal specialists and government departments and read the statutes themselves in order to find the information for her articles. When university professors Ramsay Cook and Wendy Mitchinson put together a compendium of original writings and documents about women between 1856 and 1946,[92] it was a response to the fact that there were so few sources available.

I was ready to contribute my efforts to help change this situation. So I was pleased that in the fall of 1976, I was approached by publisher Fitzhenry and Whiteside to write a book on Canadian law as it pertained to women for an innovative series they were planning—Women in Canadian Life. Pat Kincaid[93] and Jean Cochrane were co-editors for the series. Three other books were already planned: *Women in Literature*, by Molly McClung; *Women in Sports*, by Jean Cochrane, Abby Hoffman, and Pat Kincaid; and *Women in Politics*, by Jean Cochrane. Until then, my only published work had been a 1,300-word summary of the history of Canadian women for the 1977 *Encyclopedia Canadiana*. I was thrilled to be invited to write a full-length book, and I accepted. I modelled the book after the course I had given several years earlier at Women's Place. It was promoted as "a vivid account of women's roles in and contributions to the laws of Canada from the earliest days of settlement to today." After summarizing, in the first chapter, the European roots of laws and attitudes toward women, I went on to write chapters on the laws relating to all aspects of women's lives: Single Woman; Woman as Wife; Woman as Mother; Property; Separation and Divorce; Women in the Economy; and Women as Citizens.

When the book was published the next year, not only was there very little in the libraries about women's legal situation, women

still had few rights. There was
no sharing of family property,
pensions, investments, or
homes, and spousal and child
support payments were completely inadequate and difficult
to enforce. Sexual harassment
was not illegal. It was not a
crime to rape one's wife. No
one talked about abuse of
women, whether inside or outside of marriage. Abortion and
contraceptive devices had been
legally available under limited
conditions for only eight years.
Dr. Henry Morgentaler had
been actively working for only
four years to widen the availability and legality of abortion
and contraception.

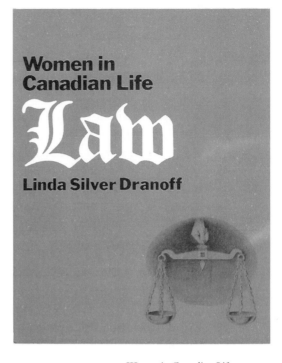

*Women in Canadian Life:
Law* was published in 1977.

The book was mostly a result of original
research into primary sources. I found and read
what secondary sources there were (not many), and
for the rest, spent long hours of research in the library. I was thank-
ful that my history and legal education had prepared me to conduct
research into original sources. I had agreed to produce a manuscript
by June 1977, a mere six months after signing on for the project, and
frequently berated myself for undertaking such a mammoth task. I
spent every weekday morning working on the book and arrived at
the office around noon to work in my "full-time" practice of law. I
used a manual typewriter. I am not even sure that "ko-rec-type" was
available to correct mistakes on the page. I would type the first draft
and then cut and paste like crazy to put the final version together. I
had to hire an extra staffer part-time to type it in final form, because
the others were busy working on the law cases. What a hectic
time that was. My friend and colleague Rosalie Silberman Abella,
who had recently been appointed to the Provincial Court (Family
Division) in Toronto, wrote the introduction.

When it came out, the *Toronto Star* lauded it as a "cliff-hanger" and gave it a wonderful review:

> ...a concise readable account of women's status in Canadian law (past and present).... The other twist...is a realistic assessment of [women's] potential rescuers. By and large, they're definitely not knights in shining armour...but other women.... What's invigorating about the book...is that it is not a political tract. But that doesn't mean that a plain story well told won't be read as a call to arms by readers of the 1970's.... Dranoff's conclusion that "laws affecting women, marriage, and the family continue to assume that marriage is society's primary vehicle for meeting the economic needs of women" can't be ignored....[94]

The review in the *Canadian Journal of Research on Women*,[95] published by the Ontario Institute for Studies in Education (OISE), called it a progressive roadmap of needed reforms and a useful pedagogical tool that "should dispel some of the dangerously exaggerated romantic views of marriage and motherhood that many young people hold." The University of Toronto *Faculty of Law Review* put the icing on the cake, calling it "excellent...a text in the new mode, to provoke thought and discussion rather than give definitive answers...."[96]

I couldn't have been happier that readers and reviewers read the book as I intended—not as a political tract but as a truthful depiction of what existed and what must be changed to achieve fairness. I was thrilled and gratified when Florence Bird called my office one day out of the blue to say that she had read the book and that it was as good as any of the research written for the Royal Commission on the Status of Women, which she had headed. Mostly, I was happy that the information was out there, accessible, and hopefully would reach a large number of women who might benefit from having it all pulled together in one place.

Chatelaine

In 1978, Betty Lee, then managing editor of *Chatelaine*, approached me about a planned new "experts" section of the magazine called "Free for the Asking." *Chatelaine* was being re-fashioned under its new editor, Mildred Istona, who had taken over when Doris

Anderson left her acclaimed twenty-year stint at the post in 1977. Betty Lee had read my book and asked if I would be interested in writing a column. She suggested I prepare one "on spec" so they could see if I could do it. *Chatelaine* liked my sample.

Before I approved my byline description as "a lawyer and author of *Women in Canadian Life: Law*," I checked with the Law Society secretary. Out of an abundance of caution, I got in touch with Mr. Scott, who had been my contact during the complaint made against me the year before. I asked him to consult the Professional Conduct Committee for a ruling on whether I was in breach of any rules by describing myself in that way. The Law Society had no objection.

The "Free for the Asking" section debuted in the January 1979 issue. The first column (the one I had written on spec) was about whether a woman had the right to use her own name or whether marriage required her to take her husband's. I was particularly interested in the subject, since I had been told after my own divorce that I had to keep my ex-husband's last name. Only later did I learn that this was a custom and not, in fact, the law. I thought women should know this.

I loved doing the column; it gave me the opportunity to be an agent of change and both inform and influence the magazine's wide readership. *Chatelaine* had a million readers, and I was told my legal column was one of its most read. In the beginning, the editors told me that the column was for information purposes only. I was specifically instructed not to express an opinion, but just to give the facts. I did what they wanted, but in choosing the subjects for the column, I was able to disseminate information on subjects that I felt could be of great help to women. Sometimes these subjects were about new laws, or the options for dealing with antiquated ones. Sometimes there was no law on a subject, and I speculated on which existing laws might have a bearing on an issue. Sometimes it was a place to encourage reforms.

There were times, especially in these early days, when my subjects were too innovative for *Chatelaine*'s editors. For example, in 1980 I wanted to write about whether a husband's consent was needed for a woman to obtain an abortion (the answer was emphatically *no*, and I wanted women to know this). The editors felt this was too radical for their readership and rejected the column idea.

JANUARY 1979 75 CENTS

chatelaine

WHAT'S NEW

AT CHATELAINE

Columnists
Gifford-Jones,
Robinson,
Dranoff, top row;
Shain, Cohen,
McCutcheon,
bottom row

Checking out the columnists

Our new *Free For The Asking* columnists who will answer your general questions on medicine, the law, psychiatry, relationships, finance and pets, were introduced to you last | *Should Know About Hysterectomy.*

Linda Silver Dranoff is a Toronto lawyer and lecturer, and author of *Women In Canadian Law.* | *Pets,* a TV-Ontario program.

Dian Cohen is a consulting economist, lecturer, broadcaster and journalist who lives and maintains in Montreal. She is the 1978 recipient of the National Busi-

ASK A LAWYER

Q. After 30 years of marriage and three children, my husband says the law requires me to support myself fully after we separate. Is this so? O. L., Toronto

A. No. Although their position...

ASK A LAWYER

Q. My 14-year-old daughter is pregnant. I want ... have an ...

A woman's need for support to be less of the can now for are more women work outside the wives to support themselves, even by 1979, women's paid employment earned about 58 percent of wh...

A court will still order support working wife in view of her income needs and her husband's ability to the other hand, if you were marr only a short time, had no children employed, you can't expect to be a...

A judge will try to establish an amou dren to maintain the standard of livin enjoyed during your marriage. If you are employed during your marriage, your... your accustomed standard of living. your husband will have to contribute as... he can afford to bring such... Furthermore, you... means or... of living...

strictions for abortion vary from province to province, this does not mean that you may insist on your daughter's having an abortion. If you forced your daughter to abort against her will, you could probably be sued for assault, and the doctor who performed the operation could be sued as well.

If you tried to arrange an abortion in the hope that your daughter would eventually agree to it, you would first have to convince a hospital therapeutic abortion committee that termination of the pregnancy is medically necessary to protect your daughter's life or health, either physical or psychological. Abortions are illegal without a hospital committee's approval, and I do that a committee would...

ASK A LAWYER

Q. All our property is in my husband's name. He says he doesn't want a will, but if

FREE · FOR · THE · ASKING

DOCTOR Cynthia Carver *examines causes and treatment of headaches*
• **LAWYER** Linda Silver Dranoff *discusses the legal options available to nonsmokers on choosing a Registered Retirement Savings ... from South America ... does not want to marry*

ASK A LAWYER

Q. My doctor tells me he must operate to remove fibroids from my uterus. He then may decide to do a hysterectomy. My husband objects. He would even refuse to allow me to abort a pregnancy—he wants more children. I feel helpless. What are my legal rights? R. M., Edmonton

ASK A LAWYER

Q. If my partner infec with venereal dis what legal action take? C.C., Regi

A. Under the laws ac women and men wh real disease, such as rhea or genital herp to take steps to sto disease. They must seek m promptly and report their the contacts to be exami necessary. In Saskatch deadline for seeking tr

Contract work: what the

ASK A LAWYER

Do contract workers have the same rights as permanent employees?

The short answer is no. Permanent employees are protected by provincial and territorial employment standards and labor laws, which set out such legal rights as:

• At least two weeks paid vacation annually;

• A ceiling on the hours of work required per week, after which overtime must be paid;

• Pay for the annual statutory holidays, usually 10 days;

• Contribution by the employer to each employee's Canada Pension Plan and Employment Insurance premiums;

as self-employed entrepreneurs.

What contractors get Contract workers sign a contract with specific terms including the period of employment, rate of pay and notice required for termination. They have only those rights spelled out in their contract. They may not get paid vacation or statutory holidays. Independent contractors must pay both the employer's and employee's share of their Canada Pension Plan premiums, and may not be entitled to Employment Insurance. The contract usually stipulates the date of termination or the notice required for dismissal. The notice periods are usually shorter than those that apply to regular employees.

Enforcing your rights If a worker believes the employer is not honoring the terms of the contract, she can sue in a court of law. Or she may believe she

Linda Silver Dranoff

So I modified the proposal and suggested instead that I write about whether a husband's consent was required for a woman to have a hysterectomy. This idea they accepted, and I was therefore able to convey the fact that a man's consent was not required for a woman to have a hysterectomy, which might affect her child-bearing capacity, and to add as an aside that the man's consent was not required for a woman to have an abortion, either. I evened things out by noting that a woman's consent was not required for her husband to undergo a vasectomy—indeed, no one seemed to have even considered the idea! By 1985, the social climate was changing, affected possibly by the new Charter of Rights and Freedoms, and I was allowed to answer the question *Do I need my husband's consent to have an abortion?*, and to be unequivocal in my answer: *no*. By 1990, my column was able to canvass whether a childless woman had *any* legal rights if her husband had a vasectomy without her consent— the answer was no.

The other columns that appeared that first year illustrate the great variety and importance of the subjects that needed exploration: parental liability when one's child injures another; a woman's duty to support her husband after divorce; rights of common-law partners; maternity leave; insurance claims on the death of a mother; a widow's property rights; whether to marry or not; discrimination against single parents in accommodation; adoption; jury duty; legal aid; settling an estate. So much to cover! It was certainly an exciting challenge, and one I looked forward to each month.

I continued to write, both in response to readers' letters and to the issues I felt were important to women. There were so many matters that arose over the twenty-five years I wrote the column that gave me the opportunity to contribute to the public discourse. My writing for women focused primarily on legal issues for the public. At the same time as I was writing about law, there was a wide variety of articles and stories—in academic journals, magazines, newspapers, and organizational pamphlets—on all sorts of subjects affecting women, all seeking to empower women with the knowledge they needed to pursue greater equality.

Left: A sampling of *Chatelaine*
Ask a Lawyer columns written
between 1979 and 2004

As much as I enjoyed it, writing was only one aspect of my outreach work. Often asked to speak at public events and to be a guest on radio and television interview and discussion programs, I used these opportunities to educate the public and lay the groundwork so people would understand the need for legal reforms, particularly as they affected women's equality rights. The requests started coming in almost as soon as I was called to the Bar. There seemed to be a thirst for accessible legal information and reasonable opinion from a knowledgeable feminist and lawyer. In 1974, the year of my Call to the Bar, I was asked to speak at conferences sponsored by Humber College, the Ontario Committee on the Status of Women (the volunteer group), and the Ontario Council on the Status of Women (the government's advisory group).

By 1976, these requests had become even more frequent. I was invited to address many organizations about all kinds of issues affecting women and the family, speaking not only to lay people but also to professionals in allied fields. I was a member of a panel "The Breakdown of the Family" for the C. M. Hincks Institute, which dealt with children's mental health (that must have been when I first met the wonderful social activist and journalist June Callwood, who was moderator of the panel, and so kind to me). In that same year, I was a speaker at a program sponsored by the Toronto Community Law Program for high school law teachers on custody issues. I judged law students in a moot court at University of Toronto Law School. And I participated in a two-day conference, "The Child and the Courts," sponsored by the Programme on Family Law and Social Welfare of the Faculty of Law, University of Toronto, at OISE. I spoke to many educators through invitations from the various Toronto boards of education or various branches of the provincial education ministry, or to conferences of the Federation of Women Teachers' Associations of Ontario.

At an Ontario Progressive Conservative Women's Policy Conference I was gratified to be asked to speak on a panel that included then attorney general Roy McMurtry, even though I was not a member of that political party. In fact, I was deliberately non-partisan and spoke to any political party when invited. I felt that my role was to educate and advocate for women's equality rights, and not to be a spokesperson for any one group.

The pace of invitations increased over the years, and it was rare for me to refuse. It gave me such a wonderful public platform to share my views and thoughts for reform and to educate the public about law. It also showed how interested people were in the law and how relevant the law was to the issues of the day. They asked questions that illustrated how vulnerable they were. This confirmed for me how complex and universal women's problems were and how important it was to find systemic solutions that would benefit most women.

By 1977 I had also started doing the occasional phone-in radio show. In May of that year, CBC Radio's *Metro Morning* asked me to do a weekly legal update called "Legal Grapevine." In December, I was on *Radio Noon* to take phone calls dealing with family law and women's rights. I appeared on City TV's *Sweet City Woman* and *You're Beautiful*, both shows appealing to women who were eager to know about their rights. Journalists called on me often for a quotable quote or background on a legal issue they were researching, and I was happy to oblige.

Picking up where I started in university, I wrote letters to the editor when something in the news exasperated me and I felt I had a point of view that had not been expressed by anyone else. For example, and using the criminal law I had learned in law school, I weighed in on Gerald Ford's pardon of U.S. president Richard Nixon in my first letter published in the mainstream press, this one to the editor of the *Globe and Mail*.

> Surely democracy does not empower a President to initiate a pardon before the normal legal procedures present to him a convict. Surely democracy must stand for the ordering of society based on time-tested principles of law, and not on the whim (even if such whim is evoked by compassion) of one person.[97]

I wrote about policy issues like MPs salaries[98] and started expressing my views on issues affecting women, such as pay equity. As early as 1976, I pressed for the use of public schools for child care.[99]

• • • • • • • • •

And so this was life by 1979, five years after hanging out my shingle. If I'd had anything like a five-year plan, I sincerely doubt it would have been this ambitious. But I had always been a person who answered the door when opportunity knocked, and I was so fortunate that it had. And by 1979, there was a ferment of activity among many feminists to advance the welfare of women in society through volunteer-run organizations such as the National Action Committee on the Status of Women, NAWL, the Ontario Committee on the Status of Women, and others, as well as through the government councils set up across Canada in response to the recommendations of the Royal Commission on the Status of Women. Shelters and help for disadvantaged and abused women were springing up. The mood among women was increasingly optimistic. We were getting somewhere.

PART 3

MAKING STRIDES, 1979–89

Chapter 8
THE LAW:
WHAT'S IN IT FOR WOMEN?
1979-82

During the 1970s, the women's movement was in full flower as we struggled to achieve equitable changes for women. The challenge for the movement was to become a voice for those who had no voice, a change agent for those who didn't think change was conceivable.

Women's needs were becoming increasingly apparent as more women joined the labour force. By 1973, 35.1 percent of all mothers held down jobs outside their homes,[100] and they came up against the challenges of balancing a life inside and outside the home. It was clear that women at this time were rejecting any remaining pressures to choose between having children and having a career (or at least a job), but they still had to come to terms with a dearth of child-care options, unequal pay, and unequal employment opportunities. Divorce was becoming more common, and women who separated were forced to face how poorly the law was treating them. There was no lobby group or organization representing the interests of divorced women; each woman was an individual labouring under the impression that her problems were unique to her. Criminal laws affecting women were being challenged. Women were working separately and together in all women's organizations that were active. I was asked to speak in June 1979 at a speaker series on a subject that seemed to summarize the period: "The Law: What's in it for Women." It equally could have been called "What's not in it for women."

At the same time, it was a period when transformation seemed possible—governments sought consensus and respected the citizens who approached them with ideas. It was not perfect—the door was only partly open, but it had not yet slammed shut in our faces. We didn't understand it at the time, but this was a golden age for citizen political engagement in Canada.

It was also a golden age for me. I was well-established and had more clients and more interesting work than I could handle. I was gaining a reputation for competence as a lawyer and successful advocacy of a client's rights. I had set a precedent in court for the right of a woman to collect costs from her husband in provincial family court, and had served female and male clients in increasingly complex cases. The 1978 changes in family laws were being tested, and I was pressing forward cases to try to make the law work for women. And I was becoming known for my activism, writing, and advocacy for women's rights of all kinds.

These were also busy years for me. Beth was now twelve, and we were planning her Bat Mitzvah. I was happily in a long-distance relationship with a fine man. I had put a deposit down on the purchase of a condominium townhouse at a time when it was rare for a single woman to buy her own home. I was gratified that my gamble was working out—I had created a legal career that suited my interests and needs and desire to make a contribution. It wasn't a conventional path but it was *my* path, and I never regretted the choices I made. My big problem was stretching time to accommodate everything I wanted to do. So when I was offered the opportunity to be a member of the Ontario government's advisory Council on the Status of Women, I worried whether I could juggle another challenge.

THE ONTARIO COUNCIL ON THE STATUS OF WOMEN, 1979–82

I looked forward to the opportunity to help set the government's agenda for women's rights and to have a direct path to the powers that be. Over the first several years of my career, I had become familiar with what women needed, through my own experiences and those of my clients, and through my growing involvement in the women's movement. When this offer was presented to me in 1979, I was excited that I would be involved in so many issues affecting women that I would not otherwise have had the opportunity to

explore in depth. While token compensation was paid, it was not close to what could be earned as a lawyer, but that didn't matter to me as long as my law practice allowed me to make a living. I figured I would squeeze in the work somehow.

(l to r), Judge Rosalie Silberman Abella, Ontario Premier William G. Davis, and Lynne Gordon, Chair of Ontario Status of Women Council, at the party held when Lynne and Linda stepped down from the Council, June 1982.

It was a unique opportunity, because the Ontario government—by creating the council, appointing members, and hiring paid staff—had a stake in the process and was more likely to listen to its chosen insiders. And we had the opportunity to have off-the-record conversations about public policy with decision-makers.

The Ontario Council on the Status of Women (OCSW) had been established in 1973 as the Ontario government's response to the recommendation of the Royal Commission on the Status of Women (RCSW). The OCSW's mandate was to advise the government of Ontario on matters pertaining to the status of women. This specifically included evaluating and monitoring existing legislation, policies, and programs, and making recommendations for new ones; identifying areas needing attention and reform; preparing position papers; consulting the public; and providing advice to government.

The advisory group's first chair was Laura Sabia who had been instrumental in persuading the government to create the RCSW in the first place. In the years between 1973 and 1979, council members had made strides including prodding the Ontario government into the 1975 and 1978 family law advances.[101] When I was appointed in 1979, Lynne Gordon was the chair, and the council reported to Ontario's first woman cabinet minister, Margaret Birch, the provincial secretary for social development, who headed what was called a "super ministry." She was responsible for the ministries of health, social service, education, and youth, as well as overseeing our work. There was no ministry for women's issues; the advisory Ontario Council on the Status of Women was "it."

The executive director of the council was Susan Gibson. She had concluded that the council needed a lawyer to advise on the numerous legal issues affecting women that were coming to the fore. There was, at that time, no lawyer on the council, and they did not have the budget to hire one. It was Susan who persuaded the government to include me among their appointments. It could not have been easy; I did not have any political connections within the Bill Davis Progressive Conservative government and was firmly committed to my non-partisan approach to women's rights. The chair, Lynne Gordon, had been a broadcaster with a specialty in consumer affairs advocacy before taking on this part-time role. Lynne was outspoken and energetic and her heart was in the right place. However, she had little experience or knowledge of Canadian women's issues at the advocacy level. As a result, and because so many of the issues at that time were legal, I was involved in just about everything. I was appointed vice-chair in October 1980, when the previous vice-chair's term ended. I attended every meeting of the full council and also chaired some subcommittees. I was involved in most of the briefs we prepared and distributed. And I suggested some ideas for further research and proposals, and then had the chance to implement them.

I enjoyed the meetings and the camaraderie with many of the other council members and staff and learned from the experts who were brought to the meetings when we were discussing an issue for which we needed outside guidance. The full council of about fourteen met four times a year. There were also five executive committee meetings once I was vice-chair, as well as other meetings and conferences to represent the council. I met and worked with some fine people with varying degrees of expertise on women's issues; regardless, we all shared a commitment to achieving fairness and equality. Among them were Bill Kelloway, one of the few men on the council and an educator at the national police college in Ottawa; Dr. Josephine Somerville, a physician; Eleanor Ryan, a public servant with the federal government and active in its union; Kay Toye, a lifelong volunteer; Roberta Jamieson, the first Indigenous woman lawyer in Ontario and later its ombudsman; and Beverley Salmon, a nurse and later the first black female Toronto city councillor. The director of the Women's Bureau of the Ontario Ministry of Labour was also an *ex-officio* member. I learned a great deal from Susan Gibson, who understood the inner workings of government and the strategies necessary to achieve a result. She remains a dear friend to this day.

"Employment Strategies for the 1980s"

One of the first briefs that all members of council worked on gathered together the most effective ideas of the time for the improvement of women's employment situation. Volunteer women's groups were also seeking to advance the position of women in the work force. But we set ourselves the task of creating a comprehensive roadmap for government policy that would improve conditions for the women—and the increasing number of mothers of young children—who were entering the workforce in great numbers. When I joined the council in 1979, the existing laws took for granted that few wives—and even fewer mothers—were likely to hold down jobs outside the home. The laws had not caught up with the reality. By 1976, 42 percent of women age fifteen and over were in the labour force,[102] and 39 percent of women with children under age sixteen had a job.[103] Of mothers with a youngest child between ages three and five, 37 percent participated in the labour force.[104] And among those with a youngest child under age three, 28 percent worked outside the home.[105]

Yet there was no protection in employment if a woman married, became pregnant, or took maternity leave. In 1979 the Supreme Court of Canada turned down pregnant Stella Bliss's claim that her equality rights under the 1960 Canadian Bill of Rights were

Ontario cabinet minister
Margaret Birch congratulates
Linda at the end of her time on
Council, June 1982.

breached when she was denied unemployment insurance.[106] Part-time workers were less protected than full-time ones. Sexual harassment was not a recognized problem much less an illegal act. Equal pay laws were mostly for women who did exactly the same work as men—a rarity. Only recently had it been changed to require equal pay for "substantially" the same work—and that did not work either. There were few organized child-care facilities.[107] The insufficient laws that did exist were inadequately enforced.

The council supported such far-reaching and fundamental changes as legislation to promote "equal pay for work of equal value" in order to achieve our goal of what we called "wage equity." The existing law was ineffective, even though it required employers to pay women the same as it paid men for doing the same or substantially the same work. In 1977, the average earnings for full-year female workers were 56.5 percent of that for full-year male workers. We wanted the government to enforce this law proactively, and not only in response to the few complaints by courageous individuals. Legislated affirmative action programs meant that it would be legal to give preference to women (the assumption always being that the man and woman in contention were of equal merit) in order to remedy past discrimination and historic imbalances. We also endorsed "contract compliance." This meant that government would not grant contracts to companies whose female workers suffered discrimination in employment.

We knew that women would not be able to advance as employees unless they found a way to care for their children while they worked. This was widely supported by the women's movement. We put front and centre the adoption of a comprehensive child-care policy and asserted that accessible and affordable quality child care is essential to the attainment of full equality for women. The report made it clear that *all* working women needed child care, not just those on social assistance. We also regarded child-care programs as a source of education for children. We were innovative in asking for all-day kindergarten and the use of existing surplus classrooms in schools for preschools. We even suggested twenty-four-hour facilities to assist professional and shift workers and for emergency situations. The council was an early proponent of tax credits for child-care expenses.

We floated strategies to train women to enter non-traditional jobs, amendments to the Human Rights Code to allow for class actions, and a prohibition of and remedy for sexual harassment. We proposed that Ontario remove its opposition to the Canada Pension Plan providing pension credits for women who had dropped out of the labour force while having and raising children. This needed approval by the provinces, and Ontario (the last holdout) had vetoed this change for six years. (In 1983, Ontario quietly approved the right of women who dropped out of the labour force to raise children, for up to seven years, to receive Canada Pension Plan benefits referable to those years.)

Women who worked part-time were not protected the same as full-time workers by labour laws, and we included the suggestion that part-time workers should get pro-rated benefits. We expanded on this later in a separate brief that made recommendations seeking pro-rated benefits for part-time workers, the inclusion of part-timers in private pension plans and collective agreements, and the expansion of child-care facilities to support part-timers in their employment efforts.

The Employment Strategies brief sought legal protections for domestic workers. We asked that pregnant women be safeguarded against dismissal or demotion under the Employment Standards Act, and that this law provide for paternity and adoption leave.

This was certainly a powerful wish list. We hoped it would gather in one place an all-encompassing agenda to show the government the employment strategies that were needed for the years ahead.

The council submitted the brief to Margaret Birch in April 1980. She thanked us and tabled it in the Ontario legislature. We knew that telling the government what it should do did not necessarily mean that they would do it. But it was important that they know about the strong public support for our ideas. The council organized its first public consultation, which was attended by representatives from fifty women's groups who spoke for teachers, nurses, Indigenous women, rape crisis centres, daycare workers, service clubs, and religious groups.

These women endorsed our brief whole-heartedly and took it back to their members to follow up with programs. We announced to the press the extent of the backing our brief had received. It was gratifying when a *Toronto Star* editorial concluded that "with one exception, the recommendations in the brief are sound and should be implemented."[108] The only thing they did not agree with was legislation promoting "equal pay for work of equal value," viewing the then existing legislation requiring "equal pay for substantially the same work" as sufficient. This was always a difficult issue to sell, as Mary Cornish and the Equal Pay Coalition would attest, given their considerable work on this issue over many years.

Lynne Gordon and I later brought the employment strategies brief to a national meeting of the Joint Councils on the Status of Women, held in Vancouver in November 1981, and discussed it with the representatives of all the government advisory councils across Canada. We proposed and secured approval for a resolution which, among other things, urged every province to adopt an employment strategy on all the issues we in Ontario had reviewed, and we also urged the appointment of a Royal Commission to study affirmative action. This was an idea whose time was ripe, and in fact, in 1983 Judge Rosalie Silberman Abella was appointed as the chair and sole member of a federal Royal Commission to inquire into "the most efficient, effective, and equitable means of promoting employment opportunities, eliminating systemic discrimination and assisting all individuals to compete for employment opportunities on an equal basis." The commission was directed to focus on women, Aboriginals, visible minorities, and the disabled, and it concluded in 1984 that the obstacles to their full equality were "so formidable and self-perpetuating that they cannot be overcome without intervention."

Of all the ideas we submitted in this OCSW brief, government support of child care has been the most intransigent. To this day, child care remains underfunded, and most governments ignore the fact that women will never achieve true equality without a public policy that supports them in raising their children. I was the one who represented the council at conferences and meetings dealing with this issue. In October 1980, for example, I participated in an event that explored whether government or the individual family was responsible for the care of children, and I concluded that my personal view—families needed help—still held true. In 1981, I attended a conference on work-related daycare, which dealt with the novel idea (for that time) of employer-funded workplace daycare, a solution that has always appealed to me.

Even though the Ministry of Education was not open to the idea of extending its mandate to include child care for those younger than kindergarten age, I continued to instigate for the use of empty classrooms for the care of young children. The idea was top-of-mind for me, and I used every opportunity to put the matter of child care on the public policy agenda. At a September 1984 invitation-only gathering of community leaders at the Partnership in Ontario Economic Conference (hosted by the Ontario government to open the new Metro Toronto Convention Centre in downtown Toronto), all the invitees sat together in plenary session, and each had the opportunity to speak to a captive audience of decision-makers and opinion-leaders. I used the occasion to challenge the minister of education, Dr. Bette Stephenson, to explore the possibility of utilizing empty classrooms for child care. She replied *definitively* that care of children was solely the responsibility of the parents and that the government should not and would not get involved. This old-fashioned and out-of-touch view saddened me. Apparently, the time was not yet right for this pioneering approach to have wide-ranging application.[109]

Sexual Harassment

The council used the opportunity of a government discussion about amendments to the Ontario Human Rights Code to focus on the subject of sexual harassment, particularly in employment. In those days, there was no law against it. It was another one of those hidden issues that women didn't talk about, at least not until Constance Backhouse and Leah Cohen wrote about it in their 1979 *The Secret Oppression: Sexual Harassment of Working Women*.[110] If a supervisor insisted on sexual favours from an employee with the stated or unstated threat of being fired if she refused, she had no apparent remedy apart from quitting her job. When a young woman in the non-traditional field of law enforcement consulted me for legal advice, I was able to put a face on this issue. She had no one to complain to at her place of work who would take her seriously. And when the word got around that she had made a human rights complaint, it made her even more of a target than before. In the end, she dropped her complaint, resigned from her position, and went into an entirely different career.

When amendments were proposed to the Ontario Human Rights Code in June 1981,[111] I presented the OCSW brief to the Ontario Government Standing Committee studying the proposed code. My lawyerly line-by-line review of the entire draft legislation concentrated on sexual harassment, which had not been previously protected, and for which new language was required. I submitted that in order to be considered sexual harassment, the misconduct had to be persistent and affect the woman's livelihood. In the end, after hearing from many interested parties, the committee did recommend to the government that the wording of the sexual harassment section take those factors into account, and they became part of the legislation. When the Canada Labour Code was amended on March 1, 1985, it also outlawed sexual harassment in the workplace in similar terms. The law has evolved since then as cases have come forward. By participating in the government process, I came to appreciate that persuasion on rational grounds rather than threats are what had an impact on government decision-makers.

"The Disinherited Spouse"

The council was persuaded to study the absence of property rights
for widowed persons in 1979 after I stumbled on an inequity in the
law that would not have been obvious to me had it not been for a
client. Certainly, no one else, to my knowledge, was aware of this
discrepancy in the law. My client told me that her husband owned all
of the family's assets in his own name and had made it very clear that
he intended in his will to leave nothing to her and everything to his
brother. She had been married for more than thirty years, was in her
sixties, and was a full-time homemaker; she would end up destitute
if he carried out his plan for his estate. She had no money or assets
of her own. She came to me to find out whether she had any legal
rights. I realized that there was no law assuring her of a share of
property in her husband's name or the right to live in their matrimonial home, and no arguable case for a share of property as she had
not contributed any cash. Her only right in law was, after he died, to
claim—as a dependant based on her need—monthly support from
his estate. She would have to act quickly after his death, and she
would have to fight his brother. The fact that she had no absolute
right to anything—and that other widows and widowers were in the
same position—was troubling. It was so unfair, and there was no
lobby group of widowed persons to even flag the problem, much
less work for public awareness and support legal changes.

I brought the issue to the Ontario Council on the Status of
Women. I believed that widowed persons should be treated the
same as divorced persons who, under the Family Law Reform Act,
had a right to share at least *some* of the property accumulated during
the marriage. Of course, as I had long ago learned, the person who
comes up with a good idea is generally expected to run with it, and
the council was no different. I was, as they say these days, "in charge
of the file."

I presented a resolution at a meeting of the council, which
was passed in 1980, "that the Family Law Reform Act's system of
division of property should be available to widows and widowers
so that assets are shared equally on the death of a spouse." We sent
a copy of the resolution to Margaret Birch, who forwarded it to
Attorney General Roy McMurtry for reply. He dismissed the issue
in his responding letter, saying that "problems did not usually arise

Linda's article for the *Toronto Star* November 1, 1982, pressed for the establishment of a Minister Responsible for the Status of Women.

The *Toronto Star* editorial of September 15, 1980, approved the Council's brief on Employment Strategies for Women in the 1980s.

'Women need voice at the top'

Advisory councils have been ignored and a new structure is now needed

By Linda Silver Dranoff
Toronto Star special

Linda Silver Dranoff is a lawyer and writer and formerly vice-chairperson of Ontario's advisory Council on the Status of Women.

It is time to rethink the entire concept of government-appointed advisory councils on women. We need a more effective way to get a fair break for women from elected decision-makers.

Councils of government appointees to advise on women's issues were set up after 1972 in most provinces across Canada and by the federal government, in response to the advice of the Royal Commission on the Status of Women. The royal commission had recommended that councils be able to establish programs and implement policy decisions and be a way for women to tell government how to achieve equity and equality for women. None of the councils was given the recommended power.

tion for appointment to its staff of women council, despite government guidelines that independence and expertise are reasons for appointment. It frequent

usly chooses members because their sex, which is not a criterion and certainly not appointment process in the lic or private sector. Some chosen because they are affected with the right political pull which is offensive only if such appointees are more committed protecting politicians than to advancing women's interests.

Not every woman has expertise to know how to achieve equality for women. It's being a woman that makes an expert on women issues; it's knowledge of laws affect men and women equally; it's knowledge of nancing and staffing care centres; practical application of affirmative action programs knowledge of

Sound ideas on equal pay

The 1,756,000 Ontario women in the labor force face many problems: They earn less than men, they rarely get into the executive suite, they have a hard time finding good day care for their children.

A brief on employment strategies for women, prepared by the Ontario Status of Women Council and endorsed recently by representatives of 50 women's groups, offers a wide-ranging approach to solving these problems. With one exception, the recommendations in the brief are sound and should be implemented.

The exception is the demand for new provincial legislation requiring equal pay for work of equal value. The concept, designed to enable comparisons of entirely different jobs — a truck driver with a secretary, for example — is seen
... as the way to eliminate the dis... en and women.

with jobs where men and women do similar work, not where the work is wildly dissimilar.

Rather than rushing headlong into new legislation, as the brief proposes the Ontario government would be better advised to enforce more vigorously its existing legislation which requires equal pay for men and women doing substantially the same work, requiring similar skill, effort and responsibility, in the same establishment.

The brief is on sounder ground, however, when it recommends affirmative action programs in which special efforts are made to promote women to higher-paying posts. The fact that the high-paid executives in a company are generally men, while women are the lower workers or, at best, middle managers.

The council is also correct to urge Park to give day care a high priority. Day care is vital if mothers of young children are to be able to continue in the labor force and t...

Our Concern is the Status of Women

"Society's most arbitrary folly is the underutilization of women's brainpower. We have made a few dents in that massive folly! In the past women have been idolized, patronized and exploited — it is time they are humanized, utilized and recognized."

Laura Sabia, Chairman
Ontario Status of
Women Council

The Ontario Council on the Status of Women pamphlet quoted Laura Sabia, its first chair, in 1974.

Some members of the Ontario Council on the Status of Women 1982 — (l to r) Seated, Josephine Somerville, Barbara Stone, Kaye Toye, Lynne Gordon, Gwen Bower-Binns, Annabelle Logan; Standing, (l to r) — Kay Howland, Marguerite Martel, Bill Kelloway, Linda Silver Dranoff, Georgie Calder upon death and that such drastic legislative interference with respect to the freedom of testamentary capacity was largely unwarranted."

Since this letter was firm in closing the matter, at least as far as the attorney general was concerned, I understood that I had to be more persuasive. I wrote another letter to Mr. McMurtry suggesting that there was no way of knowing how many such widowed persons were affected, since without a clear legal right, no widow who was disinherited would go to court seeking a share of property. At the same time, I got to work on a brief on behalf of the council to explain the analysis in a way that I hoped would justify a fresh look. The thrust of my argument was that the Succession Law Reform Act would order an estate to provide support for a widowed person only in the event of need. There was no absolute right for a widow to share her husband's assets on his death as an entitlement arising from the marriage itself—which, of course, was the thinking behind the 1978 Family Law Reform Act. I questioned why a divorced person should have greater rights to share family property than a widowed person who had stayed in the marriage "until death did them part."

At the same time, my April 1980 column in *Chatelaine* spread the word and gave the issue a public airing. The column went across Canada— Ontario was not the only province that ignored the rights of the widowed. I explained the problem and what needed to be done about it. I concluded by suggesting that women write to their MPPs asking for laws requiring that family property be shared whether or not a couple is divorced. And I gave my readers some practical advice: Don't assume the law takes care of married women's property interests. Your best protection is to be registered on the title as an owner.

The council brief was completed in the fall of 1980 and submitted to the government. We also added the subject of the disinherited spouse to the agenda at the consultation with women's

ASK A LAWYER

Q My husband and I separated in 1977 after 35 years of marriage. When he died in 1979, our home was in his name, and he willed it to his brother. Is this legal? *B.G., Sault Ste. Marie, Ont.*

A It's not fair, but it's legal. Ontario's new Family Law Reform Act does provide for an equal division of family assets. "Family assets" are defined as property (used for shelter, transportation, recreation and household purposes) owned by one or both spouses and ordinarily used or enjoyed by them or their children while they reside together. It is only in very special circumstances that a court decides to divide assets unequally.
However, the Family Law Reform Act *only applies when the marriage has broken down and a court application for property division has been made while both spouses*

This 1980 *Chatelaine* column was meant to raise awareness that a spouse could be disinherited, and the law needed to be changed.

organizations on the employment strategies brief. I spoke about the issue. I guess my passion for fairness was showing that day, because the *Toronto Sun*'s reporter led off her news report with "Linda Silver Dranoff went to bat for Ontario widows. Her swing would make George Brett cringe as she lambasted the Ontario government...." Whether I went that far or she took "poetic licence," I certainly did speak up for widowed persons whom I felt should not have to go hat in hand as mendicants to get a share of property that should rightfully be theirs. She quoted me as saying (and it does sound like me), "The government is almost rewarding marriage breakdown and punishing the persistence of the unhappily wed."

In April 1981, Attorney General McMurtry finally paid some attention to the issue. He asked the Wills and Trusts section of the Canadian Bar Association—Ontario (CBA-O) to comment on the OCSW brief. They formed a subcommittee made up of eminent practitioners in the field, including my former law school professor Maurice Cullity. Their overall view was that it would unduly confuse the distribution of estates, and that there were few people affected. It seemed to me that the process to ensure fairness for the widowed need not be complicated, but that no one cared about the few who would be adversely affected.

In February 1982, I was asked to address the Wills and Trusts Section when their subcommittee's brief was presented for approval. I remember distinctly the barrage of questions and critical comments by the lawyers present. Their major criticism was that the proposed change would get in the way of the distribution of all estates and wasn't warranted when so few were affected. My answer, which silenced them, was that it did not have to affect all estates. Give the widowed person the option to choose between taking what was provided for her under the will or under family law legislation. I submitted that it could be as simple as a box to check off on the application for probate form. Most will want what the will provides, but the law will at least protect the minority.

The speech that I gave that night took apart their brief point by point. I followed it up with a letter to the section chair, Mary Louise Dickson, summarizing what happened at the meeting and hoping for their support for the clarified way of dealing with their objections. The opportunity to make this election, I pointed out, would combine certainty, flexibility, and freedom of testamentary capacity, and would ensure that the vast majority of fair wills would not be forced into a different regime. I presented this solution to the OCSW, which in turn presented it as a submission to the government. I don't recall whether the Wills and Trusts section amended their report, but my ideas did fall on receptive ears within the government. Ultimately, the disinherited spouse was protected in law, the application for probate included a check-off box, and, to my knowledge, there have been no complaints of unnecessary complexities by lawyers who work in the area of wills and estates.

Older Women and Poverty
The extent of poverty facing older women was another issue explored by the council. Almost 600,000 older Canadian women could not afford the basic necessities of life. Nearly two-thirds of Canada's 1.1 million female senior citizens had annual incomes below $6,000.[112] Some women who consulted me in my law practice learned that they could not afford to divorce, particularly given the laws in effect in the early years of my practice.

These facts were a reflection of all the things that were wrong with the law and customs affecting women. Women did not have equal employment opportunities and equal pay with men in the labour force. Women who divorced did not receive a fair share of the family's assets, nor did they receive adequate spousal support. Wives who had not worked outside the home had no legal right to share in their husbands' private pensions or his Canada Pension Plan. A woman who worked outside the home only after her children were in school lost entitlement to her pension for those years when she had dropped out of the paid workforce. The result of these inequities was that few women were in a position to save for old age. It also explained why women uncomplainingly stayed in unhappy or abusive marriages.

On November 23, 1981, the council issued a report on the poverty of elderly women. We recommended an increase in government financial support beginning at age sixty, improvement in pension benefits unrelated to labour force participation, expansion of in-home support services for the elderly, and much more, totalling thirty-three recommendations. Many of these were eventually implemented.

Battered Wives

My work with the OCSW also broadened my understanding of feminist issues by casting light on the problem of domestic violence. I had been told by a number of my clients about the abuse they suffered at the hands of their husbands, so the subject did not come as a shock to me. However, I hadn't appreciated the enormity of this often hidden problem, or the extent to which women felt they had to accept it for their own and their children's survival.

On the heels of the Canadian Advisory Council Report in January 1980, "Wife Battering in Canada: The Vicious Circle," the OCSW studied the issue. The Canadian Advisory Council on the Status of Women report was the first of its kind and astonished people when it disclosed that one in ten married women in Canada (about 500,000 women) were estimated to be battered by their husbands every year. And yet this wasn't considered a major social problem, and there was little help for these women—whether from police, doctors, shelters or crisis centres, or the law.

In May 1980, the OCSW conducted a symposium featuring the few experts on the subject, including Linda McLeod, senior researcher with the CACSW; Trudy Don, a leading figure in the development of shelters for victims; Pat Kincaid of the Toronto District School Board, who was then doing a doctoral thesis on wife assault; and several former victims. Participants made suggestions and council presented a brief with numerous recommendations to the government.

There was so much to be done that the list of proposals was lengthy. We asked for such improvements as the education of police and Crown attorneys so that the problem would be taken more seriously. We sought substantial government financial support of shelters for victims of wife battering, an abuse registry, and mandatory reporting of incidents of family violence. I remember passionately presenting the idea of "morning after" courts to enable an immediate hearing—I had in mind what clients had told me: that their husbands felt free to do as they pleased until the matter eventually (and after a considerable period of time) came up for a court hearing.[113] I also wrote a column for *Chatelaine*, published in June 1981, providing legal strategies for victims and admonishing the police to use an existing section of the Criminal Code to arrest the abuser on the spot.

During preparations for this consultation, we discussed at a council meeting the Criminal Injuries Compensation Board set up under the 1971 Compensation for Victims of Crime Act. I remember asking the expert who attended that day to brief us as to who benefitted from this funding. We were told about victims of all kinds of violence, but wives and women who had been assaulted or raped were not included in her description. I asked why, given the wording of the Act. I was told there really was no reason, except that applications had not been made by female victims to that date—almost ten years after the establishment of the Criminal Injuries Compensation system. I suggested to the council that we write to all the women's shelters and other affected groups to alert them to this right under the Criminal Injuries Compensation Act and suggest that they advise the women accessing their services. This had a big impact and encouraged abused women to apply for this government-paid compensation.

Violence against women, and tools to cope with it, remains a serious societal problem. There are groups across Canada that provide a variety of services for abused women in need—shelters, counselling services, legal advice and representation, employment referrals, and more. But they are under-funded and under-resourced, and society still does not offer adequate help to abused and terrorized women. In 2016, a survey conducted by the Canadian Network of Women's Shelters and Transition Houses showed that on a typical day 416 women and children in Canada sought shelter to escape violence, but 73 percent of them were turned away because of lack of resources and capacity.

Some women have had little choice but to fight back on their own. In 1990, the Supreme Court of Canada, in the *Lavallee* decision[114] delivered by Madam Justice Bertha Wilson, ruled that a woman who murdered her spouse was able to use the "battered woman's syndrome" as a defence to criminal charges. The woman anticipated an imminent attack and death after a history of repeated abuse at his hands. While few women take this extreme action and rely on the battered woman's defence, the court's ruling acknowledged the ongoing terror and desperation of women in these situations.

Rape Laws

Rape laws were federal, not in provincial jurisdiction, but Margaret Birch had nevertheless asked us to comment on the rape sections of the Criminal Code as the women's movement was raising public concern about it. I was appointed chair of the subcommittee (which also included Roberta Jamieson and Dr. Jo Somerville). We recommended removal of the provision that marriage could be used as an excuse for rape of a partner and the establishment of rules limiting the opportunity for defence counsel to question a rape victim about her previous sexual history. We sought the elimination of the word *sexual* from the rape provisions of the Criminal Code because it reinforced the stereotype that rape has something to do with sex rather than what it truly was—violence. These were ideas on which many women could agree and work together to persuade the government.

In 1983, the Criminal Code was amended to change the term "rape" to sexual assault, to emphasize the violent nature of the act, and also to make it a crime for a husband to sexually assault his wife. These changes also tried to deal with consent and credibility issues. For example, there used to be a legally accepted assumption, often used as a criminal defence, that if a woman had ever had sexual relations with anyone, her credibility was in question when she said she had not consented to have sexual relations with the accused—as if to suggest that any woman who is sexually active is more likely to have consented. The 1983 changes tried to prevent questioning the victim about her previous sexual conduct, but there would be further changes needed over the years to deal with this issue. In 1991, in *R v. Seaboyer*[115], the Supreme Court of Canada dealt with a case that saw its two female jurists on opposite sides—Madam Justice Beverley McLachlin writing for the majority said the 1983 law was unconstitutional and it favoured the rape victim at the expense of the accused; Madam Justice Claire L'Heureux-Dubé dissented, saying too many judges determine relevance on the basis of myth and stereotypes about women's sexuality.

In 1992, a new "rape shield" law was enacted that defined consent as actual consent to the specific act in question ("No means No") and the victim's previous sexual history became irrelevant. The rape shield law was a result of significant consultation by then justice minister Kim Campbell with women's groups in the drafting of the law, and a rare vote of unanimity by all three federal parties in the House of Commons.[116]

The Constitution: Patriation, the Charter,
and the "Notwithstanding" Clause

In about 1979, a long-festering and significant legal issue arose for the council and for many in the women's movement.[117] It was a concern on which we were all united, but it was not only a women's issue; it affected every Canadian as well.

The topic was sovereignty—the patriation of the Constitution of Canada from Great Britain—and the creation of an entrenched Charter of Rights and Freedoms. The pressure to move on the issue came from Prime Minister Pierre Elliott Trudeau. Women's groups, including the council, wanted to ensure that women would be protected by the wording that would be chosen and, particularly, that equality rights would be entrenched in the Constitution. It had become clear that the Canadian Bill of Rights—a piece of legislation that applied only at the federal level and could be changed by a subsequent government—did not protect women's rights. Part of the problem was its wording and another was that it was not made permanent by being entrenched.

Many organizations, including the Canadian Advisory Council on the Status of Women, the National Action Committee on the Status of Women, and others lobbied for authoritative constitutional protections of equality for women and appeared before the hearings of the Special Joint Committee of the Senate and House of Commons held in November 1980. In January 1981, the minister of justice announced that section 15 of the Charter—which granted equality rights—would be worded in this way: "Every individual is equal before and under the law and has the right to the equal protection and equal benefit of the law without discrimination...."

CACSW had organized a conference to explore the impact on women of the planned Constitution. Its president was leading Canadian feminist Doris Anderson, who, having left her job as editor of *Chatelaine* in 1977, took on the presidency of CACSW in 1979. In preparation for this conference, Doris had hired constitutional lawyers Mary Eberts and Beverly Baines, Louise Dulude, Myrna Bowman, and others to prepare background papers on the

WOMEN AND THE
CONSTITUTION
FEBRUARY 14
1981

issues, including the recommended wording for the Charter that was most likely to protect women's equality rights. These papers and others were published in 1981 in the book *Women and the Constitution in Canada*.

Before the conference could be held, Cabinet minister Lloyd Axworthy, to whom Doris reported, intervened and unilaterally cancelled it. Doris firmly believed it was because he wanted to avoid any embarrassment for the government, and she said so publicly. She resigned in protest.[118]

Women were up in arms. Women's constitutional equality rights exploded into the consciousness of women everywhere. A number of activist women gravitated to each other and, calling themselves the Ad Hoc Committee on the Constitution, decided to organize an alternative conference. The Ad Hoc Committee included Nancy Ruth Jackman, Pat Hacker, Laura Sabia, Kay Macpherson, Shelagh Wilkinson, Maureen McTeer, Lynn McDonald, Maude Barlow, Kay Sigurjonsson, Marilou McPhedran, and Linda Ryan-Nye. To everyone's surprise, 1,300 women turned up in Ottawa for the event on February 14, 1981, and showed that Canadian women were determined to stand up for their rights.[119]

As discussion tools, they used the material prepared for the cancelled government conference, including proposed wording for a further equality rights section 28, "Notwithstanding anything in this Charter, the rights and freedoms referred to in it are guaranteed equally to male and female persons."

In the end, after continuing and considerable pressure was applied, the government agreed to the wording and inclusion of section 28, which first appeared in the April 1981 draft[120] some two months after the Ad Hoc gathering in Ottawa.

As usual, though, women were not permitted to rest with a hard-fought win. The concern then became the protection of equality rights in sections 15 and 28 from legislative inroads by the use of the "notwithstanding clause." This clause was a compromise measure invented on November 4, 1981. That night, the "Kitchen Accord" was negotiated by Jean Chrétien, Roy Romano, and Roy McMurtry behind the scenes in a kitchen at a federal-provincial conference[121]; it included a "notwithstanding clause" as the bargain that would get consent by all the provinces (except Quebec) to the Charter of Rights and Freedoms. The notwithstanding clause permitted Parliament or a provincial legislature to pass laws that breached the Charter protections and suspended the Charter for that purpose for a maximum of five years. The clause was an attempt to ensure parliamentary supremacy. To our dismay, equality rights was one of the Charter rights that could be suspended, so it had the potential to let governments do by the back door what they couldn't do by the front door—limit equality rights. They would also be able to suspend other fundamental and legal rights, such as freedom of assembly, religion, press, liberty, and security, and protection against unreasonable search and seizure.

I conferred with Marilou McPhedran and Linda Ryan-Nye, who continued to lead the campaign for the Ad Hoc Committee on the Constitution. I told them that as vice-chair of the OCSW, I was going to Vancouver with Lynne Gordon, the council chair, to attend the Joint Councils on the Status of Women on November 11 and 12, 1981. I asked if it would be

CHARTER OF RIGHTS
AND FREEDOMS

15. (1) Every individual is equal before and under the law and has the right to the equal protection and equal benefit of the law without discrimination and, in particular, without discrimination based on race, national or ethnic origin, colour, religion, sex, age or mental or physical disability.
(2) Subsection (1) does not preclude any law, program or activity that has as its object the amelioration of conditions of disadvantaged individuals or groups including those that are disadvantaged because of race, national or ethnic origin, colour, religion, sex, age or mental or physical disability.
28. Notwithstanding anything in this Charter, the rights and freedoms referred to in it are guaranteed equally to male and female persons.

33. (1) Parliament or the legislature of a province may expressly declare in an Act of Parliament or of the legislature, as the case may be, that the Act or a provision thereof shall operate notwithstanding a provision included in section 2 or sections 7 to 15.
(2) An Act or a provision of an Act in respect of which a declaration made under this section is in effect shall have such operation as it would have but for the provision of this Charter referred to in the declaration.
(3) A declaration made under subsection (1) shall cease to have effect five years after it comes into force or on such earlier date as may be specified in the declaration.
(4) Parliament or the legislature of a province may re-enact a declaration made under subsection (1).
(5) Subsection (3) applies in respect of a re-enactment made under subsection (4).

helpful if a resolution regarding equality rights were passed by this national women's umbrella group. They agreed that this would be a useful and persuasive tool.

The subject of the Constitution was not on the agenda for the Joint Councils meeting, but I found a way to get it discussed. Since the first session included an opportunity for each provincial chair to speak during the first morning of the meeting, I asked Lynne Gordon to raise the issue and refer to the need for an opportunity to discuss constitutional developments. A time was found and, during the discussion, I made a presentation on the implications of the not-withstanding clause and proposed a resolution, which I had created on the spot (I still have among my papers my handwritten notes for the resolution). In the end, the Joint Councils passed the resolution pretty much as I had written it:

> The Joint Status of Women Councils are relieved that the consti-tutional debate appears to have ended, but are concerned that the rancour and divisiveness remain.
>
> Canadian women's rights should have been entrenched. Entrenchment means that fundamental rights cannot be denied or abridged by any legislature without an amendment to the Constitution. The Accord said that Provincial legislatures could opt out of equality rights from time to time. This is not entrench-ment. There is no entrenchment "notwithstanding," or subject to an "option to." Women's rights to full equality with men in our society cannot be contingent or qualified.
>
> We serve notice on our legislatures that we will collectively oppose any attempt to diminish equal rights for women.
>
> We call on the provincial premiers for the deletion of the over-ride provisions (the "notwithstanding clause") from the terms of the Federal-Provincial Accord. Alternatively, we ask that the premiers recognize publicly that the equality guarantee (Clause 28) was never intended to and will never be made subject of the over-ride provision of the Accord.

After approval, it was forwarded by telegram to Prime Minister Pierre Trudeau, Attorney General Jean Chrétien, all provincial pre-miers, and other concerned parties. It was also released to the press and was featured in a *Globe and Mail* report on the conference.

Soon after, a similar resolution was submitted to the second Provincial Consultation on Women's Issues, sponsored by the OCSW, and it was approved by them. Immediately after the consultation, the OCSW sent it directly to Premier William Davis. His response was that while he preferred that there be no over-ride clause, it was a necessary price to pay for the Charter.[122] He also promised that his government did not intend to make use of it, and he doubted that any government would use it "wilfully to deny or withdraw rights." He encouraged vigilance by groups such as ours to "ensure that no government will take unwarranted action or, if it does so, it will be at its own political peril." I preferred that the clause be omitted in the first place, as vigilance was too much to expect. In fact, the notwithstanding clause was approved by the federal and provincial governments in November 1981, and the resolution went to the House of Lords in England to be passed "at the request and consent of Canada."

Not content to let the issue go, I wrote an op-ed piece—an opinion piece that appeared opposite the editorial page (hence the abbreviation "op-ed")—that was published in the *Globe and Mail* on December 23, 1981, entitled "Override: menace to basic rights?" It was the first time I had tried this means of getting my ideas across, and I was pleased that the newspaper agreed to print it. I was against the notwithstanding clause not only because of its effect on equality rights. I argued that the section 33 over-ride was

> the absolute power to unilaterally overrule the fundamental freedoms, legal rights, and equality rights of every man, woman, and child in society. This power is unfettered and unrestrained; use of the power need not be reasonable nor justified, nor must its use be proved appropriate in the context of a free and democratic society.
>
> The accord was accepted to get approval for patriating the Constitution. But will it be worth patriating if we diminish basic rights and freedoms in the process? Patriating is only a symbolic gesture, a formality; it will not represent any change in laws that will affect Canadians in any real way.

I expressed the hope (wishful thinking) that the British Parliament would agree with me. It was not to be, and the

Override: menace to basic rights?

Canadians are being misled if they think the accord means fundamental rights can't be withdrawn without amending the Constitution.

BY LINDA SILVER DRANOFF

Linda Silver Dranoff is a Toronto lawyer, author and commentator on legal subjects.

BASIC RIGHTS and freedoms we take for granted are in jeopardy — fundamental rights such as freedom of assembly, religion, press, the right to liberty and security, equality without discrimination no matter what our color, religion, sex or origin.

The "Section 33 override," which those who govern us instituted last month, is the absolute power to unilaterally overrule the fundamental freedoms, legal rights and equality rights of every man, woman and child in society. This power is unfettered and unrestrained; use of the power need not be reasonable nor justified, nor must its use be proved appropriate in the context of a free and democratic society.

How much power are we willing to hand over to provincial and federal legislatures?

The Charter of Rights and Freedoms under discussion for the past year contained the following: "(1) The Canadian Charter of Rights and Freedoms guarantees the rights and freedoms as set out in it subject only to such reasonable limits prescribed by law as can be demonstrably justified in a free and democratic society."

Linda's first op-ed piece, in the Globe and Mail December 23, 1981, challenged the "notwithstanding" clause in the Constitution.

Constitution was approved with the notwithstanding clause in place. The Queen came to Ottawa and, on April 17, 1982, signed the documents patriating the Canadian Constitution.

I was there that day in Ottawa, at the request of the CBC, to serve on a TV panel. Also on the panel were Alan Borovoy, counsel to the Canadian Civil Liberties Association, and Peter Russell, a professor of political science at the University of Toronto.

I recall that the CBC producers had called around looking for a feminist lawyer who could speak to the issues, and my name came up enough times that I was "it." Pat Hacker, a member of the Ad Hoc Committee on the Constitution, urged me to do this. Of course I said yes. I took the opportunity to exhort women, and particularly Indigenous women, to use and test the Charter equality provisions (the Charter contained new rights for Aboriginal Peoples[123]). Members of the panel had a strong difference of opinion on the notwithstanding clause—I objected to it, but Al Borovoy spoke out in its favour. He believed that governments would exercise restraint in the use of section 33, and that they would politically be unable to use the power available to them to opt out of fundamental rights and freedoms.[124]

The equality rights in section 15 of the 1982 Charter of Rights and Freedoms came into effect on April 17, 1985, three years after the Constitution was proclaimed, and I participated in welcoming it. I was a keynote speaker at the celebration of Charter Equality Rights at the "Feminist Fantasy of the Future" event sponsored by the Charter of Rights Coalition and the Women's Legal Education and Action Fund (LEAF), held at St. Lawrence Hall in Toronto. That was when LEAF began its significant work to try to ensure that court interpretations of the Charter did not erode women's equality rights. Many of the same women who were part of the Ad Hoc group also supported the development of LEAF. Four leading feminist lawyers—Beth Atcheson, Mary Eberts, Beth Symes, and Jennifer Stoddart—had researched the idea of a legal action fund for the Canadian Advisory Council on the Status of Women in 1984, and their ideas formed the basis for the establishment of the Women's Legal Education and Action Fund in 1985.[125]

Since then, LEAF has brought countless issues before the courts in order to ensure the equality rights of women and girls under the Charter of Rights and Freedoms of the Canadian Constitution. Their legal directors were exceptional leaders in feminist legal thinking—Helena Orton, Carissima Mathen, Joanna Birenbaum, and Kim Stanton among them. LEAF had the benefit of numerous volunteer practising lawyers who argued the cases in court. At the beginning, they focused only on constitutional issues; by 1987, LEAF found that

A Feminist Fantasy of the Future

WOMEN'S CELEBRATION OF THE
CANADIAN CHARTER OF RIGHTS
AND FREEDOMS

"All fantasy should have a solid base in reality."
Sir Max Beerbohm

Dinner and Cabaret
St. Lawrence Hall
April 17, 1985

Program for the event celebrating the 1985 arrival of constitutional equality rights (cover illustration by feminist artist Helen Lucas)

one-third of inquiries to its offices related to family law—the law that most affects the average person. Asked for my advice on how to apply the Charter to family law issues, I wrote a lengthy letter with suggestions. Over the years LEAF branched out to add their views in family law court cases dealing with such issues as tax that was (formerly) payable on child support received by the custodial parent, spousal support, child support, and pension sharing. I have joined many others in supporting the important work of this group since its beginning.

Minister Responsible for the Status of Women
The three years on council made it clear to me that while we made effective analyses and suggestions, we were not being heard, and our ideas were not being implemented to the extent that we would have liked, or that would make enough of a difference for women. It turned out that the advisory council structure allowed governments to distance themselves from a direct confrontation with women's reality. In 1982, toward the end of my term, we discussed this issue and decided that a better structure was needed to ensure that the impact of government laws and programs on women were taken into consideration. We needed a voice at the cabinet table, where policy was discussed and decided. We needed a minister responsible for the status of women—someone who headed an actual ministry with a staff and funding to keep an eye on women's concerns and coordinate policy among all the ministries whose policies have a bearing on women. Our small and poorly funded group on council certainly punched above its weight, but we saw that more could and should be done to bring women's issues to the fore.

The council at that time was purely advisory, had part-time members, and managed with a staff of three. Susan Gibson and Bridget Vianna valiantly and dynamically ran an office that made a significant difference, but the fact is that they had a budget of only $155,000 in 1982. We wanted a cabinet minister specifically appointed to be responsible for the status of women and a ministry with the funding to do the job we were doing with one hand tied behind our backs. We also asked that the chair position be a full-time spot.

In June 1982, the OCSW released a report entitled "Recommendations for New Government Structures for Women," which I helped prepare. It was submitted to the government, and we were thanked for our suggestions.

At the same time, I was asked to permit my name to stand for reappointment to the council for a further three-year term, once my first term came to a close. The presumption was that I would become chair. I agonized over the decision. If I took on the role, I would be over my head in work, and while it was labelled a part-time job, it would be closer to full-time for me. I wanted to do it, but I was exhausted. I had driven myself too far, and my health was suffering. During my term on council, I had an exceptionally demanding caseload in my private law practice. I had purchased a home and organized the move. I had reorganized, expanded, and moved my office. I had nurtured a long-distance relationship. I had organized a Bat Mitzvah celebration for my daughter. I was still writing, accepting speaking, TV, and radio engagements, and more.

I felt I had reached my limit. With great regret, I notified Premier Davis and Margaret Birch that I would not be seeking re-appointment. Margaret Birch sent me a wonderful letter expressing disappointment and assuring me that my advice was relevant and practical and my participation had "benefited our government and women in Ontario."

That was wonderful recognition, but I knew that I had personally benefited from the invaluable experience I got on the Ontario Council on the Status of Women. I learned how to mount a campaign to influence change. I learned to stay focused on the issues and make rational representations. I did not believe it was helpful or wise to criticize politicians' intentions or assume they had a hidden agenda. Even if they did, one could not accomplish the desired result by challenging, confronting, or ridiculing them. When I took apart the sexual harassment section of the proposed Ontario Human Rights Code, for example, I analyzed how their wording might be interpreted when cases would come before the court. I suggested alternative wording that would be more effective. When I wrote the disinherited spouse brief, I spoke of the fairness factor—that divorced women should not end up in a better position than women who had stayed in an unhappy marriage. I think this approach encouraged governments to change their positions. In fact, TV broadcaster Dini Petty commented on more than one occasion that she could support feminism because of me; she felt I was sensible and rational in my views and recommendations. It was a wonderful compliment.

I kept in touch with the council staff after I left in June 1982, and they kept me informed, particularly with the government reply to the issue of a ministry responsible for the status of women. Unfortunately, the reply was silence, and more silence. As a result, I wrote an article promoting the idea. Ellie Tesher, the *Toronto Star*'s Life editor at the time, chose to print the article and my photo on the entire front page of her section. It was headlined "Women need voice at the top." Not content to assume that the decision-makers would happen upon the article, I sent a copy to everyone I thought would benefit from such a ministry, including MPPs and those involved in many women's organizations. I added a memo to the women's groups urging them to write to their MPPs, the newspapers, and the premier, asking for a more effective structure to deal with women's issues.

Less than one year later, on April 19, 1983, the Bill Davis government responded positively and announced the appointment of the first minister responsible for the status of women. He was Robert Welch, who also served as deputy premier. He had been a family law lawyer before going into politics. He appointed veteran civil servant Glenna Carr as his first executive director. I was pleased, as I felt she understood the issues and needs of women. She told me the Ontario Women's Directorate (OWD), the bureaucratic arm of the ministry, would have a staff of fifty people, which was a significant improvement over what had been available to the council. The council continued on as an advisory group[126] and although I left the council, I continued my efforts to contribute to the advancement of women's equality rights wherever I could.

Chapter 9
CHALLENGING INEQUALITY
IN FAMILY LAW, 1979-84

Family law lawyers like me "toiled in the vineyards of matrimonial discord," as Ontario family law judge George Walsh was fond of saying, and our job was to try to resolve the legal issues arising from marriage breakdown. In the 1970s the majority of lawyers, judges, and husbands expressed attitudes during negotiations and litigation that made me very aware that they did not consider marriage to be an economic partnership. Divorce itself had become simpler in 1968 when the federal government modernized the cross-Canada Divorce Act, but the provinces were slower in reforming their property-sharing family laws. It was difficult for women to receive a fair share of the family's assets or sufficient financial support.

During the 1970s, family law reform was forced onto the public agenda to meet women's concerns. This chapter tells the story of the process that resulted in the 1978 Ontario Family Law Reform Act, a story that illustrates what went wrong with that law, and the campaign that yielded laws that mandated fairer and more equal treatment for women.

THE PRESSURE FOR CHANGE
Since 1967, the Ontario Law Reform Commission (OLRC) had been studying options on how best to acknowledge the changing economic and social conditions in the laws dealing with the family. In 1970 the Royal Commission on the Status of Women recommended new laws that would recognize marriage as an equal partnership

and acknowledge financially the woman's role in homemaking and child care. In 1971, women were shocked by the travesty suffered by Irene Murdoch, the wife of an Alberta farmer. As outlined earlier, the *Murdoch* case had stunned and alarmed Canadian women with its gross unfairness; how was it possible that in 1971 an Alberta trial judge could refuse this woman—who had worked alongside her husband running every aspect of the farm—a share of what she had helped to build? How could the Alberta Court of Appeal, in 1972, and then the Supreme Court of Canada, in 1973, support that trial decision?

The 1974 Conference on Women and the Law at Windsor devoted an entire section of the program to a discussion on how to change matrimonial property law. That same year, the Ontario Law Reform Commission[127] issued its recommendations that approved equal sharing after a divorce of property accumulated during a marriage. In 1975, the federal Law Reform Commission also supported property sharing between husband and wife, commenting that the law was far behind public opinion.

Both the federal and Ontario Law Reform Commissions promoted a deferred community of property regime; that is, property accumulated by either the husband or the wife during the marriage would be shared at the end of the marriage. The Ontario government was concerned to show women that it meant well, so it enacted stopgap legislation in 1975 to prevent a Murdoch-type decision in Ontario; the law stated that no spouse would be disentitled to a share of property to which she had contributed work, money, or money's worth "by reason only of the relationship of husband and wife or that the acts constituting the contribution are those of a reasonable spouse of that sex in the circumstances." As awkward as that sounded, the new law was promising that real change was on the way.

Ontario Family Law Reform Act 1978

Over the next three years, the Ontario government studied the OLRC's 1974 report on family law, and after public consultations, the government recommended a different way of sharing assets than anyone had previously considered. Ontario was the first common-law province[128] to try to achieve equity for women in family law when it enacted the Family Law Reform Act (FLRA) on March 31, 1978.

Attorney General Roy McMurtry's solution was far more complicated and more dependent on the discretion of the courts than the deferred community of property system that the Ontario Law Reform Commission had suggested. While the FLRA's stated purpose was unprecedented[129]—to recognize that the marriage relationship assumes that both spouses contribute, and therefore both are entitled to an equal division of the family assets—the language and structure of the FLRA was complicated. This legislation was clearly a compromise: section 4 required husbands and wives to share only limited "family assets"—defined as the family home, household contents, the cottage, and any cars owned by the couple. The courts were given discretion to vary this sharing in several different ways. In described circumstances, the courts could order an unequal division of these family assets in order to achieve an equitable result. The court could also choose, in defined circumstances, to divide "non-family assets" (including investments and business and pension assets), where the result of the division of the family assets would be unfair. Section 8 allowed a judge to order a payment of money or a share of a specific non-family asset when one spouse contributed work, money, or money's worth to the non-family assets themselves. The FLRA was not the straightforward deferred community of property approach recommended by the Ontario Law Reform Commission, and it was criticized for not going far enough—it did not provide for the automatic division of all assets accumulated during the marriage, and it gave judges (at that time, mostly male) too much discretion.

It was only recently that I learned from Karen Weiler, who had been senior counsel in the Policy Development Division of the Ministry of the Attorney General between 1974 and 1980,[130] that the cabinet was given two choices: (1) the Law Reform Commission proposal of deferred community of property, which would apply only to those married after the new law was enacted,[131] or (2) a hybrid differentiating between "family" and "non-family" assets, which would apply to all existing as well as future marriages.

She said that the family assets approach was her response to the challenges to the OLRC recommendations heard from the public at

THE FAMILY LAW REFORM ACT
OF ONTARIO SECTIONS 4 AND 8

Section 4

4(1) Subject to subsection 4, where a decree nisi
of divorce is pronounced or a marriage is declared
a nullity or where the spouses are separated and
there is no reasonable prospect of the resumption
of cohabitation, each spouse is entitled to have the
family assets divided in equal shares notwithstanding the ownership of the assets by the spouses as
determinable for other purposes and notwithstanding any order under section 7.

(2) The court may, upon the application of a person
who is the spouse of another, determine any matter
respecting the division of family assets between them.

(3) The rights under subsection 1 are personal as
between the spouses but any application com-
menced under subsection 2 before the death of a
spouse may be continued by or against the estate of
the deceased spouse.

(4) The court may make a division of family assets
resulting in shares that are not equal where the court
is of the opinion that a division of the family assets in
equal shares would be inequitable, having regard to,

(a) any agreement other than a domestic contract;

(b) the duration of the period of cohabitation
under the marriage;

(c) the duration of the period during which the
spouses have lived separate and apart;

(d) the date when the property was acquired;

(e) the extent to which property was acquired by
one spouse by inheritance or by gift; or

(f) any other circumstance relating to the acquisition, disposition, preservation, maintenance,
improvement or use of property rendering it
inequitable for the division of family assets to be in
equal shares.

(5) The purpose of this section is to recognize that
child care, household management, and financial
provision are the joint responsibilities of the

twelve town hall meet-
ings held throughout
the province. At these
well-attended meetings,
people were educated
on what the existing law
was and what the Law
Reform Commission
proposed. The attorney
general's office created a
film to make the issues
easier to understand,
and gave away 50,000
copies of the twelve-
page summary of the
OLRC report that
Rosalie Abella, Mary
Eberts, Jane Maddaugh,
and I had prepared for
the Ontario Committee
on the Status of Women.
We were delighted to
agree to the distribution
of our pamphlet. We had
done the work hoping
to educate and promote
change, but to have
50,000 copies distrib-
uted by the government
was an unexpected
bonus.

Karen Weiler told
me that many men who
attended the hearings
had vocally opposed
sharing their businesses,
investments, and partic-
ularly farms with their

wives, calling it expropriation of their property. Women had resisted the OLRC recommendation that all debts be shared as well as assets. They also disagreed with the proposal that the deferred community of property regime would only apply to those who married after the law was changed— many women wanted the rights and benefits to be retroactive and apply to their existing marriages. This difference of opinion between men and women was the cause of the compromise. In the end, the bill that was approved by the cabinet and eventually passed as the Family Law Reform Act 1978 divided marital property into defined family and non-family assets; spouses were given more rights to family assets, and sharing of non-family assets was much more limited. At the same time, the new law was made retroactive to apply to all existing marriages. Other provinces[132] followed Ontario's lead in giving spouses an opportunity to claim a share of the family's assets on marriage breakdown.

spouses and that inherent in the marital relationship there is joint contribution, whether financial or otherwise, by the spouses to the assumption of these responsibilities, entitling each spouse to an equal division of the family assets, subject to the equitable considerations set out in subsections 4 and 6.

(6) The court shall make a division of any property that is not a family asset where,

(a) a spouse has unreasonably impoverished the family assets; or

(b) the result of a division of the family assets would be inequitable in all the circumstances, having regard to,

(i) the considerations set out in clauses a to f of subsection 4, and

(ii) the effect of the assumption by one spouse of any of the responsibilities set out in subsection 5 on the ability of the other spouse to acquire, manage, maintain, operate or improve property that is not a family asset.

Section 8

8. Where one spouse or former spouse has contributed work, money or money's worth in respect of the acquisition, management, maintenance, operation or improvement of property, other than family assets, in which the other has or had an interest, upon application, the court may by order,

(a) direct the payment of an amount in compensation therefor; or

(b) award a share of the interest of the other spouse or former spouse in the property appropriate to the contribution, and the court shall determine and assess the contribution without regard to the relationship of husband and wife or the fact that the acts constituting the contribution are those of a reasonable spouse of that sex in the circumstances.

Although the FLRA had been created to satisfy competing interests, it did not satisfy all women. Typical of women's response was Doris Anderson's editorial in *Chatelaine* in October 1976, in which she criticized the bill as "too vaguely defined and far too much is left to the discretion of the judges—who are generally older and overwhelmingly male."

I was ready to work with it. I had to—as a lawyer whose clients would either suffer from or benefit from the new law, I had to try to make it work to achieve justice for my clients. In fact, I was excited by the possibilities of the 1978 legislation. It seemed that the law gave judges the discretion to reward the indirect financial contribution of the wives who stayed home to raise their children and manage their homes, supporting the work done by husbands outside the home. After all, the legislation's clear intention was to recognize the equal contribution of men and women to marriage—and that judges should exercise their discretion accordingly.

The FLRA was certainly an improvement over the previous legal situation; it had been impossible to ignore the injustices suffered by women in some cases we studied in law school. Once I represented clients and took cases forward under the new law, I witnessed how difficult it was to make the 1978 Family Law Reform Act work for women in the face of judicial discretion often working against us. One of my cases exemplified how historic attitudes toward women undermined the new legislation whose goal was supposed to have been to achieve fairness for women.

The Challenge to the Family Law Reform Act: The Leatherdale Case
Barbara Leatherdale separated in 1978, the same year as the Family Law Reform Act came into force. She seemed to be a perfect candidate to benefit from the new law. She had contributed to the family as a wage earner in a bank for half of her nineteen-year marriage, in the home for the other half as a child caregiver, and throughout as the household manager. It seemed so obvious that the new law intended that she would receive half of *everything*. Her husband was an employee of Bell Canada and owned Bell Canada shares through an employee share purchase plan, as well as some Registered Retirement Savings Plan (RRSP) pension assets. He opposed her claim to any share of the investment or pension assets. We resolved

the division of the family assets, but the issue of non-family assets went to trial.

The case was decided on January 31, 1980, less than two years after the FLRA came into effect. Mr. Justice John J. Holland presided over the trial and ordered that the Bell Canada shares and the RRSPs—in fact, *all* of the couple's assets—be shared equally. He was very clear that this was fair since there had been real teamwork and a true pooling of finances and efforts during the marriage. The husband's assets were worth $50,000 and the wife's were worth $10,000; Justice Holland ordered the husband to pay $20,000 to the wife as an equalization payment. My hope was vindicated—the new law would be good for women. The judge ruled that investments and pensions, although defined in the FLRA as non-family assets, were in fact the product of the joint effort of the spouses and therefore, according to section 4(5), had to be shared.

After he gave judgment, Justice Holland had to decide whether one spouse had to pay some part of the other's legal costs. He reviewed their settlement offers to determine whether they could have avoided a trial by the acceptance of a reasonable offer. Because Mrs. Leatherdale had received a better result at trial than she had offered to accept before trial, the judge said that "all the reasonableness had been one-sided," and he ordered Gordon Leatherdale to pay part of his wife's legal costs. Mr. Leatherdale also had his own lawyer's costs to pay.

So at trial, Barbara Leatherdale won; the law was interpreted in a way that set a precedent to benefit many women, and men who resisted this law would have to pay significant legal costs. This triumph was short-lived. Mr. Leatherdale refused to accept the trial judge's ruling and appealed to the Ontario Court of Appeal.

The Court of Appeal

On September 19, 1980, I arrived at the Court of Appeal dressed in my uniform—my barrister's robes—ready to stand up for the correctness of the trial judgment. The Court of Appeal hearings are held in the historic building at Osgoode Hall on Queen Street West in Toronto. The courtroom's carved wood interior and the grave demeanour of the judges on their raised dais added to the weight of the proceedings. The Court of Appeal hears cases in panels of three;

Mr. Justice Maurice Lacourcière, Mr. Justice John W. Morden, and Mr. Justice Donald S. Thorson were the ones chosen to hear the case.[133] At the hearing, Justice Lacourcière was the leader, and he was not sympathetic to my argument.

Justice Lacourcière took the surprising position that the application had not been made under the correct section of the FLRA and therefore the trial judge could not give the relief requested. I could hardly believe my ears, but I was unable to persuade him that he had misread the materials. In fact, the application had been made under all conceivably applicable sections of the statute, and the argument had also been made that the common law of constructive trust applied. Common law is created not by legislation but by decisions in cases, and over the years the law of constructive trust was developed to recognize—with an ownership share—a contribution of work, money, or money's worth to property in the name of another person who is unjustly enriched as a result. Unfortunately, Justice Lacourcière chose to focus only on the abbreviated wording dashed off by the referring judge who had sent the case to trial in general terms, saying the trial judge should rule "as to the proper division of family assets...." The court application that started the lawsuit specified full details of the claim as well as the sections of the FLRA that were relied on. While the trial judge had, in fact, dealt with those issues in the court application at the trial, the Court of Appeal chose not to follow suit and allowed the inadequate direction to become an obstacle that limited the rights of the wife.

Not only that. The panel interpreted the FLRA far more narrowly and restrictively than had the trial judge. In its ruling, released on November 14, 1980, the Court of Appeal reversed the trial decision and directed that the wife was *not* entitled to any part of the value of the Bell shares or the RRSPs or to receive any payment toward her legal costs. The Court of Appeal decided that Barbara Leatherdale had not made a contribution directly in the form of dollars or employment earnings to the acquisition of the shares or the RRSPs themselves (it was, after all, Mr. Leatherdale who had worked for Bell), but rather to the marriage as a whole, and therefore she could not receive a share of them. In their decision, her contribution to the marriage as a wife and mother, and to the upbringing of their child and the care of the home and family, did not count.

Deciding What to Do

I was both deflated and incensed. This decision made it clear that the FLRA would not be allowed to live up to its promise. Not only was the Court of Appeal decision unfair to Barbara Leatherdale, it also established a negative precedent with respect to every divorcing woman's future ability to achieve equity in family law. I could not tolerate the idea of this decision standing as the last word on the subject, because it would be very difficult for this interpretation to be altered unless the statute was amended. My experience taking cases forward for divorcing women and men led me to the inexorable conclusion that the legislation itself must be changed. While the exercise of judicial discretion could benefit women in some cases—the trial decision in *Leatherdale* among them—there was a greater risk that these cases would be interpreted narrowly and restrictively by subsequent judges.

The process of seeking legislative change would be the next challenge. Unless all possible legal avenues in court were canvassed first, the government would not even consider changing the law again, so soon after it had enacted the FLRA.

A further appeal, this time to the court of last appeal—the Supreme Court of Canada—had to come first. Either we would win the case and set a precedent by which the FLRA would have to be interpreted, or we would lose and set the stage for a groundswell of outrage among women that would hopefully result in a more clear and definitive law that asserted that men and women were to share equally what they accumulated during the marriage. I thought public opinion would be on Barbara Leatherdale's side.

I faced a real dilemma. Mrs. Leatherdale was willing to appeal but could not afford to take the case to the Supreme Court of Canada. Nor did the amount at issue make it worth doing on a cost/benefit analysis to her. The disbursements alone would be costly—including out-of-pocket costs for photocopying, court fees, travel and hotel, and similar expenses. I would need to prepare documents and travel to Ottawa to present an argument just to receive permission from the Supreme Court to appeal. If leave to appeal was granted, there would be more documents to prepare and more travel and hotel costs for the appeal hearing itself.

Only a few lawyers ever appear at the Supreme Court of Canada.

I had no experience in appellate work. I anguished over the decision and how I could manage its practical aspects. I was in practice only six years at that time; my daughter was thirteen, and I was her sole support. And of course, there were other clients to serve and other responsibilities and commitments. There were thirty days to resolve what to do, get instructions from my client, and prepare and file a Notice of Appeal. It would cost me more than $25,000 in lost income and disbursements, which I could ill afford. In the end, however, I just *had* to find a way to do it. I could not allow the Court of Appeal decision to stand without a fight. This was a unique opportunity to make a difference in the lives of both my client and other women. For me, this was not only an opportunity but an obligation.

I made a deal with my client to take the case forward and the major financial risks would be mine. Her only risk was that if she lost, an order might be made that she pay her husband's court costs, estimated at that time to be $850 at most; she put up the required $500 security deposit in case she was ordered to pay these costs.

If she won the case, we agreed that she would be entitled to keep the amount the court awarded, except that she would reimburse me for the disbursements I advanced—estimated at about $1,600. If the Supreme Court ordered her husband to contribute to her legal costs because she won the case, any amount collected would be paid to me in partial compensation of my fees, even though it would represent a very small portion of what my bill would have been to a paying client.

It never occurred to me to ask anyone for a financial contribution, nor to undertake a fundraising campaign. There was no organization at that time that might fund such a legal challenge. LEAF was not on the scene yet,[134] there was no Court Challenges program,[135] and there was no audacity (on my part) to pass the hat. Even if I had considered organizing a fundraising campaign, I would not have had time to do it. My hands were full just dealing with the case itself.

When it came to making this decision, the advantage of being self-employed cannot be overstated. Having my own law practice meant I did not have to account for my time to a boss or a group of partners who might have been unwilling to fund the litigation, particularly since there was little hope of financial reward. They might also have been concerned that my activism for women might lose them male clients. Lawyers who worked for large firms often had their hands (and time) tied to prevent them from engaging in cases that might negatively affect the firm. I had no such limitation. All I had to do was find the time to serve paying clients so I could make a living while still paying for staff and overhead. My solution: stringent time management and long working hours.

Challenging the Family Law Reform Act at the Supreme Court of Canada

Once we came to this understanding, I got to work. The application for leave to appeal had to be prepared quickly. To get permission to appeal, the court had to be persuaded, both in the submitted brief and in the oral argument, that the issues raised by the case had national importance. The trial transcript, containing the evidence that had been heard by the trial judge, had already been paid for by the husband when he appealed to the Ontario Court of Appeal, so at least we did not have to come up with the money for that. Judith Huddart, who was an articling student at that time, helped with the research and preparation of the documents and came with me to Ottawa. The application was heard by Chief Justice Laskin and justices Willard Z. Estey and Julien Chouinard on March 2, 1981, and thankfully, leave to appeal was granted.

The press continued to be interested in issues and cases dealing with family law because this was a matter that affected many people. I was often called for comment and explanations as this case made its way through the courts. *Toronto Star* columnist Michele Landsberg[136] wrote a supportive column on March 9, 1981, in which she described the Ontario Court of Appeal decision as "strange and ominous." She continued: "Wasn't it the whole point of Family Law Reform that a wife's work, in or out of the home, should weigh as heavily on the scales of justice as her husband's? Does it seem fair and right to anyone else that a couple's savings should go entirely to the husband?"

We prepared and filed the documents to make the case in the actual appeal, and one year later, off we went to Ottawa for the hearing before the Supreme Court. This time, in addition to Judith Huddart, my daughter also came along. Beth was fourteen, and it was a real joy to share this experience with her and, at the same time, to be a role model for fighting the good fight for women's equality rights. Ottawa feminist lawyer Shirley Greenberg opened her home to us, which spared me the hotel costs. Shirley and I had met at the first National Conference of Women and the Law back in 1974. I had just been called to the Bar and Shirley was in law school. Both of us were in the room at the end of the conference when many of us enthusiastically voted to establish the National Association of Women and Law. We had maintained our connection and, with her help, the forces of feminism came together in the courtroom at the Supreme Court of Canada to stand up for the rights of women in family law.

Arriving at the Supreme Court of Canada on March 22, 1982, I was impressed with the majesty of the place. The many steps leading to the entrance of the building lend a certain distance and air of formality to the process. The mahogany-panelled courtroom is rich in tradition. Thanks to Shirley's efforts, the courtroom spectator section was filled with feminist lawyers, which gave me a great feeling of encouragement and support.

I stood, ready to meet the challenge, and faced this panel of men in their red judicial robes embellished with ermine, all focused on me, the upstart woman lawyer who was ready to fight for the fair treatment of women. I did everything possible to appear and to be calm and self-possessed. My training and experience as a lawyer, and my history as a university debater, kicked in and provided the personal resources needed to proceed.

Leatherdale was the first case to ask the Supreme Court of Canada to interpret Ontario's Family Law Reform Act, and it dealt with the sharing of a family's business, investment, and pension assets. There had been three previous cases heard at the Supreme Court, all spouses dealing with claims to farm property arising from their significant direct and indirect contributions. In 1973, the Supreme Court denied Alberta farmer Irene Murdoch's claims. Yet in 1978, Saskatchewan farmer Helen Rathwell succeeded in securing an equal share of marital property, based on the common-law remedy of constructive trust (which compensates for one person's loss as a result of another's unjust enrichment). Then, in 1980, Ontario common-law wife Rosa Becker was granted one-half of the value of

the bee-keeping business she had helped build, also based on constructive trust.

Shirley Greenberg and Linda outside the Supreme Court of Canada, after the hearing of *Leatherdale*, March 1982

A panel of seven judges heard the *Leatherdale* case, led by Chief Justice Bora Laskin. The others were justices Roland A. Ritchie, Brian Dickson, Jean Beetz, Willard Z. Estey, William R. McIntyre, and Julien Chouinard. Justice Laskin took the lead in questioning, which made me hopeful. Here was a judge who had experience with the issues raised in the *Leatherdale* case. He had been on the panels that had heard the other three cases dealing with farm assets. He had written the dissenting judgment in the *Murdoch* case, stating that he would have ruled that Irene Murdoch was entitled to a property interest in the farm based on the common law of constructive trust, considering her extraordinary contribution of work, money, and money's worth. He had sided with the majority decision in *Rathwell*. He was on the majority panel that gave Rosa Becker a one-half interest in the bee-keeping business owned in the name of her common-law partner based on the law of constructive trust arising from her work, which set a new precedent in the law of property sharing between common-law partners.[137]

There was little opportunity to present my argument in the way that I had prepared it. Justice Laskin immediately told me not to state the facts, as the judges had read the material. He did, however, ask for my "essential submissions" and kept the questions coming. In answering them, I managed to include most of my planned argument, but not in the words or order I had expected. Are you arguing an indirect contribution to the asset?[138] (*Yes*, I said.) Are you arguing only section 8? (*No.*) Does constructive and resulting trust[139] survive the FLRA? (*Yes.*) Does equity survive? (*Yes.*) Was the question of constructive trust argued in the Court of Appeal? (*Yes.*) Was there a common intention to share? (*Yes, and the Court of Appeal ignored it.*) He then asserted that the Court of Appeal decision seemed to turn on section 8. Then Justice Laskin and I had a discussion about which section of the FLRA to use. Justice Dickson, who would be the next chief justice, took an active part in the back-and-forth. He asked why an indirect contribution could not be rewarded under section 8. Relying on previous cases dealing with farm wives that had reached the Supreme Court of Canada, Justice Dickson asked why a city wife should not similarly be rewarded for her contribution. The judges struggled with the Court of Appeal's decision, and this showed up in their eventual written reasons for their decision.

I asked the court to take the larger view and not be blinded by the nature of the asset, or the kind of contribution made, but to interpret the Family Law Reform Act broadly with a view to its intention to recognize the mutuality of a marriage. To interpret the FLRA narrowly and technically would make it ineffectual in fulfilling its purpose.

The court reserved its decision for later release. It was now out of my hands. That evening after the hearing, Shirley Greenberg threw a party at her home in our honour, inviting Ottawans who sympathized with the cause. Some of these feminists and family lawyers had been in the courtroom witnessing the hearing, and it was great to be able to chat with them about the issues. Three Ottawa residents with whom I had served on the Ontario Council on the Status of Women also came. It was wonderful to be among like-minded individuals and feel their support. I was part of a community seeking justice for women.

Nine Months Later: The Supreme Court of Canada's Decision

On being advised that the court's ruling in the *Leatherdale* case would be released in open court on December 6, 1982, I flew to Ottawa. Chief Justice Laskin had written the decision and spoke for the court.[140] The court had decided that Barbara Leatherdale would receive only the share of the investments that could be justified by her financial contribution from working and earning money outside the home during one-half of the marriage — in other words, one-quarter of the assets. The fact that she was the parent to bear and raise the child of the marriage and manage the home did not entitle her to an equal share of the assets accumulated during the marriage. Gordon Leatherdale was ordered to pay half of his wife's "party and party"[141] costs throughout all three levels of court.

Chief Justice Laskin agreed with the Court of Appeal that Mrs. Leatherdale would have had to prove a financial contribution *to the very property itself* (Bell shares, RRSPs), rather than to the marriage, if she were to succeed under section 8 of the Act. But Justice Lacourcière had ruled that he could not apply section 8 of the Family Law Reform Act since, he said, the claim had not been made based on section 8 but only on section 4. To my dismay, Chief Justice Laskin picked up the same misconception in his majority judgment. He also would not consider the impact of constructive trust and its interrelationship with the FLRA.

It was very frustrating to have my real submissions misstated. It made me realize that no matter how careful and conscientious a lawyer was in the presentation of the facts and argument, judges have their own perceptions and opinions, and the power to implement them, and will see the facts in the way that makes the point and proves the case they want to prove.

It was especially gratifying to read the lengthy dissenting judgment of Justice Estey. He pointed out that in the initiating documents of the case, Barbara Leatherdale had clearly claimed under both section 4 and the alternative section 8. In his dissenting judgment, he supported my submissions. He observed that our notice of motion and my opening statement at the trial clearly requested an order under section 8 for the division of the investment and pension assets, and the Court of Appeal had been wrong in saying section 8 had not been invoked and was therefore inapplicable.

Justice Estey also pointed out that the confusion had partly arisen because the court order sending the case to trial referred to the issues in a very general way, "as to proper division of family assets, custody, maintenance for the child, and support for the wife," and the order did not reflect the specific claims of the wife. Justice Estey supported the trial judge's view that the Family Law Reform Act should be given a liberal interpretation since the statute was meant to be remedial.

The majority decision did point out that the FLRA was a difficult and complex law to interpret. In the *Reports of Family Law*, the editor, James G. McLeod, wrote a lengthy case comment and concluded by describing the majority judgment as a "superficial analysis" of sections 4(6) and 8 of the FLRA, which failed to consider their impact on the common law of constructive and resulting trust.

Although the judgment was a partial win, the court had missed the point in ruling that only a direct financial contribution to the acquisition of an asset entitled a wife to a share. At that time, so many women were homemakers and did not work outside the home, or if they worked, were discriminated against in pay and opportunities and by the absence of child care. Constructive trust law had already been used by the Supreme Court to share a family's assets between spouses in two prior farm cases, but not this one. If this regressive case was allowed to stand, many women would have no legislated entitlement to a share of non-family assets—the business, investments, and pension. And women who had not worked outside the home could not prove that they had directly contributed to the acquisition of the asset in order to make the argument that they were entitled by the common law of constructive or resulting trust. The financial recognition of women's role in and contribution to marriage had been a premise of the 1978 Family Law Reform Act. Other provinces had based their laws on Ontario's provisions. Now the promise of that law had been undermined. I had now exhausted all the litigation options to have the decisions reflect the stated purpose of the 1978 FLRA. There was no further court to which to appeal. The court of last resort had spoken.

WHAT NEXT? THE LOBBY CAMPAIGN
FOR EQUAL SHARING LAWS

The only course of action left was to lobby for a change in the legislation itself. The campaign to change the FLRA started on the very day that the Supreme Court of Canada decision was released. The press was gathered for the result and wanted a comment, so I read the judgment as rapidly as possible inside the courtroom and was ready for the journalists who were waiting outside to report on this landmark judgment. The press surrounded me with microphones, cameras, and notebooks.

This is the gist of what I said: *The result is unacceptable. The law must be changed. There must be no doubt that a husband and wife are entitled to share equally all assets accumulated during the marriage. The Ontario Law Reform Commission Report on Family Law had recommended this in 1974, and they were right. It was unfair that Barbara Leatherdale got only 25 percent of the pension and investment assets. The decision did not acknowledge a woman's role in the marriage as homemaker and child-care provider. The Court admitted how difficult it was to interpret the FLRA.*

What an uphill battle this would be! The existing legislation had been passed on March 31, 1978, and it was only 1982. The Ontario government would be reluctant to put family law reform back on its agenda only four years later, but we had to try. Nothing ventured, nothing gained. What helped in this effort was the knowledge that most women (and many men) knew how unfair it was to ignore a woman's contribution to home and family in the distribution of assets after a marriage breakdown. Equal sharing of all that had been accumulated during a marriage was obvious to so many people. The newspapers followed the issues and many columnists wrote opinions in support of equality in marriage. Both the federal and the Ontario Law Reform Commission reports had recommended community of property to take effect only after the marriage broke down. I had promoted equal sharing of family property effective from the first day of marriage. I now realized that if any change in law was possible, the solution would have to be already in the public and political consciousness. The law commission's proposals were widely known. Clearly, that was the solution to pursue.

Ontario's family law act is an ass — and a mess

Ontario housewives called losers in

DORIS ANDERSON

Family law reform bill is welcome

Roy McMurtry, Attorney-General of Ontario, announced recently that he's going to bring in a new Family Law Reform bill in the next few weeks. That's welcome relief for thousands of Ontario couples who divorce every year. Ontario's Family Law Re-form is the

It's
as ta
Manit
new b
dollar:
payme
This
covere
about
orders
Manito
on a co
If pa
governm
or two
the deli
a man)
up in ja
efficienc
nance o
for ever
total turi

The set
000 a yea
000 that
out in we
has gone
treasury.
Manitol
lion peopl
are 8 milli
ers on well
the million.
"The sy:
every prov
Robyn Dia
Law sect
Attorney-G
Ontario ma
doesn't pay
But if a N
Ontario the

Provincial law one of the worst in Canada experts say

By Frances Kelly and **Leslie Scrivener**
Toronto Star

If you're a housewife and your marriage is on the rocks, look out if you live in Ontario.

lude, a lawyer and executive member of the National Action Committee on the Status of Women, who ranks it among the worst in Canada along with those of Prince Edward Island and Newfoundland.

Dulude is not alone in being disappointed in a Supreme Court ruling Monday that didn't recognize a Scarborough woman's work in the home, but only her years of work in a bank, in awarding her one-quarter of her estranged husband's investments.

Audrey Coville-Re
Toronto would likely ha
better in one of the west
inces.
The Ontario Court o
recently upheld a Supre
judge's ruling that her
an "enthusiastic hostess
husband's dinner parties
ness associates did not c
all that much to his suc
wealth.
Her husband, David,
to Canada from South
1961 with $200 in hi
a successfu

Family law bill 'top priority'

By Jackie Smith Toronto Star

A new family law reform act is the Ontario attorney general's top priority.

"From the point of view of this ministry, there is no more important bill," says Ian Scott, who is also minister for women's issues and native affairs.

The Liberal government has adopted the family law bill introduced by the Progressive Conservative government prior to its defeat on June 18. The bill proposes that at marriage breakdown, all assets accumulated during the marriage — business assets, registered retirement savings plans, stocks and bonds — be divided equally between the spouses. Gifts and inheritances would be excepted. At present only "family assets," such as house, car and cottage, are shared automatically.

In an intervie
women's issues, the
lor lawyer said he
ernment will give
ity during the nex
However, he says,
agenda and the bi
studied in committ
nical changes and
tions for change
Scott says, but o
much as it
If the bill is
would apply tro
was introduced
Scott believe
reassure farme
who fear losir
the new act w
ners by allowi
over a period o
Though wor
plaud passage
yer Linda Sil
worried it giv
judges to vary
Women's g
closely to see
ment handles
interest to w
Lynn Kay:
sentative of
mittee on th
has mixed
formance sc
She is ple
with grassr
skeptical a
ure to intr
pay for wc
vate secto
"The b
Progressiv
the Liber:
promised
they want
they have to hold themselves in usel
promise," Kaye says.
The government has announced it
will introduce legislation requiring
equal pay for work of equal value in
the Ontario public service; there will
be a green paper study on how it can
best be implemented in the private
sector and at hospitals and schools.
Glenna Carr of the Ontario Women's
Directorate will head a task force
studying the issue. The paper will be
tabled in the Legislature in the fall,
and public hearings will then be held.
Scott admits he is hurt by criticism

the problems women have in the work-place. Employment equity or affirm-ative action programs intended to get women into jobs they haven't been able to get into are every bit as important as equal value, he says.

But Scott is not promising a rush of big changes for women, though he is confident that his cabinet colleagues also regard women's issues as impor-tant. Government is faced with a host of competing demands. It can't do everything at once and maintain a reasonable tax structure and viable economy, he says.

Still he recognizes he has to produce real results if he is to gain the confi-dence of women's groups.

"There have been too many years of non-action for (women) to be very trusting of what (government says) may happen," says lawyer Mary Cor-nish, spokesman for the Equal Pay Coalition.

Scott says he wants careful, steady progress for women, rather than promising the moon and increasing

Fairness for divorced women

In 1982, Scarborough's Barbara Leatherdale went to the Supreme Court of Canada asking for one-half of her ex-husband's retirement savings nest egg of $40,000. The court gave her only one-quarter, reasoning that since she had worked outside her home for only nine of the 19 years of her marriage she could only have contributed to the accumulation of the nest egg during those years. The court didn't count the 10 years she had spent at home raising the couple's child.

Recently, a divorced woman asked a Toronto lawyer for help in tracing her ex-husband who is $30,000 in arrears in support payments. This is the third lawyer in as many provinces whom the woman has consulted in the last 10 years; so far, all her efforts have been futile. And she doesn't even want the money for herself; she wants it to help put her daughter through medical school.

The Leatherdale case and the divorcee's fruit-less search illustrate how Ontario needs to amend its family property laws and institute a better sys-tem for enforcing support orders made by the

poised to set up a special automated agency that will collect money on behalf of divorced persons when their former spouses fall into arrears in pay-ments. Manitoba already has such a system; in 1983, it's estimated, the taxpayers of that province saved $250,000 in welfare payments that would have had to be made to families if support pay-ments hadn't been collected.

A spokesman in the office of Attorney-General Robert Welch says that the new agency is Ontar-io's response to Crosbie's initiative. He added that the data banks likely to be accessed — to obtain addresses of defaulting spouses — would be those recording drivers' licences and health insurance coverage. It isn't likely, he said, that income tax files would be looked at; a reassurance that's wel-come since it's important to retain the confiden-tiality of income tax data.

Ontario also intends, at long last, to amend the Family Law Reform Act to provide that all assets a couple accumulates during marriage be divided

He estimates he spent——hours a day working on women's issues.
"I've never had a busier or more re-warding time," he says. "The jobs I have are really fascinating. They are very difficult . . . some problems . . . seem almost insoluble.
"We have to be very careful not to be mesmerized by issues that have re-ceived symbolic importance (such as equal value)," he says. It won't solve all

equity. Scott says he wants a "march-ing" equity program that will "march along" with equal pay for work of equal value. In pre-election promises, the Liberals said they would require mandatory employment equity pro-grams in all private sector companies with more than 250 employees and the

See FAMILY/page F2

As he dealt with equality rights cases in his law practice, his knowl-edge increased. Women he worked with educated him "politely and thoughtfully" on women's issues. When he became attorney general and minis-

Scott says he became seriously inter-ested in women's issues about three or four years ago. "I got educated in them slowly and I think my education parelleled that of the general public," he says.

the public ——— public of a second test that four is ment on it, he says.

Newspapers and columnists supported the need for reform of family law to provide fairness for women.

Equality was in the air; the timing was right. This was 1982 and women's equality rights had been recognized in the new Charter of Rights and Freedoms, after great pressure by the women's movement. It was a good time to assert equality rights in family law. Gather and focus public opinion; persuade the powers that be that full equality—full sharing of property between husband and wife—was what the public wanted. That became the strategy.

The *Globe and Mail* carried a lengthy article the next day[142] on the *Leatherdale* decision and quoted me as saying, "It's a partial victory but I wouldn't say it's a good decision for women." Louise Dulude, a lawyer, spoke to the *Globe and Mail* on behalf of the National Action Committee on the Status of Women and blasted the decision as "an absolute disaster" for housewives who don't earn wages outside the home. Dulude went on to say that "this definitely establishes Ontario family law as one of the worst in Canada."

The newspaper followed up a day later with an editorial stating that the Supreme Court of Canada had "balked" at going the distance for separating and divorced women and noted a "mixed reception" to the judgment. This national newspaper went on to say that the ruling "puts the contributions of wives in watertight compartments and places the husband's business assets beyond reach of wives who devoted themselves entirely to looking after the home and family. It gives little or no weight to the idea that a husband's business success might be psychologically linked to the support he obtains, and the confidence he gains, from a happy home life."[143]

The *Ottawa Citizen* reported on December 7, 1982, and included my advice to women to insist on marriage contracts that protected their rights to property before being so foolhardy as to agree to leave their jobs and devote their time to uncompensated housework and child care. I never knew how many women took my advice.

The issue reached the floor of the federal House of Commons in Ottawa on December 8, 1982. Two Opposition MPs from Ontario, Lynn McDonald of the New Democratic Party (a former president of the National Action Committee on the Status of Women) and Flora MacDonald of the Progressive Conservatives, tabled motions. Lynn McDonald wanted the House of Commons to express "profound regret" over the decision, which failed to recognize that women contribute to families by raising children. Flora MacDonald said the decision was discriminatory "because it fails to recognize the value of work women do in the home." Unfortunately, neither motion received the necessary unanimous consent for debate. But they did add to the groundswell of support for legislative change in Ontario.

Doris Anderson, then president of the National Action Committee on the Status of Women, described the Supreme Court ruling as only a partial victory for women, and one that did not recognize women's true role in a marriage. Michele Landsberg added her voice in a pointed column in the *Toronto Star*, saying that the FLRA "was one of the most badly written and restrictive such acts in Canada" and that the Supreme Court's decision was "a narrow legalistic interpretation of Ontario's law." The fact that it recognized only Mrs. Leatherdale's contribution as a wage earner "was another slap in the face of Ontario housewives: He gets to keep the lion's share...because all her years of housework and child-rearing and husband-serving count for zip." Hers was the kind of passionate and forthright support that helped to publicize the need for reform and to educate the public about the issues.

Then Laura Sabia weighed in. In her *Toronto Sun* column, she said that when she was chair of the Ontario Status of Women Council, she had worked for the change that became the 1978 Family Law Reform Act. She described it as "a flawed bill, half-assed— better than what we had, but weak and full of loopholes. It left far too much discretion to the judiciary." She noted the irony that Justice Laskin was, in the *Murdoch* case, "the dissenter who pleaded for equal sharing. Ten years later [he] pleads the case against the housewife. So much for judicial discretion...." She encouraged the Ontario Council on the Status of Women to push the issue.

Lawyers from all over Ontario wrote expressing concern at the result and asking for photocopies of the case. In those pre-Internet days, there was no quick click on the court website to download a copy of the judgment. How times have changed!

Other newspapers and broadcasters carried stories as well: the *Kingston Whig-Standard*; *Kitchener-Waterloo Record*; *Cape Breton Post*; CTV's *Canada AM*; CBC Radio's *Metro Morning*, *Ontario Morning*, and *Radio Noon*; the Canadian Press; and various radio shows. *Maclean's* magazine ran a full-page piece with a caption under my photo that the case demonstrated "an underlying attitude that women aren't worth as much as men."

The *Kingston Whig-Standard*'s thoughtful editorial on December 8, 1982, concluded that the law was biased against women who made an indirect contribution to the assets through years of unpaid labour in the home because of "a failure of political will," and that the Ontario government "has badly undermined its own rhetoric on the marriage partnership."

The *Toronto Star*'s lengthy feature included a comment from Allan Leal—he had been vice-chair of Ontario's Law Reform Commission and deputy attorney general when the 1978 FLRA was passed—expressing concern at the inequity suffered by homemakers. Ontario Liberal (Opposition) leader David Peterson cited the *Leatherdale* case to the *Kitchener-Waterloo Record* to support his call for reforms to permit spouses to share pension benefits. Letters to the editor flooded in about the need for family law reform.

Leatherdale was the first test of non-family assets in the FLRA to come before the Supreme Court of Canada, and it did not result in an equitable sharing of assets. Even Justice Laskin had commented on the complexity of the FLRA. No comments quoted in the newspapers expressed agreement with the views in the majority decision. Justice Estey's dissent, and his view that family legislation should be read liberally and not restrictively, was quoted widely and with approval.

The Issue Enters the Political Arena

On December 14, 1982, the opposition parties in the Ontario legislature added their voices. Bob Rae, leader of the NDP, asked Attorney General McMurtry to consider changes to the FLRA that would recognize a homemaker's contribution to the finances of the family and do away with the distinction between family and non-family assets. Mr. McMurtry answered that in light of the upcoming fifth anniversary of the FLRA, he had asked his staff to begin a review of the legislation. The widespread groundswell of dismay and concern following the Supreme Court decision had forced Mr. McMurtry to consider improving the law—just eight days after the release of the *Leatherdale* decision. On the news on that day, he said that his government had always felt the wife should share in the business assets, but "the *Leatherdale* case raises the possibility [that] the law must be changed." It seemed the attorney general was tentatively on board.

A week later, on December 21, 1982—just two weeks after the release of the Supreme Court's decision—Attorney General McMurtry rose in the legislature to formally announce a review of the Family Law Reform Act. He applauded the FLRA as progressive legislation in its time and then admitted that "it is time to pause and consider whether there may be some improvements indicated by the passage of time and the wisdom of hindsight."

He invited written submissions from any interested person or organization on any aspect of the FLRA that they felt was in need of amendment. He particularly wanted to hear from the Ontario Council on the Status of Women and the Family Law Section of the CBA-O. He asked for any and all proposals for reform but specifically asked for input on whether the provisions for sharing non-family assets needed adjustment, whether the definition of family assets was adequate, whether the legislation should be extended to widowed persons, whether the matrimonial home was sufficiently protected, and whether there were any problems in the support provisions of the FLRA.

He concluded with the reassurance that the government was "committed to the principles that marriage is a partnership of equals and that, if a marriage comes to an end, the law should ensure the spouses are treated fairly and equitably."

He asked for all briefs to be sent to him by March 1, 1983, and said he hoped to bring a bill before the House no more than a year from that time—March 1, 1984. What an accomplishment!—a formal commitment from the government to review the 1978 Family Law Reform Act. The next task was to try to focus the review.

The Task of Persuasion

It was clear that the government had to be convinced that there was sufficient credible support before it would pay attention. It would help if a broad non-partisan group emerged to lend its influential name, reputation, and support to the reform goals. The Justice Committee for Family Law Reform (JCFLR) was formed in February 1983 by me and a group of women and men who were concerned about the issues and who agreed about the need for equal sharing of a family's assets and the way in which that should be accomplished. This group included Doris Anderson, renowned feminist; Thomas Bastedo, family lawyer and bencher of the Law Society of Upper Canada; Florence Bird, journalist, retired senator, and chair of the 1970s' Royal Commission on the Status of Women; Harry Brown, broadcaster; June Callwood, journalist, author, and activist; Catherine Charlton, executive member of Progressive Conservative Women and the Empire Club; Shirley Greenberg, Ottawa family lawyer and feminist; Lynn King, family lawyer and author (and later judge); Stephen Lewis, former Ontario NDP politician; Kay Macpherson, social activist; Clifford Nelson, Ontario family lawyer (now a Superior Court judge); Laura Sabia, former chair of OCSW and a leading activist; Harriet Sachs, family lawyer (and later bencher and then judge); and Geraldine Waldman, family lawyer and Bar Association committee representative (and later judge).

There was a lot of public support for family law reform. The *Toronto Star* ran an editorial supporting the idea.[144] The *Globe and Mail* focused public attention on the petition being circulated by the JCFLR.[145] The OCSW submitted a brief to the government recommending changes in family law.[146] A Gallup poll revealed that 85 percent of the respondents said a homemaker's contribution should be compensated.[147]

Radio and TV, especially the daytime programs and those with predominantly female audiences, started focusing on how family law affected women. Our task was to educate the public about the concerns of women in terms simple enough that viewers and listeners could understand.[148] Broadcasting proved to be an effective way to get the message out.

As public interest grew about family law reform, there were more and more opportunities to speak to a wide range of interest groups.[149] I was the keynote speaker at the May 1983 conference held by the newly formed Ontario Liberal Women's Perspective Advisory Committee. The Liberal Party in Ontario at that time had been out of power since 1943, and the Progressive Conservative government of Bill Davis did not seem vulnerable. The invitation was extended by Daphne Rutherford, then a staffer in the Ontario Liberal Party's office, on behalf of the committee chair, Elinor Caplan, then a North

York alderman (councillor). According to Daphne, they wanted someone to "fire up women." They knew that I was not committed to any political party. My goal was to educate everyone about the need for equity in the law of marriage breakdown. Several months later, Ontario Liberal leader David Peterson invited me to be a guest on his cable TV show to speak about women and the law generally, including family law.

I proposed writing a feature article on the need for family law reform across Canada to the editor of *Chatelaine*, Mildred Istona, who liked the idea. The research was a huge task, as it meant that we had to pin down the law in every Canadian province and territory. *Chatelaine* assigned writer and editor Ann Rhodes to work with me, and Judith Huddart, by then a junior lawyer in my firm, helped with the research. *The Plain-English Guide to Family Law* was published in the September 1983 issue and ran a full twelve magazine pages—an almost unheard of size for a magazine feature—and reached over a million readers nationally. The headline read, "At last a basic route map through the jungle of laws, statutes, and procedures that threaten to entangle any woman faced with separation or divorce." A side benefit of outlining family law across Canada was the opportunity to illustrate the particular backwardness and unfairness of Ontario's Family Law Reform Act as interpreted by the courts. By then, some provinces (but not Ontario) had improved their statutes in light of court interpretations.

The guide included answers to many of the questions that clients were asking about ownership and possession of the matrimonial home, furnishings, recreational property, savings and investments, pensions and RRSPs, business and professional assets, and their valuation. It provided information about responsibility for debts and taxes and detailed the tax rules affected by divorce, including the impact of conduct, custody of and access to children, and spousal support. There was even a section on enforcement of court orders, noting that the extent of default in support orders was causing some women to go on welfare. As a result, the guide said that the public was paying the support that should have been paid by the husband. It outlined the legal rights of common-law partners, which were then very limited; readers sometimes assumed that common-law partners had the same rights to property and support as married partners. They didn't then and they still don't. The guide shared information about the evidence required for trial. And it concluded with a section headlined "The Marriage Contract: Oh, if only…" and told women in what jurisdictions such contracts were legal and what they should include. The article was a roaring success, so much so that *Chatelaine* printed *The Plain-English Guide to Family Law* as a stand-alone publication so that readers could write in to request a copy. I sent copies to each Ontario cabinet minister and opposition leaders, as well as to relevant members of their shadow cabinets.[150] I handed it out at my speeches on family law and made it available to anyone else who was interested, believing that once educated in the inequities of family law, intelligent people could not fail to be persuaded of the need for further family law reform that recognized that marriage was an economic partnership.

Whenever I spoke about family law reform, my goal was to persuade the audience of the merits of equality and fairness. A petition was available for the audience to sign, prepared on behalf of the Justice Committee for Family Law Reform, which sought equity in the division of marital assets. The "Petition for Fairness in Our Family Property Laws" began with the words: "We are concerned that Ontario's Family Law Reform Act does not treat women fairly nor recognize the contribution a woman makes to the economic partnership of marriage."

The petition was circulated everywhere I went, until 2,300 signatures were secured. I prepared an analysis of those signatories and was able to point out to the attorney general that they represented people from every walk of life. Whenever the result in a court case appeared unfair to women, the JCFLR held a press conference or issued a press release drawing attention to those areas where the law, in that instance, needed to be changed.

We created a mailing list of all ministers and parliamentary assistants, including the new minister for women's issues, to send them information as well as educate them on family law. We urged people to write to the identified people in government to press for changes in the law.

Brief of the Family Law Section of the Ontario Bar Association

As the attorney general had requested, the Bar Association's Family Law Section was preparing a brief, to which I contributed. In June 1983 at the meeting, when the draft brief was presented to the membership, I made an impassioned pitch for equal sharing. Most of the lawyers present were not persuaded. Many felt that lawyers should not intervene and express an opinion on public policy matters, but should limit viewpoints to drafting and interpretation issues. Thankfully, some did agree with me. Even so, few wanted to be formally associated with an equal-sharing campaign.

Several lawyers told me, privately, that they could not be seen to favour a wife getting half the assets or their male clients would flee. Another lawyer said his firm would not let him take a public stand in case it affected business. Once again, I felt fortunate to be working for myself.

In the end, the Family Law Section decided not to take a policy stand in its submission to the government. All the same, I pushed for and got the group to hold an informal straw vote of their views. Of the forty-eight family lawyers present at the meeting, twenty-seven voted for sharing all financial assets and twenty-one opted for the status quo.

Some members of the Family Law Section had not been present at the meeting, so I informed them about what had happened in their absence and asked for their help in distributing the JCFLR petition—and for their signatures. Some signed; others did not.

Brief of the Ontario Council on the Status of Women

I was consulted by the council as they prepared their brief under the leadership of chair Sally Barnes. The comprehensive 112-page brief, released on March 24, 1983, supported many of the key proposals made by the Ontario Law Reform Commission in 1974, and with which the Justice Committee for Family Law Reform agreed. The council called for an equal sharing of all assets on marriage breakdown and death and made a point of saying that the existing law makes the rights of a spouse dependent, in part, on the individual value system of the judge hearing that spouse's case. The council also recommended increased funding for family law legal aid, better guidelines on support payments, improved enforcement of support payments, including the use of jail as a penalty for non-payment, and additional shelters for battered wives.

Several months later I wrote a six-page letter to the attorney general commenting on the OCSW and Family Law Section briefs;[151] informing him of the result of the straw vote of family lawyers[152] and sharing my observations gleaned from the *Leatherdale* proceedings. I had seen first-hand how easy it was to forget that inherent in the Family Law Reform Act was the intention to recognize marriage as a joint venture—an economic partnership; while the trial judge found *as a fact* that the Leatherdales had intended the accumulated Bell shares to be a shared nest egg for their retirement, the Court of Appeal and the Supreme Court of Canada ignored this finding; and the judges had different opinions about the entitlements given in sections 4 and 8. In short, *Leatherdale* demonstrated how difficult it was for judges and lawyers to interpret the meaning of the Family Law Reform Act.

June Callwood, a member of the JCFLR, brought a smile to my face when she wrote to me in September of that year offering to help and drolly commenting: "You are going gang-busters on this family law reform issue. One day we'll put a statue of you in the park."

These were busy days, but the clock was ticking. Early in 1984, to keep up the pressure, I wrote an op-ed piece for the *Globe and Mail* entitled "Sharing the spoils of marriage," making the point that:

> Promises made by men courting their wives that "everything I own will be ours, darling" are dismissed by our courts as part of the mating ritual and not taken seriously as evidence of intention if the marriage breaks down....
>
> Promises made by the Ontario legislature in 1978 that the Family Law Reform Act was going to recognize marriage as an economic partnership, with the partners obligated to share the fruits of their labour on marriage breakdown, have been overlooked by courts in exercising discretion under the act.[153]

Mr. McMurtry had promised to announce his plans to amend Ontario family laws by March 1, 1984. When this date came and went with no specifics released, I turned up the heat. On March 26, I organized a press conference and drafted a press release to urge the attorney general to do what he had promised and pointed out that family law cases could neither be settled nor go to court until the government made its intentions clear. That same day, his policy advisor, Craig Perkins, told me that the attorney general had not yet made up his mind on the issues.

The next step was a letter to members of the cabinet and their parliamentary assistants, providing a copy of the *Chatelaine Plain-English Guide*, a copy of my letter to Attorney General McMurtry in August 1983, and a copy of the "Sharing the spoils" op-ed piece. I thanked Liberal MPP Bill Wrye for his private member's bill to have the FLRA apply to *all* assets accumulated during the marriage. The *Toronto Star* ran an editorial headed "Share divorce assets fairly," and, on the same day, the *Toronto Sun* editorialized against reform of family law.

On April 2, 1984, I wrote again to Mr. McMurtry expressing my satisfaction at learning, from his comments reported in the *Toronto Star* and the *Globe and Mail* the previous week, that he seemed to be headed in the direction of equal sharing, and I encouraged him to extend coverage to widows and widowers.

On April 6, NDP leader Bob Rae introduced a resolution calling for amendments to the Family Law Reform Act to eliminate the distinction between family and non-family assets and to replace it with a system of deferred community of property. On the same day, the *Lawyers' Weekly* featured a major article on family law reform.

Culmination of the Lobby Effort
It was April 19, 1984. The Women's Law Association of Ontario sponsored a luncheon meeting to introduce the women lawyers called to the Bar in 1984; Attorney General McMurtry would be the speaker. The invitation did not specify a subject for the attorney general's talk, so when I received the notice, I realized what an opportunity this gave me to try to further the campaign.

I chatted beforehand with the organizers and innocently asked whether there would be an opportunity for questions. "I guess so," someone answered. And so, after Mr. McMurtry spoke, the moderator asked for questions from the audience. I did not waste a moment:

Mr. Attorney General, when will you bring in family law reform providing for equal sharing of all assets accumulated during marriage between husband and wife, not just the family assets like the house, car, recreational property, but now also savings, investments, pensions, and business assets? When will you recognize the contribution to the financial worth of the family of women who manage the home and raise the children?

He hesitated. I had hounded him so much by that point that he might have been forgiven for deflecting the question with a *we're thinking about it* or even *we're taking it under advisement*—the kind of answer a lawyer gives on an Examination for Discovery that says neither yes nor no. He didn't. Instead, he announced that his government had decided to proceed with legislation to provide for equal sharing of all assets. And he acknowledged that I had been persuasive. The applause, in which I heartily joined, was enthusiastic. Needless to say, I left the meeting on cloud nine.

He did indeed make good on his word. The very next day as I was leaving court, I ran into Simon Chester, a lawyer who worked as a policy advisor with the attorney general. He congratulated me. He added, with a wink and a grin, "Well, Linda, now you see how policy is made." I was flabbergasted. "Do you mean the decision was made on the spot after I asked the question?" He replied with an amused "No comment" followed by "Gotta go." I followed this up by sending him some information on family law reform issues, and, on May 2, received a response, which included these words: "It was splendid to see you on the street last week and to learn that your campaign has yet one more (distinguished) supporter...." He signed it, "Yours cryptically."

On May 30, 1984, I followed up with Attorney General McMurtry by letter and delivered the signatures of the 2,300 people who had signed my petition.

You were kind enough to say on April 19th when you addressed the Women's Law Association that I had convinced you of the necessity of reforming Canada's family laws by implementing the Ontario Law Reform Commission's deferred community of property system.... I look forward to seeing the family law bill promised for June.

June came and went, and the legislature closed down for the summer. The problem was that once the attorney general said he was going to change the law, family lawyers could no longer settle cases based on the existing law without taking into account the possibility that equal sharing laws were on their way. In order to push the decision-making along, I publicly expressed concern at the impact of the delay on separated spouses. Friendly columnists responded to the publicity. Doris Anderson wrote a particularly helpful column in the *Toronto Star* in July 1984, pressing the government to reveal its detailed legislative plans. Calling Ontario's family law a "social dinosaur," she criticized the Ontario Progressive Conservative government for "playing fast and loose with the lives of thousands of people" by "shutting up shop for the summer without passing a new bill on family law reform." She quoted my words: "The longer the delay, the more women get shafted."

EXPANDING THE LAW REFORM AGENDA

I received a letter from Mr. McMurtry expressing gratitude for the opinions of the 2,300 who had signed the petitions. He confirmed that he was working on property law reform, but that it was taking longer than expected. The review had exposed many other matters that needed attention. I treated this as an invitation to express my thoughts on other problems. And so, on September 17, 1984, I sent my further ideas for change and improvement, focusing on issues surrounding spousal support.

Spousal Support

Many lawyers interpreted the FLRA to mean that if a woman received a share of property, she would not also receive monthly support payments, except perhaps a small amount for a short transitional time. I didn't read this as the law at all; in fact, any such assumptions were completely unrealistic. Family property was rarely worth enough; the income it could produce if the proceeds were invested after a sale would not support the wife and any children in most cases. And a wife and mother's ability to earn a living to support herself and help provide for the children was unpredictable, if she had not worked outside the home during the marriage.

So it was unfair to set up a trade-off between property and

support. Even in the *Leatherdale* case, the husband had tried to over-turn, at the Court of Appeal, the indefinite monthly spousal support ordered by the trial judge; in my view, the only reason the Court of Appeal let stand the spousal support order was because they chose not to grant the wife a share of the investment and pension assets.[154]

Other unfortunate wording in the 1978 law was the require-ment that the court consider, as one of the factors in setting spousal support, whether or not the wife was able to become "financially independent," as if that were the goal. I did not think it was fair to expect complete financial independence, although it was reasonable to expect a woman to earn what she could, and to oblige the hus-band to pay the difference to the extent that he could. The question should only be a wife's ability to *contribute* to her own support. After all, when these women married—and limited their careers as a result—the social contract of the day promised that they would be supported by their husbands.

This misreading of the law needed to be repaired to clarify that long-term support was contemplated by the statute, that a wife who received a share of property was not thereby disentitled to regular financial support, and that her practical ability to earn a living and contribute to her support was the key factor in determining support, not a vague expectation of self-sufficiency.

While Mr. McMurtry was reviewing these issues in Ontario, the federal government was also considering reform. On January 19, 1984, the minister of justice, Mark MacGuigan, tabled in Parliament proposed amendments to the 1968 Divorce Act, including a provi-sion permitting limited-term spousal support. *Here we go again*, I thought. I wrote an op-ed piece published in the *Toronto Star* that challenged the unfair self-sufficiency rules,[155] and I also pressed my interpretation of the support law in court.

My own clients were encouraged not to negotiate away their support rights and be prepared to take their cases to trial, not only for their own benefit, but also in the hope that a positive decision from a judge would set a precedent for other women. *Jarvis* v. *Jarvis* was one of the cases that raised a number of significant support issues. When she married at age twenty, Gail Jarvis left a modest job at her husband's urging and, in accordance with the expectations of the times, devoted herself to being a wife and, eventually, mother of three. At the trial, held in June 1983, I called evidence from an expert on the financial situation of women in Canada. Economist Monica Townson testified that a forty-four-year-old woman with a grade twelve education, out of the workforce for twenty-five years, had poor job and earnings prospects. The type of work available to her was in the clerical, sales, or service sectors—*if* there were any vacancies in these high-unemployment sectors. Her potential earnings for full-time work were $9,000 to $12,700 a year, and for part-time work less than $6,000 a year, all according to Statistics Canada figures for 1981. Ms. Townson also added up the costs this woman would incur by going to work, such as wardrobe, transportation, and, most of all, child care.

The statistical facts were so powerful that they surprised even the presiding judge, Mr. Justice George Walsh, who had a long history as a family law lawyer before he was made a judge. He had been ready to assume that a divorced woman was able to be self-supporting through employment. Thankfully, he was also capable of adjusting his assumptions based on the evidence in the case. It showed me how important it was to enter the best possible evidence in the court proceedings to prove your points so that it was less likely that judges would act on their own beliefs and suppositions. Justice Walsh's interest was piqued. He asked whether there was a retraining program that might make Mrs. Jarvis self-supporting and was stymied when Ms. Townson answered "No." She testified that the number of clerical and sales jobs was diminishing, because these jobs were being threatened by the introduction of computers. Justice Walsh ended his questioning by asking, "So you are saying if you are age forty-four and have a grade twelve education, there is no chance?" It was clear that Gail Jarvis was not able to get a job that would make her self-supporting. Now the question became, how much did she need and how much could her husband afford?

The testimony made it clear that my client needed financial support for herself and their children from her husband, who at that time earned about $200,000 a year as an executive of Imperial Oil. His salary was $170,000, which was an excellent income, and he could well afford to provide for his family. Accounting evidence was presented that identified that the value of the husband's benefits and bonuses added about another $30,000 to his annual compensation package. I argued that the value of the bonuses and benefits should be considered as income for the purpose of determining the amount of support. To my knowledge, no one had ever argued this before, and the husband and his lawyer challenged it. I brought in Jack Marmer, a leading forensic family law accountant to substantiate (1) that over a period of years, the husband had a pattern of receiving these bonuses and benefits as part of his compensation package, (2) the dollar value of these benefits, and (3) that if the husband did not get the benefits from his employer, he would have to pay for them from his salary.

Another issue in contention was whether spousal support should be payable indefinitely and whether the amount should be automatically adjusted each year in keeping with increases in the cost of living. In those days, a wife had to hire a lawyer and possibly go to court for an order increasing the amount of support. While a change in her circumstances might still justify such a process, I thought that modifications due to inflation were straightforward and should not require a court hearing. I asked Mr. Marmer to give evidence on the history of the husband's annual salary increases, and to show that these increases exceeded the increases in the cost of living. The husband's lawyer contested an automatic cost-of-living clause on the basis that no judge had ever ordered one in a family law case.

In the end, Justice Walsh ordered the husband to pay $6,000 a month in child and spousal support, with annual increases to keep pace with the cost of living, provided his base salary increased by at least the same percentage as the cost of living. The amount would be reduced as each child became independent; once she was on her own, Mrs. Jarvis was entitled to $3,000 per month indefinitely. The judge based his ruling on the husband's income being $200,000, which included bonuses and benefits. The husband was also ordered to pay part of his wife's legal costs. Mrs. Jarvis won everything she had asked for.

Unfortunately, Justice Walsh did not refer in his Reasons for Judgment to the expert evidence of Monica Townson as to what an unskilled mother could earn, nor did he explain why he was per-suaded to order indefinite spousal support. Had he done so, the case might have set a precedent to guide lawyers and judges in future cases. What he did do was state *as a fact* that "the wife...has never worked and has no marketable skills" and that he had made his order on that basis. The outcome for Mrs. Jarvis was gratifying, but the case did not serve as a precedent to help other women. Instead, lawyers ignored the ruling and continued to make assumptions about the acceptability of time-limited support. However, the case did stand for the judicial acceptance of cost-of-living increases and that bonuses and benefits were to be used in determining support. These new principles were applied to cases from then on.

In my September 1984 letter to the attorney general, I proposed that he include in the legislation the opportunity for the judge to order automatic cost-of-living increases, the inclusion of benefits and bonuses in calculating a payor's income, and the right of a spouse in need to indefinite support.

Not surprisingly, Mr. Jarvis appealed the trial decision. Included among his objections were that the support amount was excessive, that the wife should have been ordered to work, that no law existed requiring an automatic cost-of-living increase, and that his bonuses and benefits should not have been considered in determining his income. Mrs. Jarvis won the appeal on all grounds. One of the three Appeal Court judges expressed surprise that no court had previously affirmed the validity of cost-of-living increases in a family law case, saying that it only made sense. I let the attorney general know about the Court of Appeal result to motivate him to include these provisions in any new law.

Enforcement of Support Obligations

I also encouraged Mr. McMurtry to improve how spousal as well as child support court orders were enforced. My practice had taught me how difficult it was to collect support when payments went into default. Courts did not (and still do not) take responsibility to automatically enforce their own orders. If her husband defaulted, the wife had to hire her own lawyer to try to collect. That lawyer could, for example, register the judgment as a lien against any property of the husband's, or as a garnishment against his wages or his bank accounts. But if a wife did not have enough money to support herself, she likely did not have enough to pay a lawyer to collect on a support judgment. Enforcement was more difficult when the husband moved to another province.

It was even more difficult to collect when the parties had settled the case by agreement before trial. In these cases, the wife had to endure a costly and complex litigation process by first getting a judgment based on the agreement and then seeking to enforce the amount in that judgment. There was a better way. New Brunswick and British Columbia already had laws in place permitting a party to a settlement to register the agreement with the court so that it could be enforced as if it were a court order. I suggested to the attorney general that Ontario add this to the new legislation.

More effective enforcement of court orders was essential, regardless of whether they were ordered by a court or settled by agreement. What was the point of having an order if you had no reasonable and cost-effective way to ensure that it was paid? The bottom line was that the available procedure was cumbersome and expensive, and most women could not pursue it. Some of them went on welfare instead. At that time, researchers found that 75 percent of men ordered to pay support were in some degree of default. In 1979, Ontario alone had a known backlog of more than $32 million in unpaid support bills, and 48,000 women were forced on social assistance, at a cost of $16 million a month. It just made sense that a government agency should be established to do the enforcement on behalf of the women—a step Manitoba had already taken. Another selling point had to be that if the husbands paid up, their wives and children would not need to seek social assistance. In other words, the cost to the government of establishing an agency might be more than offset by the savings in payments for social assistance. Could anyone disregard this logic?

My letter to the attorney general contended that the overwhelming expense to the average litigant, usually a sole-support mother, including the cost of lawyers and the expense of tracing defaulters' whereabouts, could be prohibitive on a cost/benefit analysis, due to the modest amount of most support orders. I supported my position with concrete information about the Manitoba model. I had met Robyn Diamond,[156] who was on staff in the Manitoba attorney general's department, at one of the meetings on the patriation of the Constitution and the Charter, and we'd hit it off. When I sat down to write to Mr. McMurtry about enforcement issues, I first called Robyn to get an update on how the Manitoba system was working.

Based on the information she shared, I was able to advise the attorney general that the Manitoba system had been very successful, with an 85 percent rate of compliance with court orders compared to the previous 85 percent *non*-compliance rate. The program was also successful on a cost/benefit analysis. Robyn advised that the cost to administer the system in the previous year had been about $400,000. Over the same time period, a total of $8.6 million was collected for wives. Of this, $640,000 was collected from defaulting husbands whose wives were being supported by social welfare funding. This money was repaid, so the Government of Manitoba actually came out *ahead* by $240,000.

I suggested that the attorney general work with the federal government to use social insurance numbers filed in tax returns to locate defaulters and advise any enforcement agency or individual recipient accordingly. I even added that jail should be mandatory in flagrant cases. It had been my experience that no judge at that time would send a defaulting husband to jail, even if the default was blatant, the defaulter was in contempt of court, and there was no other way to punish him.

The Matrimonial Home

A wife's interest in her matrimonial home could be defeated by an unscrupulous husband. In a reported case, without his wife's consent, the husband had put mortgages on their home and cottage—both registered in his name. He swore false affidavits that neither were matrimonial homes, received the monies from the mortgages, and left the country. I proposed that the spouse not registered as the owner should be permitted to unilaterally register a Designation of Matrimonial Home, which would serve as actual notice—a warning—to the mortgage lender as well as a purchaser that there was a spouse who was not on title, but who had an interest in the matrimonial home.

• • • • • • • • •

The *Murdoch* and *Leatherdale* cases had demonstrated that the legislation must be changed to ensure that women receive their fair share on marriage breakdown. Lobbying and education had persuaded the Ontario government to do something to acknowledge women's role as mothers and homemakers, and to deal with the adverse impact of judicial discretion on the interpretation of the law. I had done everything I could think of to persuade the government that changes had to be made and what those changes must be—equal sharing of all property acquired during marriage, indefinite spousal support, automatic cost-of-living increases, including bonuses and benefits in calculating support, court enforcement of agreements, an enforcement agency to ensure the payment of support, and real protection for sharing of the home. Newspapers, broadcasters, opposition politicians, and women's groups were involved in the struggle and added pressure on the government. The opposition parties were engaged and active. And then we waited.

Chapter 10
ACHIEVING EQUALITY
IN FAMILY LAW, 1984-86

The Ontario government's response to proposals for reform of family law was widely anticipated, and there were critical issues at stake.

Would the government make a definitive statement requiring husbands and wives to share all assets, including business, investments, and pensions? Would a wife's contribution as a homemaker and mother be recognized financially? Would widowed persons have the same claim to property as divorced persons? Would a woman's career sacrifices be acknowledged? Would indefinite rather than limited-term spousal support be part of the landscape? Would the expectation of self-sufficiency be abandoned in favour of the hope that a woman would contribute to the extent that she could? Would cost-of-living clauses be legislatively sanctioned? Would benefits and bonuses be considered an integral part of a payor's income? Would judicial discretion be tempered? Would a government enforcement agency be established to collect support? Would agreements be enforced as if they were court orders? Would the matrimonial home be better protected? People who had already separated, and their lawyers, were wary of concluding agreements with such dramatic changes to the law possible and pending.

MEETING WITH THE ATTORNEY GENERAL
The attorney general took me up on my offer to meet with him, and a meeting was set for October 1, 1984, to discuss some of these

further ideas for family law reform. It was just the two of us. We had met a number of times before—the first time in 1976, when we had appeared together on a panel at the Ontario Progressive Conservative Women's Policy Conference. In his speech that day, Mr. McMurtry had demonstrated his understanding that the contribution of homemakers might be undervalued if the system was too reliant on judicial discretion when he said that spouses should not have to go begging to the court for a share of what they had helped to build.

It was satisfying to be able to connect directly with the person who actually had the power to put family law reform on the government agenda. The meeting lasted about an hour, and Mr. McMurtry was very gracious. He greeted me with respect and warmth. I came away feeling as if he genuinely understood the issues and sympathized with the need for change. The challenge to the 1978 Family Law Reform Act could not have been easy for him, since he was the attorney general who had produced the first family law legislation only six years earlier. It took a special kind of man to agree to review a law he had himself brought in and that was itself progressive for its time.

In our meeting, he shared with me his concerns about not alarming the public; he was afraid this would happen if he were to describe the law as a dramatic new step. He preferred to see the process that was underway as evolutionary, and that was fine with me as long as significant reform happened. He felt that the 1978 FLRA was a good piece of legislation. I didn't disagree. We both believed that it could have been interpreted by judges and lawyers to mean that business and investment assets should be shared. He said that he intended to introduce new family law reform legislation within the first two weeks of the next sitting of the legislature, or, if an election were called, to present a White Paper[157] for discussion purposes during the election campaign. (I didn't clue in at that time to the implications of his referring to a possible election. It had been only about three years since the last one.)

We talked about the possibility of his ministry sponsoring a consultation in order to canvass, in one place and time, all the issues being reviewed. He wanted it to happen within the next four to six weeks and said he would welcome my thoughts on the guests and the program. It was such a satisfying meeting. I felt involved in the process and gratified that my views were being valued.

I followed up the meeting with a letter in which I outlined the type of guests who might be invited and what the program might look like. His staff started organizing the conference and having detailed planning discussions with me. They had settled on the date of December 11, 1984, and booked the Toronto Sheraton Centre. They were anticipating 150 to 200 people. A panel was in the works, and I was told, "We know we want you on it and that's all we know."

ROADBLOCKS ON THE PATH
TO REFORM: POLITICAL UPHEAVAL

It was all going exceedingly well...until it wasn't. Before the consultation could be held or the promised legislation introduced, Bill Davis resigned as premier on October 8, 1984, triggering a leadership contest to determine who would take over for him as leader of the Progressive Conservative Party and, therefore, premier of Ontario. Mr. McMurtry wrote to me a few weeks later saying he had to reflect further on how to proceed. The planned path for family law reform had hit a major roadblock.

As it turned out, Roy McMurtry was one of the candidates who came forward seeking to replace Bill Davis as premier. The others in the running were Frank Miller, Larry Grossman, and Dennis Timbrell. The Progressive Conservatives were, at that time, considered the natural governing party of Ontario, so it was reasonable to assume that one of the four would become and remain premier. I decided to try to make family law an issue in the leadership contest, to ensure that family law would be reformed no matter who came out on top. I wrote to all of the candidates, asking them to publicly announce where they stood, hoping they would get on-side and that their views on family law reform would be a factor in the leadership race. Frank Miller was the only one who spoke out definitively against family law reform. The others articulated some version of approval, but the most sympathetic was Roy McMurtry, who, in November, issued the White Paper that he'd talked to me about at our meeting the previous month.

In the midst of all this, in mid-October 1984, my six-year long-distance relationship with Harvey ended. We couldn't figure out a way to be together, and we no longer accepted being apart. I was heartbroken. I ploughed into work and the campaign for family law reform. I also began work on another book, *Every Woman's Guide to the Law*.

This leadership race was a bit of a departure for me. I had made it a point not to be politically identified with any party, but to share my views with all parties. Because I thought it would be helpful to women's interests if I assisted Roy McMurtry, I prepared a twenty-page outline entitled "Women's Issues: Policy Suggestions and Analysis."[158] It focused on family law reform and also included specific policy suggestions regarding child care, equal pay, affirmative action, part-time worker benefits, pension reform, contract compliance, violence against women, poverty, and access to abortion. It was my effort to acquaint Mr. McMurtry with all the policy issues affecting women. I was pleased when he even challenged the other candidates to a debate specifically on women's issues—which they refused.

As the leadership campaign heated up, it appeared that family law reform had turned into a divisive issue. On December 20, 1984, the *Toronto Star* reported Mr. McMurtry's comments that the public was being deliberately misled by allegations that the proposed law would kill small business. He pointed out that all three of his leadership rivals had been in the cabinet that approved the proposals for family law reform. Yet now they all had one reason or another to object or await further consideration. I knew that the concern that a business might have to be sold to pay a spouse was being blown out of proportion; a trade-off of one asset for another was always possible, or a payment could be extended for a period of years so as to diminish the effect on an ongoing business. However, what Mr. McMurtry did say, according to that article, was that if he couldn't manage to clear up confusion on the issue, he would introduce some family law reforms but leave out the division of non-family assets.

I wrote to him the next day, asking him to confirm whether he was quoted accurately so that the Justice Committee for Family Law Reform would know how to properly respond. In the meantime, I was corresponding with the other leadership candidates to get them to take a clear public stand. I also joined with members of the newly formed Women's Lobby Coalition, organized by Business and Professional Women's Clubs of Toronto, Federation of Women Teachers' Associations of Ontario, National Action Committee on the Status of Women, Equal Pay Coalition, International Women's Day Committee, Ontario Committee on the Status of Women, and the YWCA of Metropolitan Toronto. The Coalition had tried to get the leadership candidates to discuss other women's issues, such as abortion and equal pay; the coalition added family law reform to their list.

The legislature adjourned and family law reform had not been tabled. In fact, NDP leader Bob Rae charged that family law reform "had been scuttled by the dance of the dinosaurs...who lost their courage on the way to the Tory convention...."

On January 4, 1985, PC campaign volunteer, feminist, and lawyer Jane Pepino wrote to me on behalf of Mr. McMurtry, in response to my letter, reassuring me that should he become premier or remain attorney general, he intended to introduce the legislation, including division of non-family assets, at the earliest possible opportunity. She attributed the delay to objections from other leadership candidates and their supporters in caucus. That worried me, because it was not clear what would happen to family law reform if Mr. McMurtry was not chosen leader.

On January 17, 1985, the Justice Committee for Family Law Reform issued a press release headed "Ontario Women Beware! P.C. promises of equal sharing of a family's entire assets in new family laws may be in jeopardy depending on who is the new premier." The press release summarized the responses we had received from the leadership candidates. They ranged from McMurtry's unequivocal endorsement of equal division of a family's entire assets, to Timbrell's qualms about the effect of sharing business and farm assets, to Grossman's endorsement only of the existing FLRA, to Miller's indifference (saying, "This issue you raise will be dealt with," but without saying how).

Needless to say, I was disappointed when Frank Miller was chosen leader. When he took over for Bill Davis as premier on February 8, 1985, the matter of family law reform was *not* on his agenda. All appeared lost. One potentially bright spot was that Miller appointed Robert Welch as his attorney general. Mr. Welch had been the province's first minister for women's issues, and I believed that as a former family lawyer, he might be sympathetic to family law concerns.

Another promising moment was when Premier Frank Miller appointed Dennis Timbrell as minister responsible for women's issues. Within two weeks of his appointment, Mr. Timbrell invited me to join him at an International Women's Day celebration. He was specific: "Since I have been recently appointed to this portfolio, I view this occasion as an excellent opportunity to respond to your questions and [have you] share your concerns with me on women's issues."

The government bureaucracy continued its path toward family law reform. Merike Madisso, a research officer in Ontario's Legislative Research Service, prepared and released, in May 1985, an analysis for all MPPs of three problems with the 1978 Family Law Reform Act arising from cases decided under that law. She focused on the unfortunate distinction between family and non-family assets; property rights on death and the unfairness of family law for widows and widowers; and the ability of an unscrupulous spouse to usurp ownership of the matrimonial home. She then laid out proposals for reform. After lengthy conversations with me, some of which she quoted in her paper, she concluded that reforms were needed.

Premier Miller called an election soon after he took office, which gave a further opportunity to put the issue on the front burner. By then, both the Liberals and NDP—the leading opposition parties—were in favour of family law reform and said so during the election campaign. Premier Miller's PCs were not.

The Ontario Advisory Council on Women's Issues[159] sent a questionnaire to each party, seeking its position on various women's issues, and then issued a press release with the results. Premier Miller said that he would amend the Family Law Reform Act but would not say how. I was asked for comment by the *Toronto Star* and didn't hesitate to call Mr. Miller's response "outrageous." "To go now to the electorate with only a promise to address the issues, without saying how, is destructive of Miller's credibility."[160] The *Star* followed up with a strong editorial favouring family law reform,[161] saying that it was inexcusable that Premier Miller was the only provincial party leader who would not promise equal division of all assets accumulated during marriage if a marriage breaks down. The editorial quoted me: "In no case has any Ontario woman been able to get a court order for half of the assets accumulated in marriage because of her contribution as a housewife or income earner."

The general election was held on May 2, 1985. Not only did the PCs lose a significant number of seats but they also lost their majority in the legislature. They secured fifty-two seats, the Liberals under David Peterson took forty-eight, and the NDP under Bob Rae won twenty-five. By May 29, an Accord was signed between the Liberals and the NDP to work toward governing together under the Liberal banner. Meanwhile, Miller and his party tried to hang on to office. On June 3, 1985, I spoke to Denise Bellamy, then on the staff of the Ontario Women's Directorate.[162] She told me that "Miller said the first bill was going to be on the Family Law Act. He was told that he had to bring in full community [of property]. The Throne Speech is tomorrow. We'll see a bill tomorrow."

THE FAMILY LAW ACT IS ANNOUNCED

The next day, I received an invitation from the ministry of the attorney general to be among the attendees at a press conference at the Sutton Place Hotel on June 5, 1985, a date that is burned into my memory. The new attorney general, Allan Pope, announced what Roy McMurtry had not had an opportunity to finish: family laws were being changed, and new laws were on their way. On June 4, the first reading of Bill 1 of the new government had been tabled in the legislature as "An Act to Revise the Family Law Reform Act."

Mr. Pope also announced the new and important Support and Custody Orders Enforcement Act (SCOE), with a promise to create a government office to actually enforce support orders on behalf of recipients. He followed up with a copy of the draft legislation and asked for my comments and suggestions as quickly as possible "so that any necessary improvements or adjustments can be made as they proceed through the legislative process."

Mr. Pope pointed out that even though Bill 1 of each new legislature was supposed to be a technical "housekeeping" bill, he was departing from that tradition to show that family law reform was the Conservative government's "highest priority."

Only twenty-one days later, Allan Pope and the Frank Miller Progressive Conservative government were out of office. Frank

Miller could not make a minority government work, nor withstand the vote of no confidence on June 18. By June 26, Miller had resigned and David Peterson took over as premier with the support of the NDP. When Peterson appointed Ian Scott as attorney general, I couldn't believe our good luck. Mr. Scott had been an eminent trial counsel and a noted civil libertarian. The education process would be brief. Indeed, Ian Scott and the David Peterson government did support family law reform. Peterson appointed Murray Elston as minister for women's issues, and Daphne Rutherford, then working inside the new government in a staff position (and whom I had met in her previous role with the Liberal Party), arranged for me to have lunch with her and Mr. Elston in order to bring him up to speed.

Bob Rae and the New Democrats, whose Accord was maintaining the David Peterson Liberals in office, also supported family law reform. Even so, the Accord—which required the Liberals to proceed with specified legislation to ensure the NDP's continued support—did not mention family law reform.

I called my contacts to find out what was going on. I spoke to Elinor Caplan, who had been elected as part of the new Liberal government. I had met her back when she was a member of North York Council and first chair of the Ontario Liberal Women's Perspective Advisory Committee. She explained that just because it was not in the Accord did not mean that it was not on their agenda. "We didn't want it to look as though the NDP made us do it." The office of NDP MPP Marion Bryden reported to me that "the Accord shouldn't be interpreted as 'all the legislation,' that family law reform is just as important as it always was. The more difficult things are on the [Accord] list." Perhaps most reassuring was the letter that Bob Rae wrote to me on the very day the Accord ousted Miller's PCs from office: "We want you to know that the issue of family law reform continues to be important to us and will be until we have achieved the necessary changes...."

LEGISLATIVE AND PUBLIC REVIEW
OF THE DRAFT FAMILY LAW ACT
This was an exciting time. I was thrilled to see the hard lobbying work of the previous three years bearing fruit. We had a consensus. Carrying on the process that was started by Roy McMurtry and

continued by Allan Pope, Ian Scott did introduce the Family Law Act in August—saying it was the new government's most important bill. In fact, Mr. Scott made family law reform his top priority, and it was the first piece of legislation presented by the new Liberal government. Now it had to go through the public and legislative review process. I wrote to him with my congratulations as well as comments on the specific terms and language of the legislation. I was so delighted to see that many of the recommendations I and others had made in the long push for change had found their way into the bill. There was to be an equal division of assets between husband and wife, and a judge could vary this only if the result would be "unconscionable" rather than, as formerly defined, "inequitable." This use of the word "unconscionable" restricted judicial discretion, and it became one of the key sources of heated discussion about the bill.

This bill was introduced for second reading in the legislature on October 22, 1985. Bob Rae sent me a copy of the Hansard debates and a letter with his appreciation for sharing my expertise and views with him, and I was publicly acknowledged in the legislature for my role in working for family law reform and educating the public. Marion Bryden spoke at length in support of the bill and traced the history of its development and the NDP's long record of support for equal sharing of family property. She referred to the *Leatherdale* case and paid tribute to me.

Not everyone, however, liked the terms of Bill 1. The Family Law Section of the Canadian Bar Association–Ontario established a subcommittee to comment on the specifics of the bill, but not on its philosophical underpinnings. In fact, then CBA-O president J. Alex Langford wrote a cover note to the brief:

> An Act to Revise the Family Law Reform Act is undoubtedly the most significant proposal for change in the relationship between the men and women of this province in the province's history.... CBA-O is pleased to be of whatever assistance it can to the Legislature, not in commenting upon policy, which is the expression of political will, but in helping the Legislature smoothly implement that which it has chosen to do.

Needless to say, I thought lawyers had a larger role to play. On November 14, 1985, the Section met to discuss and approve their subcommittee's draft brief on the government bill and recommended, among other things, that the test to set aside a 50/50 division should be "inequitability" and not "unconscionability," that the matrimonial home should not get special treatment, and that the bill should not be retroactive to the date of its announcement.

The government scheduled public hearings before its Standing Committee on the Administration of Justice to permit all interested parties another opportunity to present their views before this all-party committee. There were representations by those who disagreed with the thrust of the legislation, including the Canadian Organization of Small Business (concerned about the impact on owners of small businesses), the Advocates' Society (wanting greater judicial discretion), and law professor Winifred Holland (suggesting the FLRA was good enough). There were those who agreed with the need for the law, even if they wanted particular tweaks, including Business and Professional Women, National Association of Women and the Law, and the Ontario Liberal Women's Perspective Advisory Committee, among others. I prepared a brief on behalf of the JCFLR and the National Action Committee on the Status of Women, and on November 20, 1985, it was my turn to present.

I applauded the basic premise of equality in the draft legislation and made sure to underline that any variation of a 50/50 division had to meet the threshold test of unconscionability. It was known that other submissions would criticize that wording, including the Advocates' Society represented by family law lawyers Rodica David and Susan Lang, so I explained why it was important to keep the stringent test as it was in Bill 1. In doing so, I talked about what went wrong with the 1978 Family Law Reform Act, pointing out that judicial discretion, relying on the use of the criterion "inequitable," had not resulted in a single case in which a homemaker received 50 percent of the assets accumulated by the couple during the marriage. I reminded the committee of the 1974 Report of the Ontario Law Reform Commission, which had recommended that the only circumstance in which there should be judicial discretion is when "strict application of the rules of the equalizing claim would lead to grossly inequitable results."

I cautioned the committee that if they changed the test from unconscionable to inequitable, and allowed too great a discretion to the judges, then they would not be changing the present situation. One of the main reasons that new legislation was needed was the way in which judicial discretion was used to weaken the original intention of the 1978 legislation.

One of the committee members asked me if we couldn't trust judges to be fair. My response:

> Certainly you can rely on the judiciary to try to be fair and to aim for that. But if you simply leave the word "fairness" or "equity" up in the air, floating around loose without any definitions to tie it down, then everyone will go from his or her own gut. He will define by his own gut feeling what is fair to him. That will depend upon what his life history has been—how his mother and father treated each other, his own relationships at home; whether the judge is divorced or is not divorced; if his wife left him or he left his wife. All those things are going to tutor his understanding of what is fair. I do not think that as a legislature you want to do that. You want to require fairness to have a specific, legally-based definition. You want rule of law. Rule of law means it has to be written down in some way. If you have a rule by general feelings of inequity, that is rule by man, rule by specific judges and their own feelings.

They asked numerous questions. One committee member expressed frustration with the different views among the family law bar and, in particular, the contrast in views on "unconscionable" versus "inequitable" found in Rodica David's submissions and mine. This is how I answered her:

> I heard Ms. David of the Advocates' Society give...an example... about where legislation does not allow sufficient flexibility. She felt she would lose half her home if she married and the word "unconscionable" was there. If that is the case, and she is saying the word "inequitable" would satisfy her, she is really saying that the word "inequitable" will allow anyone to get out of the 50-50 division, which is what I am saying it will do. If you are going to set up a scheme whereby using a word is going to let anyone get out of it, what is the point of going through the exercise?

I asked that specific words be put into the law to enable judges to order transfers of property between spouses to equalize the assets. I proposed that the judge could order that the spouse who is continuing the operation of the business or farm pay or transfer to the other some alternative property of equal value in place of their interest in the business or farm.

I put forward numerous ideas—my brief contained almost a line-by-line review of the draft legislation, along with responses to ideas contained in other briefs. For example, I noted that the CBA-O recommended that the right to a private pension should be shared, but only when it is actually paid out. I worried that if the pensioner died before the pension vested, this would leave the survivor without benefits. I suggested that the value of the pension should be evaluated on a lump sum basis and that this lump sum be reviewed as part of the whole asset picture when the matter was resolved after marriage breakdown. I assumed the pensioner would keep his pension and the non-pensioner would get some other asset in exchange, such as the home.

On November 25, 1985, Ian Scott came to talk to the Family Law Section of the CBA-O about their objections to various provisions of Bill 1. The meeting was held the day after the Standing Committee started its clause-by-clause review of the draft legislation. He dealt with each of the items in the CBA-O brief. He confirmed that, in his view, marriage is a social and economic partnership that should have real consequences if terminated, including sharing any increase in net worth. He reinforced that the government stood firm on the use of unconscionability as the guideline for departing from the 50/50 sharing of assets. He commented that he had not considered the depth of the family law bar's disapproval of the special treatment of the matrimonial home, but agreed with the Ontario Law Reform Commission and reaffirmed that the special status of the matrimonial home would remain in the bill. He also confirmed that the date of the announcement—June 4, 1985—remained the effective date for implementation of the terms of the law.

THE FAMILY LAW ACT, 1986

The bill made its way through the legislative process and was completed by January 24, 1986, when it was proclaimed into law, to take effect on March 1.

The Justice Committee for Family Law Reform had—at last—accomplished its mandate. The new law provided for equal sharing between husbands and wives of all assets accumulated during the marriage, with gifts and inheritances received during the marriage excluded from sharing, except if they went into the matrimonial home. Property owned at the date of marriage was also protected from sharing. The spouse with higher net worth would make an equalization payment to the spouse with lower net worth. Widowed persons had a right to claim the same equal share as divorced and separated persons simply by checking off on a form a choice between the provisions received under a will or the share provided by the Family Law Act. There were special protections for the matrimonial home: no matter whose name was on title, both spouses had to consent to any sale or mortgaging of the home, and neither spouse could exclude the other from residing in the home. Spouses could file a designation of matrimonial home on title to protect their interests. Unfortunately, sufficiently strong clarifying words were not added to direct judges to rearrange assets to achieve equity. But cost-of-living clauses were authorized—any court order for support could attach a cost-of-living clause for automatic increases to take place. Bonuses and benefits were specifically required to be disclosed in the mandatory financial statements that parties had to complete. A spouse was required only to *contribute* to his or her own support and not to become financially independent; the law did not require him or her to become self-supporting within three years. The government had established an enforcement agency to help collect the support payments. Separation agreements could be registered with the court, and support provisions would be enforced by the new government agency as if they were court orders.

ENJOYING THE MOMENT

The Ontario Women's Directorate held an event on February 28, 1986, to celebrate the new law, and I spoke. I was introduced by Ian Scott, who recognized my role with a very laudatory tribute. Then the Ontario Liberal Women's Perspective Advisory Committee organized an all-day conference on March 1 to launch the new legislation. Again, I was one of the invited speakers and introduced by Ian Scott. I was elated at the passage of the legislation and the opportunity to talk about its excellent features. I knew that education was now an important part of advancing the usefulness of the law. I received a standing ovation for my work in achieving family law reform. It was an exciting occasion, and I couldn't have been happier. My speech started with plaudits for democracy.

> For me, today is a day to celebrate the democratic process. The law governing division of property between spouses was unfair to women. We pressed for change by showing the patent unfairness of the law…. And eventually the political process yielded a victory, by government being responsive to people's expressed wish for change. I applaud the commitment of this government in its efforts to achieve for women and men fairness…Some of you know how hard I have fought for change—well, let me tell you, victory is sweet.

I was witnessing first-hand how the history of family law was interwoven with the history of the evolution and empowerment of women, and how essential the advances for women in family law were to the fair and equal treatment of women.

On a personal level, this was a wonderful time. I received numerous letters of congratulations, but a highlight was a pair of letters from the attorney general of Ontario.

On March 4, 1986, Attorney General Ian Scott wrote to acknowledge "the truly significant contribution you have made to the form of this new law." He followed it up two days later with another letter:

> The new Family Law Act and the major portion of the new Support and Custody Orders Enforcement Act have now come into force. I am writing to you to acknowledge your contribution to the legislative process that produced these two Acts.
>
> In the course of the Legislature's deliberations on these important pieces of legislation, it was of great benefit to me personally and to my colleagues in the House to have your comments and suggestions…. I believe the result of this process is very fine legislation of which we can all be proud and which will serve us well in the future….

Senator Florence Bird, who had been chair of the Royal Commission on the Status of Women, delightfully wrote, "Congratulations. Hurray. Attagirl." I was also credited in the media with the role I had played in achieving family law reform. The *Globe and Mail*'s Ian Brown interviewed me for a feature article. During our conversation, he commented that "several lawyers are having nervous tics about it. It struck me as a progressive and radical piece of legislation. Everywhere I turn I find your name." In the article, Brown wrote:

> Romance has always been a male invention. Linda Silver Dranoff, a family lawyer and feminist who almost single-handedly lobbied the new legislation into place, sees it as a concrete answer to the economic oppression of women. "There are a lot of men who don't accept that there is a lot of unfairness. It's a habit. They have to break the habit of thinking of women as subservient...."[163]

But not everyone, it seemed, wished to publicly acknowledge my contributions and expertise. Early in 1986, the CBA-O hosted a full-day professional conference to educate and inform practising family law lawyers about the interpretation of the new Family Law Act (FLA). The co-chairs and organizers were prominent members of the family law bar—Philip Epstein and Malcolm Kronby. I was not asked to speak or participate in any way. The same thing happened two years later, when the same lawyers co-chaired the first conference on family law since the FLA was enacted, which was jointly sponsored by the CBA-O and the Law Society of Upper Canada, the two main organizations of the legal profession. I was taken aback by these slights but I should not have been surprised. I had reason to revisit this twenty-five years later when, in March 2011, the Ontario Bar Association sponsored a retrospective conference on the Family Law Act. It was co-chaired by two other leading members of the family law bar—Stephen Grant and Gerald Sadvari—and, once again, I was not invited to participate.

These events, bookending a quarter-century of practice in family law under the Family Law Act, highlighted the difficulties of trying to practise family law as a feminist, trying to reform the law to be fair, and wanting to be a collegial member of the family law bar. While the male family law lawyers were generally courteous to me, many treated me as an outsider throughout my family law career.[164] An exclusive group of these and other male family law lawyers met frequently, calling themselves "The Academy." I learned about it many years after it was formed. The guys dined together, went on trips together, cottaged together, discussed legal interpretations of cases, and negotiated opposite each other. To my knowledge, only one woman had ever been asked to join the group, and she later committed what they regarded as a *faux pas* that led them to ostracize her, professionally as well as personally for a lengthy period of time.

Given this uneasy history, it was all the more gratifying when, in 2003, the Family Law Section of the Ontario Bar Association honoured me with its Award of Excellence in Family Law. I was the eighth family lawyer to receive the award and the first woman. I had been nominated a number of times, but was not chosen until a behind-the-scenes tussle changed the rules. A number of the women lawyers on the Family Law Section executive banded together[165] and insisted that the award be given based on stipulated criteria rather than discretion, and ensured that the entire Section executive voted for the recipient rather than just the inner circle. It was only then—in the first year under the restructured rules (and seventeen years after the Family Law Act was enacted)—that I was chosen for my contribution to law reform and for my achievements as a practising family lawyer. I was very happy to receive the acknowledgment and grateful to those who wanted me to have it. Judith Huddart, by then my valued law partner and compatible colleague in so many of the things I did, was asked to introduce me. My family also attended; it was a fine evening. I had practised law my way and it had worked out. I had achieved my own definition of success.

· · · · · · · · ·

Almost everything I had worked for was contained in the Family Law Act 1986. These ideas form the basis of current family law, and they have endured for more than thirty years. On a daily basis I experienced in my law practice the appreciation of those women whose lives were enhanced and improved by the new law. When consulted by women who wanted to know their rights, I could say, without hesitation: *The law recognizes your contribution to the marriage, and so you get half of what you and your husband accumulated during the marriage, including his pension, investments, and business.* And I would see the anxiety leave them and the smiles of relief and happiness on their faces. There were more family law and other battles to come, but on March 1, 1986, I was content that the crusade for family law reform was won.

Signing *Every Woman's Guide to the Law* at the book launch held at the Toronto Women's Bookstore, November 1985

Chapter 11
CRUSADING FOR
WOMEN'S EQUALITY IN THE 1980S

The 1980s continued to be an exciting period in the women's move-ment, and governments seemed to be listening to us. We had achieved significant family law reforms, and kept going—there was so much more to do. The goals set by the Royal Commission on the Status of Women in 1970 guided our path and were taken up and fostered by government status of women councils and volunteer organizations across Canada, as well as *Chatelaine* magazine and others among the media. Feminist issues were the issues of the day—the right to an abortion, maternity leave, equal pay, employment equity, pen-sion rights, family law, child care, violence against women. We were involved in politics and public policy, including contributing our voices to debates around the Constitution, the Meech Lake Accord, and Free Trade—the Free Trade Agreement (FTA) was the biggest issue for the Mulroney Progressive Conservatives in their 1988 re-election campaign, and we were concerned it would affect the job market for Canadian women and men, and control over our own country. The party leaders came to talk to women and focused on our concerns. No government could ignore the voices of women.

The family law reform campaign helped me to understand the inner workings of the political process and how to influence change from the outside. I continued to be an activist to advance women's equality in connection with many different public policy issues. I was sometimes on the organizing committee or in the background as an idea person and problem-solver. I often found a way to use my writing, speaking, and strategic skills and experience to advance the causes I was interested in and to use the platforms available to me to contribute to public awareness.

My second book, *Every Woman's Guide to the Law*, was published in June 1985. This comprehensive reference guide to Canadian law gave advice on matters that particularly affected women in the family, as wives, mothers, and single parents; in the workplace; and as members of society entitled to human and public rights. It began with a prologue urging women to take charge of their own lives and suggested the many ways they might do that, even within a traditional marriage.

I also continued my speaking and broadcasting efforts on the issues affecting women's rights. In 1985, I started a long stint as a legal and women's issues expert on City TV's *City Line* phone-in show. This show, then hosted by Dini Petty, was on air live Monday to Friday between 10 a.m. and 11 a.m., and I appeared at least once a month. At first, each program focused on a particular area of law. It soon became clear, however, that viewers just wanted their questions answered. So I would sit at a desk with Dini in front of a studio audience for the full hour, cameras rolling, and answer whatever questions came my way. I really enjoyed the challenge, the interplay, and the opportunity to advise viewers on how to deal with difficult situations they were facing. Callers appreciated feeling as if they were in my office having a personal consultation. I used the forum to educate and enlighten women about legal issues and to point out areas in need of reform. If I didn't know the specific answer, I always knew at least enough to give them some guidance and direction. My columns for *Chatelaine* gave me lots of subject matter for the show, and the research I did for those and for *Every Woman's Guide to the Law* stood me in good stead when I answered questions off the top of my head.

I was on the program for eleven years between 1985 and 1999. After Dini Petty left, I continued with the new host, Marilyn Denis. Both were a pleasure to sit and chat with, even though there was a studio audience as well as viewers at home. I laugh when I recall that my anxiety in connection with the show had less to do with what I would have to say and more to do with my appearance. I worried over what to wear, and since I had to be sure not to repeat outfits too often, I kept a card file of what I wore on each show. The whole experience affected how I chose my wardrobe, since patterns and wild colours looked out of place on TV. Then there was hair and makeup. City TV had a makeup artist on staff but not a hair stylist, at least not for me. So I had to be sure to "do" my hair before I arrived at the studio at 9:15 or so for makeup. And even that became a problem after a while—since there were other demands for the makeup artist, she would just do the basic foundation and powder. As a result, I learned how to do my own makeup before I arrived at the studio.

I have strong recollections of my appearances on *Speaking Out*'s ninety-minute discussion and phone-in program on TV Ontario, along with pre-eminent American feminist Betty Friedan, to talk about the women's movement in Canada and the United States. *Speaking Out* invited both of us to appear on their programs in January 1983 and again in 1986. Betty Friedan had sparked widespread interest in women's issues when she wrote *The Feminine Mystique* in 1963,[166] and she continued at the forefront of the American feminist movement for the rest of her life.

She acknowledged readily on the shows that women in Canada were far ahead of those in the United States. On one of the programs, seemingly from nowhere, she tore a strip off the host, Harry Brown, painting him as a misogynist apparently just because he was a man. I defended him; he was a supporter of women's rights—as host of the CBC radio show *Metro Morning* and as a member of the Justice Committee for Family Law Reform. I cautioned Betty Friedan against lumping all men together in the same category. Afterwards, we went out for coffee. She told me about the constant infighting in the American women's movement, its difficult internal politics, and the enormous effort it took to build a movement. She was intrigued by how Canadian women had managed to achieve so much. After all, we had just successfully lobbied for equal rights in sections 15 and 28 of the Charter of Rights and Freedoms, while to this day American women still do not have an equal rights amendment in their constitution.[167]

During 1985, I had an idea for a feature article called "Judging the Judgments." *Chatelaine* liked it, and it was published in their March 1986 issue. The theme was that the law, developed mostly by male legislators and judges, does not always reflect women's needs. I assessed recent Canadian legal cases affecting women and realized that some should have been labelled "good, but..." Although each case benefited a particular woman, the judgments often left the law unchanged. Other judgments that I criticized turned out, on closer scrutiny, to be even worse. In some instances, courts restrictively interpreted potentially progressive legislation, like the 1978 Family Law Reform Act. In Charter of Rights cases, judges were forced to make decisions that appeared to erode women's equality because discriminatory statutes had not been amended to conform to the Charter. I reviewed six family law cases on property, pensions, support, and enforcement; I highlighted cases on women suffering discrimination in employment opportunities; I examined five cases that trivialized sexual attacks on women and didn't hold the assailants sufficiently accountable. I had observed the role of judges in the battle for equality for women and thought the facts should see the light of day.

And then there was politics. Many feminists were involved in elections, and we tried to put our issues in front of the public during political campaigns and on the "to do" list in party platforms. We achieved much success in this effort. In Ontario, the Accord between the Liberals and the NDP that governed the province for two years after June 26, 1985, created a blueprint of progressive policies that would be legislated by agreement, many of benefit to women. The government even gave LEAF a million dollars to do its important work.

Feminist issues were the issues of the day in the 1980s, and we accomplished many of our ambitious goals in addition to family law reform.

PAY EQUITY: A LONG-STANDING PROBLEM
One of our most ambitious goals was legislation to achieve equal pay for work of equal value, also known as pay equity, both in the public and private sector. In the 1980s, politicians began to pay more attention to satisfying this demand of the women's movement.

The first efforts to create laws to secure equal pay had started in the 1940s when lawyer Margaret Hyndman, as president of the Canadian Federation of Business and Professional Women's Clubs

(BPW), led the campaign for the women's clubs. On January 1, 1952, the Female Employees Fair Remuneration Act became law, making Ontario the first province to put equal pay legislation into effect. Ellen Fairclough introduced a similar private members bill in the federal Parliament in 1955, but it was defeated. However, the Ontario law mandated "equal pay for equal work"—which meant that only jobs in which men and women did the very same work could be compared. Ineffective, this was changed in the mid-1970s to "equal pay for substantially the same work," which also didn't work. "Equal pay for work of equal value" and then "pay equity" became the goals. All along, enforcement was lax and improvement negligible. An aggrieved person had to stick her neck out and register a complaint, risking her job.

I felt in my bones that until they were paid equally with men, women would never be able to take an equal place in society or take charge of their own lives, care for their children, and contribute to their family's well-being. This became even more crucial if her marriage broke down, especially if her husband defaulted on his support obligation, as many did. A woman who was paid equally with men would be less likely to be trapped in a bad or abusive marriage, would be better able to pay for good child care where there was no government program, and would have a better chance of taking care of herself in her later years. Equal pay is a major key to equality and independence. It is also a fundamental human right of women to be paid wages that are free of the systemic gender-based discrimination that places less value on women's work than on men's work of comparable value. Equal pay for work of equal value and pay equity had, by the mid-1980s, become the new mantras to define this issue.

Equal pay was an issue needing remediation, and many women—and some men too—were dynamically engaged in efforts to make it happen. In 1976, the Equal Pay Coalition of thirty-nine constituent organizations was founded and, given persistent unequal pay conditions, continues today under the sustained and exceptional leadership of labour lawyer Mary Cornish to lobby for equal pay for work of equal value. When the OCSW promoted the idea of "wage equity" in its 1980 brief "Employment Strategies for the 1980s," there was little support for it within government. But in October 1984, less than a year before the Accord was signed in

Ontario, Judge Rosalie Silberman Abella, sole commissioner of the federal Royal Commission on Equality in Employment,[168] issued a report recommending the implementation of "employment equity" to proactively establish working conditions that counteracted systemic discrimination in the workplace. While the report was not specifically about pay equity, it set out a rationale and process to achieve fairness in the workplace. The federal government implemented many of the ideas in the report when it enacted the 1986 Employment Equity Act affecting federally regulated private sector companies and Crown corporations.[169]

In Ontario, equal pay for work of equal value was included in the 1985 Accord signed by the Liberals and the NDP for action in the first session of the legislature. Ian Scott, in his role as both attorney general and minister for women's issues, pressed forward with the promised equal pay for work of equal value laws. He relied upon Elaine Todres, the director of policy and research in the Ontario Women's Directorate, for background and support. She prepared a consultation document for public discussion, called a Green Paper, released in November 1985 to encourage widespread discussion of how to resolve the discrimination facing women in the workforce. There were fears in the business community and in the cabinet about both pay equity and employment equity. In the end, Ian Scott chose to leave out employment equity and concentrate on pay equity.[170]

The pay equity legislation was challenged by many, on questionable grounds as far as I was concerned. Pay equity laws were criticized as harmful to the economy, just as family laws had been challenged as bad for business. I decided that it was important to weigh in on this issue. I was interviewed on radio and television and wrote an op-ed piece that the *Toronto Star* published on December 2, 1986, headed "Let's give equal pay law time to work." While I applauded the law as the best we had seen to date, I also pointed out ways to achieve more effective enforcement. I commented that the new law was tougher and more effective legislation than we had asked for in our 1982 brief of the Ontario Council on the Status of Women and that it should be given a chance. I also wrote about pay equity in my column in *Chatelaine*. It was important to support government efforts when they were proceeding in the right direction.

When Ontario's Pay Equity Act was passed in 1987, it surpassed all previous legislative attempts to promote equal pay for women in Canada. The innovative act required both public- and private-sector employers with ten or more employees to take the initiative in adjusting pay patterns. Those employers with one hundred or more employees had to develop pay equity plans with their employees or unions. The Pay Equity Commission was established to educate Ontarians about pay equity and to respond to complaints. A tribunal was also established to adjudicate on disputes that could not be resolved by the commission. In 1987, women earned 64 cents for every dollar that men earned. We hoped the new law would improve this unjust situation.

Women in Ontario understood that it mattered who was running the government, that without sympathetic and open-minded legislators at the helm, we could not assume further progress. Unfortunately, the ten-year progressive period we were enjoying in Ontario from 1985 to 1995—with two years of the Liberal/NDP Accord followed by three years of Liberal majority government, followed by five years under the NDP—did not continue in Ontario, and was not matched at the federal level.

THE SWING TO THE RIGHT: THE 1984 FEDERAL ELECTION
In March 1984, Pierre Elliott Trudeau resigned as prime minister and leader of the federal Liberal Party. I was one of ten individuals (and the only woman) asked by the *Toronto Star* to assess his performance; I was the only one to note and comment on his advances for women:

> He has been a strong leader, with an amazing ability to get and keep power. The history books will probably applaud him for the Constitution and rightly berate him for the War Measures Act. But women should not forget to appreciate his early initiatives in 1967 for divorce reform and legalization of abortion when he was justice minister. Too bad he did not maintain his drive as [a] leader for social change where women are concerned.[171]

Trudeau was replaced as Liberal leader by John Turner, and a federal election was called for September 4, 1984. The women's movement revved up to try to ensure that the political parties all understood the issues and would enact measures needed for women's equality. The Liberals had governed Canada (with the exception of approximately one year) since 1963, and women had made progress during that period. There was greater freedom of reproductive choice as contraception and abortion, under certain circumstances, had been legalized during the Liberal government of Lester B. Pearson, when Pierre Trudeau was minister of justice. In 1967, the Liberal government had established the Royal Commission on the Status of Women. And in 1968, a new Divorce Act gave spouses greater freedom to leave a bad marriage.

By 1984, the Canadian women's movement had achieved a high level of maturity and prominence. Politicians were beginning to realize that they had to pay attention, or at least *appear* to be paying attention. The National Action Committee on the Status of Women under the magnificent leadership of Chaviva Hošek[172] was able to get agreement among the parties to have a women's debate. The three leaders—Progressive Conservative Brian Mulroney, Liberal John Turner, and the NDP's Ed Broadbent—went at it on August 15, 1984. It was a great achievement and still ranks as the only time in Canadian electoral history when there was an official debate entirely devoted to women's issues.[173]

Not surprisingly, there was a huge lineup of women to witness this event. More than two thousand stood for two hours outside the Royal York Hotel[174] in downtown Toronto to get into the live debate. The event was televised by all of the major networks in a pooled effort. I was thrilled to be present to actually hear the men compelled to debate issues such as abortion, affirmative action, daycare, equal pay for work of equal value, poverty of single and older women, pension credit splits, social programs, and world peace. It was exhilarating to watch the political leaders attempt to persuade women to support *their* party. The questioners included Kay Sigurjonsson, the executive director of the Federation of Women Teachers' Associations of Ontario, and to this day, I remember her brilliant final question to the leaders: "You've all made a lot of promises tonight. Given how dismal your record is, I ask you on behalf of all Canadian women: *Why should we trust you now?*" We in the audience, who had been cautioned at the beginning to be silent throughout the televised debate and had done so to that point, couldn't help ourselves. Hoots and shouts and applause cheered the question. Kay had struck a chord that resonated with all of us. The question—which was, in effect, unanswerable, despite the big point it had made—took the three men by surprise. In one form or another, each party leader gave a "trust me" response.

During the same election campaign, Myra Sable Davidson and Lynn Kinney, both businesswomen and active in various issues of the women's movement, joined forces to spearhead a series of three non-partisan "Lunches with Leaders," where each of the three major party leaders was the guest of honour at a lunch held at the Harbour Castle Hotel ballroom in downtown Toronto. The letterhead naming supporters was a who's who of the women's movement of the day and ensured three well-attended events. The honoured guest was required to answer questions, all of which were on women's issues. We were all excited at the possibilities, with politicians so keen to get our votes.

The first lunch was held May 25, 1984, and attracted an audience of about three thousand. NAC president Chaviva Hošek introduced Progressive Conservative leader Brian Mulroney. It had been pre-arranged that I would ask the first question. While I can no longer recall the exact question, I do remember how difficult it was to craft, and that *Globe and Mail* journalist Alan Stewart referred to it the next day as complex enough to "set any politician off on a tortured twisting through a maze of obfuscation and hemming and hawing."[175] To my chagrin, Mulroney slid around it with a one-word answer: "Yes."

I was nonplussed and later tried to figure out how I could have phrased the question differently, but in retrospect, I imagine Mulroney was capable of sliding through any question that was asked. He continued to give very brief answers to subsequent questions and to make a lot of promises.

The second lunch was held on August 24, 1984, and featured Liberal leader and prime minister John Turner, who was presented by *Globe and Mail* journalist Judith Finlayson. The third lunch was held a week later and featured New Democratic Party leader Ed Broadbent, introduced by former NAC president and former *Chatelaine* editor Doris Anderson. The *Toronto Star* assessed the three lunches as a "truly big deal." Journalist Lynda Hurst said John

Turner had mastered the buzzwords, Ed Broadbent understood the issues, and Brian Mulroney? Well, she described him as "the human promissory note" who will "soon suffer an amnesia attack and conveniently forget all the commitments he made during the women's-issues TV debate."[176]

I was worried about the record of the parties in keeping promises and wrote an op-ed piece for the *Toronto Star* headed "Election promises: Women won't settle for less than action":

> This is the first time women have been an election issue in Canada. The leaders have been forced to bone up on the issues, have expressed dismay about injustices to women, and have promised changes.... People who want fairness for women will choose to vote for the party whose promises they like, whose policies they support, and whose commitment they trust.[177]

Then I analyzed the promises made, and focused on the big one:

> Must women wait for the economy to improve? This is the most important issue of the campaign for women's votes.... Brian Mulroney said that he is "earnestly and genuinely committed to equity for women" but "no-one will be able to make good on their commitment to women unless the economy improves."

To me, this simply wasn't true. It was an old excuse, and I did not understand why problems in the economy should end up on the backs of women. I made my point strongly:

> Slave owners in the U.S. South in the last century said they were ready to free the slaves—when their cotton-based economy could afford it. The blacks would *still* be slaves if their liberators had not corrected discrimination despite the economy.

The current economy was based on the sacrifices of women, who were paid less than men for work outside the home and who did a disproportionate amount of work inside the home. Governments have choices, and the Liberals had spent $5 billion bailing out Canadair and DeHavilland, corporations in the airline industry, but applied negligible amounts to child care. Mulroney had promised millions for increased military spending, but made no specific promise for child care. There were inconsistencies between the promises and the record and the logic. And I ended the piece with these words: "Whichever party wins, it will have the help of women's votes and trust, and must fulfil their promises or be booted out at the next election by outraged women with long memories."

These words were as much wishful thinking as a threat to the candidates for election. In the end, Brian Mulroney and his Progressive Conservatives won with a record showing. The PCs formed a majority government with 211 seats, the Liberals were the official Opposition with only forty seats, and the NDP won thirty seats. At the same time, a record crop of women was elected—twenty-seven, about 10 percent of the members of Parliament and the largest representation of women to that date.

One year later, the *Toronto Star* ran an article analyzing whether Mulroney had followed through on his promises; Cathy Dunphy had interviewed a wide variety of women in the women's movement. The headline was "Women criticize Mulroney's inaction." My comments led the article:

> "We don't seem to be a priority on Mulroney's agenda. I don't sense we're that important...." She says the attitude is symbolized by Mulroney's recent economic conference. "He promised an economic summit with women heading the agenda. I remember him making that promise. But women didn't head the agenda. While women were there, our issues weren't."[178]

I continued writing letters to the editor. I wrote about Mulroney's budget cuts to the CBC[179] and his sale of Air Canada, and I challenged the Mulroney government about the budget plan to reduce social programs: "The social safety net was once described by the prime minister as 'a sacred trust.' The new budget shows how meaningless these high-sounding statements have become and how politicians can abuse the language."[180]

The women's movement kept Brian Mulroney under close scrutiny. The fact that his was a majority government, which could do what it wanted, made it more difficult. To his credit, and that of Flora MacDonald, his minister of employment at this time, he did pass the Employment Equity Act during his tenure. Nevertheless, Brian Mulroney and his government made a number of serious policy decisions that were directly contrary to what he promised during the election campaign, or that had never been mentioned at all during the campaign. There were more challenges to come from Mulroney and his Progressive Conservatives, including the Meech Lake Accord and abortion rights.

THE MEECH LAKE AND CHARLOTTETOWN ACCORDS, 1987–92

It seemed like an ordinary day in April 1987 when I woke to hear a radio news broadcast that Prime Minister Mulroney, together with both federal opposition leaders and all provincial premiers, had agreed to the Meech Lake Accord. It was described as the instrument by which Quebec would be brought back within the Canadian constitutional fold (Quebec had objected in 1981 to Pierre Trudeau's patriation of the Constitution and the Charter without its approval). The Accord defined Quebec as a "distinct society," but that was not all it did. I was concerned that it also decentralized a number of federal government functions, gave more power to the provinces, limited federal spending powers, changed the system of appointments to the Senate and Supreme Court of Canada, and more.

Here we go again, I thought. Yet another politician is taking the country apart to conform to his idea of what Canada should look like. Passed off as simply a way to bring Quebec back under the constitutional umbrella, the Accord in reality was about so much more.

Later that day, the news reports carried a story that Deborah Coyne, a law professor at the University of Toronto, was organizing a campaign against the Meech Lake Accord and holding a meeting at the law school that very day. I rearranged my schedule and went to the meeting, where a non-partisan organization of Canadians from all walks of life, called the Canadian Coalition on the Constitution, was formed. I was a founding member. Many Canadians lent their support, including Harry Arthurs, Farley Mowat, Eugene Forsey, June Callwood, Doris Anderson, Adrienne Clarkson, Izzy Asper, Desmond Morton, J. M. S. Careless, Ramsay Cook, Michael Bliss, Sharon Carstairs, Lorna Marsden, and Keith Davey.

We all agreed that the changes proposed in the Accord would fundamentally weaken and irrevocably alter the nature of Canada, gravely undermine the capacity of the federal government to act on behalf of all Canadians, and potentially imperil our long-term

Meech pact deals away powers without consent

LINDA SILVER DRANOFF
s Dranoff, a Toronto lawyer and author, is a mber of the Canadian Coalition on the Constit-ion and on the steering committee of a national men's coalition on the constitution.

HE CAVALIER ATTITUDE toward the rights of Canadians being dis-played by those entrusted with power is appalling. Canadians have t been asked to decide whether the Meech ke constitutional accord should be al-ved to change the basic structure of their ntry in a way that depletes national wers. Nor have they consented to making ebec's status more important than equal-rights, freedom of religion and the press, e right to have an election every five rs, and all the other provisions of the arter of Rights and Freedoms.

If Canada were a business corporation, d Prime Minister Brian Mulroney were chairman of the board, he wouldn't have d the power to sign a corporate equiva-t of the Meech Lake accord and then sent it to shareholders as a fait accomp-. Without shareholder approval, a board of ectors cannot make such basic changes the structure of the corporation as alter-ing its bylaws or the rights of shareholders, disposing of substantial assets, or changing the nature of the corporate undertaking.

The Meech Lake accord does much more than recognize Quebec's distinct status within Canada. It will touch the lives of Canadians in ways we cannot fully grasp, and there must be sufficient time to explore and discuss it thoroughly.

New rules will take precedence over the founding 1867 Constitution and the 1982 Charter of Rights. The balance of powers will be altered irrevocably, shifting national powers to the provinces and jeopardizing national social programs.

Deadlocks likely

Handing every province the power to veto future changes in political institutions and to appoint judges and senators may lead to deadlocks. The accord effectively creates a new and different constitution.

A corporate board of directors is in a position of trust. If a board were to make structural changes as basic as those in the accord, it would be overstepping its authori-ty and be subject to court action.

The Mulroney Government is also in a position of trust. A 211-seat majority should not give automatic permission to the leader of the party in power to dictate fundamental change.

In a democracy, the governing party is a trustee and should not, without the consent of the governed, deal away powers that go to the heart of a 120-year-old constitutional framework. There was no mandate in the 1984 federal election to undertake serious constitutional change.

By refusing to reconsider their accord seriously and by counting on party disci-pline to back them, the Prime Minister and the premiers have not allowed for genuine approval, either in Parliament and the leg-islatures or among the citizens. Democra-cies rely on periodic elections to assess the performance and credibility of their lead-ership. The lack of constructive "loyal opposi-tion" raises the question: just who inside the legislatures is speaking for Canada's national future?

It should not be the responsibility of peo-ple outside government to act as the "loyal opposition" and prove the accord has seri-ous implications. The onus is on the signato-ries to prove it is wise and beneficial in all respects, not just in relation to "getting Quebec in'" — everyone wants that.

They also must prove that what the ac-cord says is so clear, judges will not fail to interpret it as intended. The document should at least be referred to the Supreme Court of Canada in advance to settle current differences of opinion over meaning. Fur-ther study will do no harm to any person or institution — or to Quebec — but substantial harm can be done to Canada as a national entity if this accord is ratified hastily.

Free vote needed

If the Prime Minister and 10 premiers were so sure their deal would stand up to scrutiny, they would allow a free vote in Parliament and the provincial legislatures to ensure the integrity of the democratic process. This constitutional change affects Canadians more than capital punishment, the most recent free vote in Parliament. Backbenchers of all parties in all provinces should be allowed to exercise their judg-ment independently.

---

survival as a single, sovereign, bilingual, and multicultural nation.

This op-ed piece published by the Globe and Mail September 21, 1987 challenged the Meech Lake Accord.

Under Deborah Coyne's leadership, this organization maintained a strong lobby cam-paign against the Meech Lake Accord. One of the things we did was challenge the constitutionality of the Accord in the Federal Court of Canada. The case was dismissed for lack of jurisdiction, citing the political nature of the issue.[181] At the same time, several women's groups banded together[182] to deal with the impact on women of the Meech Lake Accord, and I served on the steering committee for that coalition.

My role, as had become customary, was to analyze the legal issues and write about them. On September 21, 1987, the *Globe and Mail* published my op-ed piece entitled "Meech pact deals away powers without consent." It set out the issues and expressed my concerns that those entrusted with power were displaying a cavalier attitude toward the rights of Canadians. We had not been asked to decide whether we wanted to change the country's basic structure or deplete national powers. We had not agreed to make Quebec's status more important than equality rights, freedom of religion and the press, the right to have an election every five years, and other provi-sions of the Charter of Rights and Freedoms and the Constitution. We had not consented to let the Meech Lake Accord alter the balance of powers, shift national powers to the provinces, and jeop-ardize national social programs. I pointed out that deadlocks could result if every province was handed the power to veto future changes in political institutions and to appoint judges and senators. I felt strongly that in a democracy, the governing party is a trustee and should not, without the consent of the governed, deal away powers that go to the heart of our 120-year-old constitutional framework. I was dismayed that the lack of a constructive "loyal Opposition" within Parliament led to the question of just who was speaking for Canada's national future.

I tried to leverage the effect of what I wrote by sharing it with those who were in a position to use it. Since, by the terms of the Meech Lake Accord, the Ontario legislature (and each of the other provincial legislatures) had to ratify it by the deadline of June 24, 1990, I wrote directly to Ontario premier David Peterson and attorney general and minister for women's issues Ian Scott. I included a copy of the op-ed piece that had appeared in the *Globe and Mail*. Ian Scott responded with a promise to hold a full and open public hearing process prior to any final decision on the Meech Lake Accord.

On October 18, 1987, the Ontario Advisory Council on Women's Issues sponsored a day-long education and strategy meeting of more than twenty women's groups.[183] Delivering the keynote address gave me the opportunity to put all of my concerns together in one place. I called it a "Primer on the Meech Lake Accord," and I was determined to be thorough. In forty-eight typed pages, I outlined the history of the Constitution of Canada between 1867 and 1980; I described Pierre Trudeau's plan for the Charter and patriation of the Constitution between 1980 and 1982; and I summarized the history of the impact of the Constitution on women. I dealt with the potential impact of the Meech Lake Accord—the distinct society clause, women's equality rights, decentralization and the shifting balance of powers, amendment procedures, national social programs, appointments to the Supreme Court of Canada and Senate, immigration, and more. I highlighted the possible impact on women's equality rights: "It is the view of all women's groups who presented submissions to the Joint Parliamentary Committee, and my view, that... the Charter and equality rights may be interpreted secondary to Quebec's place as a distinct society."

I pointed out that we were told by politicians not to worry. To me it sounded like *There, there, girls, don't worry your pretty little heads about this....* We were admonished that if we were against the Accord, we must be against Quebec, which simply wasn't so. Quebec had every reason to object to being bypassed by Pierre Trudeau in 1981. But there was so much more to the Accord than the distinct society clause.

I encouraged everyone to make a presentation to the legislative committee holding the Ontario public hearings and to seek a free vote in the provincial legislatures. I concluded with dramatic language:

> The Meech Lake Accord represents a political earthquake. It has arisen suddenly and we don't know what damage will be left when the earth under our feet stops rumbling. It has become an implacable force, which has proceeded like a juggernaut, and as remorseless. There are too many problems with it to think we can tinker with it. It must be stopped.

The primer was distributed widely by the Ontario Advisory Council on Women's Issues. It was also translated into French by the New Brunswick Council on the Status of Women, which gave it broad distribution in Quebec and other French-Canadian areas of the country.

Over the next several years, I spoke about the Meech Lake Accord at every opportunity, as a guest speaker at a number of events and in interviews on a number of radio and TV programs.

Attorney General Ian Scott sent me a copy of the speech he made in the legislature on November 25, 1987, when he tabled the constitutional resolution. In it, he explained in some detail the provisions of the Accord and what it meant to him and his government. Overall, he said that the potential effects of the provisions of the Accord were either overstated by the Opposition or worth the compromise, although he admitted that the process left something to be desired. Above all, he affirmed that the Accord was an "honourable and historic reconciliation of Quebec within Canada." In establishing the public hearings, he said the Accord "cannot be analyzed against some purely hypothetical or abstract alternative. The Accord must be analyzed in light of the absolute necessity of achieving national reconciliation." I respected his view but could not agree with it.

On March 8, 1988, I made my own presentation to the Ontario public hearings on the Meech Lake Accord, and in it I expressed some of what has motivated me throughout my public policy activism:

> I speak as a proud citizen of Canada, who feels that the public interest of the country as a whole has been underrepresented in the Meech Lake negotiations. I am not here to represent any special interest groups, although I could identify myself with many.
>
> You should understand that my background and perspective does, however, inform my perception and judgment about this important matter. You could define me as a woman, and dismiss me as only representing women's interests, but I hope you will not do that. I am also a practising lawyer, which helps me to understand what happens when legislation comes to be interpreted in the courts. I am Canadian-born and educated, with an Honours History degree from the University of Toronto, and an LLB degree from Osgoode Hall Law School and throughout, a student of politics. My grandparents were immigrants to this country, but I remain grateful two generations later for the opportunities I have had in Canada. And if you want to know still more about why I feel compelled to speak out, understand that I am a mother who wants her daughter to live in the best possible Canada.
>
> …The future of our nation, as a nation, is at risk, and I feel it is the responsibility of every citizen to speak out. Citizens must do more than vote at election time, or our representatives may forget who gives them their power. We must stand on guard for our country when we see that our leaders and the opposition parties are not. We must speak for Canada when our elected politicians do not.

On March 28, 1988, Premier David Peterson sent me a five-page letter explaining the province's position in favour of the Accord, but this also did not persuade me.

Along with many others, I continued to be watchful. On April 23, 1988, I noticed that the *Globe and Mail*, in reporting that Justice Willard Estey would be retiring from the Supreme Court of Canada, suggested that his replacement probably would be chosen by the method set forth in the Meech Lake Accord. I sent a letter to the editor, which was published, in which I pointed out that "since the contentious Meech Lake Accord is not law, and in fact may never become law, it would be illegal to apply it in this context." I also sent a copy to Justice Estey. His reply to me illuminated his position on the Accord itself: "I am not in any way inclined to go into politics but I am inclined to have something more to say about Meech Lake if the discussions toward ratification, without any change, continue."

Opposition to the Accord grew. This included the new premier of Newfoundland, Clyde Wells,[184] who just happened to be a constitutional lawyer who had advised both Pierre Trudeau and the Canadian Bar Association on constitutional issues. Brian Peckford had been premier when the Accord was ratified by the Newfoundland legislature, but Clyde Wells said he was ready to rescind the ratification and resubmit it. He was against the Meech Lake Accord for reasons similar to those of the Canadian Coalition on the Constitution. He said he was willing to discuss possible changes, but added that "the concerns I have are so substantial that the chances of getting changes that would meet them are very remote."[185]

Prime Minister Mulroney stood his ground. He wrote to all the provincial premiers on February 10, 1989, saying:

> I simply consider that reopening or renegotiating the constitutional accord signed on June 3, 1987, and since ratified by eight provinces and the federal government, would present such insurmountable obstacles and represent such a risk to the country's future that the burden of proof must lie with those who claim they could reconstruct unanimous support for an improved accord.[186]

Concerned about what the prime minister had said, I wrote a letter to the editor of the *Globe and Mail*, which was published on March 1, 1989; I put the onus back on Mulroney to prove the Accord's merit. I suggested that it was the Accord *itself* that was a risk to the country's future.

At the time that the Meech Lake Accord was initially approved by the federal and provincial leaders, polls concluded that the public supported it. By the time of the deadline for ratification, in June 1990, polls showed the opposite. The legislature of Manitoba did not ratify it, as a result of the lack of support by Indigenous leader and MPP Elijah Harper, who swung the vote to the negative side. Nor did Newfoundland ratify it. So it never became law. Former prime minister Pierre Trudeau's strong objections were also a powerful force.

Undeterred, Prime Minister Mulroney, after intensive negotiations among federal, provincial, and territorial governments and Indigenous groups, pulled together a new version of the Accord. The Charlottetown Accord, as it was called, was submitted to Canadians in a referendum on October 26, 1992. The referendum was to placate those of us who had objected to the undemocratic process that had created the Meech Lake Accord. The Charlottetown Accord was defeated, with a national "no" vote of 54.3 percent against a "yes" vote of 45.7 percent.

I welcomed the defeat but I was nonplussed to note that the federal government nevertheless began to implement some of the Meech/Charlottetown changes behind the scenes, such as giving Quebec more control over immigration. Ironically, this just showed that many of Quebec's concerns *could* have been addressed effectively without changing the basic constitutional structure of Canada.

And then, in 2006, a minority Conservative government under Stephen Harper pushed through Parliament in five days a declaration that Quebec is a "nation" within Canada. I objected in a letter to the editor of the *Toronto Star* that the decision "was impulsive (five days from conception to birth) and undemocratic (negligible opportunity for public debate)."[187] I was concerned that many seemed to vote "holding their noses" in the hope that the vote was purely symbolic.

CANADA PENSION PLAN AND EQUAL SHARING
The challenges kept coming as the inequities faced by women became more apparent. The treatment of wives in the Canada Pension Plan (CPP)—an area related to family law—was not even-handed.

The Canada Pension Plan Act had been enacted in 1966 by the federal government. Both an employer and employee contributed, and on retirement the employee was entitled to a monthly pension. The husband was more often the sole breadwinner in the family during the years after 1966 and as a result earned the right

Inequities deprive women of pensions

By Linda Silver Dranoff
Special to The Star

Anna F., a homemaker and mother of three, divorced after 22 years, had the door slammed in her face recently when she tried to claim the government-advertised share in her husband's Canada Pension Plan. She discovered that she, like many others, was deprived of a pension share because she divorced between Jan. 1, 1978, and Aug. 26, 1983. Her separation agreement was silent about the Canada Pension Plan, but instead contained a standard clause releasing all property rights.

Jake Epp and his federal ministry of health and welfare openly admit that this is an inequity, but they have failed to follow through on promises to correct it. While they did change the law for post-1983 divorced spouses, they did not make the new law retroactive to pre-1983 divorced people.

The 1978 law had been hailed as a breakthrough for divorced homemakers who had not worked for wages and accumulated their own pension credits. It required husbands and wives to share the Canada Pension Plan credits earned by them during the time they were married and living together.

The federal health and welfare ministry publicly announced from 1978 onward, that pension credits would be divided no matter what was written in separation agreements. Spouses were not allowed to waive their rights, and the standard "release clause" in a separation agreement would not be interpreted to include a release of rights to pension plan credits.

That is, until several husbands challenged the credit-splitting, and the Pension Appeals Board interpreted the law differently by deciding in the 1983 "Preece" case that if spouses sign a separation agreement with a standard clause, "releasing all rights," they must be presumed to intend to also release pension plan sharing rights.

First, Monique Begin and then Epp, successive federal ministers of health and welfare, admitted the intention of the legislation had always been to share pension credits as joint assets. Both promised to amend the legislation.

Begin was not in office long enough to do it. But Epp brought in a new law in October, 1986, that was supposed to fix the problem. It said that the right to a split of pension credits cannot be waived by a separation agreement, but added the unfortunate exemption that such an agreement could be expressly permitted under a provincial law.

Only Epp decided to make the new law apply only to agreements signed after June 4, 1986, and not retroactively to those who had divorced prior to the Preece case, that is between 1978 and Aug. 26, 1983. Why? Epp wrote to me that, "The federal government considers that it would be improper to retroactively abrogate agreements made in good faith." This, even though everyone signing such agreements knew or must be taken to know, what Canada Pension Plan policy was between 1978 and 1983.

Epp said he was concerned about the problem and promised to rectify, "those cases where it can be shown that an agreement was signed on the basis of advice that spousal agreements would not affect a division of Canada Pension Plan credits." These, of course, were most of the cases.

But Epp and the Conservative government have not done anything to help the women who divorced between 1978 and 1983. The women affected either suffer now if they have already retired, or will feel the pinch when they retire.

LINDA SILVER DRANOFF: Toronto family lawyer says pension law works against divorced women.

Bad enough not to change the law to solve the problem. But it gets worse. Epp and his people have actively worked against these women.

Since Aug. 26, 1983, the health and welfare ministry has scrutinized all separation agreements when divorced spouses applied to share pension credits, and they have refused to authorize sharing of credits when a release clause was in the agreement.

Some women have appealed this first-level refusal to the review committees, set up by the legislation to act as a sort of "jury," and some of the review committees have allowed a woman's claim to share the credits. Anna F. won the right to share her husband's pension from a review committee.

But the Ministry of Health and Welfare did not allow this to stand, and, as in many other similar cases, instead registered an appeal to the next and final level of appeal, the Pension Appeals Board. And the board continues to apply the Preece case like a "rubber stamp," even though the law has since been changed to conform to Canada Pension Plan policy.

In Anna F.'s case, the Pension Appeals Board acknowledged being "acutely aware" that legal counsel had relied on pension plan policy in advising their clients, and that they knew that subsequent legislation changed the statute to conform to the policy of the department. But they dismissed her case anyway.

to receive a CPP pension on his retirement. The law did not require the homemaker to receive any share of his pension, whether they were still together or whether they had separated or divorced. The Royal Commission on the Status of Women recommended[188] that the government study the options and find a way for CPP to be shared between husbands and wives, either by sharing pension credits or by allowing homemakers to pay into the CPP themselves to earn credits. The National Action Committee on the Status of Women supported pension credit splitting[189]; it passed policy resolutions in 1977 allowing for voluntary sharing of credits and later endorsed mandatory sharing.

As of January 1, 1978, under Pierre Trudeau's Liberals, the federal government enacted a law that said that upon being notified by application within three years after a divorce was granted, the CPP was required to divide pension credits between the husband and wife. At that time, few spouses knew or were told about this; only about 2 percent of those who were entitled to apply did so within the three years after their divorce. In cases where a party did know, the husband's lawyer would sometimes demand that the wife give up her right to share pension benefits in exchange for something else the wife really wanted, like custody of the children. For many

Published by the *Toronto Star* September 3, 1988, this article warned women of inequities in Canada Pension Plan law.

women, the prospect of sharing pension credits was so far away that they released them in exchange for immediate benefits. The minister of health and welfare, Monique Bégin, who had feminist credentials—she had been the executive secretary of the Royal Commission on the Status of Women—set a policy (but did not change the law) that separation agreements and court orders could not take away the right to share pension credits between husband and wife on divorce. The government split the pension credits, notwithstanding any release clause in a separation agreement. It was known to the legal community that this was the policy of the Department of Health and Welfare, and many lawyers let release clauses remain in agreements knowing that the CPP split would happen anyway; it was one thing less to fight about.

This was the situation for a woman who consulted me. She had applied to share her husband's pension credits, relying on ministerial policy in the face of her separation agreement to the contrary. This was another time that work on a client's file brought to my attention the need for legislative change.

Her claim was denied because of a decision made by the Canada Pension Plan Appeals Board in 1983 in the *Preece* case.[190] A husband had challenged any sharing of his CPP pension with his ex-wife, and won. The board ruled that agreements negotiated between a husband and wife could remove the right granted in the Canada Pension Plan Act to share pension credits. I wrote to Minister Monique Bégin to suggest that her policy to invalidate such release clauses in agreements should be enshrined as law. She answered me on October 21, 1983, saying the intent of the legislators was to recognize that pension credits earned by one or both spouses during a marriage are a "joint asset." She added that in view of the Pension Appeals Board ruling, it appeared that the legislation should be changed, and her advisors were reviewing it.

The Liberal government in which Monique Bégin served lost the 1984 election to Brian Mulroney's PCs, and Jake Epp took over as minister of health and welfare. I was not aware of anyone else working on this particular pension issue, so I thought it best to write to him before he made any final decisions on this issue.

In my letter,[191] I described briefly the history of the problems and focused on three issues: (1) release clauses in agreements should not invalidate a person's entitlement to share the spouse's CPP pension credits; (2) any new rule should be made retroactive to when the sharing law was first passed; and (3) the pension plan credits should be divided without a formal application by the divorced spouse within three years after the decree is made absolute. With respect to retroactivity, he replied: "The federal government considers that it would be improper to retroactively abrogate agreements made in good faith."[192] This, even though everyone signing such agreements knew or must be assumed to have known what Canada Pension Plan policy was between 1978 and 1983.

The revised law was introduced in October 1986 and enacted effective January 1, 1987, so that credit splitting became mandatory, but only in cases of divorce occurring on or after January 1, 1987. And because the split was mandatory, no application was required and the three-year rule was repealed. I was happy with two out of the three changes, but concerned that the new law was not made retroactive. Nor did the new law help the client whose situation had made me aware of the issue. She had won her case in front of the CPP Review Committee, which ruled that she should receive an equal sharing of her husband's pension since she had signed the agreement before the 1983 *Preece* case became law, during a time when ministerial policy applied. However, Jake Epp, notwithstanding his promise to try to find a way to rectify those cases where parties had relied on ministerial policy, appealed the Review Board's decision to the Pension Appeals Board. Not only did he *not* rectify the situation, he worked actively against her. The case was heard in June 1988. The board was straightforward in its denunciation of ministerial policy and regarded itself as bound by the law expressed in the statute and not by statements of policy contained in a departmental brochure. The board expressed regret that the new legislation was not retroactive.

This was very disappointing not only to my client and me, but also to a number of other clients who were awaiting the results of the decision. If the law was that they were to share CPP pension credits, then why put so many obstacles in the way? At first, the obstacle was that the benefit was unknown, and that there was a time limit for application. Then, when the sharing became enshrined in law no matter what the separation agreement said, it did not apply retroactively. I highlighted this inequity in a column I wrote for the *Toronto Star* published on September 3, 1988, titled "Inequities deprive women of pensions."

To my knowledge, couples who separated between January 1, 1978, and August 26, 1983, and who also signed standard separation agreements with full release clauses, continue to be prevented from sharing their partner's CPP credits. Other couples are now protected.

ABORTION

The quintessential women's issue, central to women's rights, is the absolute entitlement of women to control their reproductive powers and the freedom to decide whether or not to bear a child. It should not be up to a government, controlled primarily by men, to tell a woman what to do with her own body. Indeed, abortion was a criminal offence under Canadian federal law until 1968, when the Pearson Liberals legalized it, but only if a hospital committee of three doctors approved and the woman's life or health was in jeopardy.

Not everyone agreed that this law solved the problem. The Vancouver Women's Caucus wanted abortion removed from the Criminal Code and organized, in 1970, what was called the Abortion Caravan[193] to make the cross-country drive to Ottawa. Seventeen of them started out in three vehicles and supporters joined them along the way from women's groups across the country. They arrived at the House of Commons on Mothers' Day 1970 and demonstrated in the public gallery of the House of Commons, closing it down. They were not arrested, but they did get the attention of then prime minister Pierre Trudeau, who made it a point to talk to them when he was in Vancouver. They said the problem affected every woman. No promises were made, but these women had proclaimed that this was an important issue for all women.

Dr. Henry Morgentaler took up leadership in the battle for freedom of reproductive choice. His inspiring efforts to secure for women freedom of choice about whether or not to abort a fetus included his willingness in the 1970s to go to jail. Once he was released from prison (in 1974, juries in Quebec twice refused to convict him, as did an Ontario jury ten years later), Dr. Morgentaler set up clinics, taught doctors how to perform safe abortions, and faced down picketers and protesters and legal challenges. He spoke up against laws that "compelled the unwilling to bear the unwanted."

Pro-choice committees formed on an ad hoc basis to help and support Dr. Morgentaler, who continued to be in financial and personal jeopardy because of his strong stance. The Canadian Abortion Rights Action League (CARAL) was founded in 1974, by a number of pro-choice activists including Norma Scarborough, Eleanor Wright Pelrine, and Judy Rebick. I participated on The Issue Is Choice committee, which sponsored events and raised funds for Dr. Morgentaler's legal defence and I also was involved on strategy committees to deal with the continuing battle to maintain the legality of abortions. When issues arose and I got a call or note seeking my attendance, I showed up if I could, as did many others in the women's community.[194] As a lawyer, I was in a position to understand the legal issues, and the media platform I had established allowed me to contribute to keeping the public informed.

Morgentaler's legal challenges culminated in 1988, when the Supreme Court of Canada ruled that the law that prohibited abortion, unless it was approved by a hospital committee of three doctors after proof that the mother's life or health was in danger, was unconstitutional under the principles of the 1982 Charter of Rights and Freedoms. It was determined that this law restricted a woman's right to control her own reproductive life, which infringed her constitutionally protected guarantees to security of the person, to liberty, and to freedom of conscience. As a result, abortion was decriminalized and the choice as to whether or not to have an abortion was left to the woman and her own doctor. The most compelling words in the judgment were those of the first female Supreme Court of Canada justice, Bertha Wilson. For me—and I'm sure for many others—Justice Wilson spoke for women that day in bringing into play the Charter guarantees of liberty and freedom of conscience:

> It is probably impossible for a man to respond, even imaginatively, to such a dilemma, not just because it is outside the realm of his personal experience (although this is, of course, the case) but because he can relate to it only by objectifying it, thereby eliminating the subjective elements of the female psyche which are at the heart of the dilemma.

No male consent needed for abortion

By Linda Silver Dranoff
Special to The Star

The media and courts have treated recent abortion-injunction cases as if they represent a brand new issue arising as a result of the absence of an abortion law. In fact, men have been bringing these applications for injunctions since abortion was legalized in this country more than 20 years ago. The absence of an abortion law is irrelevant and all the public attention paid to the case of Barbara Dodd and others is no justification for a new federal abortion law.

Dodd, 22, has been the focus of attention since her boyfriend Gregory Murphy, 23, took steps to obtain a court injunction to stop her having an abortion in Ontario.

The fact is that there is not now, nor has there ever been, a law saying that a pregnant woman, in order to get an abortion, needs the consent of the man who impregnated her (be he husband, boyfriend or casual lover).

No such paternal consent requirement existed under the old law, which stipulated only that a hospital committee of three doctors must consent. No consent requirement can be assumed by the courts unless legislated.

Some men have been successful in using the court system as a club in this guerrilla warfare against a woman's access to abortion. These scattered "victories" are not precedents. But a precedent-setting Ontario case (Medhurst, 1984) concluded that the husband had no right in law to require that his consent be sought or that he even be consulted.

The Supreme Court of Canada made it very clear what it thinks of consent requirements in a January, 1988, decision favoring Dr. Henry Morgentaler. The court struck down the old law, ruling that the requirement of committee consent breached Charter of Rights guarantees.

Chief Justice Brian Dickson spoke of abortion controls as a profound interference with a woman's constitutional guarantees of personal security. Madame Justice Bertha Wilson wrote of a pregnant woman's right to have the liberty to follow her own conscience.

In compelling words, Wilson pointed out that "it is probably impossible for a man to respond, even imaginatively, to such a dilemma not just because it is outside the realm of his personal experience (although this is, of course, the case) but because he can relate to it only by objectifying it, thereby eliminating the subjective elements of the female psyche which are at the heart of the dilemma."

In this context, when the law was so very clear, and direction had been given at the highest levels of the judicial system, the trusting public must wonder what went wrong in Mr. Justice O'Driscoll's court in the Dodd case and in Mr. Justice Viens court in the Daigle case in Quebec.

When one side is unrepresented, should the judge have an obligation to know the law? Should the lawyer representing the father have an obligation to present the other side of the case? Should there be a judicial management system to supervise the judges? A judicial training institute to ensure that judges apply decided law rather than create law? Should judges be trained to distinguish between the law and their personal predispositions? How do we get judges to apply Supreme Court of Canada decisions?

Think of what would happen if a woman were forced to have a child on the premise that the husband would raise the child. The fact is that the law does not require the husband to take custody although it gives him the privilege of asking for it.

Think, too, of the implications for men if the same rights of control over the male procreative function were given to women. Would men think it fair if they had to seek a woman's consent to them getting a vasectomy?

A new law is not needed at all; nor did the Supreme Court of Canada in the Morgentaler case "invite" a new law. All that happened is that one member of the court said, in an *obiter dicta* (an aside, a by-the-way, which binds no one), that Parliament could conceivably think up some kind of fetal-protective legislation which would not offend the Constitution.

Surely it is time to recognize that laws preventing abortion are an exercise in futility because women will have abortions anyway.

If society limits access to safe abortions, women with money will find a way to have safe abortions, while poor women will be forced to have unsafe abortions or deliver unwanted children. And who will care for these children in a world where child care is often unavailable and too many need food banks in order to eat?

LINDA SILVER DRANOFF: Toronto family lawyer is the author of *Every Woman's Guide To The Law.*

This piece made sure a woman knew that she did not need her husband or boyfriend's consent if she chose to secure an abortion. It was published in the *Toronto Star* July 22, 1989.

After the 1988 Supreme Court of Canada case, Dr. Morgentaler opened clinics in many places across Canada to provide safe medical abortions. He challenged in the courts those provincial governments that tried to close him down or deny health plan coverage to women for abortion services.

Access to Abortion

The next challenge was the delivery of abortion services. After decriminalization, it was up to the provinces to provide abortion services to their own citizens. Elinor Caplan, who was at that time minister of health in David Peterson's Liberal government, told me how Ontario's policy came about. The day the Supreme Court of Canada decision was released, she knew the media would be asking for Ontario's view. The premier was in Switzerland at a conference, and she did not think it advisable to delay taking a position until he returned. So she went into the media scrum and announced that Ontario would respect the Supreme Court of Canada decision and that the Ontario Health Insurance Plan (OHIP) would pay for abortions at those hospitals that provided them. The headlines were "OHIP will pay." When Peterson returned a few days later, he quietly chided her for acting without consulting him or the cabinet, and she apologized. As she said to me, "On this one, I would rather ask for forgiveness than permission." She told me that this was a highlight of her career. For me, it emphasized just how important it is for right-thinking women to be in positions of power and influence inside the government. Elinor Caplan had been there for women before. A steering committee[195] (on which I served in 1987–88) to create a centre for women's health—to be open twenty-four hours a day, focus on women's well-being, and provide access to abortions— had secured her support. A centre was eventually put in place. Again in 1987, she "forcefully backed the establishment of a women's health care clinic at Peterborough's Civic Hospital" to include abortions in the face of objections by doctors, but with the support of a local community referendum. The *Toronto Star* applauded this as "a gutsy action from the rookie health minister."[196]

Throughout his life, Dr. Henry Morgentaler maintained his determined efforts to provide legal and safe abortion services to women, and all Canadian women are in his debt. I was very proud when he was made a member of the Order of Canada in 2008, despite strong opposition from the anti-choice forces. He had truly made an extraordinary contribution to Canadian women and families.

Whose Consent Is Required?

Even after the Supreme Court of Canada decision in 1988, some men continued to try to prevent their partners from having an abortion. I thought, *Not again! Don't they know that only the woman's consent is required?* I had learned that back in law school, where I wrote a paper in 1972 for a class on legal philosophy entitled "The Philosophical Implications of the Legal Presence in Matters of Abortion." I focused on a case in the headlines of a woman whose husband sought an injunction against her, her doctors, and the hospital to prevent her from aborting her fetus without his consent. The woman and her husband already had three children, and she had permission from the hospital abortion committee. The husband, the judge, and the hospital all assumed that the husband's consent was needed. The judge granted the injunction, and the woman, unrepresented by counsel, caved in "for the sake of peace in the family," as she was quoted to say.

I felt that the legal system had been used as a club and not as a measured, rational application of the rule of law. I believed then, as I do now, that a woman can be trusted to make a responsible decision about an abortion, and that the decision is a difficult one. I don't think anyone other than the woman, in consultation with those she chooses, should be making decisions about her body. Even though I thankfully never had to make that choice myself, some women do, and I wanted them to have the power to do so within the law. Indeed, I questioned whether the legal system should ever be involved in decisions about abortion.

But the issue of consent kept surfacing. In 1989, Guy Tremblay persuaded a Quebec court to order an injunction to stop his girl-friend's scheduled abortion, and it made headlines across Canada. I immediately wrote an op-ed piece, published by the *Toronto Star* and headlined "No male consent needed for abortion."[197] I wanted to make sure readers knew what the law actually was.

The girlfriend, Chantal Daigle, appealed the ruling to the Quebec Court of Appeal, but it was upheld, so she appealed further to the Supreme Court of Canada, which granted an emergency hearing. Finally, the highest court overturned the injunction. By then, however, Ms. Daigle had taken the law into her own hands. She had no time to wait—she was near the end of the first trimester, the safest time to have an abortion. She went to the United States and had the abortion a week before the Supreme Court made its ruling. But the court did settle the law about consent, and did rule *definitively* that a husband or boyfriend had no right to prevent his partner from having an abortion.

Another Law?

Still, the battle wasn't over. Brian Mulroney's government tried twice to replace the law struck down as unconstitutional in 1988 and brought back into the public eye by the *Tremblay* v. *Daigle* case. In 1988, the government came up with a bill that would have prohib-ited all abortions *except* when the woman's life was endangered, and only if one doctor agreed in the earlier stages of pregnancy and two doctors agreed in the subsequent stages.

A group calling itself Canadians for Choice joined forces in the 1980s, and we worked with Dr. Henry Morgentaler to raise funds, provide moral support, respond to the court cases regarding consent to abortion, and challenge the necessity of any new law on abortion.

The group organized a major campaign to fight the proposed legislation, including full-page newspaper ads and the preparation of briefs to parliamentary committees; it was supported by many organizations. The Canadians for Choice steering committee was composed of Harriet Bomza, Linda Bronfman, June Callwood, Myra Sable Davidson, Selma Edelstone, Suzanne Grew Ellis, Florence Mintz Geneen, Jane Hill, Nancy Ruth Jackman, Michele Landsberg, Marilou McPhedran, Norma Scarborough, and me. Canadians for Choice itself was a coalition of major organizations and individuals who believed in a woman's right to freedom of choice and equitable access regarding abortion. The organizations included the Canadian Association of Sexual Assault Centres, Canadian Labour Congress, Canadian Abortion Rights Action League, Canadian Union of Public Employees, Law Union, National Action Committee on the Status of Women, National Association of Women and the Law, Physicians for Choice, and more. Members also included Rebecca Cook, Bernard Dickens, Susan Fish, Margo Lane, and Dr. Henry Morgentaler.

Mulroney's first attempt to pass the legislation failed to make it past the House of Commons. I have always been proud of the fact that it was an almost-unanimous vote against this bill by women of all parties that helped to defeat it. I've always wanted women to act together in sisterhood. While there are, of course, a variety of views among women, I feel that if women can find a way to stick together, nothing but good will come of it. This has not happened as often as I would have liked, but on that day in August 1988, the women in Parliament stuck together and were a critical factor in swinging the vote. This was at a time, remember, when there were 253 male members in the House and only twenty-nine women members, so obviously there were a good number of sensible men also affecting the outcome. Canada became the only country in the world with no law limiting abortions.

In 1989, while the *Tremblay* v. *Daigle* case was before the Supreme Court of Canada—but before the decision was made—the Mulroney government tried yet again to make abortion an offence under the Criminal Code. The proposed law would have re-criminalized abortion and reinstated a "doctor's consent" requirement. Public outcry by both the pro-choice sympathizers and the anti-abortion forces stoked up the heat of the debate.

In a letter to the editor of the *Toronto Star*, I challenged the government's apparent haste to write a new abortion law.

> Why is the federal government rushing to enact abortion legislation? Why not wait for the Supreme Court of Canada decision in the Daigle case? Why not accept that a law exists (i.e., the 1988 Supreme Court of Canada decision on Morgentaler)? Why doesn't the government take a thoughtful approach and wait for its new Royal Commission on Reproductive Technologies to consider and report before casting in stone a new law? Haste on this issue is likely to cause more trouble than it will cure.[198]

In the March 1990 issue of *Chatelaine*, my column on the legal implications for women of this further proposed legislation concluded that as far as I was concerned, whatever law the government might introduce would be declared unconstitutional by the Supreme Court of Canada.

In 1990, Canadians for Choice prepared and presented a brief to the Parliamentary Committee on Bill C-43, "An Act Respecting Abortion," which was signed by the steering committee. There was much public and parliamentary debate, and a vote in the House of Commons favoured (but by only nine votes) re-criminalizing abortion. However, the bill that went to the Senate in January 1991 resulted in a tie vote. As a consequence, the bill did *not* pass, and the federal government decided to abandon further lawmaking on the subject. Despite whispers and threats, no subsequent government has sought to re-open the debate.

· · · · · · · · ·

We had come through the 1980s having achieved many advances for women in the law. We had full equality in family law legislation; we had a minister appointed in Ontario to be responsible in the inner circles of government for the status of women; pay equity laws were in place; abortion had been decriminalized and the choice to abort or not was up to the pregnant woman; men and women shared their contributions to the Canada Pension Plan; women had equal rights with men under the Charter of Rights and Freedoms; victims of domestic violence had greater protection; sexual assault laws were modernized; we had seen the Meech Lake and Charlottetown Accords defeated. And we had organizations such as LEAF, NAC, and NAWL in place to help guard what we had achieved.

We had made strides. But we had also inflamed a backlash. Just two examples illustrate what we had to face by the end of this decade. Edward Greenspan, a prominent criminal defence lawyer, started making speeches in 1986 alleging that feminists were intimidating the judges and taking over the agenda. He was still at it a decade later when in 1999 he wrote an angry, intemperate letter in the *National Post* regarding a judgment by Supreme Court of Canada justice Claire L'Heureux-Dubé, concluding that "the feminist perspective has hijacked the Supreme Court."[199] He could not have been more wrong. It was always challenging to push back against the stubborn forces of bias as our advances seemed to threaten some people. In fact, as Constance Backhouse noted,[200] his was "an attack on every effort that feminists had made to create a fairer legal framework for sexual assault...and a massive misreading of decades of law reform work."

And then on December 6, 1989, at the École Polytechnique de Montréal, a twenty-five-year-old lone gunman named Marc Lépine massacred fourteen female engineering students, claiming he did so to fight feminism. During his rampage, he separated the women in a classroom from fifty men and told the men to leave. They did, leading feminist and physicist Ursula Franklin to ask why fifty men had abandoned their fellow students and made no effort to intervene or subdue one crazed individual.[201] This horrific event is commemorated annually on December 6 as the National Day of Remembrance and Action on Violence Against Women, established in 1991 by the Canadian Parliament.

We could not let these setbacks stop us. We had made gains. Now it was important to protect and enhance them. This was easier said than done.

Rosemary Speirs, Elinor Caplan

Nancy Ruth Jackman, Beth Atcheson

Ethel Teitelbaum, Dian Forsey, Sylvia Bashevkin, Dorothy Davey, Linda Silver Dranoff, Ceta Ramkhalawansingh

Linda Nye, Laurel Ritchie

Norma Scarborough, Shelagh Wilkinson

Jean Townsend, Linda Silver Dranoff   Mary Cornish, Pat Hacker, Kay Macpherson

Linda Silver Dranoff, Helen Lucas, Kay Sigurjonsson

Elisabeth Sachs, Lynne Sullivan, Marilou McPhedran   Beth Symes

Norma Scarborough, Virginia Rock, Michelle Swenarchuk, Shelagh Wilkinson, Nancy Ruth Jackman,
Kathleen O'Neil, Doris Anderson, Linda Silver Dranoff, Sally Armstrong, Judith Finlayson, Laurel Ritchie

PART 4

RESISTANCE AND RESOLVE, 1989–

Chapter 12
AT A CROSSROADS

It was 1989 and I had been in practice for fifteen years. My clients, I believe, knew me as a caring and conscientious advocate. I was breaking new ground in my profession and was an active member of the women's movement. I was still writing a monthly column for *Chatelaine* after ten years and had published two books. I was active in TV, radio, and public appearances and was a continuing regular on *City Line*. I played a role in many of the issues arising from cases being decided and legislation being floated. I contributed to public policy discussions such as the Free Trade debate in 1988—I thought the Free Trade Agreement was not good for Canada.

I certainly was busy. I recently found among my papers a summary of my work in 1988 outside the practice of law. In addition to the above, it added up to twenty-three TV and radio appearances, one feature article in *Chatelaine*, three op-ed pieces for the *Toronto Star*, and one for the *Globe and Mail*, five speeches, a presentation to lawyers at a Law Society program, and one to educators at a Women in Educational Administration conference. I also spent two three-week stints at the Leighton Artist Colony at Banff in 1988 and again in 1989, to combine a vacation with a chance to write uninterrupted and in a beautiful natural setting.

FAMILY LIFE
As always, I set aside time for my family. Beth was completing her education in political science and journalism and was preparing to

live independently. I had been an active and involved mother as she grew up, but still, I had worried that the intensity of my professional and outside commitments would affect her. It turned out that I had nothing to worry about, according to a "report card" she unexpectedly gave me when she attended a feminist Passover Seder dinner held at our home. After dinner, the women were sitting around chatting and the conversation turned to their feelings of guilt over not having enough time for their children. Beth reassured them. "My mother was a single parent from the time I was a year and a half and she was very busy, what with law school and all, and I feel I turned out okay," she told them. "I didn't suffer because of it. There *is* such a thing as quality time." Boy, did I feel good! I had passed that test with flying colours, according to my own daughter. I had raised an independent-minded and smart feminist daughter who was also kind and compassionate, charming, and lots of fun. I was even more relieved when, several years later, she chose to marry Opher, a fine man with feminist views who took on his fair share of the household and child-care work.

My mother had passed away in 1987, and my family grieved for its matriarch. Gradually, I took on the role of helping keep our close and loving family together. Our family had grown. My siblings, our spouses, and children could barely fit at a large dining room table. My sister, Judy, and her husband, Bill, had a daughter, Shaina, and I was bestowed the title of honorary grandmother. I took my new role seriously.

I got into the habit of calling my dad every evening between 10 and 11 p.m. to make sure he was okay and to hear about his day and tell him about mine. It was a responsibility I happily took on, and from which I benefited. Dad had maintained a watchful eye and deep interest in me through the years, and we had great discussions.

PROFESSIONAL CHOICES

In 1988, the lease on my downtown office space was coming up for renewal, and in the face of substantial increases in rental costs, I had to decide whether to sign another five-year lease or buy an office condominium so that I could stabilize the costs. I knew that if I bought an office, I was limiting my options; I would not be able to expand the practice without selling and relocating, and I would

be making it more complicated if I chose to seek a judicial appointment, run for politics, or join a large law firm.

Judith Huddart and Linda at the Law Society Medal Ceremony and reception, 2006

I had often been asked whether I was interested in becoming a judge. Certainly, more women were advancing to the bench in the 1980s and also entering politics. I had considered both, but did not pursue either. As time passed, I knew that the decision must be made once and for all, and in the context of deciding about my office, I decided my future. I concluded that I liked to be in control of my own life far too much to work in a large organization where my time would be controlled and my ability to speak out would be limited. Judges need to be seen as objective, which would have required me to hold my tongue about my personal views.

Then there was politics. I have always had an interest in public policy and made an effort over the years to contribute to public discourse as an interested citizen. However, I had decided early on that I could be most effective in the advancement of women's equality and law reforms by trying to influence public policy as an engaged citizen. As a politician, I would have had to choose a political party and stand up for its positions and follow the leader's directions, not necessarily advocate for the public interest as I saw it.

If I joined a large law firm (I had received several such invitations over the years; I was seen as a "rainmaker"—one who could attract clients to the firm), I would have had to work unconscionably long hours, take in clients I didn't necessarily want to represent, be responsible as a partner for the errors of others, and possibly be prevented from my social justice and law reform activities.

Thankfully, I had figured out how to do everything I wanted to do under the mantle of my own small law firm. I had put myself in a position where I could accomplish more from where I was. As a lawyer, writer, and activist, I felt that I could contribute more to my society (and do so more openly) than I could as a judge or a politician. So I bought an office condo large enough for a three-lawyer firm, and that is where I practised—as my own boss—for the rest of my law career. Judith Huddart, who had been with me since her Call to the Bar in 1982, eventually became a partner. It was a happy association based on trust and compatibility of values, as we thought alike and practised together amicably.

PERSONAL CHOICES

I had settled in and figured my life would continue in its well-established pattern. Then everything changed. Jack Marmer, the forensic accountant whom I had retained as an expert on many of my family law cases, separated from his wife and, a couple of months later, asked me out for lunch, which he transformed into dinner on a Saturday evening. It was a surprising evening. Jack and I had worked together periodically for about seven years, and I knew him on a professional basis as a brilliant and caring man of integrity. But that evening revealed more about the man, and I was intrigued. I thought of my Aunt Sally's optimistic words when I would, over the years, express resignation about meeting a worthy husband. She said, "Let life surprise you." It truly did.

We began to date each other exclusively, and our personal compatibility was evident from the outset. He introduced me to his three children and their spouses, his mother and sister, and their families, who were warm and welcoming to me and mine. My daughter met him early in our relationship and liked him; so did the rest of my family.

It did not take long for Jack to ask me to marry him. I needed time to think it through. Falling in love wasn't enough for me—the marriage had to make sense on all kinds of levels. I had seen in my professional as well as my personal life what could go amiss if the wrong decision was made. He had to understand that I was not a traditional woman of his generation and would not be a traditional wife. He had to be an equal and accept me as a peer.

I was scheduled to leave for my writing vacation shortly after Jack's proposal. The Banff retreat gave me time and a peaceful setting in which to consider my future. Jack was eight years older than me, but was surprisingly open, flexible, and fair-minded for a man of his generation. He was successful in his own right, and his ego didn't require him to disparage me to elevate himself. Jack appreciated and respected me for who I was. It was fortunate that we had come to know each other as congenial professionals. Without that history, I doubt that I would have risked a personal relationship. Also, I was relieved that he had been raised, lived, and worked in Toronto. I would not have considered another long-distance relationship.

When I returned to Toronto from Banff, I said yes. We negotiated our marriage contract ourselves, and the process turned out to be an eye-opener. When we analyzed the cause of disagreement on several thorny issues, it became clear that I was negotiating for him and he was negotiating for me. While we each wanted to protect ourselves if anything went wrong, we still wanted the outcome to be fair to both of us. This has, in fact, been a hallmark of our marriage. It was also, I now believe, a result of our experience in our professional practices. Jack's forte was not only to provide his lawyer clients with information, but also to find a financial solution that would promote settlement. I knew how to settle differences without causing a war. With that level of know-how, combined with vast stores of goodwill, we put our own contract together readily.

We married the following year. We chose one of the first female rabbis to officiate. Beth was my maid of honour and Jack's eldest son, Mark, was his best man. Jack and I were the only speakers at the lively party that followed the synagogue service. I was sorry that my mother did not live to meet Jack; I know she would have liked him. My mother, who was a role model for tolerance and strength of character, had always wanted a good marriage for me, as in her view it was the most important thing in life. I think she would have been pleased to know that I had a good marriage, eventually, and just as pleased that I had managed to combine it with a career that allowed me to contribute to my society. However, my dad was very much present at the wedding and beaming from ear to ear. He liked Jack and felt that with this marriage, all was right in my world. I added to my busy life the roles of wife and stepmother, and wonderful relationships with Jack's children, Paula and Alan, Shawn and Barbara, Mark and Leslie.

Fast forward twenty-seven years. Jack and I have a happy and successful marriage, and our families joined together harmoniously. Given my professional experience, I know how unusual this is and consider myself extremely fortunate. It is ironic and amazing that I ended up experiencing a full and eventful career while also enjoying a large and loving family. Now, I am a mother and stepmother to four, mother-in-law to four, grandmother to eight, and great-grandmother to two. Having it all was improbable, and I feel inordinately lucky that it all came together for me.

The grandchildren in 2003: (first row) Robert; (second row, l to r) Aaron, Benjamin, Kevin, Zak, Laura, Maxwell; (third row) Leah

Linda at the Parliament Hill statue
of the Famous Five after receiving
the Governor General's Award in
Commemoration of the Persons Case,
October 2001

Speaking after the presentation of
the Governor General's Award in
Commemoration of the Persons Case,
October 2001

AS IF THAT WASN'T ENOUGH...

The achievements in my personal and professional lives were deeply fulfilling, and it was hard to imagine how life could get any better. But then the legal community, the women's movement, and the world beyond began to honour my contributions.

I was surprised at the level of recognition I received. After all, I did not choose a traditional career path or goals. Normally a person does not earn kudos by working for women's legal equality and social justice. And yet, even the establishment at the highest levels ended up acknowledging the importance of these issues and my contributions to them. In a way, this showed that it is possible to live the life that is meaningful to you, instead of the life that meets the expectations of others—and to be respected for it.

The legal profession honoured me: the Canadian Bar Association–Ontario (CBA-O) in 1993 with an Award for Distinguished Service, its Family Law Section Award of Excellence in 2003, and the Feminist Legal Analysis Section's Award for Commitment to Equality in 2005. The ultimate tribute from the legal profession was the Law Society Medal in 2006, the highest honour given by lawyers to a very few lawyers "for service according to the highest ideals of the legal profession." The legal profession came through for me.

I was given honours that specifically recognized my contribution to Canadian women and girls, such as a 1995 YWCA Toronto Women of Distinction Award; the City of Toronto appreciation, in 2004, in honour of the seventy-fifth anniversary of the Persons Case; and the Women's Legal Education and Action Fund (LEAF) recognition, in 2010, in honour of the twenty-fifth anniversary of the founding of the organization and my contribution to equality rights.

I particularly cherish the memory of being one of the five women recipients in 2001 of the annual Governor General's Award in commemoration of the Persons Case from then governor general Adrienne Clarkson. The award celebrated the efforts of the five Canadian women who won the court challenge in 1929 that finally included women in the definition of "persons" in law. At the reception following the ceremony, my father was so pumped with pride that he greeted Governor General Adrienne Clarkson with so much

Joseph Silver, Linda's dad, greeting
Governor General Adrienne Clarkson
enthusiastically at the reception
following the presentation of the
Governor General's Award in
Commemoration of the Persons Case

warmth that he leaned forward and gave her a kiss. I told him that he was breaching protocol, but the governor general was very gracious—she smiled and responded to him with warmth and kindness. This was one of the award events that allowed a recipient more than a handful of guests, and eighteen of my family members came to Ottawa for the celebration—what a great day that was! Jack's son Mark followed it up by presenting me with a framed commemoration of the event, which I treasure.

And then in 2012, I was thrilled to receive the Order of Canada, Canada's highest civilian honour "for a lifetime of outstanding achievement, dedication to the community, and service to the nation…they have all enriched the lives of others and made a difference to this country." The ceremony

ORDER OF CANADA CITATION

Linda Silver Dranoff has been instrumental in advancing equality in Canadian family law. As a lawyer, she has argued many precedent-setting cases that have directly benefited women by recognizing marriage as a social and financial partnership. Notably, her lobbying efforts resulted in essential reforms to family law legislation, including equal sharing of all matrimonial property between spouses following a separation or death, and automatic cost-of-living adjustments in support payments. As well, she has written several books and a long-running law column in *Chatelaine* magazine aimed at average Canadians, helping to make our laws more accessible and widely understood.

paid tribute to Canadians whose contributions embodied the motto of the Order of Canada: *They desire a better country*. My father was not alive for this one, nor was my brother Marty. My mother didn't live to see me receive any honours. But I know that they would have joined Judy, Stevie and Sandy, Laura, Beth and Opher, and the rest of the family in being overjoyed at this extraordinary recognition for a lifetime of contribution in the public sphere to our wonderful country. None of this had been foreseeable, which made it all the more unforgettable.

Linda received the Order of Canada
from Governor General David
Johnston at a ceremony held at
Rideau Hall, May 2014.

Chapter 13
THE STRUGGLE TO
SUSTAIN PROPERTY SHARING

Yes, we came through the 1980s having achieved many advances for women in the law. But it became increasingly apparent that for every advance, there was a retreat, for every achievement there was a need to be watchful to ensure that the gains were enduring. The best examples and those closest to my daily life were in family law, where new challenges arose all the time and where I had new reasons to dig in my heels for the rights of women.

After the Family Law Act became law in 1986, I set about using it as a tool in my daily practice. It did not take long to experience the resistance of some spouses and their lawyers, and even a few judges, which made me realize that the battle for equal sharing of family property was far from over. It had just moved to a different battleground.

Once the law was in the wind, some wealthy spouses turned to lawyers and accountants to find a way out of sharing with their wives. Some recommended transferring assets into a trust and naming the children as beneficiaries and the husband as sole controlling trustee. Others came up with inventive interpretations of the FLA, finding or creating loopholes in the law that might intimidate the other spouse into backing off.

Some lawyers failed to even acknowledge the law—the lawyer would vigorously assert an untenable position in order to pander to a client's unreasonable expectations. This would cause apprehensiveness and insecurity in the other spouse. I recall one instance when I was arguing with a fellow lawyer that stock options should be valued as income and not as a capital asset. Not only did he challenge the assertion, he also ridiculed my reading of the Act. Shortly after our conversation, I came across a very recent article in a professional journal on the subject of stock options that confirmed my interpretation and contradicted his. The very same lawyer had written the article! When I called him on it, he refused to concede, and so the issue could not be resolved without a trial.

THE LEGAL SYSTEM AS A CLUB

Others found lawyers who were willing to use the legal process as a sledgehammer to slow down and make torturous the inevitable, hoping their client's wife would give up either in exhaustion or after having spent all of her money on legal costs. In these cases, clients had to hang tough and rely on the courts to help them get justice; they had to withstand the threats of their mates and the obduracy of their mates' lawyers.

I was taken aback sometimes by the vigour and aggressiveness of the negative response by some to the FLA. I had a memorable case that demonstrated to me just how far a husband would go, especially if he had a supportive and inventive lawyer. It also demonstrated how determined the female client had to be to stand up to the personal rigours of living in the midst of conflict.

Elisa Van Bork came to see me in 1986, two years after she and her husband had separated following thirty-one years of marriage and three children. The couple had immigrated together to Canada from Holland in the 1950s. They had established and worked together in their family lighting business, which she helped operate from the basement of their home. Her previous lawyer had allowed the case to languish after starting divorce proceedings. Her husband was voluntarily giving her modest support of $2,250 a month, but keeping from her the significant assets registered in her name. He controlled their finances with a tight fist, as if everything belonged to him alone. I took on her case hoping to be able to settle it. The Family Law Act had been proclaimed earlier that year, and I amended her Petition for Divorce to add claims to share property under the FLA. I suspect this took the husband by surprise; he certainly reacted strongly to the proceedings.

While the lawsuit was in process, financial decisions still had to be made and the couple's investments managed. They had used some of their savings to lend money out in exchange for mortgages. They had each declared on tax returns half the income they had received from these mortgages. As these matured and the borrowers wanted to pay them off, the husband pressured the wife to sign each discharge document and allow him to receive all the money. She asked that her share of the proceeds be paid to her. He warned the mortgagors of dire consequences if they talked to me, provided me with information, or paid his wife anything. Each mortgagor (the person who owes the money on the mortgage and whose property serves as collateral to the mortgage loan) was forced to bring legal action to get his mortgage discharged. The courts ordered the mortgages discharged, with payment made to both the husband and wife. So the husband appealed the rulings. The couple also had invested in land syndication groups, and the husband threatened to sue anyone in the syndication group who provided me with information or his wife with money. He took the position that where his wife's name was on title, she held the property in trust for him, although she had not signed any written agreements to this effect.

He refused to share the income from the lighting business with her, although she had worked in the business, behaved as a partner, and had declared half the business income on her tax return. He alleged for the purpose of her family law claim that she was not his business partner, even though during their marriage he had declared her as his partner for tax purposes, and Revenue Canada, after an audit, accepted her partnership status.

He even changed the locks to a recreational farm property outside Toronto that was owned entirely in his wife's name. After she tried to enter this unoccupied property, he reported to the police that there had been a "break and enter," and the police came to interview her. Of course, they did not pursue it when they learned she was the owner, but it showed how far her husband was prepared to go to intimidate and defeat her.

He refused to detail and document all of their assets, which would have helped his wife to pursue her case, even though the law required it and court orders had ruled that he comply. In response to a motion seeking production of specific documents, I was told

Law can leave spouse in a bind

By Linda Silver Dranoff
Special to The Star

There must be something wrong with family law "reform" when a hard-working 61-year-old farm wife and mother of six loses her rightful share of the $5 million dollar farm she and her husband struggled to build.

Gordon Atkinson, 69, a Barrie-area farmer, had sole title to the farm and, during their marriage, pledged it without his wife Ruth's knowledge as security for a $3.5 million bank loan, which he invested and lost in the stock market.

When Ruth Atkinson and the bank vied for rights to the farm, the court, in a recent decision in Barrie, gave the bank priority.

Now a $200-a-week sales clerk with no assets to her name, she is meeting her expenses with the help of one of her children.

The average person must instinctively feel that the result is unfair. But the court had no choice. The current Family Law Act was clear. The law does not protect the rights of the spouse during the marriage unless that spouse has legal title as owner or part-owner. Nor does it prevent one spouse incurring debt without the consent of the other. You can do what you want with your own property.

What the law does is require the spouses to calculate their assets (less debts) at date of separation and the one with a greater share of the assets must write a cheque to the other to equalize their shares. No lender need protect the potential rights of the other spouse.

The lack of protection for the spouse without title to assets, usually women but not always, is a disgrace. Family laws have changed twice in Ontario in recent years, once in 1978 and again in 1986. But none of the reforms have, during the marriage, guaranteed fairness for spouses, nor protected assets other than the home from improper use by the spouse with title.

What protection exists relates only to the matrimonial home. A lender must ensure that a spouse agrees to any transfer or mortgage of a property that he should know is a "matrimonial home". And when the home is only in the name of one spouse, you can register on title the fact it is a matrimonial home to forewarn of the need for the spouse's consent.

What's the solution? A change in the law would help. The question is, how strict and strong must our laws become to provide true protection to avowed marital partners?

The most straightforward option is a true Community of Property system which shares property from Day One of marriage. This marital property regime considers all property accumulated by either spouse to be jointly owned, managed and controlled. Neither partner could do anything with family property without the consent of the other. This option has never been seriously debated in Ontario, but it may be the only way to maintain joint control during the marriage, unless greater protections are built into the existing system.

A less severe solution would be to require the signature of both spouses before permitting any sale or mortgaging of property owned by a married person.

So laws could be passed. But the history of family law shows that laws can be circumvented, most notably by marriage contracts, which have become the way many rich, and even not so rich, marrying persons avoid the family law requirement of equal sharing. Or a court's restrictive interpretation of the legislation can result in receipt of less than 50 per cent.

The other and more immediate solution is for non-owner spouses, particularly women, to watch out for their own interests.

How do you do this? Make sure your name is also on title to every single piece of property owned by the family. This way, your signature will be needed before any mortgages or sales can be made. You won't need the law to protect you; you will have protected yourself.

Sign a marriage contract before any indication of trouble, requiring shared ownership of all property. And if your spouse won't agree to this, wonder what kind of a "partner" he will make. If he says, "Honey, trust me," run for the hills. And if he later says, once your name is on title, "Sign here" on an official-looking document, read it carefully, and consult your own lawyer before signing.

Become a true partner, and don't assume "it's ours, honey" just because he says so. See it on title and keep a copy of the document.

If separated wives of the future should learn anything from this case, it's that you can't assume either your mate or the law will take care of you. You must take care of yourself. But it would be nice if the law would take more of a hand.

☐ Linda Silver Dranoff is a Toronto family lawyer, Chatelaine columnist and author of Everywoman's Guide To The Law.

From the *Toronto Star* July 7, 1988

to come to his lawyer's office and pick out what we wanted. When I got there, I found forty-two boxes of old bills and receipts—mostly junk—and was told to go through them to find what I needed, if I could. In the face of a court order to produce completed tax returns, he filed and produced blank returns containing only his name and signature, which made it impossible to evaluate his true financial position.

In the six years it took to move the case to trial, there were ten orders made by masters and fifteen orders made by judges. There were three orders arising from appeals. Once judges made orders, it was up to the husband's lawyer and me to agree on the precise wording. This too presented challenges. We could rarely agree, so we had to schedule meetings with the court registrars whose job it was to resolve the wording of judges' orders. There were numerous appearances by both Mr. and Mrs. Van Bork for examinations before trial, many of which occurred only after orders were made to compel attendance. Just before trial, Mr. Van Bork brought four more motions that were adjourned to be dealt with by the trial judge.

This husband and his lawyer did everything they could to try to intimidate the wife and, when that did not work, he and his lawyer focused on me. First his lawyer registered a complaint against me with the Law Society of Upper Canada, and then tried to get the court to defer all proceedings until the Law Society completed their investigation. The Law Society refused to get involved. Then they brought a motion to the court asking that I be found in contempt. While the judge hearing the argument dismissed it, I still had to prepare written material and turn up to argue the case, which added time and expense. These actions looked to me like efforts to "persuade" me to drop the case, given how vigorously I was championing my client's interests. It accomplished the opposite result: I dug in my heels.

Before trial, I amended the petition again, adding claims to penalize the husband for his extreme use of bullying tactics during the years it took to get the case to trial. A claim was added for damages for breach of fiduciary duty, on the basis that Mr. Van Bork had an obligation to manage funds that were in Mrs. Van Bork's name in her interest and not his. A request was included for punitive damages, a remedy for high-handed conduct. An application was made for compounded pre-judgment interest because Mr. Van Bork had thwarted her access to her capital at the same time as it was increasing in value.

It took until just before trial and a judge's order before the husband even delivered a response to the amended petition with his position on the Family Law Act issues. Mr. Van Bork had not complied with court orders for production of information, and there was no reason to believe this would change. I had no choice but to proceed to trial despite the absence of most of the information I had wanted. I decided that the efforts we had gone through unproductively would prove to the judge the husband's flagrant disregard of his legal obligations.

This was probably the worst case I ever dealt with. The combative bully manoeuvres seemed to be aimed at making my client drop the case because she could not afford to continue the battle. Right and justice and law were irrelevant in this scenario. I believe their assumption was that no lawyer would or could continue to battle a case that was so difficult, expensive, and time-consuming. Indeed, the case stretched the resources of our small three-person firm to the limit, and past it. My client had no access to funds with which to pay me, and her husband was doing everything possible to stop her getting any. I kept the case because otherwise Mrs. Van Bork would have ended up destitute. The new Family Law Act would have been of little use to her, as she would not have been able to afford to go to trial to get a court order. Having achieved the FLA, I simply could not let it be defeated by a campaign of intimidation.

It was late November 1992 before we got to trial in front of Madam Justice Ellen Macdonald, who had been a family lawyer prior to becoming a judge. The trial lasted twenty-six days at intervals, concluding May 7, 1993. The longest interval was caused by Mr. Van Bork's lawyer's dispute as to the authenticity of a document that had been signed by Mrs. Van Bork. The judge permitted a delay of several months in order to allow him to secure expert evidence. When we finally returned to court, his so-called expert's credibility was discredited. But in the meantime, I had to hire my own expert. Once again, I had to bring myself back up to speed, and once again, the costs of the trial mounted.

Judgment was issued six months later, on November 19, 1993. Justice Macdonald saw Mr. Van Bork for exactly what he was, and said so in her judgment:

> When Mr. Van Bork was asked why he chose to take these positions in the face of the laws of the province of Ontario, it was apparent from his reply that he did not agree with the law. He was adamant that it should have no application to him. His commitment to this position has distinguished these proceedings from most other family law litigation in this province since the inception of the Act. Mr. Van Bork had the financial means to be unrelenting in his position and, were it not for the fact that Mrs. Van Bork's solicitors were prepared to see her through to the end, she would have had an extremely difficult time continuing to pursue her legal rights....The legal costs were extremely high in this matter and were driven by Mr. Van Bork's intransigence.[202]

Justice Macdonald noted that she suspected the family was worth about $2 million at the time of separation in 1984, and by trial, it was "at minimum, in the range of $4 million. There was little reliable information as to value. Mr. Van Bork's evidence seemed designed to confound the court and, on a number of occasions, it occurred to me that he was deliberately doing so to lead the court to error."

Justice Macdonald concluded that she could not rely on the husband's credibility as he gave his evidence "in a confusing and evasive manner" and his financial disclosure "made no sense." She commented that he "was prepared to compromise his integrity to a shocking extent." She damned his conduct, saying, "The convoluted history of the proceedings is illustrative of his determination to defeat Mrs. Van Bork's claims without regard to the consequences to her, her advocates, and to those who had long professional associations with him." He had even contorted the facts to fit within his interpretation of the Family Law Act, trying unsuccessfully to attribute the seed money for their investments to a small inheritance from his mother that he had received before the marriage. The judge found that he "participated in shocking subterfuge with respect to the actual will of his mother by providing a copy of the same to Mrs. Van Bork's solicitors which he knew to have been altered in a material way." In her judgment at trial, Justice Macdonald ordered payments to Mrs. Van Bork of about $1.8 million, together with monthly support of $5,000 per month for three years and then $3,500 per month for her lifetime.

To my regret and disappointment, the judge did not adequately punish Mr. Van Bork for his conduct. I had hoped the case would set a precedent as a warning to husbands who used the legal system as a club. While the judge said she had no doubt that he'd used the litigation process as a weapon against Mrs. Van Bork, she refused to order damages for breach of fiduciary duty or punitive damages. She also denied the claim for unequal division of assets or compounded pre-judgment interest back to date of separation, to make up for the fact that Mr. Van Bork had pocketed the income and increase in value of their assets over eight years.

I wanted the court order to be an enforceable ruling, and not something the husband could successfully ignore. So I asked and the judge took the unusual step of ordering that Mr. Van Bork be restrained from dealing with any of the assets in his name, Mrs. Van Bork's name, or their joint names without Mrs. Van Bork's consent until he satisfied all his obligations under the judgment. Concerned that he might find a way to justify ignoring even this order, I immediately filed a copy of the judgment, which included this freeze order, with every person or institution we knew about or suspected he had financial dealings with, in order to alert them to their obligations to obey the court order. As a result, I am happy to say that Mrs. Van Bork did receive every penny to which she was entitled by the trial judgment.

Thereafter, Justice Macdonald heard an unusually long period (seven days) of submissions between December 1993 and July 1994 as to the obligation for payment of legal costs. She concluded that the net effect of the settlement offers was that Mrs. Van Bork achieved results at trial that provided her with far more in terms of assets and income than she was prepared to accept by way of compromise to get the matter settled without the cost of a trial, and that Mr. Van Bork's offer gave Mrs. Van Bork little alternative but to proceed to trial.

The judge fixed the amount of the costs and ordered that Mr. Van Bork contribute the sum of $447,930.80 toward Mrs. Van Bork's legal fees, disbursements, and GST. I did not charge a premium for success or interest on my unpaid accounts over the years when I had worked without compensation, as the bill based just on time spent was significant. Not content to let it go at that, Mr. Van Bork kept the fight going and appealed the trial and costs decisions to the Court of Appeal.

Normally a trial decision is held in abeyance while an appeal is pending, but I asked the Court of Appeal to order the immediate release of some of the funds coming to Mrs. Van Bork. On March 2, 1994, Mr. Justice George Finlayson ordered over $1 million to be paid out to Mrs. Van Bork forthwith. It seemed the Court of Appeal judge had the husband's number too.

The appeal of the trial decision was eventually heard in 1997, *eleven years* after Mrs. Van Bork had initially consulted me. Mr. Van Bork had certainly succeeded in delaying the outcome, although he had failed to prevent an order for sharing of their family net worth. The husband lost most of his issues on appeal and was ordered to pay his wife's appeal costs. Mrs. Van Bork wrote to me with gratitude when the matter was coming to an end. She acknowledged that without me carrying the case forward, she would not have had any chance to get what was legally hers, nor would she be receiving the support money to which she was entitled. So, the eleven-year nightmare was over; Mr. Van Bork lost and had to pay up. He was not, however, punished for abusing the legal system or for having withheld what legally and financially belonged to his wife. We never did find out exactly what he was worth. It became very clear to me that laws by themselves will work to achieve equity only if law-abiding people are involved. When individuals refuse to obey the law and figure out how to use the system to support their stubbornness, then those seeking equity need to find lawyers who will stand up for them, and courts with the strength and willingness to make the tough decisions. Underfunded legal aid plans are inadequate to the task. And few lawyers can afford or are willing to prop up on their own the promises of the legal system to deliver justice. The legal system still has to figure out how to deal with this kind of litigation misconduct.

JUDICIAL DISCRETION

There were other forms of resistance to the new Family Law Act 1986. The exercise of judicial discretion sometimes defeated the purpose of the legislation. I had seen many judges ignore the opportunity in the 1978 Family Law Reform Act to compel spouses to share their investment, business, and pension assets. When the Family Law Act replaced the FLRA in 1986, an issue to be resolved was whether a judge had the jurisdiction under the FLA to order transfers of property between spouses in order to achieve the equal sharing required by the law. The law did state, in sections 9 and 10, that after a court makes an order, it can "transfer property to a spouse or order the partitioning and sale of any jointly owned property, and give any ancillary orders." The meaning was obvious to me, but not, apparently, to everyone.

The issue arose in the *Humphreys* case, which I took to trial in April 1987, one year after the FLA came into effect. We asked for an order that the wife retain the home and the husband keep the cottage, both of which were in joint ownership. If those two assets were not exactly equal in value, I proposed that a sum of money should be paid by one to the other to equalize these assets. It seemed to me a straightforward request. I was not prepared for Mr. Justice Patrick Galligan's angry and sharp words, or for his manner, which seemed to me to ask, *Why are you bothering me?* Justice Galligan appeared to perceive the FLA as a choice by legislators to exclude judicial discretion and replace it with predictability—definitive and specific rules—even where the legislation did not say so. He was unyielding in his view that the court did not have the right to rearrange the parties' assets. To my dismay, he read the law as giving him no discretion at all. As a result, only the parties acting by agreement could rearrange their assets. If they could not agree and went to trial, the judge would only order the properties sold and the cash proceeds divided.

Many judges—and therefore lawyers recommending settlements—followed Justice Galligan's lead to interpret the law literally and restrictively, using very little discretion. Justice Galligan's words continue to resonate with lawyers and courts to this day. The result has been what he predicted—that his perspective would encourage settlement because there was no other way to rearrange assets. The settlements did not always end up being fair, but if a party wanted to receive an asset that was entirely or partially owned by the other, that party would have to give up something in the settlement in order to achieve it. And spouses learned that if they could not agree on the disposition of a jointly owned asset, the court would likely order it sold.

When I saw the way the law was being interpreted, I wrote to Attorney General Ian Scott, expressing concern and some suggestions for clarified wording in the legislation. He chose to wait for a clear case to come from the Court of Appeal before he reviewed family laws again. He said it was important not to change the law too often or predictability would be compromised. I certainly understood that, but was disappointed at the inroads being made in the legislative intent. It demonstrated to me yet again that changing the law is not always enough. When those implementing the law disagree with it, they can often find a way to make their views count.

FAIR SHARING OF PRIVATE PENSIONS

Private pensions were not shared between spouses until 1986, when the Family Law Act made it a requirement of law. Unfortunately, the wording of the law left a good deal open to interpretation. I should not have been surprised when women were faced with the least generous interpretation of the new statute. As it turned out, the *Humphreys* case, which had interpreted the issue of judicial discretion to rearrange assets, also dealt with the significant pension issues requiring interpretation. It was one of the first cases, if not *the* first case, to reach the court under the new Family Law Act. I had to become an overnight expert on pensions, since we had learned relatively little about this highly specialized and complex area of law when we went to law school. I can still remember the intense learning curve.

Justice Galligan had already disappointed me with his rigid view of judicial discretion when it came to rearranging assets under the FLA, but he did not hesitate to use his discretion to interpret the pension provisions when it came to setting rules for the valuation of the husband's defined benefit plan.

The Family Law Act provided that pensions would be shared at their lump sum value, like all other assets. This meant that an actuary had to be hired to do the valuation, though it was not clear what appraisal method the actuary should use in a family law case—how to assess and take into account the income taxes that would be levied when the pension was paid out, whether the survivors' pension should be appraised, and other evaluation issues. In choosing the method to be used, the judge chose the one that paid the wife the least. This may not have been his goal, but it was certainly the result of his analysis.

Once a lump sum value was determined, the issue was how to pay out the receiving spouse's share. The pension owner was not entitled to receive his pension until he retired, and separate legislation, the 1987 Ontario Pension Benefits Act, did not permit money to be paid out from the pension plan until the plan member stopped working, retired, or died. Nor did that law permit a spouse to negotiate for more than 50 percent of the pension, so that trade-offs with other assets were more limited. Moreover, the person with the pension often had no other assets to trade with. Many families had a home and a pension and little else.

I thought that it would be more equitable and practical if a husband and wife shared the pension income when the pensioner received it. But the only way to do this effectively and protect both spouses was to divide the membership in the pension plan into two separate memberships, one for the husband and one for the wife. For this to work, the pension plan administrators had to agree to co-operate, as there was no law forcing them to do so. The way the Family Law Act 1986 was written, it was almost impossible to make this kind of arrangement. Mind you, that did not stop some lawyers from negotiating their clients into what came to be called an "if and when" agreement, requiring the pension income to be paid out to both spouses "if and when" it was received. I regarded this as a risky arrangement. If the husband did not live to receive his pension, the surviving wife would not be entitled to receive anything at all. If the husband retired and did receive his pension, he might fail to pay his wife her promised share out of his monthly cheque. She might have a hard time chasing him for payment and would be limited by what other assets he might have available to make up any arrears.

As a result, I did not recommend the "if and when" method for parties with pensions in the Ontario jurisdiction. I was pleased when the federal government came up with an option that was less risky for the non-member spouse. Legislation was passed that required the federal pension plans—dealing only with pensions in the federal jurisdiction, such as government employees, banks, airlines, and Crown corporations—to split the monthly payment between the spouses. I tried to get the Ontario government to pass a similar law, and by 1989, they had agreed to review the issue. Murray Elston, whom I had met when he was minister for women's issues, was, in 1989, the minister of financial institutions, which included the Pension Commission of Ontario. I was retained to advise the ministry on the family law aspect of his pension review.

The ministry's consultation paper put forward two recommendations I had proposed. First, the pension plan member should be able to split his entitlements with his spouse at the time of separation or divorce and, in effect, create from then on two separate memberships in the pension plan. And second, a couple could negotiate the sharing of any percentage of the pension plan. For example, there were times when the only assets the couple had were the home and the pension, and depending on their respective values, they might wish to transfer the home to the wife together with a smaller percentage of the pension, in order to equalize assets. Unfortunately, the government did not proceed with its tentative plan. I learned that they dropped it because of the strong objections of some pension plan administrators, who did not want the extra administrative work.

I continued trying to clarify and improve pension law whenever and wherever I had the opportunity. I was on a Bar Association panel in September 1988 with a pension lawyer and a pension actuary where I pressed for a secure and safe "if and when" division plan. I wrote a column in *Chatelaine*'s November 1996 issue, and for *CARP*[203] *Magazine*'s February 2007 issue, declaring that law reform was long overdue.

I added this concern in many of my speeches and broadcast opportunities. Successive governments were not responsive, even though the Ontario Law Reform Commission, the Canadian Institute of Actuaries, family lawyers, the Ontario Bar Association, and a number of pension plan administrators and unions had pressed for action.

It was not until 2012, after further prodding by a report from the Law Commission of Ontario, that the Ontario government led by Liberal premier Dalton McGuinty brought in some improvements. These included new rules requiring the co-operation of the administrators of Ontario pension plans. Plan administrators were compelled to provide an actuarial valuation for family law division purposes, on the request of a plan member. Plan managers were also obliged, unless the spouses agreed otherwise, to divide up the funds held in their pension plan to the credit of a spouse. They would then transfer the share coming to the pensioner's spouse into the spouse's own pension plan, Registered Retirement Savings Plan (RRSP), or Registered Retirement Income Fund (RRIF). It has turned out to be a workable compromise. And it only took twenty-six years to accomplish!

SHARIA LAW

Vigilance means keeping our eyes open to challenges from surprising places. As late as 2003, a threat to the Family Law Act—and the advances it entailed to give equal rights to all women in all aspects of family law—appeared from an unexpected source when the Islamic Institute of Civil Justice (IICJ) was established to resolve family law disputes for Muslims through arbitration. The problem was that they intended to make their decisions according to religious law—Islamic Sharia law—rather than Ontario family law. Their plan was to use the authority of the 1991 Ontario Arbitration Act, set up to deal with commercial disputes, so that their family law decisions would be enforceable by the Canadian courts. If Muslims did not submit to a Sharia arbitration, they risked being ostracized as apostates.

This raised a furor, led by moderate Muslims and particularly the Canadian Council of Muslim Women (CCMW), who wanted to be governed by Ontario family law and not by Sharia law, which they said had outmoded and, in some cases, abusive attitudes toward women. Although several other faiths had arbitrated family law matters for their co-religionists, there had been no public objections raised. In this case, as a result of concerns raised by some Muslim women, many Canadian women's organizations expressed trepidations at the effect of this plan on our Muslim sisters, and members of the public contacted local MPPs, the attorney general, and the minister responsible for women's issues. I was particularly apprehensive that if the government legitimized private religious arbitration of family law disputes, Muslim women would not benefit from our many years of hard work to entrench equality rights in family law for everyone.

Alia Hogben, the president of the CCMW, asked for my help in preparing and presenting the viewpoint against Sharia family law, as well as for strategic advice. For his part, Premier McGuinty felt the uproar and asked his attorney general, Michael Bryant, and minister for women's issues, Sandra Pupatello, to advise him. They appointed Marion Boyd to look into the matter.

Marion Boyd had served as both attorney general and minister for women's issues in the NDP government that ran Ontario between 1990 and 1995. I hoped that she would understand how important it was to sustain secular law; she was a feminist with a history of activism. She was not, however, a lawyer, and that may have been a challenge when it came to making recommendations on this issue.

Ms. Boyd heard a wide variety of views between July and September 2004. Her report, *Dispute Resolution in Family Law: Protecting Choice, Promoting Inclusion*, recommended that religious law rather than secular law be permitted to govern in Muslim family and inheritance law disputes *and* that any such rulings be enforced by the government of Ontario as if they had been rulings of the Ontario courts. She also proposed that a spouse be permitted to waive the right to have independent legal advice (ILA) even though

Ontario law does not legitimize and enforce an agreement without ILA. Boyd thought the requirement of ILA was "costly, legalistic, and time-consuming." I was dumbfounded. I knew this rule had been established to protect the vulnerable, and I was certain that a Muslim woman subject to Sharia family law fit this criterion. I also knew that the arbitration system contained no accountability or redress if the parties waived independent legal advice and the right of appeal.

Boyd's main solutions to safeguard the process were to allow the Ontario courts to set aside the arbitrated agreement if (1) it was unconscionable, (2) it resulted in a party going on social assistance, (3) each party did not have ILA (unless they had waived it), (4) each party had not received the faith-based statement of principles that were intended to govern the arbitration, (5) each party had not been advised first of Ontario law applicable to their situation, and (6) if the arbitrator had not certified that he had screened the parties separately for domestic violence and was satisfied that they were signing the agreement voluntarily.

I was deeply disappointed with the Boyd Report. I did not believe that the complex process that it recommended would provide women with the guarantees that were enshrined in the Canadian Constitution nor the significant advances contained in the Ontario Family Law Act. Women had not come this far only to have our rights removed by a back-door route. I was apprehensive that the complicated proposals could threaten the primacy of secular law, the separation of church and state, and potentially lead to other multicultural and multi-religious communities choosing to arbitrate family law matters by applying their own religious laws and then asking the state to enforce them. I made a number of telephone calls and spoke to people who might want to add their voice. Many of those concerned became involved in the public discussion.

Marion Boyd's report was released in December 2004 to mixed reviews. *Globe and Mail* columnist Margaret Wente summarized succinctly what many people felt when she wrote:

> Pinch me, quick. What century is this, anyway?...Ms. Boyd has promised all sorts of safeguards so that a woman can appeal a decision she thinks is unfair. All the woman has to do is overcome

the immense social pressure to conform, and withstand the shame and ostracism she will experience if she tries to defy the spiritual leaders of the community and her entire family.... Here's what I think: Religious laws have no place in the legal system. One Canadian law should be good enough for all. Period. Full stop.

The YWCA Toronto issued a press release in which its executive director, Heather McGregor, wryly observed: "To my knowledge, nowhere in the world did women wake up one day to find enlightened men in positions of power handing over equality. We have always had to fight for our rights. Ms. Boyd's proposal flies in the face of this historical fact.... We believe that this proposal has the potential to throw women in Ontario back decades."

It was important to persuade other lawyers as well, and hope for their support. I wrote an article for the newsletter of the Family Law Section of the Ontario Bar Association, *Matrimonial Affairs,* whose editors wrote an editorial that "such arbitration could undermine women's equality rights and be a step backwards for all women in Ontario." I also appeared on a panel organized by Sandra Demson for the Family Law Section of the Ontario Bar Association to discuss the issue. Appearing with me were Marion Boyd herself along with University of Toronto Faculty of Law professors Lorraine Weinrib and Anver Emon. It was a lively and respectful discussion.

By then, I was the "expert" within the family law bar on this issue, so when the Law Society program "The Six Minute Family Lawyer" was being planned, I was asked to summarize the issue for the education of the members of the family law bar.

The provincial government was under great pressure to invalidate Sharia law, indeed all religious laws, for family law purposes, notwithstanding the Boyd Report recommendations. In the end, Premier McGuinty decided against accepting Boyd's recommendations, saying that his government was committed to equality principles and women's rights, and Ontario courts would only enforce family arbitrations that applied the family law of Ontario and Canada. While this battle, at least, was won, it served as an important reminder that the fight for equality rights and the need to be resolute and watchful continue.

Chapter 14

SPOUSAL SUPPORT CHALLENGES

When it came to the implementation of the Family Law Act 1986, property-sharing issues were just one area in which watchfulness was required. Another—of equal concern to those of us on the frontlines of the battle for equal rights—was spousal support.

I had tried to protect and enhance the rights of women to spousal support ever since I started practising family law. The new FLA had made it clear that a spouse was *not* required to become self-supporting within a predetermined period of time; she was required only to *contribute* to her support. Now it was important to ensure that cases were decided accordingly. In June 1987, I accepted a request to lecture to family law lawyers and show them what evidence to present at trial. I knew it was essential to make workplace realities *real* to judges and then hope they would act on this evidence—and reflect the rationale in their reasons—so that a body of law would be created that established the recognition of these realities as a precedent. In that presentation, I explained the difficulties faced by male judges in dealing with the realities of a woman's life:

> Bringing the reality of a woman's life before the court can be an awesome task. It is particularly difficult because most judges are men, with different life experiences, expectations, needs, and interests and often a failure to appreciate the reality of a woman's life and the limitations related to her child-bearing function. It is this gap in experience which makes it necessary to provide

evidence to put in the record of the court hearing.

The judge doesn't know instinctively how difficult it can be for a woman to find work, and how time-consuming childcare and household work is. But he does have his own life experiences, expectations, needs, interests, and resentments. For instance, note the language in *Messier* v. *Delage* when the court begrudges her her support, and referred to a spouse as being a "drag on the other," wanting a "lifetime pension" and to "luxuriate in idleness."

I included in the materials the entire transcript of economist Monica Townson's testimony in the *Jarvis* case, and described the facts in the case.

Despite these early efforts at education, there were no precedent-setting cases confirming that spousal support should not be time-limited until 1992, when a landmark Supreme Court of Canada decision[204] was released. Madam Justice Claire L'Heureux-Dubé, who wrote the decision for the court, had been a family law lawyer before being elevated to the bench, and she had a perceptive and compassionate perspective on the issues and the inequities facing women. She ruled that it was unreasonable to demand total self-sufficiency from a long-time homemaker, if she quit working or never worked, and lost skills, income, seniority, benefits, and opportunity in order to look after a family. The need for self-sufficiency was only one factor in a support award. Support was in addition to a division of property and was required even if the wife worked outside the home full- or part-time. The law to that date had contributed to the feminization of poverty in Canada. She overruled the Manitoba judge who, when terminating Mrs. Moge's spousal support, had said, "She cannot expect that Mr. Moge will support her forever." In the process, the Supreme Court of Canada gave direction to the contrary to all lawyers and judges in Canada.

I was jubilant that this issue had finally been dealt with at Canada's highest court. I was also proud that LEAF, through its legal counsel Helena Orton, made a significant impact on the presentation of the case by intervening at the Supreme Court and presenting the feminist perspective. Lawyers would now have to tell their clients that the Supreme Court of Canada had spoken on the subject. They surely would not advise their clients to "roll the dice" by going to trial, as they would know that any trial judge was bound by this ruling.

Courts across Canada followed the lead of the Supreme Court of Canada and began to award spousal support in higher amounts, for longer periods of time, and more frequently to women who had assumed a traditional role of wife and mother in marriage and suffered economic disadvantage. There were at least 2,962 published cases (by December 2016) that referred to and were guided by *Moge*. As a result, it became possible as a practising lawyer to help women clients cope with the financial fall-out from divorce. I was always happy to be able to advise a client that she had rights, clearly stated in law, to spousal support for an indefinite term, based on her need. I also wrote about it in my *Chatelaine* column and *Every Canadian's Guide to the Law*, and discussed the issue in my radio and TV appearances, so that women would know their rights.

Eventually, I was even able to advise that the courts had confirmed that a wife, even if she was working part-time, was entitled to seek "top up" support, given the modest income of secondary wage-earners. I was pleased to be able to set a precedent in just such a case. A client of mine in her late thirties was working part-time (twenty hours a week as a medical secretary) so that she could care for her ten-year-old son before and after school and also avoid additional child-care costs. This was considered reasonable by Madam Justice Janet Wilson in the *Magder* case.[205] My client's husband had brought a court application to reduce the child support he had been paying. He thought that his ex-wife should be working longer hours and paying a greater share of the costs to raise their son. He had remarried and had more children and gave that as a reason not to pay as much for the child of his first marriage. I was able to persuade the court that his obligation to his first child should not be secondary to the children of the second marriage. The Ontario Court of Appeal panel upheld the ruling. Both the trial and appeal courts ordered that the husband was to pay part of my client's legal costs.

A CHANGING CLIMATE

By the late 1990s, some women who were suffering the negative effects of the limited-term support orders from the previous twenty years came forward. Many who had settled for limited-term support returned to lawyers and then courts seeking the reinstatement of support because they were unable to support themselves. Usually the agreements they signed were absolutely clear and unequivocal about support termination under any possible circumstance. No lawyer could offer hope to such a client; there were no cases, no precedents.

The changing climate of opinion started in 1997 when Madam Justice Marie Corbett, writing for the Ontario Divisional Court in the case of *Santosuosso* v. *Santosuosso*,[206] reversed a trial judge who had upheld a 1987 final settlement, which had restricted a forty-three-year-old homemaker coming out of a twenty-three-year traditional marriage to two years of monthly support. She had agreed to, thereafter, be responsible for her own support "regardless of any change in circumstances no matter how catastrophic...." The agreement met all the traditional conditions for a valid agreement: it was executed properly; the parties had had independent legal advice; and they did not suffer duress from the other spouse.

However, Mrs. Santosuosso was unable to secure a full-time job, while her former husband was a full-time tenured professor. The Divisional Court ordered that he augment her earnings by paying her $500 per month of support with no time limit, reasoning that the agreement was based on the parties' expectation that the wife would be able to become self-supporting; her failure to do so was held to be a "radical unforeseen change in circumstances."

Santosuosso was ground-breaking because it did not take an agreement at face value but, instead, saw it as only one factor—and not the defining factor. *Santosuosso* was widely followed across Canada. This case was the first positive sign of sympathy from the courts for the plight of divorced and separated women who had gone along with recommendations from lawyers that they give up their support rights after a defined period of time, taking their advice that they had little choice but to do so. The *Santosuosso* decision made a lot of sense to me, of course, and I wrote about it where I could in order to circulate the information. I noted that it had taken one of the growing number of female judges to understand the issue and make the appropriate decision, supported by one male colleague in a three-judge bench (the other male judge dissented).

It is also noteworthy that the lawyer who represented Mrs. Santosuosso was James G. McLeod. He was a full-time law professor at the University of Western Ontario, and the long-time and respected editor of the *Reports on Family Law*. I have no idea of the financial arrangements between him and his client, but given her financial circumstances, I doubt that she was able to afford the court hearings. The *Santosuosso* case shows that sometimes the law is only improved when there is a lawyer willing and able to take a risky case forward.

In 2000, in the case of *Bailey* v. *Plaxton*, an ex-wife who had given up spousal support ten years earlier found her home ownership threatened by her inability to make the payments. She had agreed to accept three years' spousal support of $2,000 per month ending in 1990 and made a sincere effort to establish herself in a career. She applied to the court for support from her ex-husband, including interim support pending the final disposition of her claim, despite the fact that so much time had elapsed since her support ended. Her lawyer, Harold Niman, took the risky case forward, and Ontario judge Frances Kiteley took the unusual step of awarding her the sum of $5,000 per month in interim spousal support pending trial.[207]

Justice Kiteley found that the wife's economic hardship arose from the breakdown of the marriage and that she was allowed to make the order under the 1985 Divorce Act, notwithstanding the parties' agreement, which was only one factor that the newer version of the Divorce Act required to be taken into account. She held that the husband was well able to pay the support ordered, pending trial. She found as a fact that his annual income was $300,000 and that in the prior year he had earned a performance bonus of $100,000. He, by then, had a net worth of $5 million. The husband appealed the interim order unsuccessfully. The case never went to trial, but a judicial decision later reported that it had been settled with the payment of $7,000 a month indefinitely, indexed annually in accordance with changes in the cost of living and binding on his estate.[208]

From then on, lawyers had to ensure that the initial agreement was actually fair to be enforceable. But many women continued to suffer. Many did not try to challenge their settlements.

Harold Niman acknowledged in the January 2001 issue of the Family Law Section newsletter that he and other lawyers were wrong for many years in thinking that women were only entitled to rehabilitative or limited-term support. It was gratifying, if frustrating, to read this acknowledgment so many years later—after many women had suffered injustices by the misinterpretation of the law.

The cases of *Moge* v. *Moge*, *Bailey* v. *Plaxton*, *Santosuosso* v. *Santosuosso*, and *Magder* v. *Magder* brought significant improvements for women in family law. Looking back over the history of this family law issue, I was intrigued to realize that women judges— Claire L'Heureux-Dubé, Frances Kiteley, Marie Corbett, and Janet Wilson—had a great impact on ensuring that women's needs and concerns were considered important in family law cases. This was an important effect of the appointment of more women to the bench and called to mind the question framed by Madam Justice Bertha Wilson in a famous speech "Will Women Judges Really Make a Difference?"[209] Well, it certainly seems they have.

Through the 1990s, courts also gradually began to make higher and higher awards of spousal support. By 1999, the trend was to equalize the couple's income after divorce. In the 1999 Ontario case of *Andrews* v. *Andrews*,[210] a husband earning $200,000 appealed a trial court order requiring him to pay spousal and child support that gave the wife and children 60 percent of the parties' total disposable income. This was a huge advance and one I tried to implement in every case after that. Sixty percent was a vain goal in most settlements, but the existence of the *Andrews* case meant that in many situations, one could successfully argue for the case to be settled without a trial on the basis that at least 50 to 55 percent of the family income would be paid to a wife for herself and the children.

DOING THE MATH

Once the law agreed that women should be paid a fairer amount, it was necessary to find a way to calculate it. I had been using an informal rule-of-thumb formula as a tool to make it easier to negotiate and resolve a fair spousal support payment and to present my proposals to the court. I shared it with the profession in a Bar Association program in 2000 and a Law Society lecture in 2001. I showed colleagues how to factor in differing circumstances such as long- versus short-term marriages, children versus childless families, employed versus unemployed parties, and so on. Following the direction pointed out to us by *Andrews,* my formula was based on income-sharing between the parents and not budgets, and it allowed for the differing tax treatment of child and spousal support. The formula was based on the presumption (shared by other lawyers as shown by the results of an informal survey of family law practitioners) that such a tool (as opposed to a rule or legislation) would be useful.

Spousal Support Advisory Guidelines

I was initially pleased when family law Professors Carol Rogerson[211] and Rollie Thompson[212] began a project in September 2001 with the financial support of the federal government. It was published in December 2002.[213] Their twenty-three-page background paper canvassed at length every possible method for calculating spousal support used in various (mostly American) jurisdictions, and it included mine as the only Canadian spousal support formula they found to study. The authors appear to have based their approach on my formula, and where I allowed for discretion, they took it to the next step and suggested a precise method of allowing for some of the many variables. They recommended unequivocally that there should be no legislated guidelines. What was proposed was an informal "advisory" guide, based on income sharing. The professors were careful to point out that "they will not have the force of law."

The most significant change wrought by the guidelines was the resurrection of time-limited support with no stated justification. While the authors acknowledged that support law by then frowned on time limits except in short-term marriages, they then proceeded to recommend time limits. It had taken so many years for the legislation and the courts to correct this misapprehension. I was appalled that these new guidelines might return some credibility to limited-term support.

The level of detail in the formula reduced the opportunity for negotiation and increased the chance of lawyers taking fixed positions. I thought it was likely that a computer program would be developed (it was), and lawyers would not put their minds to the fairness issues. Lawyers would want to do at least as well for their client as the formula allowed, and so anyone wanting to argue exceptional circumstances would have to persuade their client to risk going to court and finding a judge who would not choose to apply the advisory formula.

I warned lawyers and the authors of the study that all that would be needed was for a couple of judges to apply the formula as is and treat it as gospel, in written reasons, for its intended "advisory" status to become law by way of precedent. I could not do anything to prevent this from happening. There was no politician or government official to lobby, because this was only a funded "study" and not an act of a legislature.

My concerns ended up being spot on. The Spousal Support Guidelines took on the force of law because some judges exercised their discretion to apply them, and some lawyers accepted them in negotiations. Even the authors became concerned that their guidelines were being applied as if they were mandatory and without adjusting for numerous factors that were supposed to be considered. Eventually, Professors Rogerson and Thompson came out with warnings and cautions that lawyers should apply the *entire* advisory guidelines and not just selected parts.

THE BATTLE TO MAINTAIN THE GOVERNMENT ENFORCEMENT AGENCY

At the same time as the FLA was enacted in 1986, so too was the first Ontario enforcement agency to ensure payment of child and spousal support. The Support and Custody Orders Enforcement Act (SCOE) permitted the agency to garnishee wages and bank accounts and register a support order or agreement against the land of the person obligated to pay the support. Court orders and agreements were registered with the agency, which was set up and ready to go by July 2, 1987. It was a well-planned and effective agency and it fulfilled its purpose admirably.

I wished, however, that it had also been allowed to enforce orders dealing with property sharing between spouses. The landmark 1980 case that highlighted this need was *Becker* v. *Pettkus*, in which common-law spouse Rosa Becker was recognized by the Supreme Court of Canada as an equal partner and entitled to a one-half share of the bee farm she had run with her partner for twenty years; the court ordered Lothar Pettkus to pay her $150,000 for her half-share. In doing so, it upheld the ruling of the Ontario Court of Appeal written by Madam Justice Bertha Wilson. According to the news reports of the day, Pettkus used every legal trick in the book to deny her the $150,000. In November 1986, Rosa Becker shocked the community when she committed suicide. She left behind a message that her suicide was a protest against a legal system that awarded her $150,000 six years earlier but did nothing to ensure that she received the court-ordered amount.

I wrote a column for the *Toronto Star*, published November 14, 1986, headlined "How to stop tragedies like Rosa Becker's." If her death was to mean what she had intended, I sought to outline a positive and workable solution. I wrote that she had highlighted the fact that in failing to enforce its own orders, the legal system lets people down. Since divorce was liberalized in 1968 and since family property became sharable in 1978, thousands had become involved in lawsuits for the first time in their lives. And they were bewildered and frustrated by the complex and technical rules and procedures of the courts. I emphasized that we as a society needed to polish up the sometimes tarnished image of our legal system.

Ian Scott had set up an Ontario Courts Inquiry with the mandate to look into the "organization, structure, and jurisdiction of all courts in Ontario, the accessibility of the courts to the people of Ontario, and the service provided by the courts to the people." I

Guest Column

Linda Silver Dranoff

How to stop tragedies like Rosa Becker's

Rosa Becker — her name represents a landmark Supreme Court of Canada case that recognized the property rights of a common-law wife. How unfortunate she should have felt so alienated she chose self-destruction.

Becker, a farm worker, won a court award in 1980 of half-interest in a bee farm she had operated with her common-law husband. But it is reported that Lothar Pettkus, with whom she lived 20 years, used legal tricks to prevent her from getting the money. She finally shot herself in despair last week.

In her act of suicide, she left behind the message that she saw her death as a protest against a faulty legal system that awarded her $150,000 but did not see to it that she received it.

In accusing the legal system, she has opened a subject that deserves dispassionate debate.

Where the legal system lets down the Rosa Beckers is in its failure to enforce its own orders. We have never expected our courts to provide this service. But more average people now are involved in lawsuits than was the case a few years ago.

From the *Toronto Star*
November 14, 1986

thought the Inquiry should be asked to also advise on the issue of enforcement of property under the aegis of the new enforcement agency. I sent a copy of the *Toronto Star* piece, along with a covering letter outlining my suggestions. He replied, saying that his ministry was exploring options. Ian Scott had been an accomplished trial lawyer before he went into politics and would understand the enforcement difficulties that litigants had. What he could do about it, both politically and financially, was another matter, but at least the issue would be reviewed. With him, as previously with Roy McMurtry, I felt that Ontario had an attorney general whose legal background helped him to understand the problems and whose heart was in the right place; they both saw their role as being public servants. Unfortunately, enforcement of property rights and property-based court orders were never added to the mandate of SCOE and, to this day, court orders must be enforced by the one to whom money is owed. But at least I knew that I had tried.

Succeeding governments made inroads into the agency's ability to enforce even support payments. When Mike Harris's Ontario Progressive Conservative Party was elected in 1995, there was immediate talk of all kinds of changes in keeping with Harris's ideology, which he named the "Common Sense Revolution." I didn't think his views always represented "common sense" at all, on a number of fronts, but I will stick to family law issues. Soon after he took office, his government—apparently in order to save money—threatened changes to the enforcement agency, by then called the Family Support Plan (FSP) instead of SCOE.

I received from a confidential source[214] a copy of an internal government document describing the issues and the plans. The memo warned that recovery of social assistance payments could be jeopardized by the proposed FSP budget cuts, the closure of eight regional offices, the firing of most of the staff, and centralization of the plan—that is, there would be no net saving to the government if social assistance costs went up because support payments to women went down. The structure would be changed so that, in future, no one caseworker would be familiar with any one file. Whoever picked up the telephone would face a steep learning curve each time a new and complex case was presented to them. I worried that it would be the women and children who would suffer. The government was even planning to charge each caller two dollars, including women whose child support was not being paid. The intention was to make 335 out of 350 employees "surplus" and then hire back some of them on contract.

I shared my worries with both the Feminist Legal Analysis Section and the Family Law Section of the CBA-O, and on their behalf, I prepared a submission in March 1996. The major thrust of the submission was that there was no need to cut funding for this well-respected program since it not only paid for itself but also saved money in the social assistance system. It was both self-sustaining and profitable. This was illustrated with information from the confidential memo. It cost the government $22.8 million to run FSP, which was expected to recover $49.8 million in fiscal 1995–96 for social assistance. Ontario could fully offset the cost of services and provide a similar amount as net return to the government. Also worrisome was that the changes would cause the plan to lose its collective operating memory. And I fretted about further cuts to the justice system: "To cut from anywhere in the justice system is to cut bone and sinew from an emaciated corpse." No one could doubt my passion on the subject.

Much of the material made its way into an op-ed piece for the *Toronto Star*, published on March 1, 1996, and headlined "Myopic cutters pose grave threat to Family Support."

On March 28, 1996, Judith Huddart, as chair of the Feminist Legal Analysis Section, Ruth Mesbur, as chair of the Family Law Section, and I met with Attorney General Charles Harnick to discuss the proposed changes to the Family Support Plan, following upon the submission to the attorney general from the CBA-O. We presented our point of view and he appeared to listen. He was soothing and reassuring. He said he thought that his ministry was trying to create a new plan that represented a much tougher approach and streamlined the plan in a way that would not weaken it. "We are going to hire a higher level of personnel," he said. He also said that $17 million of the $23 million it took to operate the Family Support Plan went to salaries "to shuffle paper." What an odd statement that was, when keeping records was part of their job. He asked for our backing for the penalty of motor vehicle licence suspension for the non-payment of child support, which we were happy to give.

At the same time, we expressed other concerns, including the impact of all kinds of cuts that had been made by the Harris government to the justice system. We spoke of fewer available legal aid certificates to needy people, the unconscionably long lines in the Family Law Division offices because of reduced staffing, the adverse impact of the cuts to shelters for battered women, the growing number of unrepresented litigants, and more.

Harnick promised to be in touch, but we did not hear further from him. The bill containing the legislation was in fact presented to the legislature not long after we met, and in it the name of the agency was changed again. The Family Responsibility and Support Arrears Enforcement Act 1996 included all the features that were in the leaked memo, despite the government's denials. The Standing Committee on the Administration of Justice held perfunctory hearings, where I presented with others on behalf of the Bar Association. Using the majority they had in the legislature, the government pushed through the changes with little further discussion. I was appalled.

From then on, support became more difficult than ever to enforce. If the court order was not specific as to the amount owing, the Family Responsibility Office (FRO) would not act. For example, if the order provided that the father was to pay the child's university tuition, but the amount was not inserted in the order (usually because it was unknown when the order was given), the FRO refused to enforce it, and enforcement had to be undertaken by the individual recipient. People waited on the telephone for hours for an actual person to talk to, and then, if the correct information had not been entered into the computer, they could not be helped. A party was allowed to withdraw from enforcement by the agency, which became a negotiating point from then on—some women were forced to agree. Family lawyers hearing the complaints of clients were frustrated, but we were stuck with it. While the government took money from the program, they did not make the economically sensible decision. The appearance of saving money seemed more important to them than doing what was right and cost-effective.

The FRO continued to have problems. Since those 1996 changes and even today, the ombudsman of Ontario has received more complaints about this government agency than any other. The bottom line is that only one-third of payors are fully compliant with court orders, one-third pay partially, and one-third pay nothing. And it took until 2011 for the Liberal government of the day to realize that the system would be more efficient if every case had an assigned case worker, as was the situation when the agency was originally established. But it is still a fact that FRO currently has only four hundred employees to cover 180,000 cases. Some battles, it seems, rage on.

Chapter 15
PROTECTING THE
CHILDREN OF DIVORCE

Feminists, both inside and outside the legal profession, are also concerned about the children affected by divorce. The hidden story of divorce is the wrenching impact it has on children. In my law practice, the cases involving children were the most difficult and heartbreaking. Parents have to find a way to resolve the children's living and care arrangements and continue to parent from separate homes. The issues include custody, access, and decision-making about such things as schools, as well as determining the costs to raise the child and how these costs will be shared. Often, children have difficulty coping with the destabilizing alterations in their lives. The "best interests of the child" has been the governing principle, which considers the individual circumstances in each family—this adds cost and complexity to the process. The preparation of cases for court requires a lawyer to present evidence about details of the child's daily life and the parent's ability to handle the particular child's needs.

CARING FOR THE CHILDREN: WHO DECIDES?
When the parents, who know their children best, cannot agree, they hire lawyers to try to negotiate a resolution. If this does not work, the case may go to court, and a judge has to decide. But lawyers and courts are often ill-equipped to decide the best interests of children. Few lawyers are educated in the psychological effects of divorce on children. Negotiation itself is a skill requiring sensitivity and tact as

well as firmness and persistence. Lawyers who practise this art try to settle a case amicably, but it isn't always up to them if the parties resist settling. The best lawyers are firm with their clients, giving them realistic, effective, and ethical advice. When lawyers have to litigate—which is adversarial, aggressive, and inconsistent with a caring approach to the feelings and needs of children—they tend to bargain with whatever is available. Some trade off custody or access in exchange for property or support concessions.

I tried to be both assertive and caring; one gets more with honey than with vinegar—it was best for everyone to be able to have a civil relationship at the end of the dispute. If the process was confrontational and antagonistic, then no matter who "won," it was a war that would damage the children and affect the ability of the parents to work together in the children's interests.

If the matter had to go to trial, reaching an agreement became even more difficult. Parents felt threatened and, just as soldiers in a war, would use whatever equipment was available to survive. A mother whose custody was challenged might gather the children closer, as if to protect them, but her real goal may have been to protect *her* relationship with them. The father would then feel that his paternal relationship was at risk, and he might change his previous patterns of behaviour. Some fathers would become more involved in their children's lives in order to build a case for custody; mothers might then resist his access visits in order to avoid "losing" the custody fight.

And because the children could not help but become involved in the struggle between their parents, things often escalated. The custodial parent might resist the continuation of a close relationship with the other parent. Some would regard the closeness as an act of disloyalty. The children, in turn, would experience a conflict of loyalties and eventually feel as if they had to choose between their parents in order to feel less conflicted. And when the conflict between the parties was so great that they both genuinely felt that the children would suffer being in the custody of the other parent, the result was what Master[215] Stuart McBride used to call "a holy war." Then the only way to resolve matters was for the court to lay down the law.

In the early years of my practice, many of the hard-fought cases were resolved only by court proceedings. Gradually mediation by social workers and psychologists and, later, for the toughest cases, assessments by professionals assisted the judges to reach their decisions. Judges often redirected children's issues to mediators in the hope that the parties would sit down with a professional and be helped to come to their own agreement. This was the best route when it worked—when the professional involved had just the right combination of compassion, candour, and wisdom, and when the parties were rationally able to consider the best interests of their children over themselves. But when these attributes were missing, mediation ended up being only an extra cost and a delay, and the parent who had day-to-day custody benefited because a status quo was established.

Around 2000, collaborative law developed as an alternative process methodology to deal with all family law issues. Both parties had their own lawyers, with specialized training in psychology and interest-based mediation. The parties and their lawyers agreed to be reasonable and act in good faith, and to work through four-way meetings instead of going to court to resolve matters. If this did not work and litigation was needed, the lawyers agreed not to act any more, and the parties had to find new lawyers. Encouraged by Judith Huddart—one of the first in Ontario to take up collaborative law and indeed a founding member of both the Toronto and Ontario collaborative associations—I practised collaborative law toward the end of my career and found it a useful adjunct to my practice in selected cases.

I tried to "speak for the children" through my writings in a way that I could not as a lawyer dealing with a specific case. A lawyer acting for a parent who also tried to represent the interests of the child was often viewed with suspicion by the other side or the court; you were thought to have a hidden agenda favouring your own client.

I came to the conclusion that children were not being adequately protected by the courts. In October 1987, I wrote a piece for the *Toronto Star*; the headline highlighted my overall view: "Divorce court rulings ignore children's plight."[216] I pointed out that by making it easier for parents to divorce, we had inadvertently created a new social policy about the family that ignored the impact on children in both intact and divided families. The message was

Divorce court rulings ignore children's plight

Over the past 18 years, by making it easier for people to divorce, we have inadvertently created a new social policy about the family. For in deciding what happens at the end of a marriage, we guide everyone's expectations of family life in first and reconstructed families.

One significant set of expectations affects children. The message? Children are not important; money is.

Divorce and separation judgments and settlements permit children to suffer reduced personal and economic security. The prevailing wisdom assumes they are so adaptable they can cope.

But is it realistic for children to adjust without harm to losing their home, changing their friends and familiar places, and perhaps living in impoverished circumstances, at the same time as losing their father's presence and their mother's nurturing at home?

Loss of security

Orders and settlements now emphasize a "clean break." That means dividing the home, the income, the children and other assets between the husband and wife. The "best interests" of the children must be considered in custody and access arrangements, but rarely influence property distribution, the amount of support or decisions about occupation or ownership of the family home.

Guest Column
Linda Silver Dranoff

have the financial ability to provide comparable housing and so the children's standard of living is reduced.

Some who lived in a home may end up living in a highrise apartment or welfare housing, with other children and influences with which they have no experience. Sometimes, there is no housing available, especially since some landlords are reluctant to rent to single parents.

And children have less economic security. Many divorced mothers (usually the custodial parent) work, partly because some lawyers and judges have translated family laws to require women to strive for personal self-sufficiency while contributing to their children's support.

This goal ignores the realities of the working world where women do not have an equal opportunity to be self-sufficient. Today, despite the significant numbers of sole-support female heads of households, many women are not paid enough to support their families.

Drop in income

From the *Toronto Star*, October 15, 1987

that children were not important, but money was. Judgments and settlements in divorces and separations resulted in children living in reduced personal circumstances and without economic security. The prevailing wisdom assumed that children were so adaptable, they could cope. I was not so sure.

I also questioned the "clean break" philosophy, which means the matrimonial home is usually sold rather than held for the sake of the children, and challenged the notion that the custodial parent must be employed full-time, when part-time work might, in fact, be better for the children. It was never possible to know the impact these articles had, but at least I had stated my views.

JOINT CUSTODY: CONTROVERSIAL CURE-ALL

By the mid to late 1980s, joint custody was pressed as the best presumptive choice by the burgeoning and persuasive fathers' rights movement. Few judges seemed to want to choose one parent over the other unless an assessor recommended it or the selection was obvious. Joint custody was seen as a way for both spouses to continue to parent. However, it failed to deal with a key issue: if the parents could not get along in a marriage, what was the likelihood that they could jointly parent when they were apart? Joint custody had the potential to create a fertile ground for continued anger and arguments between the separated parents.

The first published court cases were decided quite sensibly by judges who declined to order joint custody unless the parents consented and displayed an ability to co-operate. When the fathers' rights activists pressed the government to insert a presumption of joint custody into legislation, the issue pitted the women's movement against the fathers' rights movement. Women favoured voluntary arrangements—they saw joint custody as a tool that could be used by abusive husbands against their wives and children. The fathers' rights movement felt that mothers were favoured and that this presumption would redress the imbalance. Their attempt to insert joint custody into the 1986 amendments to the federal Divorce Act had been circumvented by women's groups, but the idea lived on. Judges were frequently being asked to make joint custody orders and eventually some did, even without the agreement of both parents.

I observed that involuntary joint custody was not good for children and wrote a cautionary article for *Chatelaine* in May 1987 to bring some of the difficult issues to public attention. To be beneficial to children, joint custody required co-operation, shared values, similar parenting styles, mutual respect, commitment, and flexibility. Research had already shown that it did not work when parents were hostile, angry, or abusive; could not distinguish their feelings from those of their child; or believed their ex-spouse was a bad parent. I worried that children would become a bargaining chip in negotiations over property and support, and that many women would give up financial benefits for the sake of getting custody. It was not right to make the children the winning tickets in the divorce lottery. Parental co-operation, maturity, and reasonableness could not be created by laws.

ACCESS ENFORCEMENT CHALLENGES

Some fathers took the position that if the mother prevented access to their children, they should not have to pay child support. Judges never considered this to be in a child's interests. When mothers began to benefit from the collections by the support enforcement agency, the fathers' rights movement began to press for laws to help them enforce access orders.

In 1988, Ian Scott, the Ontario attorney general and minister for women's issues, tabled legislation trying to set up some rules for the enforcement of access, including make-up time when access was denied, reimbursement of expenses, appointment of a mediator, and supervised access. It appeared that neither the women's perspective nor the best interests of the children involved had been adequately taken into account, and that enforcement of access might be wielded as a tool to talk mothers out of support payments. Before the bill was tabled in the legislature, I attended a briefing at the Ontario Women's Directorate and expressed my concern and tried to persuade the powers that be that the courts already had sufficient options to deal with access issues, if the judges chose to use them.

Around the same time, I wrote a guest column for the *Toronto Star*, saying the proposed law would only complicate child access.[217] "There ought to be a law" is a familiar cry of anguish in response to such problems, but in my view, the province's well-intentioned Bill 60 would create more problems than it would solve. Several possible solutions were offered, such as a supervised access centre to facilitate access in difficult family situations, or an extension of the support enforcement law to include access. I concluded that if the government was determined to pass a law rather than provide a service, then it should at least limit the law to cases where there was a persistent course of wrongful denial of access.

This material gave others some ammunition to use in the campaign against the draft law. The Family Law Section of the CBA-O also submitted a brief, stating that the committee was divided on the need for an access enforcement bill. They suspected, based on their law practices, that access problems addressed by the bill were not a universal problem and decided that the bill would create problems where they did not previously exist.

In the end, the government chose not to proceed with the legislation.

REALITY CHECK: A MEMORABLE CASE IN POINT
It could take superhuman effort and many years to resolve a case involving custody of and access to children. One had to be determined and patient and focused on the main goal—protecting the children and their relationship with both their parents to the extent possible.

I tried to avoid going to court by settling cases on reasonable terms. However, there were times when it was impossible not to get drawn in, even where the possibility of settlement was slim to non-existent. In one memorable case, which lasted many years, I acted for the father of two young boys who were five and three years old at the time when the father retained me. It started as a simple consultation, set for 2 p.m. on a Thursday in 1999. The young man was in his early thirties and was referred to me by his mother, who had been present at one of my speeches on family law. Some consultation! When he sat down, he showed me a letter dated Tuesday, two days prior, which had been delivered to his place of work on the Wednesday morning on behalf of his wife's lawyer, asking him to have his lawyer contact her with a view to putting interim arrangements in place. That is why he contacted me for a consultation and told his wife the previous evening that he had done so. But then he also gave me court documents that had been served on him *that very Thursday morning* at his workplace.

Had I known when he called for the appointment that this was already a court battle, my secretary probably would not have made the appointment. Given my previous experience with cases involving children once the courts were involved, I knew that I probably would not be able to negotiate a settlement. Any parent who initiated court proceedings without any effort at settlement was gearing up for a fight. In this case, the content of the court documents and the wife's use of the court process were outrageous.

The application was for an emergency hearing to be held the very next day, Friday. The mother wanted sole custody, with *no* access to the father, and an order that he be put out of the matrimonial home. The mother's affidavit alleged that he had been violent toward his wife. It also attached a copy of the letter that his wife's lawyer had delivered to him the previous day. The affidavit said that since her lawyer had received no response to the letter, they were bringing this emergency application.

It was shocking that any lawyer would use the power of the court in so underhanded a manner. The allegation that the father had not answered the letter within two days, when the letter itself had set no such stringent time limit, was appalling. He was given no time to get counsel and prepare for the so-called emergency hearing. The judge would have to deal with the application in some way since the wife had alleged "physical violence" on one occasion. There was no way of knowing how it would be dealt with if the father turned up on his own at the court without any documents or ability to present his side of the matter. So, like it or not, having time to do it or not, having inclination to take on a custody case or not, I could not set this pleasant young man adrift on his own to face those odds. So with him in my office and me at the computer, I set about drafting a responding affidavit, putting forward his side of the story, including an immediate response to the allegation of violence. We set out in the affidavit precisely what happened:

> My wife calls "physical violence" an instance which occurred after a lengthy attempt at conversation, while I professed my deep love for her and begged her to come with me for counselling, while we were in bed together. She callously turned to me and said I want to go to sleep and wouldn't talk to me. In anger and frustration, I applied the toes on my bare right foot to her posterior, with light force (and I am sorry I did it). She sat up in bed, continued the conversation briefly, and I left the bed of my own initiative hurt by her coldness to me, and slept in the children's room. She did not complain to me of bruises, she did not seek medical help, she did not call the police.

With no time to serve the affidavit on the opposing lawyer and no time to file it with the court, I turned up with the affidavit and my client the next morning at court to challenge his wife's application. The judge saw through the attempt to use the law to dump the husband from the lives of his wife and children after a ten-year marriage. The judge dismissed the application and ordered that the wife pay the husband $1,000 toward his costs of the motion. With that avenue lost to her and the damage to her credibility on the record, it was reasonable to think that she would have little choice but to try to settle. Maybe she would be willing to talk, since her husband had shown that he was not going to let her oust him from his children's lives.

Madam Justice Gertrude Speigel was conducting mediations at family law case conferences, and she was exceptionally good at it. She had the ability to be kind and compassionate to the parties, but at the same time firm and decisive in expressing her opinion about how the law would apply to their circumstances and what common sense would dictate. She promoted numerous settlements during her time at the Family Law Division. This would be an excellent opportunity to try to settle the case before trial.

After three or four case conferences, much anguished discussion and debate, and ineffective mediation with a psychologist, followed by an assessment, we finally arrived at a separation agreement. Even though my client and I had our doubts about a joint custody arrangement, we also knew that it would be difficult to obtain a sole custody order, given the trends in the courts. Nor did he want to exclude his wife from a full role in the children's lives. In the end, the judge recommended, and the parties accepted, a joint custody arrangement with joint decision-making and a detailed parenting plan; this included a commitment by the parents to keep the children in the school they were then attending until completion of grade five. The mother had a little more time with the children than he did, and so, applying the rules under the Child Support Guidelines (discussed later in this chapter), he paid her some child support. The father was Jewish but the mother was not. When they married, she had agreed that their children would be raised and educated in the Jewish faith. This was confirmed in the separation agreement; it was also agreed that they would attend a mutually acceptable religious school and have Bar Mitzvahs. Details of who was to pick up and return the children, who would take them to the doctor and dentist, and other details of their daily lives were worked out eventually.

This should have ended the matter, but the mother was unwilling to talk to the father. The initial agreement had included a provision for an annual review of the parenting plan schedule. Each time this occurred, the issues were sent to mediation, but they could not be resolved. So the father sought my help again.

Two years later, the issue of religious education arose. The mother would not agree that the children attend the father's synagogue with him. Mediation was unsuccessful. So litigation became necessary to determine a plan for the children's religious schooling. Justice Speigel assisted us once again and helped hammer out a resolution: a compromise synagogue was chosen for the children to attend. It was one where the mother said she felt more comfortable. Even so, she rarely attended or shared their events. Eventually the boys had their Bar Mitzvahs in that synagogue, but she chose not to attend.

This was *still* not the end of this matter. For a case I took on reluctantly and only because of the injustice to my client in the way the case was initiated, we were now in an ongoing legal war.

The boys pressed their father to find a way to permit them to live with him, or at least to spend more time with him, and they were vocal about it. They could not persuade their mother to follow their wishes, and worse—she responded by trying to keep them even more isolated from the father during her time with them. There were persistent communication problems—the mother called any contact from the father "harassment" and "abuse," even though he was calling the boys only during times permitted by the separation agreement. The mother blocked from her phone the father's phone calls, his parents' telephone number, and the numbers of all of his family members. When the children were with their mother, she refused to let them call their father. She even refused to permit them to call the friends they saw when they lived with their father. The mother would not talk to the father about any issues that needed to be resolved. The boys tired of their mother's conduct and became more insistent to both parents. But every attempt to deal with the issue was rebuffed. The older boy ran away from his mother four times.

The mother's conduct was inexplicable to me. The father had done nothing to warrant her extreme position. He had always been a strong and loving father and had an excellent relationship with his sons. But given the mother's refusal to interact with her ex-husband, this so-called joint custody arrangement did not work at all. The case illustrates that joint custody is only workable when the parents can communicate with each other and put the best interests of their children first. This was more like parallel custody, with the children living separate lives with each parent.

When the boys were eight and ten, the continuing difficulties were brought to a head by the mother's announcement to them that she planned to move from one end of the city to the other and to register them in a different school district. She did not seek the father's consent, even though the original agreement had required it, and also specified that they would remain in that school district until at least the end of grade five—one child had one more year there and the other three years. She even went so far as to propose that the parties exchange the children halfway between their homes near an exit on a highway. The boys were very unhappy about her plans, which would limit their time with their father. He would be unable to take them to school at the other end of Toronto and still get to work on time. As a result, he would have no choice but to give up some time with them. He asked me to intervene.

The original agreement had required the parties to attend mediation when certain issues arose, and so, once again, they trotted off to talk to the professional they had dealt with previously. Again, she was unable to facilitate a resolution. The mediation process by its very nature requires both parties to compromise to reach a settlement. This mother was not flexible, nor would she consider the needs or the stated wishes of the children. She blamed the father for the children's wanting to spend more time with him, but would not consider that her difficult relationship with the children had a bearing on the situation. The children met with the mediator and expressed their strong desire to spend more time with their father. Nothing came of their request. However, the mediator did prepare a report for use at trial. She wondered if the issues between the parties would have escalated to such an extent if the mother had simply listened to and accommodated her boys' requests to spend more time with their father. The agreement had provided for an assessment if mediation was not successful, but the mother refused to participate in that process.

So, five years after the initial court "emergency" motion was brought by the mother, and two years after the court's involvement in determining the children's place for religious education, this family had to go back to court for help in resolving all the basic issues of family life. Given the short time frame involved by then (there was about a month to go before school started), there seemed no option but to mount a legal challenge to the mother's unilateral action and seek a court order that the children remain in their customary and agreed-upon school district. At the same time, the father asked that the children be allowed to spend more time with him. In the process, everything that had happened over the years had to be detailed in the initiating court documents. The changes in the parties' personal circumstances were also relevant—both parents were in new relationships, and the father's wife was expecting a child. The father also asked for an increase in the vacation time with the boys. The original agreement had limited his vacation with them to one week, and while provision was made for an increase as the children got older, the mother did not permit it.

A judge made a temporary order that there was to be no change in the children's address or in their school until the motion was heard. Several weeks later, the motion was heard by another judge; she ordered on an interim basis that the children remain in their customary school, and she required the parties to attend an assessment required by the agreement, and thereafter return for a case conference. The mother persisted in her refusal to attend.

The case inched its way forward to trial and both parties amended their pleadings to ask for sole custody, as joint custody with unequal time was not working. The mother decided not to move out of the children's school district and agreed to permit four weeks' vacation for the father and children. These were the only changes.

On the eve of trial, at the trial management conference, the mother arrived without her lawyer. She said she had dismissed her counsel as she was no longer able to afford her services. The judge pressured me to try to settle the case. There had been many attempts, but I agreed to try once more, only if the mother was actually willing and interested in resolving the matter on an equal-time basis. I suspected the courts would not shift custody at that stage, but they might at least equalize the time with each parent. I put it to the mother that I would set aside the entire day of Friday in the hopes that we could work out a true and equal joint custody arrangement. She agreed. Having won the principle of equality, and with my client's agreement, we agreed to meet at 9 a.m. on Friday morning.

Knowing that you have to start from somewhere in order to resolve anything, I prepared a draft "minutes of settlement" with every conceivable detail specified as to who would do what and used it to focus the discussion. It took into account all the difficulties that had been brought to my attention over the years. That was Thursday. We met Friday morning at my office, with each parent having a copy of the draft. We worked all day, and in the end came up with an extremely detailed sixteen-page document with every possible issue and variable resolved. The basic structure was parallel parenting and not joint custody. The parents took turns with the children; they resided one full week at a time with each parent, alternating weeks, with the children moving from one parent to the other on Friday mornings at school to minimize contact between the parents. The arrangements for every holiday, including professional development days at school, were specified. They divided all vacations equally except that the children spent all Jewish holidays with the father and Christmas week with the mother. Passports, decision-making, extra-curricular program choices and transportation, place of residence, choice of school, communication by Internet message board—all were identified. It was the most detailed agreement I had ever been part of, but it was necessary in order to avoid, if at all possible, the need for more court involvement or even mediation. The wife had arranged for the lawyer she had dismissed to give her independent legal advice and advise her on the document, and that lawyer suggested a handful of small changes, which were ironed out. By the end of the day, at about 8 p.m., the minutes of settlement were signed. I went to court Monday morning for a court order in terms of the settlement signed, and was happy to have it over with, just as the father and boys were. This was in 2005, six years after the father had first consulted me. The boys were now eleven and nine years of age.

When the boys were twelve and fourteen, they found their own lawyer to talk to and help with their concerns about living with their mother. One day in 2008, they turned up with their things at their father's home after school and waited for him to come home. The mother called the police, who came to his home and talked to the boys. Given what they were told, the police officers refused to forcibly remove the boys from the father's home.

Then, in a surprising turn of events two years later, the mother disappeared, moving away from Toronto to parts unknown. By then, I had given up litigation and was working through the transition to my retirement. So my client had to find other counsel when, unfortunately, he had to go to court for a formal custody order. The mother had left without signing any papers transferring custody or at least giving the father permission regarding medical appointments, passports, et cetera. After eleven years of war, it was finally over.

The father kept me informed about how well the boys were progressing, and it was gratifying to learn that they had somehow survived the trauma of their childhood. With the formal custody order in hand, he was finally able to make arrangements for which the mother had always refused permission—counselling, orthodontic work, passports, and travel. The father was grateful to me for what he described as "saving" the boys and his family.

This case illustrates how difficult it is for the legal system to deal with issues of custody and access. The attempt at resolution is traumatic not only for the children and parents but for lawyers and judges too. In the end, a litigious battle involving children is a human tragedy. The final result negotiated in my office on the eve of trial was the one that should have been in place from the beginning, but the mother had to face a trial date and a potential loss of custody before she would agree to share the boys equally with the father. By then, it was too late to repair her own relationship with her sons.

THE CAMPAIGN FOR FAIRNESS IN CHILD SUPPORT

Child poverty has been an intractable problem in Canada. Many government policies contributed—a failure to implement an accessible child-care program for working parents, low government benefit programs, a failure to legislate a reasonable minimum wage. But from my perspective, few policy-makers and judges recognized that when divorce was liberalized, the financial needs of children were overlooked. Child support orders were inadequate and difficult to enforce.

Poverty-Stricken Children of Divorce

As a mother as well as a lawyer, I sympathized with the increasing number of single parents receiving insufficient child support. Most child support orders did not take into account the *real* cost of raising a child. Lawyers lived every day with the examples contained in the 1988 statistics from the Department of Justice, which showed that about 66 percent of divorced mothers and their children lived below the poverty line, even though they were receiving support, in contrast to 16 percent of divorced men paying support. We appreciated the American statistics too. Around that time, U.S. researcher Lenore Weitzman[218] found that divorced women and their children suffered an immediate 73 percent drop in their standard of living while their ex-husbands enjoyed a 42 percent rise in theirs. We heard the anguish expressed by clients and knew the statistics reflected reality.

As a single mother, I understood what a parent had to do to raise a child alone, and that a contribution to the cost of food and clothing and other basics did not answer the need. Much child poverty arose from divorce and inadequate financial arrangements for the children, and it was evident that something should be done about it as a matter of public policy. My January 1993 *Chatelaine* column bemoaned the paltry amount of child support payments and pointed out that they seldom covered the custodial parent's actual expenses for the children. It concluded by saying that anyone who agreed should write to the federal government (and gave the appropriate contact information).

And Then There Are the Taxes

Inadequate child support orders were not the only problem—the payments were taxable. Support payments in agreements and court orders were tax-deductible to the paying parent while the recipient had to pay tax as if support were earned income, instead of reimbursement for expenses. It was difficult to persuade a judge or master to take into account the correct amount of income tax payable on support orders, and to increase the order accordingly. The result of the tax impact could mean that the husband paid less child support (because he paid less tax), and the mother received less actual money. In any event, court orders ignored the fact that the custodial parent spent time and effort caring for the children that was not then and is not now compensated.

This Income Tax Act requirement was challenged as unfair by Quebecker (and custodial parent) Suzanne Thibaudeau; her case was heard by the Federal Court of Appeal on May 3, 1994. She argued that the amount of child support was already so low that to take off an additional amount for taxes would adversely affect her child's well-being. She asked for these tax rules to be declared invalid under the Charter of Rights and Freedoms. Mr. Justice James K. Hugesson acknowledged in his decision for the majority of the court the unfairness of the child support system.[219] The court ruled that single custodial parents (most of them women) should not have to pay income taxes on child support payments they receive from the other parent (most of them men). The court said that the income tax law was unconstitutional and infringed on the equality provisions of the Charter of Rights and Freedoms, since it discriminated against single custodial parents. He was saying what I had tried to persuade many a judge to say: that the amount of child support must be increased to realistically reflect the tax payable by the receiving spouse.

So that the court decision would be widely known and understood, I wrote an op-ed piece for the *Toronto Star*. The headline was "Court righted taxation injustice," and I couldn't restrain my delight: "As a 20-year veteran of the family law wars, I must say hallelujah and it's about time that the previously little-known injustice suffered by separated and divorced persons across Canada, was set right by the Federal Court of Appeal."[220]

However, the federal minister of justice, Allan Rock, decided to appeal the Federal Court of Appeal decision to the Supreme Court of Canada. At the same time, he appointed the secretary of state for the status of women, Sheila Finestone, to head a task force of Liberal members of Parliament to investigate how the child support system might be improved.

The Finestone Task Force

The task force was expected to have a series of round-table discussions with citizens and provide advice to cabinet and invited me to be among those making submissions. The hearings were lively and certainly made the government aware that the issue was of great concern to many people. At the hearing at a crowded, hot community centre in east-end Toronto on July 6, 1994, I said my piece. I was astonished at the boos and hisses that greeted my use of the word "feminist" when, as part of my self-identification, I described myself as chair of the Feminist Legal Analysis Section of the Ontario Bar Association. It turned out that there was a large group of fathers' rights activists present, some of whom blamed feminists for the fact that they had either lost custody or were having difficulty getting access to their children; they believed that fathers should not pay child support if they were denied access to their children. Many of them thought that the legal system favoured women over men, which was not my experience. However, it was true that in those days custody was more often granted to the mother than the father, on the basis that this was the woman's traditional role.

The *Globe and Mail*'s front page reported on this commotion the next day. The paper also recounted that the fathers' rights people demanded the removal of Sheila Finestone "on the grounds that she is a male-bashing supporter of women's rights." The reporter pointed out that the hearing made it clear that much more was at stake than taxation. The workings of the justice and tax systems were called into question, as was the treatment of men, especially divorced fathers. The men present felt there was substantial criticism of men, especially those who failed to support their children. But the *Globe*'s reporter commented that Revenue Canada figures said 98 percent of those who receive child support were women, that the most conservative estimates suggest that 40 percent of those ordered by courts to make payments do not do so, and that unpaid child support amounted to more than $400 million a year. Statistics Canada figures showed that 62 percent of single mothers lived below the poverty line in 1991.

This forum enabled all kinds of family issues to be debated. I had always worried about how a single parent coped with the paltry amount of child support usually ordered, combined with the modest spousal support and the expectation that women would be self-supporting. Some women turned up to the hearings representing themselves or groups. For the two-hour morning session, I was the only family law lawyer present and there were seven custodial mothers making presentations, four non-custodial fathers, the president of the Congress of Black Women of Canada, and three tax experts, all of whom supported the abolition of the tax on child support.

The powerful message that came out of the hearings was that tax was merely the tip of the child support iceberg. Equally important issues were child poverty resulting from minimal child support orders and the difficulty enforcing support orders. The task force was told repeatedly that judges were out of touch with the real cost of raising children and, as a result, gave capricious support awards. Sheila Finestone reported that judges were reluctant to receive training on these issues.

As I was leaving, two task force staffers stopped me to say thank you. They told me that they had received an avalanche of mail arising from my January 1993 *Chatelaine* column. They said that this had helped put the issue on the political agenda, so that when the *Thibaudeau* case hit the headlines, it was not the only child support issue the government needed to deal with. My impression was that these public servants had tried to get these issues on the agenda but could not do so without public pressure. My focus on this inequity had reached the attention of the powers that be, and I waited to see what would come of it.

Political Action
On July 25, I wrote to Minister of Justice Allan Rock and Minister of Finance Paul Martin suggesting the priorities: (1) abolish the inclusion/deduction tax system of child support; (2) validate existing agreements unless one of the parties disagrees; (3) establish a legislated system of child support guidelines to determine the proper amount of support payable (I felt that since judges and lawyers were not being realistic about what it costs to raise a child, guidelines based on the paying parent's income would be simple enough to establish and make it more likely that equitable amounts would be ordered or agreed to be paid); and (4) allow the legal fees that were paid to obtain a support order to be fully tax-deductible. (This was an add-on: I considered it unfair that a party to family law litigation was not able to deduct their legal costs as an expense spent to earn income, whereas a businessman could deduct legal fees spent in a commercial case.) I also pointed out that if the goal was to mitigate single-parent and child poverty, then a more appropriate method would be to improve child tax credits, enrich the equivalent-to-married credit, or add financing for child-care centres and programs.

Early the following year, the chief of the family law research section invited me to a consultation at the minister of justice's regional office in Toronto. The issue on the table was primarily the taxation of child support. The government was proceeding with its review of child support tax law, even though the government had won its appeal—the majority of the Supreme Court of Canada decided,[221] on May 25, 1995, to overturn the Federal Court of Appeal judgment in the *Thibaudeau* case and ruled that the tax rules did *not* infringe the equality rights guarantees in the Charter of Rights and Freedoms as the family as a whole benefited from the tax regime. The majority failed to acknowledge that it was the father rather than the mother or the children who received this actual tax benefit. Several anti-poverty groups as well as NAC and LEAF had intervened.

Of special interest to me was the fact that the majority who ruled in favour of the status quo were all men and the two dissenters were women—Madam Justice Claire L'Heureux-Dubé and Madam Justice Beverley McLachlin. The women judges understood the equities of the situation. Justice McLachlin, in her dissent, noted that the legal regime had been enacted in 1942 when few women worked outside the home and paid little or no tax on their support payments. She quoted from the House of Commons debates of the time, which were all about benefiting the husband in view of his likely remarriage. She noted that no one appeared to consider the ex-wife and the income she needed for the care of the children.

Fifty years after deductibility of support payments became law, 56 percent of married women were now in the workforce, and therefore their working income combined with their support income created a sizable tax obligation that ate into the funds available for the children. Justice McLachlin stated that in practice, judges do not correct this inequity. Either they do not consider the tax impact, or any adjustment made is inadequate to cover the additional tax that the custodial parent must pay. Justice McLachlin also noted that a survey of 147 judges conducted by a Nova Scotia Family Court judge in 1990 concluded that in only a minority of cases was there any evidence of the tax impact on child support, and that a majority of judges did not calculate the tax consequences.[222] She wisely observed that these practical problems are not remedied by the fact that the custodial parent can appeal a judgment that does not adequately take the tax impact into account, or apply to the court to increase child support under new circumstances. She understood that these corrective mechanisms put an unfair burden on the custodial parent.

Once again, the voices of women suffering inequities had been heard at Canada's highest court, although not by the male majority. However, the two female dissenting judges clearly understood the negative impact of the tax laws on mothers. It became apparent that the dissent was read very closely by the minister of justice and his staff.

This had happened previously in 1993 when the dissenting voices at the Supreme Court of Canada were the same two female judges—Madam Justice Claire L'Heureux-Dubé and Madam Justice Beverley McLachlin. Self-employed lawyer Beth Symes had challenged the law that did not consider child care/nanny costs tax-deductible whereas a man's golf club fees were. Symes could not work without child care, but it was still deemed a personal not a business expense. Her counsel was the leading feminist constitutional litigation lawyer of the day, Mary Eberts. I wrote about it in *Chatelaine* and in my books, always highlighting the dissent of the two women judges. The dissent said that the tax laws should be adapted to reflect the changing role of women in the workplace and the family. Unfortunately, this is still an unresolved issue for working women.

On March 6, 1996, Allan Rock released his child support strategy, which featured excellent principles and goals. He seemed to ignore the majority decision of the Supreme Court of Canada in *Thibaudeau*, when he could just have left things alone and relied on the court's ruling. Instead, he introduced legislation ending the tax on child support—the payor of support could no longer claim a tax deduction and the recipient no longer had to pay tax on child support payments. He set up a predictable system of Canada-wide Child Support Guidelines—the amount of child support to be determined by a chart based on the payor's income. He strengthened enforcement procedures using federal powers; if the payor could not be traced, the government would check their income tax files to locate a current address. So non-paying parents could run, but they could no longer hide as easily. Existing agreements and their tax consequences were validated, but only if the parties agreed and left the agreement unchanged.

While the plan was positive, it contained matters of concern. My main worry was that it was the government that was benefiting from the legislative change and not the children of divorce. Also, the child support amounts in the chart needed to be increased. I said so in my op-ed piece for the *Toronto Star*, published on March 22, 1996:

> I wish it were not necessary to write this. I wish the government really had accomplished what I have to believe it set out to do, and which it trumpeted in the recent budget: ensure that children of divorce get adequate support by removing the tax

consequences and establishing child-support guidelines for the courts. Otherwise what was the purpose of the exercise? But the end result appears to be that the payers (usually men) lose little to nothing and the women and children get the short end of the stick, again.

I had asked my husband to analyze and compare the old and new system and calculate the amount each parent would end up with: the husband in disposable income and the wife in spendable child support. As a forensic family law accountant, the chart Jack prepared as the illustration to my article proved that there would be less money available for the children while the fathers would have only slightly less disposable income for themselves. Meanwhile, the government would end up with $250 to $400 million more in taxes as a consequence of the change in the tax structure. I urged the government to go "back to the drawing board."

Allan Rock responded by writing a letter to the editor of the *Toronto Star*. He admitted that the government would add about $200 million to its coffers as a result of the change, but said any additional money would go toward an enriched Working Income Supplement, which he estimated would aid about 700,000 low-income working families. This would not necessarily help any of the individual women who received child support. I sent a copy of my article to journalists, politicians, and heads of influential women's groups, asking them to add their voice to the quest for improvements. Other family law lawyers also expressed their views supporting improvements.

A Good Day for Children

The final plan that was enacted effective May 1, 1997, was a federal system of Child Support Guidelines that resulted in more generous child support awards for children than the government had initially planned, calculated according to charts. It was applicable across Canada as all provinces agreed to it (except for modifications made by Quebec). The basic amount of support was based on the payor's income only, and an additional amount was allowed for "extraordinary expenses" such as university education and orthodontic expenses, which were shared by both parents (if the custodial parent was also working). At the same time, child support payments no longer attracted tax consequences. It was such a welcome change, and it enabled lawyers to resolve child support matters at far less expense to the client—more settlements and less litigation.

May 1, 1997, was a good day for children.

What Are a Child's Best Interests?

When I was growing up, parents were expected to keep their marriage together for the sake of the children. This hope evaporated when people faced the reality that children were seriously affected if they lived in a conflict-ridden home with two battling parents, and divorce laws were liberalized. But it has taken a long time to acknowledge the effect of divorce on children, especially if the parents continue the struggle from their separate homes. Fights over custody, access, decisions, extra-curricular activities, extended families, choice of schools and courses, financial support—you name it, parents clash over it. Everyone talks as if they know what the best interests of the child are, but each person has their own definition, and some parents confuse their own needs with those of their children. Judges, lawyers, and parents keep trying to invent presumptions, rules that can apply across the board. Rules after all, would make the results of disputes more predictable and would encourage settlements. But each child is different. For me, the best rule is to avoid litigation whenever possible and to negotiate an agreement that meets the needs of the child, and vary it as circumstances change. Children cannot manage conflict, so the parents have to find a way to work together and create a conflict-free home or homes for the child.

Chapter 16
VIGILANCE

Since 1989, the goals and efforts of second-wave feminism were to sustain the legal and societal advances we had made and the organizations that gave our movement the structure and support to carry on. We were learning how politicians made promises they didn't keep, gave funding they didn't maintain, and passed laws they didn't enforce. The accomplishments of one government could be removed by the next. Consider this small but telling example: Thérèse Casgrain, who had been a lifelong Quebec feminist activist, was honoured by the Pierre Trudeau Liberals in 1982 by the establishment of the Thérèse Casgrain Volunteer Award. The Brian Mulroney Progressive Conservatives discontinued the award in 1990, but the Jean Chrétien Liberals reinstated it in 2001. In 2010, Conservative Stephen Harper eliminated and then repackaged it as the Prime Minister's Volunteer Award. In 2016, the Justin Trudeau Liberals restored it, renaming it the Thérèse Casgrain Lifelong Achievement Award.[223]

I personally had lawyered and lobbied and written during a fifteen-year period from 1974 to 1989 when it was possible to proactively urge and achieve legal and practical change. But those days began to fade as more right-wing governments took over and either weakened or obliterated the advances we had made. So we learned we had to be vigilant and build a community to carry on with or without government support. My form of vigilance was to highlight, write, and speak about continuing concerns and to contribute to the organizations working for women that had endured.

I began to consider retirement from the day-to-day practice of law in the first decade of the twenty-first century, when it seemed I had done everything I could to help both individual clients (with personal solutions) and the community (with systemic solutions). I started by withdrawing from trial work in about 2007; I stayed with cases involving negotiations and collaborative practice for another five years. But I continue my involvement in women's issues as an activist, maintain my membership in and support of all the organizations to which I am committed, and focus now on my writing about law and the women's movement. I have made it a goal to ensure that I leave a record of the history of the times in which I participated, and to preserve personal archival materials. And I want to share what I have learned from my years as an advocate and activist—including that you must be wary, vigilant, and proactive to keep the gains, and achieve more.

These are some of the lessons I learned by observing the political manoeuvring that seemed to surround and obstruct the laws and programs developed or promoted to achieve women's equality.

BEWARE POLITICAL MANOEUVRING
There were myriad ways in which women's rights and needs and the laws protecting them were ignored, undermined, and subdued. Laws alone were never enough to ensure the relative permanence of improvements. A new government might reverse policies and programs that reflected the societal consensus under the prior government. Often the changes were ideologically driven, radical, and unilateral. I tried to stay vigilant and alert to the inroads and onslaughts of ideological change-makers, and speak and write about it when possible. It was challenging to mount campaigns against policies when governing parties were becoming noticeably less responsive to citizens' concerns.

The techniques used to defeat the advances made by the women's movement were sometimes blatant, but often they were very subtle and could slip by public notice. Opponents both within and outside government chose a variety of cagey paths: defunding, delay, diversion, resistance, rule-changing, destruction, and sometimes a combination of strategies. Consider the following "sneak attacks," some of which were successful while others were stopped by concerted efforts on the part of people willing to go to bat.

Undermining Pay Equity

One ploy often used by those in power is to leave a law or agency in place but cripple it by reducing its funding. Just ask former Ontario premier Mike Harris.[224] Created by the Ontario Liberals in 1987 and improved by the NDP in 1993, the pro-active and effective Pay Equity Act and the Pay Equity Commission had decreased the pay gap between women and men. Then the Progressive Conservative Harris government undermined it by reducing funding for pay equity in the public service, which reversed the trend. The Service Employees International Union mounted a successful court challenge, but the government entered resistance mode and defied for a long time the court order to pay up.

Delay was another tactic used on this front. It took the Public Service Alliance of Canada *thirty years* to get its pay equity complaint against Canada Post heard—their eventual victory had been stalled by Canada Post's appeals and then delays in paying what the court ordered. The case had been launched in 1983, and a victory was declared at the Supreme Court of Canada in 2011. It took another two years before Canada Post started to pay the affected women workers or—given the passage of time—their estates; the process is ongoing.

Child Care—Always on the Back Burner

Politicians in power have used every trick in the book to withstand effective, accessible, affordable child-care places for children. Change the subject. Change the solution. Divert attention. Make promises but don't keep them. In 1993, Liberal Jean Chrétien became prime minister and the Liberal Red Book of progressive policies promised a universal, accessible, and well-funded national child care program.[225] It did not happen. In 2003, Chrétien's successor, Paul Martin, readied a national plan with the approval and support of all the provinces. On the brink of implementation, an election was called.

I was one of those who worried that a Conservative victory might threaten women's advances. I voiced this concern by writing an op-ed column for the *Globe and Mail* on June 26, 2004, reminding women how previous Conservative governments had eroded their equality rights. I noted, in particular, that a similar group—Mike Harris's Ontario Conservatives—had made heavy cutbacks to social programs affecting daycare, pay equity, employment equity, women's shelters, welfare, and more. The Paul Martin Liberals returned to power in 2004 with a minority government, and Stephen Harper and his Conservatives were stalled—that time—in their path to power.

Two years later, however, Paul Martin's minority government fell and Harper's right-wing Conservative government took over, also as a minority. Within weeks, Harper unilaterally cancelled the planned national child-care program, without any discussion in Parliament and even though all provinces had agreed to support the program. The motivation for the decision was clearly ideological rather than financial, as there was a sizable surplus in the federal coffers, and money had been budgeted for it. The Harper Conservatives replaced the plan for more child-care spaces with a taxable cheque of $100 per month for certain families, which was not enough to enable a family to pay for a child-care spot (if one could even be found).

Child care has always been a major yardstick by which to measure women's equality, and here we were again, obstructed. I was part of an ad hoc group that came together to try to stop the cancellation of the national plan, but it was difficult to develop an effective strategy to influence a government that did not seem responsive to public opinion.

With the Liberals back in power in 2015, a renewed effort to advance child-care programs may be effective. However, there is no indication at this writing that the Liberals will do anything more than an enhanced payment program to families. There continues to be a significant need for the construction of child-care places to be available at reasonable cost for working families across Canada.

Crippling Status of Women Canada

Women had achieved a voice at the top through the federal agency Status of Women Canada, established in the 1970s with a mandate to seek equality for women. When Stephen Harper was elected prime minister in 2006, he found a way to cripple the agency without abolishing it. The Harper Conservatives eliminated twelve of Status of Women Canada's sixteen regional offices, cut 40 percent of its budget, and changed its operating rules. They expunged its equality-seeking mandate and specified that the agency was not allowed to support or fund any activity that could be defined as lobbying. But because the agency still existed, the actions went largely unnoticed by the public and were mostly ignored by the media.

Just before the 2008 election, I wrote an article published in the on-line magazine *Straight Goods*, in which I pointed out the damage done to the good work of the previous thirty years. Sadly, the Harper government was re-elected in 2008 with another minority government—and again in 2011 with a majority government—and Status of Women Canada (SWC) did not recover from the 2006 wrecking ball.

It seems to be getting its footing back under the Justin Trudeau Liberals, elected in October 2015. The equality-seeking mandate was quietly returned to the SWC website to describe the work of the agency, and on July 1, 2016, the government restored advocacy activities as eligible for government funds. Still, women must remain watchful to ensure these goals continue.

Suppressing Employment Equity

Employment equity was another issue that was central to the possibility of women achieving equality. The first sign of government interest in dealing with this ongoing problem came in 1983, when the Pierre Trudeau Liberals established the Royal Commission on Equality in Employment and appointed Judge Rosalie Silberman Abella as commissioner.[226] The commission's job was to inquire into "the most efficient, effective, and equitable means of promoting employment opportunities, eliminating systemic discrimination, and assisting all individuals to compete for employment opportunities on an equal basis" by examining the practices of government agencies and Crown corporations. I was one of many consulted in the commission's impressively wide-ranging investigation of the problem.

Judge Abella reported in 1985 to Prime Minister Brian Mulroney and his minister of employment, Flora MacDonald, who implemented some of her suggestions in the 1986 federal Employment Equity Act. The act obliged federally regulated private-sector companies and Crown corporations to create plans and file reports showing that they intended to achieve employment equity for women and other disadvantaged groups. Employment equity was the term used by the Abella commission to identify what had previously been called affirmative action—a term that had fallen into disfavour because of its association with mandatory quotas.

The challenge to equality of opportunity for women—whether it was called affirmative action or employment equity—was the misguided assumption that women with no merit would be hired ahead of talented men. This was never the belief of anyone I ever talked to in the women's movement, but was used as an excuse to stall advances for women.

A companion piece of policy—the Federal Contractors Program—required large provincially regulated companies to institute employment equity programs as a condition to getting certain government contracts. In 1995, the act was amended to apply also to the federal public service.

The Abella commission report was important, and the federal legislation arising from it was promising. However, the government legislation was toothless—the only penalty was for failure to file reports and *not* for failure to achieve employment equity.

However, the commission had a wide-ranging impact beyond the federal sphere. The Toronto Women in Film and Television—led by Barbara Barde and Elaine Waisglass—had organized professional research on the employment issues facing women in film and television. They invited me to consult on employment equity issues in the federally regulated field of broadcasting. The survey results showed clearly that women in this field were treated unfairly, that there were pay inequities, few employment opportunities, and limited access to government funding and to the powerful jobs, and, as a result, little opportunity to influence programming. I saw the research as confirming the systemic discrimination seen everywhere affecting women.

They asked me to contribute a chapter to their book of analysis entitled *Changing Focus: The Future of Women in the Canadian Film and Television Industry*, published in 1991. I wrote about the need for strong laws enforced by government and backed by pro-active programs to try to create the attitudinal and structural changes necessary to achieve equality. It was clear from the Abella commission report that voluntary programs and self-regulation were not effective, and broadcasters could not be relied upon to regulate themselves when it came to women's equality. I said, try these for a change: permanently fund employment equity programs; put some teeth into employment equity legislation, and make the achievement of equity mandatory; make the rules unequivocal with stringent penalties for non-compliance; make managers personally accountable; use the licensing power to promote equity and discourage sexual stereotyping; appoint many more women to boards; refuse government contracts to companies that had no employment equity plans. This roadmap set the goals, but implementation has been just as intractable in the broadcasting industry as it is elsewhere.

Another effort to come to grips with employment equity was made by the Ontario NDP government in 1993 when, under Bob Rae's leadership, it enacted the Employment Equity Act, which was comprehensive employment equity legislation affecting more than 17,000 companies and 75 percent of all Ontario workers, including all public service employees and businesses with more than fifty employees. Employers were required to establish employment equity plans that would identify and take positive measures to eliminate systemic employment barriers. The legislation was disparaged by opponents as a quota system, but it didn't specify quotas; it only required companies to have goals and then plan for their achievement.

This provincial legislation so angered Mike Harris's Ontario Conservatives that when they came to power in 1995, they not only dismantled but destroyed the NDP's efforts on this front. When they repealed the law, they even took the outrageous and unheard of step of requiring companies that had already complied with the 1993 legislation to *destroy* information they had secured. The government offices carrying out employment equity were closed and the entire staff was dismissed. These tactics made the operation even of voluntary employment equity programs more difficult and actively *prevented* the improvement of women's employment situation in those places that had already begun to implement the law.

I saw this destructiveness at work again when Stephen Harper's federal Conservatives quietly undermined the federal Employment Equity Act, which had been enacted in 1986. Even though the law was never tough enough and the Senate, in fact, had produced three reports—in 2007, 2010, and 2013—with recommendations to make it work more effectively, the Harper government weakened it further. In 2012, hidden away in a section of a federal budget omnibus bill, the effectiveness of the program was reduced—while the federal Employment Equity Act and the Federal Contractors Program continued to exist, their rules and funding were undercut and usefulness eroded. The omnibus bill methodology had started with Ontario premier Mike Harris in the 1990s to render numerous legal changes less visible by dumping them all into one piece of legislation. Prime Minister Harper took this stratagem a step further by burying many issues into a budget; opponents found it more difficult to object because they didn't want to defeat the budget, which was the financial underpinning of the government.

Cancelling Court Challenges Programs

Destruction was once again the method used by the Harper Conservatives when the Court Challenges program was excised completely in 2006. But they weren't the first—the program was initiated in 1978 by the Pierre Trudeau Liberals to deal with language rights, and was expanded to include equality rights in 1985 by the Mulroney Progressive Conservatives, who then terminated it in 1992. Reinstated in 1994 when Jean Chrétien's Liberals were in power, this program had helped women's groups and others to challenge discrimination before the courts, and particularly to apply the Charter's equality rights in effect since 1985. The circle has gone around again, and the Justin Trudeau Liberals announced in 2017, as this book went to press, the reinstatement of a Court Challenges program. Unfortunately, the funding is very modest—$5 million a year of which $3.5 million is for human rights, which includes equality rights—and administrative set-up costs will take a large piece of it. There are more potential claimants for the $3.5 million—a small pie divided into more slices. Women must ensure that organizations such as LEAF, which defends equality rights, receive needed funding.

Failure to Oppose

It might be easy to develop the impression that the women's movement had its sights set only on the ruling party. Nothing could be further from the truth. In Canada, where minority governments are often in power, one never knows when the official Opposition might take over the government, and because of that, Opposition leaders and shadow cabinet members are never off the hook.

It's also worth remembering that the role of an official opposition party is to…well…oppose! But when it came to protecting the gains made by the women's movement, the Opposition more than once let us down. Yes, Harper's Conservative government had diminished women's hard-fought rights during its terms as a minority government from 2006 to 2011, but the Liberals as the official Opposition in those days allowed them do it. In 2009, I gave them some advice in a letter to the editor published in the *Globe and Mail*,[227] suggesting that they pay attention to the Conservative's erosion of pay equity rights, the dropping of an effective child-care plan and the Court Challenges program, and the weakening of Status of Women Canada. I encouraged them to "stand up for us in a real way" and to remember that the Conservatives were governing as a minority. Sadly, the Liberals during that time let us down. The party did not have consistently strong leadership after Paul Martin stepped down following his election defeat in 2006. Between 2006 and 2013, when Justin Trudeau was chosen leader, the Liberal Party had four leaders—interim leader Bill Graham, then Stéphane Dion, then Michael Ignatieff, then interim leader Bob Rae. However, that minority status did not last, and things became worse. In May 2011, the Harper Conservatives received a majority in Parliament. From that point on, they seemed to feel and act even more unrestrained to ignore the needs of women—until 2015, when the Harper Conservatives were defeated and Justin Trudeau and the Liberals came into power with the promise of a more progressive approach. So far, Prime Minister Justin Trudeau has appointed an equal number of women and men to cabinet, increased the amount of the child-care benefit, and set up the Inquiry into Missing and Murdered Indigenous Women. While there is every indication that his government will be more amenable to improvements in the status of women, continuing vigilance and involvement by women is necessary to ensure that promised and necessary advances are in fact made.

Is Electoral Reform the Answer?

All of these fluctuations in policy and programs were possible because successive governments had used their power to do what they wished, whether or not there was a consensus in society. There was a time in Canadian history when the prevailing custom was for even a majority government to seek a consensus of the populace before making a major policy change. Increasingly, this approach seemed a relic of the far distant past. If majority governments governed only for the benefit of themselves and those who voted for them, then the rest of us would be left to fend for ourselves in a divided society.

I grew up and have always voted under the present electoral system, called "first past the post" or "winner-take-all," an arrangement by which the winning candidate is the one who gets the most votes, even if they don't add up to or even come close to a majority. While this may be fair when only two people are running, it is not fair when there are three or more people or parties in contention. Over the years I have become convinced that a form of proportional representation would be best for everyone, including women.

Unless the popular vote matters, it is *very* difficult to elect the people who truly represent the electorate. There are too few women in politics, and too few feminists. I think we need them. Whenever someone I knew and respected was prepared to run for office, no matter for which political party, I financially supported their candidacy.[228]

Doris Anderson led the way in championing proportional representation as the solution to the dearth of women elected under the first-past-the-post system. She travelled around the world to research the issue, and in her 1991 book, *The Unfinished Revolution,*[229] she reported that countries with proportional representation elected more women to public office. She campaigned for electoral reform in Canada and in 2000 co-founded the lobby group Fair Vote Canada and served as its first president. Doris invited me to be on the advisory board to show the widespread support there was for this goal, and I agreed.

Then, in 2001, Equal Voice was founded[230] to get more women elected to Parliament, with political journalist Rosemary Speirs as founding chair. At its first organizational meeting, Doris Anderson spoke about the need for proportional representation, and it became one of the goals of Equal Voice. I also joined this group.

There seemed to be lots of support for electoral reform. In 2002, the (federal) Law Commission of Canada started a research and public-consultation project on electoral reform. Their report was tabled in the House of Commons on March 31, 2004, and it called on Parliament to scrap the first-past-the-post voting system and institute Mixed Member Proportional (MMP), where two-thirds of the seats would be chosen based on the current riding system, and one-third by lists for proportional top-up based on the percentage of the popular vote that a party received in the riding. While the report was being discussed, an election changed the federal Parliament from a Liberal majority to a Liberal minority, only to be followed two years later, in 2006, by the election of a minority Conservative government. Prime Minister Harper not only ignored the report, he abolished the Law Commission of Canada, and nothing further was heard regarding proportional representation on the federal level.

The Ontario government, however, was persuaded to start a process to evaluate electoral reform. In 2006, Dalton McGuinty's Liberals set up a Citizens' Assembly to undertake this task. The Citizens' Assembly represented a new kind of democratic decision-making and a first for Ontario, with ordinary citizens recommending policy. The Assembly brought together 103 randomly selected Ontario citizens to learn, consult, deliberate, and come to a decision on an electoral system to recommend for Ontario. The chair was George Thomson, a former judge and public servant. The assembly was guaranteed its independence from government and direct access to Ontario voters through a referendum if it decided to recommend change.

The assembly reported in May 2007 and endorsed an MMP system similar to the one recommended by the Law Commission of Canada. Voters would have two votes: one for a local candidate and a second for a party. Each party would nominate local candidates as well as a "party list" of candidates for the entire province, in the order it wanted them to be elected; ninety MPPs (70 percent of the legislature) would continue geographic representation by being elected from local ridings, and thirty-nine MPPs (30 percent of the legislature) would be elected from the party lists, based on each party's share of the total party vote.

The lists, naming individuals in order of selection, would be created by each political party *before* the election, using an approved and transparent method. We anticipated that the parties would be pressured to put many more women on their lists, as this is what had happened elsewhere. A party would have to achieve a threshold of at least 3 percent of all ballots cast to get a seat from the list. The proposal had features of well-functioning proportional systems in Germany, New Zealand, Scotland, and Wales. In Germany, 32.2 percent of members are women, and in New Zealand 30 percent. Most of the women and minorities came from the party lists.

The referendum took place on October 10, 2007, only four short months after the assembly had released its report. This was not enough time to mount an effective campaign, especially in view of the obstacles set in the way. Defunding, resistance, rule-changing—the government used all of these methods to undermine the Citizens' Assembly that they themselves had established. The government of Ontario pulled the plug on financing for the Citizens' Assembly, whose members had anticipated that they would be able to travel the province to explain their process and recommendations. As a result, few Citizens' Assembly members were seen or heard from during the referendum campaign. Instead, Elections Ontario, a government agency, was given the job of educating the public, and did a poor job of it. Their literature did not clarify the complexities of the proposal and did not even distribute the material prepared by the Citizens' Assembly for public education purposes. Then the government set an impossibly high standard of victory. Premier McGuinty changed the rules and said he wouldn't enact the proposed system unless the referendum achieved a 60 percent "super majority" of voters as well as majority approval in at least sixty-four ridings. Even worse, the government did not defend or even comment on the MMP proposal.

The MMP plan was left to flounder, except for a modest amount of media attention and the efforts of those of us who did the best we could to make up for the fact that the government seemed to have washed its hands of proportional representation. I was one of those pressed into service by both Fair Vote Canada and Equal Voice to write about and speak to groups to explain and defend the proposal, and I was glad to do so.

In the end, however, it wasn't enough; the referendum result was a clear and disappointing no. Only 37 percent of those who voted were in favour of MMP, and in only five out of 107 ridings did a majority opt for it.

Proportional representation is still a good idea, and I continued to support the work of Fair Vote Canada and Equal Voice. I also used the many opportunities presented by subsequent election results to point out the failure of the first-past-the-post system. After yet another federal election in 2008 with skewed results, I couldn't resist sending a letter to the editor, published in the *Globe and Mail*, in which I pointed out that the election "proves that our electoral system is on life support—and we should be pulling the plug on it to put Canadians out of our misery."[231] I declared that the current system was not effective in a Canada with five political parties, and every election proves it. Consider this: in 1993, the Chrétien Liberals won 60 percent of the seats with a mere 38 percent of the votes; in 2011, the Harper Conservatives won 54 percent of the seats with just 39.6 percent of the popular vote; and in 2015, the Justin Trudeau Liberals won 54.4 percent of the seats with only 39.5 percent of the vote. At the same time, the NDP, Greens and Bloc Québécois received more votes than was reflected in their seat count.

During the 2015 election campaign, at a time when the Liberal party was in the political wilderness, Justin Trudeau vowed to make it the last election under the first-past-the-post system. However, in 2017, after achieving a majority government, he withdrew this oft-repeated promise of electoral reform. I continue to hope that activists (now led by Fair Vote Canada and Leadnow) will be able to persuade Trudeau or his successors that the MMP form of proportional representation should be chosen.

TELL IT LIKE IT IS
Vigilance takes many forms. Woven through my life's work was my writing, which I used to educate the public on what the laws were as well as to alert them to hazards and propose reforms. My column

in *Chatelaine*—which lasted for twenty-five years—was my most consistent opportunity to do this.

Initially, *Chatelaine*'s editors kept its columnists on a leash; they did not want to offend the magazine's traditional readers. But when the climate of opinion was less socially conservative, they were eager to print columns that showed the magazine as a trendsetter. By the late 1980s, *Chatelaine* editors were more willing to address, and indeed *asked* me to write about, more trendy subjects. For example, I wrote columns on AIDS in its early days, from the perspective of the legal rights of an infected woman (at a time when few women were infected). In the 1980s, there were few criminal and civil remedies available to deal with men who recklessly transmitted AIDS when they knew they were infected but didn't tell their partners. I suggested novel legal avenues that were not obvious at that time.

I wrote about non-smokers' rights before there were any. In the early to mid-1980s, a reader asked how to get someone to "butt out," and I suggested ways that were in the law but did not directly deal with non-smokers' rights, such as occupational health laws, workers' compensation, building codes, et cetera. Initially, the smokers on the editorial staff had not wanted me to write about this subject, feeling that smoking at that time was a "human right." It never was.

I was always careful to be responsible and feared anyone taking my advice carelessly. When I wrote about the legalities of ending a life due to terminal illness, I expressed the law very cautiously. I did not want anyone to point to my advice as giving them permission to pull the plug on a loved one. This issue arose a number of times in different ways, and I was able to canvass the issues from every angle.

I wrote in 1979 in favour of paternity leave, and about sexual harassment in 1981. Over the years, rape and sexual abuse were explored from every legal perspective—marital rape, incest, the use of counselling records to challenge the victim, date rape, and much more as lawmakers were being pressured to get the law right to protect women. I answered the question in the November 1980 column: Should I Report a Rape? Women were warned about the health impact of breast implants by alerting them to the successful lawsuits against breast implant manufacturers. Women were told how little protection they really had in the workplace and the need for improved equal pay laws. Daycare came up—I considered how

a working mother could find daycare and laid out the legal requirements for a woman to operate her own daycare centre. Legal rights
in marriage and divorce and common-law rights as they expanded
over the years were explained. There were columns about support
obligations, custody and access issues, and duties to stepchildren.

Questions were answered dealing with first marriages, second,
and subsequent marriages, estates and wills, pensions, powers of
attorney, and living wills (before and after they were legal). I wrote
about the law and sex—legal options in a sexless marriage, and how
adultery affected rights in a divorce. I started writing about same-sex
rights in the 1990s when human rights laws across Canada began to
protect gays and lesbians from discrimination and court cases entitled same-sex couples to share benefits. The gay community, freed
from the taint of criminality by the decriminalization of homosexu-
ality in 1969, challenged the laws that marginalized them, using the
1985 protections entrenched in the Charter of Rights and Freedoms.
Since then, same-sex rights have multiplied, so that now, same-sex
marriage (and divorce) is part of the law of the land.[232]

I described laws involving children, a parent's legal responsibilities, criminal laws involving sex and teens, rights of children born
outside marriage, protecting children from child pornographers,
molesters, cults, and abduction. I described fetal rights, surrogate
parenting, and rights and duties of sperm donors. By 1995, the social
climate had changed enough that my column was able to advise a
single woman of the legal ramifications of having and raising a child
alone. I clarified the legal issues involving the purchase of a home,
mortgages, insurance, and investments. I tried to help readers access
the legal system by explaining how to manage a small claims court
action, how to be a self-represented litigant, and how to get legal aid.

Over the twenty-five years (1979–2004) that I wrote the
Chatelaine column, I canvassed every conceivable subject and trend
that the average person would need to know about or be interested
in. And I was never at a loss for a topic. Cases and events in the news
provided fodder. I got many letters from readers with questions and
comments, which were helpful in choosing subjects for the column.
I felt that the information I provided and the perspective I gave on
the issues were a public service and something readers would otherwise not be able to access.

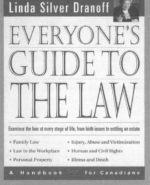

I also wrote books. In 1977, I wrote *Women in Canadian Life: Law* and in 1985, *Every Woman's Guide to the Law.* By 1997 I added a third book—*Every Canadian's Guide to the Law*[233]—an encyclopedic guide for every Canadian that provides information on the laws that affect individuals from birth to death, starting with the rights of a fetus and ending with settlement of an estate. And the book dealt with everything in between: working life, marriage, divorce, human and civil rights, criminal charges and civil remedies, property ownership, illness, retirement, and access to the legal system. I explored new trends that were reworking and transforming the law into another version of itself. I included all the issues about which women needed information. I demonstrated the flexibility of the law by showing the way it evolved in response to changing social values. I also presented options for law reform and encouraged readers to be a part of the democratic law-making process, suggesting ways to do so. The book has been in print for twenty years through four editions so far.

While both the *Chatelaine* column and the books were great platforms for the dissemination of knowledge and the discussion of important ideas, there were times when the issue was "live" and I felt the need to comment right away. When those types of issues came up, I would write a letter to the editor. I pressed for the use of public schools for child care,[234] stood up for pay equity, questioned paltry child support,[235] and clarified the law of common-law partners.[236] I also supported other women. When Flora MacDonald—a member of Parliament since 1972, the first secretary of state for external affairs (now minister of foreign affairs), and a victim of her own party[237]—was described in the *Toronto Star* in 1982 as "frantic," I was irritated by the newspaper's choice of language and penned a letter to the editor:

> If MP Flora MacDonald were a man, a week in her life might have been headlined "hectic" but certainly not ridiculed as "frantic," a word suggesting hysterical frenzy and usually misapplied only to women (Aug 1). Flora MacDonald obviously serves her constituents well. She works hard and devotedly, and deserves our respect.

In October 1986, I was outraged that Elinor Caplan lost her Ontario cabinet position because of a potential conflict-of-interest error by her husband, so I wrote a letter to the editor:

> Ontario MPP Elinor Caplan has not acted in breach of her public duty, according to all reports. Consequently, she should be returned to her Cabinet positions. Since when do we tar and feather our good public servants for trusting their spouses and staying out of their affairs? The continuing indignation is unseemly.[238]

After 2006, with advocacy groups de-funded by the Harper Conservative federal government, there have been fewer people in a position to blow the whistle on injustices affecting women in particular, so I have done what I could. For instance, in 2008, I highlighted Newfoundland's reported discrimination against oncologists who treat female disorders in terms of their rates of pay. In a letter to the editor of the *Globe and Mail*, I wrote:

> The women's equality perspective is missing. The cancers these doctors treat affect women exclusively, and the doctors are female. Newfoundland raised the pay of other oncologists by 35 percent but left out those who practise this female specialty. Patients are affected by underfunding of support services, pathology, equipment, pharmaceuticals, hospital beds, operating rooms, and access to clinical trials. The Health Minister says he will solve the problem by sending women away for care. This is adding insult to injury, as treatments can be periodic rather than concentrated.

Laura Legge, June Callwood, and Doris Anderson attended the launch of *Everyone's Guide to the Law: A Handbook for Canadians*, April 1997.

The result would take women away from their families and affect their employment at a vulnerable time.[239]

I was one of a number of voices that caused the government to deal more fairly with this issue.

I also wrote about public policy issues—MPs salaries[240] and the deregulation of Bell Canada in 1984 among them. By 2004, the Liberals were veering to the right, and in the run-up to the election, Prime Minister Paul Martin—with a surplus in the government coffers—was promising to send everyone a cheque, even as he cut social programs. In a letter to the editor, I wrote:

> I completely disagree with the federal government's plan to distribute part of the surplus by sending everyone a cheque. This is not in the public interest. Use the money for health care, education, child care, public broadcasting, and other programs and support services for citizens. To justify his plan, the Prime Minister would have to convince us that there are no unmet societal needs. I would like to see him try to do that.[241]

I was also very concerned about the significant downloading of federal responsibilities to the provinces. I wrote a letter to the editor of the *Globe and Mail*:

> At the same time as Ottawa is blessed with a significant surplus... Ontario and other provinces are underfunded.
>
> Let's not forget that when Paul Martin was finance minister, the federal government engaged in extensive downloading to the provinces of increased responsibility for costly programs without also downloading dollars to help pay for them.
>
> The provinces have been crying for help ever since. It's time for this inequity to be addressed and our taxpayer dollars to be more fairly distributed among the provincial governments.[242]

I took a good deal of personal satisfaction from my writing. I feel that ideas sent out into the universe have some impact—even if, as the author of those words, I don't know where they land or what use is made of them. Over the years, however, I have discovered a happy side benefit to this work. It seems that my public involvement—the letters, the books, and, particularly, my column in *Chatelaine*—allowed me to serve as a role model. A number of young woman lawyers have approached me over the years to acknowledge that when *Chatelaine* arrived at their homes, often in small-town Canada, they would grab it to read. I was told that they felt that if I could be a lawyer, so might they be able to. It was a great source of pride to me that I inadvertently helped many young women find their way by my example.

BUILD COMMUNITY

I have always believed that it's important for women to stick together and to work together for common goals and to maintain advances. Some wonderful moments have come as a result of this type of teamwork. A particularly memorable example came with the opportunity to entrench a feminist view of law into the establishment structure.

Executive of the Feminist Legal
Analysis Section of the Ontario
Bar Association 2011: (l to r seated)
Maryellen Symons, Janet Green,
Patricia DeGuire, Jean Franklin
Hancher, Sheryl Smolkin; (standing
l to r) Lorin MacDonald, Linda,
Judith Huddart, Michelle Kemper,
Christi Hunter, Paulette Pommells,
Joan MacDonald, Gia Gray

Feminist Legal Analysis Section

The idea germinated in the spring of 1992,
after I attended an all-day CBA-O program
on feminist legal analysis. The conference
was chaired and organized by Professor Mary
Jane Mossman of Osgoode Hall Law School
and Professor Sanda Rogers of the University
of Ottawa.

The subject was so controversial for a Bar Association event that
I attended in order to support it by bearing witness and participating.
The discussions were so enlivening and, at that time, revolutionary
that I didn't want it to stop. I stood up at the end of the program
and proposed that what was started that day should continue as a
section of the CBA-O, with regular meetings and frequent programs
on the feminist analysis of law. The audience cheered.

A number of the women lawyers present congregated afterwards and expressed enthusiasm and so, with that support, I went
to the association and asked for their endorsement of a Feminist
Legal Analysis Section. They surprised us by responding positively.
However, they asked that we first form a more informal committee
to determine the level of interest. Of course, having spoken up,
I was the one expected to implement my suggestion. We created

the Feminist Legal Analysis Committee, which we called "FLAC." We liked the name, as it presaged standing up actively for feminist views of law. Our first presentation was in September 1992, and we attracted excellent attendance—145 women crammed into the room with more than thirty-five turned away. People were extremely attentive throughout the evening. The energy and enthusiasm was boundless—people would not leave; they must have stayed an extra half hour talking.

We were so successful that the Council of the Bar Association agreed after the unusually brief time span of one year to elevate our standing to become a full section. I have always been grateful to the leadership of the Bar Association, at that time and since, for their support and encouragement of our feminist section, an unprecedented group and the first of its kind in Canada. I was particularly grateful to Erica James, who was the president both when we were a committee and also when we were accepted as a Section; she was a keen supporter of our group and attended many of our meetings.

We continued to call ourselves FLAC, even after we became a section. I served as chair for three years and continued to serve on the executive and as an advisor for many years thereafter. Then, my law partner, Judith Huddart, took over and served as chair for two years after I stepped down. She was followed by Danielle Bush, Joy Casey, Maryellen Symons, Marlo Shaw, Jean Franklin Hancher, Michelle Kemper, Joan MacDonald, Shelley Quinn, Sabrina Bandali, and Ashley Waye.

Our goal was threefold: (1) to provide a setting where academics and practising lawyers could exchange ideas and provide an intellectual underpinning in practice for the feminist understanding of law, (2) to provide a collegial and congenial setting for women lawyers to meet and advance the position of women in the legal profession, and (3) to provide a feminist voice and perspective to positions of the Bar Association that otherwise would only express a more mainstream view.

We accomplished all three. We presented an exceptional array of interesting programs with intellectual depth and practical inspiration. We provided the wonderful women who have been active on the section executive an opportunity for friendship and collegiality in a common cause, and those less active with inspiring programs. And we

Michele Landsberg, Doris Anderson, and Linda enjoyed the FLAC Award dinner for Mary Eberts, May 2002.

contributed to formal positions taken by the Bar Association, such as to briefs on health law, rules of professional conduct, rules for re-entry of lawyers who have taken time out of their practice (for example, to have a family), arbitration of family law disputes, restructuring of the Human Rights Commission, division of pensions between separating spouses, laws affecting seniors, changes to the Family Law Act, pay equity, and Madam Justice Bertha Wilson's Canadian Bar Association Task Force on the position of women in the legal profession.

Through FLAC, we were able to maintain vigilance by organizing feminist programs on all the important women's issues of the day—including those with respect to sexual assault, new reproductive technologies, pension and tax issues, domestic workers, Indigenous women and equality, midwifery, mediation, sexual harassment, product liability issues such as breast implants, multiple discrimination, international law, protecting equality rights in the era of privatization, immigration, family law issues, violence against women and children, human trafficking, environment, pay equity, women in politics, pregnancy discrimination, and so much more.

We encouraged and supported the women who ran to be benchers of the Law Society, and we had programs for women lawyers on mentoring, marketing, starting and running a feminist law practice, coping techniques for women lawyers, articling, and alternative careers.

Madam Justice Claire L'Heureux-Dubé receiving FLAC's first Award for Commitment to Equality in 1996 from Linda.

We had so many brilliant and knowledgeable feminist speakers over the years.[243] In fact, the leading lights of the feminist legal community and the non-legal feminist community all participated in our events at one time or another, contributing their knowledge and expertise to the rest of us.

We gave our commitment to equality award to some spectacular feminists: Madam Justice Claire L'Heureux-Dubé, Doris Anderson, Anne Derrick, Michele Landsberg, Mary Eberts, Professor Ursula Franklin, Professor Emily Carasco, Mary Lou Fassel, Kate Hughes, Brenda Cossman, and Sukanya Pillay. FLAC also presented me with the award in 2005.

FLAC gave many women lawyers the opportunity to work together as feminists for the benefit of all women, including women lawyers, and to practise sisterhood in the open. However, the "feminist" label became an epithet to some, and the Bar Association was concerned that some women might not join under that label. Under pressure from the Ontario Bar Association, in 2013, the executive of FLAC agreed to change the name of the group to the Women Lawyers' Forum (WLF) in order to be more universally appealing, and in keeping with the name of the national Canadian Bar Association group that had evolved over the years after our ground-breaking Feminist Legal Analysis Section was founded. I was disappointed to lose the name, but I was assured that nothing else would change. I was relieved when I attended an executive retreat of the newly named WLF to find that every one of the executives present self-identified as feminist and planned to continue what FLAC had started—and they have been doing so. The Bar Association made a video for its website to mark the transition and the history of FLAC's first twenty years.[244]

The Report on Gender Equality in the Legal Profession

While FLAC was working through the Ontario Bar Association (OBA—formerly known as the Canadian Bar Association–Ontario) to give feminists a voice and a place to experience community, the national Canadian Bar Association (CBA) decided to deal with issues facing women in the legal profession across Canada. The CBA asked former Supreme Court of Canada justice Bertha Wilson, who had retired in 1991, to conduct a task force on gender equality in the legal profession.

Justice Wilson met with many of the women lawyers and judges who had graduated over the preceding fifteen years, and she was the only one to meet with the female judges, as they would only talk to her in confidence and off the record. Some of us conducted small group discussions for her in order to get a sense from individual lawyers of their experiences and to share our own. I remember with blistering clarity the group of young corporate lawyers from the big downtown Toronto firms who scoffed at me for advising them to get the experience they needed at the large firms and then go out on their own with other women lawyers. I said that in my experience and to my knowledge, the large firms were unlikely to accommodate their need for home/work balance if they chose to start a family. Their response: the firms *must* accommodate us.

The Wilson Report, called *Touchstones for Change: Equality, Diversity, and Accountability*, was issued in 1993; it was damning in its denunciation of the inequalities faced by women in the legal profession. Justice Wilson highlighted the sexism still rampant at that time and the fact that women earned less than the men and were less likely to attain partnerships in large law firms. Many of the women revealed substantial sexual harassment within the legal profession. The report focused on strategies for achieving gender equality in every sector of the profession and made 250 recommendations for change. Above all, Justice Wilson told firms they had a duty to accommodate family responsibilities and to eliminate sexual discrimination and harassment. An action plan to guide the necessary changes was also released.

Ursula Franklin and Michele Landsberg congratulate Linda following her acceptance of the FLAC Award for Commitment to Equality, 2005.

No one has done a follow-up of the Touchstones study to determine if and to what extent its recommendations were implemented, but in 2005, Ontario's Law Society of Upper Canada established the Retention of Women in Private Practice Working Group. They

(l to r) Mary Ross Hendriks, Linda, Judith Huddart, Sandra Demson, Patricia DeGuire at the 10th anniversary celebration of the OBA Feminist Legal Analysis Section, 2002

did so because of the large numbers of women leaving private practice, primarily because it had not adapted to their realities, such as childbirth and taking on a significant portion of family responsibilities. I thought back to the women I had met in the Touchstones seminar in 1992, and how sure they had been that firms would have to accommodate their needs. The Law Society Working Group reported in 2008 with suggestions for improvements, such as the establishment of a parental leave program for sole and small firm practitioners, a practice locum service, and the creation of the Justicia Project. In this initiative, the Law Society would work with a group of large and medium-sized law firms across the province to implement programs aimed at improving the retention of women. There has been no report to date on the effectiveness of these programs for women lawyers.

The Wilson report shone a light on the issues and solutions for women lawyers that continue to need attention and improvement. The national Women Lawyers' Forum gives women lawyers the opportunity to work together in common cause. I've often said that women need an old girls network, since the old boys have mostly not let us in to theirs. Sadly, many men still have a tendency to slot

Mary Eberts and Kay Sigurjonsson at the FLAC Award Celebration for Ursula Franklin, 2007

us in as support workers. We need structures of our own—places where sisterhood can be practised. With the number of women's organizations out there, it could seem as if this work is done. It's not. We need a deeply entrenched commitment to sisterhood to sustain the progress we've made.

Sustaining the Feminist Community

And what progress it's been! Consider: the Royal Commission on the Status of Women set the agenda; the National Action Committee on the Status of Women, the Ontario Committee on the Status of Women,[245] the Equal Pay Coalition, and Status of Women councils across Canada worked to see that the RCSW report was implemented; women lawyers, with our advocacy training and skills, led the way on many campaigns and set up organizations to benefit all women; the National Association of Women and the Law did research and briefs; and LEAF ensured that the Charter of Rights and Freedoms would work for Canadian women.

Other organizations provided specialized services. Women educators including Sheila Roy, Pat Kincaid, and Veronica Lacey formed Women in Educational Administration Ontario (WEAO).

(l to r) Sally Armstrong, Marilou McPhedran, Shelagh Wilkinson, Carolyn Bennett, Michele Landsberg, and Linda at the party celebrating the release of the special issue of the *Canadian Women's Studies Journal* on the legacy of Doris Anderson, March, 2008

The Barbra Schlifer Clinic in Toronto, for many years under the leadership of lawyer Mary Lou Fassel, provides personal and legal counselling services to women experiencing violence. The YWCA—in Toronto under the leadership of Heather McGregor—focuses on help for women and girls who need shelter and jobs and are escaping violent situations. Others created shelters for abused women and women in need—for example, Interval House, which Trudy Don founded so many years earlier, continues. The Canadian Women's Foundation formed in 1991 to encourage philanthropy benefiting women under the leadership of Rosemary Brown, Mary Eberts, Dawn Elliot, Nancy Ruth Jackman, Kay Sigurjonsson, Elizabeth Stewart, Julie White, and Susan Woods.

Many of the traditional women's clubs continue. Coalitions formed whenever a need arose. And women met informally to plan and to keep their spirits up. I joined with a group, initiated and led by Barbara Caplan, Kay Sigurjonsson, and Ethel Teitelbaum, of politically engaged women of all parties. We called ourselves Wednesday Women, and we met every other month for twenty years to socialize, discuss, and intellectually strategize on the political issues of the day.

I was active in many of these groups, in one way or another. I attended, I donated, I supported, and I lent my name and reputation and ideas. I was glad to serve and learned so much from the people I served with.

As time went on, feminist lawyers were recognized and accepted for their achievements and ability to contribute to the mainstream. These are just a few not already mentioned. In 1987, Mary Eberts chaired the Ontario Task Force on Midwifery, which led to the 1992 law that regulated and licensed midwives, a benefit to many women. Maureen McTeer was a member of the Royal Commission on New Reproductive Technologies, which reported in 1993; in 2004, a new law was enacted. Janice Rubin led the CBC Workplace Investigation Regarding Jian Ghomeshi on the issue of workplace harassment, which reported in 2015. Constance Backhouse was chair of the Task Force on Misogyny, Sexism, and Homophobia in Dalhousie University Faculty of Dentistry, which reported in 2015. In all these cases, the fact that the lawyers were also feminists did not prevent them being asked to serve and advise, as it might have done years earlier.

Activist women did not engage only in political and policy work. We knew how to party! One of the biggest celebrations we ever had was the eightieth birthday party for Doris Anderson on November 9, 2001, at Toronto's Royal York Hotel. It started small—the idea and leadership came from journalists Michele Landsberg and Sheila Kieran, who had both worked with Doris at *Chatelaine*. A gang of us "Dames for Doris" were the organizing team[246] to salute Doris's achievements and rejoice in the hard-won progress of Canadian women in the twentieth century. The gala also raised funds to endow a graduate scholarship at York University in Doris's honour. The keynote speaker was Governor General Adrienne Clarkson, who had in her early days contributed to *Chatelaine* as a journalist. We sang and laughed and applauded and had a wonderful time, filling not only the ballroom but a huge overflow room.

· · · · · · · · ·

Unfortunately, not all of these efforts at community building have survived or sustained their early strength and support. Women's organizations, in particular, have been hard hit. NAC, now defunct, used to be the public voice of the women's movement representing at its strongest seven hundred organizations, conducting an annual lobby with cabinet ministers in Ottawa. It was government-funded (about 90 percent of its budget) until successive governments, beginning with Mulroney's Progressive Conservatives in the mid to late 1980s started slashing. Most of the serious cuts to NAC's funding were done by the federal Liberals. NAWL's funding was completely wiped out by the Harper Conservatives in 2006 — so they had to close their offices, fire their paid staff, and reduce their programming. They continue their work to the extent that donations and volunteer time allow. LEAF's funding was also slashed, but it continues with some endowment funds, fundraising, and lawyers willing to volunteer their time to take cases to court. The Federation of Women Teachers' Associations of Ontario was a major source of support for feminist efforts until it merged in 1998 with the Ontario Public School Men Teachers Federation to form the Elementary Teachers' Federation of Ontario (ETFO), after the men brought a court challenge about their separate status.

Other organizations carry on, helped by funding and support from like-minded individuals, including the stalwart backing from philanthropists including Nancy Ruth Jackman and Shirley Greenberg. It is essential that all women appreciate the importance of women's organizations to our ability to promote change as needed, as well as sustain and entrench the advances made by feminists over the years.

Conclusion
OVER TO YOU

As I look back over the years I have spent working as a lawyer and activist in the women's movement, I can say without hesitation that I've been blessed to live at a time when positive change was possible and one person could make a lasting impact on society. I recognize that I might not have grasped the opportunity to contribute as I did had I not developed the confidence to trust my own insights and instincts. I hope that you, dear reader, particularly young people starting out on your own path, find a way to trust *your* insights and instincts, to summon the courage to become your own person and live life on your own terms. Trust your own judgment about who you are and what you need. Assert with confidence your goals, and do the best you can to succeed according to your own definition of success. I was so lucky to have been able to carve out a way to become the kind of lawyer I wanted to be and achieve the goals I set for myself, while operating within a world that had very different expectations of me.

I hope that every woman reading this book understands the importance of working together with other women in sisterhood. I have always believed that it is only when women work together that beneficial change can be sustained. When you are in a position to help others, it is an opportunity. Remain vigilant to ensure that the advances my generation made are not taken away from you. Be aware of the areas that still require attention, and do what you can to be agents of further change. Speak, as I tried to do, for women who otherwise have no voice.

Identify yourselves as feminists. I have always been proud to be called a feminist, and to call myself one. To me, it is a venerable description of a person who believes in fairness and equality. I realized back in the early days that some people would ridicule whatever we called women's battle for equality and fairness. So I and many others stood firm in the face of scorn by continuing to valiantly use the feminist appellation. I know that today, some younger women feel uncomfortable being identified as feminists. Is it because they think that all of the battles have been won, or that the label is no longer necessary? Whatever the reason, I encourage them to look at this issue with an open mind and consider the importance of maintaining the historic and iconic name.

In the battle for fairness, it is important to acknowledge that there are many men who are feminists, who have supported the goals of the movement, and who sought equality for their wives and daughters. There are men who have mentored and befriended women. A few male judges and lawyers rose above the biases of their colleagues. Some male politicians saw the justice in women's claims for equality, and fought for women at the cabinet table or from opposition benches. I have known and loved some wonderful men in my time—my father, husband, and brothers among them—but I have also known those who are jealous, vindictive, and hostile. Women and men must work together for a fair and just society; we cannot transform society without men onside.

I encourage women to keep working for real reforms, such as a national plan for universal and accessible child-care programs and facilities, full access to abortion, practical help and legal assistance for women suffering violence, and financial support for the centres caring for them, pay and employment equity in all sectors—including independent contractors and precarious workers, more feminists in politics and on corporate boards, access to legal justice, and more. Remember how ingrained the justification for discrimination is, and how much of the battle remains to be won. We still have to change the inbred bias reflected by the words of one judge in a discrimination case in the late

1960s, when he commented that the female plaintiff "was not being discriminated against by the fact that she receives a different wage, different from males, for the fact of difference is in accord with every rule of economics, civilization, family life, and common sense."

It was exciting and thrilling to be part of the second wave of feminism, and all the issues and events that sprang forth, one after the other. It was exhilarating to be part of the historic events for women and for the women's movement, and to be there at the beginning of significant organizations and events.

I use the term "women's movement," but we weren't a superbly structured, military-type organization. We were individual women who came together on an ad hoc basis to fill critical needs. We asked for the support and help of other like-minded women; whoever had time gave time, whoever had ideas gave ideas, and whoever had a name that might lend credibility gave that too. I know that this was how my lobby effort for family law reform began. I saw a need and created a way to fill it.

There were many others doing the same thing. Doris Anderson found herself at the helm of Canada's biggest women's magazine, *Chatelaine*, and used that perch for twenty years to focus on the women's issues she felt were most important. In the process, she brought visionary thoughts and information to Canadian women on such shocking-for-its-day subjects as abortion, discrimination in employment, abuse of women, and more. She found herself in charge of the federally funded Canadian Advisory Council on the Status of Women at the height of the battle for the Constitution, and she resigned over the government's cancellation of a planned conference on the Constitution and women's issues. Two other formidable individuals—Marilou McPhedran and Linda Ryan-Nye—stepped in to lead the ad hoc committee that took its place, and sent out the word to like-minded women who came to Ottawa in droves to support the cause of constitutional equality for women.

The handful of committed women who founded the Women's Legal Education and Action Fund (including Nancy Ruth Jackman—later a senator, and lawyers Beth Atcheson, Mary Eberts, Marilou McPhedran, and Beth Symes in Ontario, with others from coast to coast to coast) knew that the Charter's fine words providing for equality rights were not enough; an organization was needed to ensure that those words were implemented for women's benefit. LEAF intervened in court cases destined to have a systemic effect on equality rights, and numerous women litigation lawyers pitched in to help. Mary Cornish, a Toronto labour lawyer, founded the Equal Pay Coalition to work toward equal pay laws and then tenaciously persisted to ensure that the laws passed actually were as effective as possible. Beth Atcheson, Constance Backhouse, Lorraine Greaves, Diana Majury, and Beth Symes founded the Feminist History Society, with the impressive goal of recording the history of second-wave feminism—the Society has to date produced seven books.

Four Supreme Court of Canada judges found a way to eloquently contribute from the bench, and not just through their decisions. Justice Claire L'Heureux-Dubé, Justice Bertha Wilson, Chief Justice Beverley McLachlin, and Justice Rosalie Silberman Abella wrote decisions that reflected an understanding of women not otherwise available in the courts. Moreover, Justice Abella advanced the cause of women's equality when she sat as chair of a royal commission on employment issues, where she coined the term "employment equity." At the request of the Canadian Bar Association, Justice Bertha Wilson took on the task of analyzing the status of women in the legal profession, and making recommendations for improvements.

June Callwood, a persuasive journalist and activist, founded Jessie's for teenaged girls, Nellie's for women in need, and Casey House for people living with AIDS—all because she saw a need and acted to fill it. Ursula Franklin, a brilliant university professor, was an activist for peace through the Voice of Women and a visionary and spokesperson for feminism. Maude Barlow founded and continues to lead with great effectiveness the Council of Canadians, an organization that speaks for all Canadians in social justice matters. Michele Landsberg wrote columns on feminist issues—a single individual with a powerful voice. Journalist, human rights activist, and *Homemakers* editor Sally Armstrong raised awareness of women's issues and particularly the plight of Afghan women on her own at a time when no one else was paying any attention. Fiona Sampson founded the Equality Effect to use human rights laws to help rape victims in Kenya achieve justice and safety. Political scientist Sylvia Bashevkin analyzed why women's representation and women's issues were stalled in Canadian politics. Elaine Todres, from her powerful position within the Ontario government as deputy minister, contributed to pay equity laws. Chaviva Hošek was a gifted spokesperson for the women's movement as president of the National Action Committee on the Status of Women and later pressed women's concerns onto the public agenda as a member of the Ontario provincial Parliament and key policy advisor to then prime minister Jean Chrétien.

When businesswomen Myra Sable Davidson and Lynn Kinney decided in 1984 to organize Lunches with Leaders, it was, at the outset, just the two of them with an idea and a plan. The child-care lobby was informed by the energetic and knowledgeable efforts of such women as Martha Friendly, Laurel Rothman, and Julie Mathien. Nancy Ruth Jackman and Shirley Greenberg not only were involved in feminist activities, but were also philanthropists who generously directed large amounts to women's movement organizations and activities. The support of Ontario's Federation of Women Teachers' Associations of Ontario (known as FWTAO) was of incalculable value, particularly in the early days when FWTAO provided office space and staff—led by Executive Director Kay Sigurjonsson—to help the early women campaigners for change. And there were others, as the pages of this book attest.

As issues came up over the years, the effort to make beneficial change for women often started with an individual or a small group with an idea and determination. In my view, this is how transformations are made. It starts with an individual who has a vision and a commitment to a better world, and it finds a consensus among compatriots on the same wavelength. I encourage those who follow us to do the same, to never ask, "What can one person do?" but rather to say, "This is what needs doing, and this is what I will do about it."

Constance Backhouse

Flora MacDonald

Linda Silver Dranoff, Laurel Broten

Susan Gibson, Carolyn Stamegna, Linda Silver Dranoff, Jean Franklin Hancher

Judith Finlayson

Barbara Caplan, Linda Silver Dranoff, Marilyn Roycroft

June Callwood

Marilou McPhedran, Naomi Black, Jean Augustine, Sally Armstrong

Chaviva Hošek, Sylvia Bashevkin   Nancy Ruth Jackman

Judy Rebick, Doris Anderson, Lorna Marsden, Mary Eberts, Kay Sigurjonsson, Linda Silver Dranoff

LIST OF ACRONYMS

BPW: Canadian Federation of Business and Professional Women's Clubs

CACSW: Canadian Advisory Council on the Status of Women

CBA: Canadian Bar Association

CBA-O: Canadian Bar Association—Ontario

CCMW: Canadian Council of Muslim Women

CEW: Committee on Equality for Women

FFQ: Fédération des femmes du Québec

FLA: Family Law Act of Ontario (1986)

FLAC: Feminist Legal Analysis Committee/Section of the OBA

FLRA: The Family Law Reform Act of Ontario (1978)

FRO: Family Responsibility Office

FSP: Family Support Plan

FWTAO: Federation of Women Teachers' Associations of Ontario

JCFLR: Justice Committee for Family Law Reform

LEAF: Women's Legal Education and Action Fund

MMP: Mixed Member Proportional

NAWL: National Association of Women and the Law

NCW: National Council of Women

OBA: Ontario Bar Association

OCSW: Ontario Council on the Status of Women

OLRC: Ontario Law Reform Commission

OWD: Ontario Women's Directorate

RCSW: Royal Commission on the Status of Women

SCC: Supreme Court of Canada

SCOE: Support and Custody Orders Enforcement Act

SWC: Status of Women Canada

UTDU: University of Toronto Debating Union

VOW: Voice of Women *and* Voice of Women for Peace

WLAO: Women's Law Association of Ontario

WLF: Women Lawyers Forum of the Ontario Bar Association

ENDNOTES

[1] Dr. Elizabeth Bagshaw opened the first family planning clinic in Canada in 1932 and was never prosecuted. It was not until 1969 that contraception was legalized. See Linda Silver Dranoff, *Women in Canadian Life: Law* (Fitzhenry and Whiteside, 1977), 39–40.

[2] The law was modified in 1969 to permit an abortion with the approval of a hospital committee of three doctors whose role it was to determine if the woman's life or health would be in jeopardy if she carried the pregnancy to term.

[3] This eased in 1968 with the passage of a federal Divorce Act, which allowed divorces after three years' separation, or earlier if specified marital misconduct was the cause. Later, in 1985, the law further loosened with the availability of a divorce after one year's separation.

[4] The Female Labour Force Participation Rate in Canada for married women in 1941 was 3.74 percent, according to the 1941 Census, vol. III, table 7, vol. VII, table 5.

[5] Protective legislation included rules about the weight of objects women were permitted to carry, restrictions on women working in bars, and more. See Dranoff, *Women in Canadian Life: Law,* 70–73.

[6] Gail Cuthbert Brandt, Naomi Black, Paula Bourne, Magda Fahrni, *Canadian Women: A History* (3rd edition: Nelson, 2011), 409.

[7] Brandt, *Canadian Women: A History*, 409.

[8] See Catherine L. Cleverdon, *The Woman Suffrage Movement in Canada* (University of Toronto Press, 1950, 1974).

[9] See www.thecanadianencyclopedia.ca/en/article/franchise/#h3_jump_2.

[10] This changed in 1977 when the Canadian Citizenship Act allowed a mother to choose Canadian citizenship for her child. Dranoff, *Women in Canadian Life: Law*, 97.

[11] The Ontario Human Rights Code—the first in Canada—was enacted in 1962 to protect against discrimination. A federal Bill of Rights was passed in 1960.

[12] See, for example, Mary Jane Mossman, "'Invisible' Constraints on Lawyering and Leadership: The Case of Women Lawyers," *Ottawa Law Rev.* vol. 20: 567 (1988); Mary Jane Mossman, *The First Women Lawyers* (Hart Publishing, 2006).

[13] Dranoff, *Women in Canadian Life: Law*, 84–87.

[14] Dranoff, *Women in Canadian Life: Law*, 75; Byron G. Spencer and Dennis C. Featherstone, 1970 DBS p. 12; Statistics Canada, 1971 Census, vol. III, Catalogue 94–706, Table 14, Catalogue 94–774, Table 8.

[15] Nellie McClung was a politician, author, and social activist. See Veronica Strong-Boag and Michelle Lynn Ross, eds., *Nellie McClung: The Complete Autobiography* (University of Toronto Press, 2003). Emily Murphy was the first female magistrate in Canada and the British Empire in 1916. Irene Parlby was elected to the Alberta legislature in 1921 and became the first woman cabinet minister in Alberta. Louise McKinney was the first woman elected to a legislature in Canada and the British Empire in 1917. Henrietta Edwards founded or co-founded a number of organizations for women, including YWCA, National Council of Women, and Victorian Order of Nurses.

[16] See Brandt et al., *Canadian Women: A History*, 390–95.

[17] There were others, too, such as the Federated Women's Institutes, YWCA, Victorian Order of Nurses, and the Women's Christian Temperance Union.

[18] Brandt et al., *Canadian Women: A History,* 393.

[19] Brandt et al., *Canadian Women: A History,* 393.

[20] Dranoff, *Women in Canadian Life: Law*, 79, and Sylva M. Gelber, "The Labour Force, the G.N.P. and Unpaid Housekeeping Services" in *Women's Bureau*, 1970. Information Canada 1971.

[21] Dr. Marion Powell opened, in 1966, the first municipally funded birth control clinic in Canada when she was medical officer of health for Scarborough. www.womenscollegehospital.ca/about-us/our-history/our-pioneers/dr-marion-powell.

[22] For more information on these women, see Ursula M. Franklin, *The Ursula Franklin Reader: Pacifism as a Map* (Between the Lines, 2006); Kay Macpherson, *When in Doubt, Do Both* (University of Toronto Press, 1994); and Marion Douglas Kerans, *Muriel Duckworth: A Very Active Pacifist* (Fernwood Publishing, 1996).

[23] See Thérèse F. Casgrain, *A Woman in a Man's World* (McClelland and Stewart, 1972), and Micheline Dumont, *Feminism à la Québécoise* (Feminist History Society, 2012), part two.

[24] Monique Bégin, "The Royal Commission on the Status of Women in Canada: Twenty Years Later" in Constance Backhouse and David H. Flaherty, eds., *Challenging Times: The Women's Movement in Canada and the United States* (McGill-Queen's University Press, 1992), 22–38.

[25] See Wendy Robbins, Meg Luxton, Margrit Eichler, Francine Descarries (Eds.), *Minds of Our Own: Inventing Feminist Scholarship and Women's Studies in Canada and Québec*, 1966–76 (Wilfrid Laurier University Press, 2008).

[26] See Kathy Megyery, *Women in Canadian Politics: Toward Equity in Representation* (Dundurn Press, 1991); Heather MacIvor, *Women and Politics in Canada* (University of Toronto Press, 1996); Sylvia Bashevkin, *Women, Power, Politics: The Hidden Story of Canada's Unfinished Democracy* (Oxford University Press, 2009).

[27] Lorna R. Marsden, *Canadian Women and the Struggle for Equality* (Oxford University Press, 2012), 189–94.

[28] See for example, Judith Finlayson, *Trailblazers: Women Talk about Changing Canada* (Doubleday Canada, 1999); Judy Rebick, *Ten Thousand Roses: The Making of a Feminist Revolution* (Penguin Canada, 2005); and Marguerite Andersen, ed., *Feminist Journeys* (Feminist History Society, Ottawa, 2010), all books reflecting in their own words the wide array of individuals who participated in and contributed to the advancement of feminism in Canada.

[29] *Citizens' Forum* started as a weekly radio program in 1942 and was later simulcast as a TV program too. It was a discussion show that addressed major policy issues. Listeners voted on upcoming topics, and the Canadian Association for Adult Education produced printed pamphlets so listeners could read up on debate topics in advance, contribute informed questions during broadcasts, and have local discussion groups. The subtext was that the ideas of the average person were important. I got the message that my thoughts and views could be openly and publicly expressed on important public policy matters. It provided me, and others, with wonderful encouragement to participate in the policy issues of the day.

[30] See Robert Bothwell, *Laying the Foundation: A Century of History at the University of Toronto* (University of Toronto Press, 1991).

[31] The Co-operative Commonwealth Federation; in 1960, this became the New Democratic Party (NDP).

[32] He would go on to become leader of Ontario's NDP from 1970 to 1978 and Canadian ambassador to the United Nations from 1984 to 1988, among other posts held.

[33] I later came to learn about the work of the Famous Five and the Women's

Clubs, but at that time their efforts were not widely known or taught in Canadian history classes. See Introduction within.

[34] The beginning of second-wave feminism in Canada is generally thought to have started about 1960 with the formation of the Voice of Women. By 1966, a number of traditional women's organizations joined together under Laura Sabia's leadership to form the Committee on Equality for Women (CEW); these included YWCA, Women's Christian Temperance Union (WCTU), National Council of Women of Canada, National Council of Jewish Women, Imperial Order Daughters of the Empire, Federated Women's Institutes, and the Canadian Federation of Business and Professional Women's Clubs. They were part of the lobby effort to secure a Royal Commission on the Status of Women. See Brandt et al., *Canadian Women*, 390–95, and the Introduction to this book.

[35] There were other pressures too. See David Kilgour, ed., *A Strange Elation: Hart House, the First Eighty Years* (Toronto: University of Toronto Press, 1999), 133–47 for a full discussion of Hart House and women.

[36] I later came to learn what it would have been like for me in the diplomatic service when I read Margaret Weiers's book on this subject. But I also learned that until 1971, married women could not be part of the Foreign Service, and in fact, Margaret Weiers had had to leave for this reason when she married in 1955. See Margaret K. Weiers, *Envoys Extraordinary: Women of the Canadian Foreign Service* (Dundurn Press, 1995). Also see www.usask.ca/greenandwhite/issues/2010/fall2010/features/cover_story.php.

[37] I had studied the Russian language during the evenings in third year, but with my full course load in honours history, my part-time jobs, and my extra-curricular activities, I simply could not find the time to do the homework.

[38] This is equivalent to about $32,000 in 2016.

[39] This is equivalent to about $40,000 in 2016.

[40] The Royal Commission on the Status of Women reported in 1970 a "nation-wide demand for child-care services" (p. 261).

[41] By the late 1990s, seven out of ten mothers with children under age 16 were working for pay. Brandt et al., *Women in Canada: A History*, 437.

[42] *Obiter Dicta*, September 22, 1970.

[43] The term actually originated in a women's caucus of the Student Union for Peace Action among young women tired of being restricted to support roles instead of leadership roles. It expanded into a nationwide movement, and in 1970 organized the March on Ottawa for a repeal of the abortion laws. See *Report of the Royal Commission on the Status of Women* (Ottawa, 1970), 352.

[44] Monique Bégin followed this stint with an election win in 1972 to the House of Commons and then an appointment to the Pierre Trudeau cabinet in 1976.

[45] See Crystal Sissons, *Queen of the Hurricanes: The Fearless Elsie MacGill* (Feminist History Society and Second Story Press, 2014).

[46] Judy La Marsh, *Memoirs of a Bird in a Gilded Cage* (McClelland and Stewart, 1969), Pocket Book edition, 1970, 306.

[47] La Marsh, *Memoirs of a Bird in a Gilded Cage*, 315.

[48] The organizations included National Council of Women, YWCA, United Church Women, Business and Professional Women's Clubs, Catholic Women's League, IODE, Federation of Women Teachers' Associations of Ontario (FWTAO), and Voice of Women. See Kay Macpherson, *When in Doubt, Do Both* (University of Toronto Press, 1994), 150–53.

[49] Doris Anderson was editor from 1957 to 1977 of *Chatelaine* magazine and brought numerous women's issues to public attention through the magazine.

[50] The numbers that Laura Sabia threatened would march for the creation of a royal commission differed in different accounts. Kay Macpherson recalled "a million" in *When in Doubt, Do Both* (p. 150), while the first *Globe and Mail* report on January 5, 1967, said that she would ask the two million members of the Committee for Equality's thirty-three constituent organizations to plan marches on Ottawa. By 1975, Laura Sabia told a *Chatelaine* interviewer that she had said, "I can march 3 million women to Ottawa." (see Cerise Morris, *No More Than Simple Justice: The Royal Commission on the Status of Women and Social Change in Canada,* unpublished Ph.D. thesis in the Department of Sociology, McGill University, 1982).

[51] La Marsh, *Memoirs of a Bird in a Gilded Cage*, 316.

[52] The chairs after Laura Sabia (1971–74) included Grace Hartman (1974–75), Lorna Marsden (1975–77), Kay Macpherson (1977–79), Lynn MacDonald (1979–81), Jean Wood (1981–82), Doris Anderson (1982–84), Chaviva Hošek (1984–86), Louise Dulude (1986–88), Lynn Kaye (1988–90), Judy Rebick (1990–93), Sunera Thobani (1993–96), Joan Grant-Cummings (1996–99), Terri Brown (2000–02), Sungee John (2003–05), and Dolly Williams (2006–?).

[53] F. Folk, "On Women in Law," Articling Newsletter (Osgoode Hall Law School, 1971), 4 and 8.

[54] F. Folk, "On Women in Law," 4.

[55] *Osgoode Hall Law Journal* (August, 1972), vol. 10, no. 1, 177–90.

[56] For example, one of the three persons who interviewed me at McCarthy & McCarthy told me twice that they were "obviously interested" and if I were to get another offer, to please let them know before deciding.

[57] One of my female classmates had powerful connections, but even so could not get a job at one of these large firms.

[58] The conference was held March 14–16, 1974, and I was called to the Bar on March 22, 1974.

[59] She is now a judge of the Ontario Superior Court of Justice.

[60] The speakers included sociology professor Margrit Eichler; film-maker Judy Steed; history Ph.D. candidate Veronica Strong-Boag; federal government lawyer Eileen Mitchell Thomas; lawyers Julien Payne and Maureen Sabia of the federal Law Reform Commission Family Law Project; Crown prosecutor and professor Mary Jane Binks Rice; Barbara Landau, psychologist and member of the Ontario Status of Women Council; family lawyer and junior counsel on the *Lavell* case Frances Smookler; Katherine Cooke, chair of the federal Advisory Council on the Status of Women; law professor Mary Eberts; Voice of Women activist Kay Macpherson; president of Quebec's Council on the Status of Women Laurette Robillard; Laura Sabia, Ontario's chair of the Ontario Status of Women Council as well as the National Action Committee on the Status of Women; and lawyer Martha Hynna, who had been a research assistant with the Royal Commission on the Status of Women.

[61] These quotes and the ones that follow from the conference are contained in an unpublished typed transcript that I found among my papers. It will be placed in public archives.

[62] At that time, the Ontario Human Rights Code provided "No self-governing profession shall exclude from membership or expel or suspend any person or member because of race, creed, colour, age, sex, marital status, ancestry, or place of origin...."

[63] Reported by Mary Jane Mossman in "Contextualizing Bertha Wilson," (2008), 41 S.C.L.R. (2d), 15.

[64] Christopher Moore, *The Law Society of Upper Canada and Ontario's Lawyers 1797–1997*, (University of Toronto Press, 1997).

[65] In Canada, lawyers graduate with the licence to be both a solicitor and barrister. A barrister engages in litigation in the courts, whereas a solicitor does all legal work except court matters. Even though we are able to do both, many lawyers choose whether or not to do litigation as part of their practice.

[66] Laura Legge, Transcript of Interview, Archives of the Law Society of Upper Canada, July 29, 2004, at 54 and 61, cited by Mary Jane Mossman in "Contextualizing Bertha Wilson," 14.

[67] Laura Legge, Transcript of Interview, 101, cited in Mossman "Contextualizing Bertha Wilson," 16 and 30.

[68] At the request of the editors, I wrote a eulogy for the Ontario Bar Association's Family Law Section's Matrimonial Affairs newsletter when she passed away in 2010 at age 87, and I described her as "a pioneer and an exemplar of integrity and service to her clients" (*Matrimonial Affairs*, vol. 22, no. 2, November 2010).

[69] Stephen Harper's Conservative minority government, upon taking office in 2006, changed the funding criteria for the Status of Women Canada's Women's Program, to bar women's equality advocacy groups from receiving funding and challenge their charitable status. NAWL was one of numerous women's organizations affected. With its funding cut to the core, NAWL faced extinction. In September 2007, NAWL closed its national office and laid off all its staff. Somehow, to their credit, a small volunteer cadre has continued on a modest level.

[70] www.collectionscanada.gc.ca/women/030001-1108-e.html.

[71] *Attorney General of Canada* v. *Lavell*, [1974] S.C.R. 1349, 1973 CanLII 175 (SCC) 38 D.L.R. (3d) 481; 11 R.F.L. 333.

[72] These included individuals and such groups as the Alberta Committee on Indian Rights for Indian Women, University Women's Club of Toronto, and North Toronto Business and Professional Women's Club.

[73] Powerful feminist lobbying resulted in this wording in the 1982 Charter, section 15 (1): "Every individual is equal before and under the law and has the right to the equal protection and equal benefit of the law without discrimination...."

[74] This is an excerpt from a letter that Jean Chrétien sent to the conference coordinator, Gabriella Lang, dated April 10, 1974, which is part of the proceedings of the National Conference on Women and the Law.

[75] What also helped was the new Charter of Rights and Freedoms that took effect in 1985. Sandra Lovelace took up the battle and brought the issue to the United Nations International Human Rights Commission, which ruled in her favour. In 1985, section 12(1)(b) of the Indian Act was repealed by the government of Canada. However, the children continued to be disenfranchised. In 2009 Sharon McIvor won her struggle to change this, although the law continues to be unsettled on how to truly reinstate the descendants of the women who lost Status.

[76] *Thompson* v. *Thompson* [1961] S.C.R. 3, 1960 CanLII 14 (SCC).

[77] *Murdoch* v. *Murdoch* [1975] 1 S.C.R. 423 at 444.

[78] *Murdoch* v. *Murdoch* [1975] 1 S.C.R. 423 at 445.

[79] *Murdoch* v. *Murdoch* [1975] 1 S.C.R. 423.

[80] In 1976, Irene Murdoch eventually won a $65,000 lump sum of support, secured against one-quarter of the ranch. Mr. Justice Bowen of the Alberta Supreme Court, through an inventive use of the law, proceeded on her counter-petition for corollary relief, even though the husband had already secured the divorce itself. Her husband had to pay most of her legal costs of the proceeding before Mr. Justice Bowen. See *Murdoch* v. *Murdoch*, 1976 CanLII 260 (AB QB); [1977] 1 W.W.R. 16; 1 Alta LR (2d) 135; 26 R.F.L. 1.

[81] *Chatelaine*, January 1974, cited in Valerie J. Korolnek, "The *Chatelaine* Legacy," in *Canadian Woman Studies Journal,* vol. 26, no. 2, 2007, 14–21.

[82] This was a group formed in 1972 to press for implementing the recommendations of the Royal Commission on the Status of Women. Its formation was reported by *Globe and Mail* society columnist Zena Cherry with the words "Here, one hopes, is a more calm group than some of the other radical ones." She also reported that the initial Steering Committee was composed of Aline Gregory, Lynn McDonald, Lorna Marsden, Aideen Nicholson, and Brigid O'Reilly.

[83] Margaret Weiers, *Toronto Star*, "Women want the law to be fair to them and men, too," October 30, 1974.

[84] Mary Cornish focused on labour and employment law and spearheaded the Equal Pay Coalition; Lynn King practised family law and became a family court judge and author; Harriet Sachs practised family law and became a bencher and Superior Court judge; Geraldine Waldman practised family law and was appointed a family court judge.

[85] Beth Symes practised administrative law and civil litigation regarding equality rights and employment, becoming first chair of the Ontario Pay Equity Hearings Tribunal and a bencher; Frances Kiteley was a family law lawyer, bencher, and Superior Court judge; Elizabeth McIntyre is a labour and human rights lawyer.

[86] Aitken Greenberg practiced family and employment law. Shirley Greenberg went on to make major contributions to women. In 2005, she endowed the Shirley Greenberg Chair for Women and the Legal Profession at the University of Ottawa Faculty of Law, as well as the Shirley E. Greenberg Centre for Women's Health at the Ottawa Hospital.

[87] It was therefore particularly gratifying when, in 2006, the Law Society bestowed on me its highest honour—the Law Society Medal.

[88] The provincial family court dealt with custody and support, but not property. So people with property needing any family law rulings went to the higher courts.

[89] *Thomas* v. *Lindsay* (1976) 13 O.R. (2d), 530.

[90] *Lesser* v. *Lesser* (1985) 44 R.F.L. (2d) 255 (H.C.J. Walsh, J.); affirmed (1985) 51 O.R. (2d) 100 (Ont. C.A.); [1985] O.J. No. 650 (Walsh J.).

[91] Among first-wave feminists, Marie Gérin-Lajoie was notable for writing about the laws affecting women under the Quebec Civil Code, in her *Treatise on Everyday Law*, first published in 1902. Nellie McClung wrote many books including *In Times Like These* (Toronto: McLeod and Allen, 1915), which she dedicated "to men and women everywhere who love a fair deal, and are willing to give it to everyone, even women…"

[92] Ramsay Cook and Wendy Mitchinson, eds., *The Proper Sphere: Woman's Place in Canadian Society* (Oxford University Press [Canadian Branch], 1976).

[93] Pat Kincaid was an educator. After the book was completed, she occasionally asked me to speak at events for teachers and, later, asked me to be on the advisory board of Women in Educational Administration of Ontario, a group of senior women in the schools. I served on it for many years and met some remarkable women in the process, including the eminent Ursula Franklin.

[94] *Toronto Star,* February 11, 1978, "For Canadian women: Law primer's a cliff-hanger," review by Anne Carey.

[95] *Canadian Journal of Research on Women*, OISE, Spring 1978, review by Margret Andersen. She also added, "Abortion is treated tactfully, completely and without sentimentality."

[96] *University of Toronto Faculty of Law Review* (1978) 36 (1) U.T. Fac. L. Rev. 150, review by Margaret McCallum. She quoted this from the book: "It used to be said that the hand that rocks the cradle rules the world. Out of this metaphor arose many romantic assumptions which many women mistakenly accepted."

[97] *Globe and Mail*, September 11, 1974.

[98] *Globe and Mail*, April 28, 1975.

[99] *Globe and Mail*, December 13, 1976.

[100] See Linda Silver Dranoff, *Women in Canadian Life: Law*, 76. In 1979, 47.4 percent of married women were employed, accounting for one in four employed women. See Alvin Finkel, *Our Lives: Canada after 1945* (James Lorimer, 1997; 2nd ed., 2012).

[101] Brandt et al., *Canadian Women: A History*, 531.

[102] Linda Silver Dranoff, *Every Canadian's Guide to the Law*, 4th edition (Harper Collins, 2011), 128. This rose to 58.3 percent in 2006.

[103] Dranoff, *Every Canadian's Guide to the Law*, 128. This soared to 73 percent in 2009.

[104] Dranoff, *Every Canadian's Guide to the Law*, 129. By 1999, this rose to 66 percent and 69.4 percent by 2006.

[105] Dranoff, *Every Canadian's Guide to the Law*, 129. This rose to 61 percent in 1999 and 64.3 percent by 2006.

[106] See *Bliss* v. *Attorney General of Canada* [1979] 1 S.C.R. 183. It was not until 1989 that the Supreme Court of Canada ruled that discrimination on the basis of pregnancy was the same as discrimination on the basis of sex, using the 1985 Charter of Rights and Freedoms. *Brooks* v. *Canada Safeway Ltd.* [1989] 1 S.C.R. 1219. LEAF was an intervener in this case.

[107] Dranoff, *Every Canadian's Guide to the Law*, 129. Statistics were not even collected about daycare until 1971, when there were only 17,391 regulated daycare spaces in Canada for children under age thirteen. By 2001, there were

593,430 daycare spaces, but this didn't come close to meeting the need. That same year there were 3,308,700 children under age 13 in Canada who had mothers in the paid labour force.

[108] *Toronto Star*, September 15, 1980.

[109] There were a few private child-care organizations that started to rent space in schools in the 1980s, such as PLASP (Peel Lunch and After School Program) in the Regional Municipality of Peel. In Toronto, the Victoria Day Nursery and West End Crèche were longstanding organizations primarily focused on welfare mothers.

[110] This ground-breaking book documents the at-that-time-unknown pervasiveness of sexual harassment: Constance Backhouse and Leah Cohen, *The Secret Oppression: Sexual Harassment of Working Women* (Macmillan, 1979). Constance Backhouse shared some of the events that surrounded the early feminist efforts to eradicate sexual harassment in Constance B. Backhouse, "Sexual Harassment: A Feminist Phrase That Transformed the Workplace" (2012), *Canadian Journal of Women and the Law,* 24:2: 275–300. Available at SSRN: http://ssrn.com/abstract=2268095.

[111] Bill 7, An Act to revise and extend Protection of Human Rights in Ontario.

[112] This is the equivalent of about $17,000 in 2016.

[113] In 1997, Ontario instituted the first specialized domestic violence courts in Canada.

[114] *R. v. Lavallee* [1990] 1 S.C.R. 852.

[115] *R. v. Seaboyer* [1991] 2 S.C.R. 577

[116] See Dranoff, *Every Canadian's Guide to the Law*, 293–94, 308–11.

[117] See Brandt et al., *Canadian Women: A History*, 566–70 for the background and events. See also Mary Eberts, "Women and Constitutional Renewal" in CACSW, *Women and the Constitution in Canada* (CACSW, 1981).

[118] This story is told by Doris Anderson in her book, *Rebel Daughter: An Autobiography* (Key Porter, 1996).

[119] The story is told in detail by Penney Kome, *The Taking of Twenty-Eight: Women Challenge the Constitution* (Women's Press, 1983).

[120] Peter W. Hogg, *Constitutional Law of Canada* (Thomson Canada Ltd., 2003), 1117.

[121] Jean Chrétien was then federal minister of justice. Roy Romanow was the attorney general of Saskatchewan and Roy McMurtry was the attorney general of Ontario.

[122] Letter from Premier Bill Davis to Lynne Gordon, December 8, 1981.

[123] At the time, Aboriginal (or Native Peoples) was the preferred term.

[124] Provincial governments in Alberta, Saskatchewan, and Quebec, as well as the Yukon Territory, did invoke the notwithstanding clause more than fifteen times, but so far, it has had little real impact. Either the attempt was abandoned or overruled by a court.

[125] M. Elizabeth Atcheson, Mary Eberts, Beth Symes, and Jennifer Stoddart, *Women and Legal Action: Precedents, Resources and Strategies for the Future* (Canadian Advisory Council on the Status of Women, 1984).

[126] The Ontario Council on the Status of Women continued for another thirteen years, until its existence was terminated by the government of Progressive Conservative premier Mike Harris in April 1996.

[127] In the same year, the Alberta and Saskatchewan Law Reform Commissions also issued their reports.

[128] All Canadian provinces except Quebec are governed by common law. Quebec is ruled by the Civil Code, which in 1970 was changed to provide for the equal division of property acquired during marriage.

[129] "...to recognize that child care, household management, and financial provision are the joint responsibilities of the spouses and that inherent in the marital relationship there is joint contribution, whether financial or otherwise, by the spouses to the assumption of these responsibilities, entitling each spouse to an equal division of the family assets..."

[130] Karen Weiler is now a judge on the Ontario Court of Appeal.

[131] See the Report on Family Law, Ontario Law Reform Commission, 189, Summary of Recommendations, chapter 4, no. 2, "The matrimonial property regime should be the basic regime for Ontario, applying to all persons married after the effective date of the legislation by which it is created..."

[132] Legislation was passed by Manitoba and Prince Edward Island in 1978, Alberta and British Columbia in 1979, Saskatchewan, Newfoundland, and Nova Scotia in 1980, and New Brunswick in 1981. See Atcheson, Eberts, Symes and Stoddart, *Women and Legal Action* (Canadian Advisory Council on the Status of Women, 1984), 28.

[133] At that time, there was only one woman on the Ontario Court of Appeal—the first ever—Madam Justice Bertha Wilson, appointed in 1976. Later, on March 4, 1982, just before the *Leatherdale* case reached the Supreme Court of Canada, she became the first woman appointed to the Supreme Court. There had been a lobby campaign to persuade Prime Minister Pierre Trudeau and Justice Minister Jean Chrétien to appoint the first woman to the Supreme Court of Canada. In February 1982, the Ontario Council on the Status of Women, while I was a member, lobbied for the appointment of the first woman to the Supreme Court of Canada.

[134] The Women's Legal Education and Action Fund became active in 1985, once the equality sections of the Charter of Rights and Freedoms were proclaimed into law.

[135] The Court Challenges program was created in 1985 and cancelled in 1992, both by the Progressive Conservative government of Brian Mulroney; its purpose was to provide financial assistance to important cases in order to advance equality rights. In 1994, the Chrétien Liberal government reinstated the program, but it was cancelled again by the Harper Conservative government in 2006.

[136] Michele Landsberg was a passionate writer and activist for feminist issues throughout her career as a columnist, mostly at the *Toronto Star*. See Michele Landsberg, *Writing the Revolution* (Feminist History Society and Second Story Press, 2011).

[137] *Murdoch* v. *Murdoch* [1975] 1 S.C.R. 423; *Rathwell* v. *Rathwell* [1978] 2 S.C.R. 436; *Becker* v. *Pettkus* [1980] 2 S.C.R. 844.

[138] Indirect contribution means that a woman who does housework and raises children enables her husband to save up for a home.

[139] The law of constructive and resulting trust arose from interpretations by judges in cases that came before them, and it said that a person who uses another's money or labour and applies it to acquire assets may owe some portion of the proceeds to that person.

[140] *Leatherdale* v. *Leatherdale* [1982] 2 S.C.R. 743, 30 R.F.L. (2d) 225 (SCC); (1980), 31 O.R. (2d) 141, (1980), 19 R.F.L. (2d) 148 (Ont. C.A.); (1980) 14 R.F.L. (2d) 263 (HCJ).

[141] "Party and party" costs are defined as a portion of a winning party's costs to be paid by the losing party. The amount usually ended up at about one-quarter of the actual costs incurred, so half of these would represent one-eighth of a litigant's actual costs.

[142] *Globe and Mail*, December 7, 1982.

[143] *Globe and Mail*, December 8, 1982.

[144] *Toronto Star*, March 7, 1983.

[145] *Globe and Mail*, March 17, 1983.

[146] March 24, 1983.

[147] *Toronto Star*, "Most feel divorce courts must pay housewife: Poll," February 28, 1983.

[148] In these hectic days, I appeared on numerous television and radio shows, including City TV's *Sweet City Women* and *You're Beautiful*; Women's Television network; TV Ontario's *Speaking Out, Policy Options*, and *Moneysworth*; CBC TV's *Fifth Estate, In Touch, Take Thirty*, and *Midday*; CTV's *Canada AM, The Shirley Show, Lifetime, Joyce Davidson Show*, and *Toronto Today*; Global TV's *Daybreak* and *Point Blank*; CHCH TV's *The Cherington Show;* CBC Radio's *Metro Morning, Radio Noon, Later the Same Day*, and *As It Happens*; and CFRB's *Andy Barrie Show, Valerie Pringle Show,*

and *Betty Kennedy Show,* among others.

[149] Including Humber College Centre for Women, the North York Board of Education, the Toronto Board of Education, the Metro Toronto Separate School Board, Canadian Advisory Council on the Status of Women, National Association of Women and the Law, the Law Union, Canadian Federation of University Women, Canadian Bankers Association, the Granite Club, Association of Women Executives, and numerous women's organizations and other organizations.

[150] The shadow cabinet was composed of Opposition members who each focused on one cabinet post; for example, one person would specialize in keeping up to date on foreign affairs, another on agriculture, and so on.

[151] Letter dated August 25, 1983.

[152] Mr. McMurtry referred to this in his White Paper on Family Law Amendment, November 13, 1984, 2.

[153] *Globe and Mail*, January 12, 1984.

[154] This matter had not been raised at the Supreme Court of Canada.

[155] *Toronto Star*, "No-Fault Divorce makes sense but Support Rules too weak," February 10, 1984.

[156] Robyn Diamond was the first director of Manitoba's Family Law Branch of the Attorney General's department (1982) and has been since 1989 a judge of the Family Division of the Manitoba Court of Queen's Bench.

[157] A White Paper is an authoritative government policy document used to inform citizens about complex issues under review in order to seek their opinions.

[158] This document is dated November 21, 1984.

[159] In late 1984, the Ontario Council on the Status of Women, on which I had served between 1979 and 1982, was renamed the Ontario Advisory Council on Women's Issues.

[160] "Miller silent on women's equal pay question," by Jackie Smith, *Toronto Star*, April 16, 1985.

[161] *Toronto Star*, April 22, 1985.

[162] Denise Bellamy later became a judge of the Ontario Superior Court of Justice.

[163] *Globe and Mail*, June 7, 1986.

[164] A paper written by Constance Backhouse for a professionalism seminar at the Law Society resonated with me, as it showed the extent historically of male lawyers' bias against female lawyers, which extended to the bench and even to the Supreme Court of Canada. She noted that Madam Justice Claire

L'Heureux-Dubé characterized her early years on the Supreme Court as akin to an "old boys' club" where she and Madam Justice Bertha Wilson were "isolated" and "felt the sting of exclusion." pp. 2-14 and 2-15. Constance Backhouse, *Gender and Race in the Construction of "Legal Professionalism": Historical Perspectives*. www.lsuc.on.ca/media/constance_backhouse_gender_ and_race.pdf. She is Professor of Law and University Research Chair at the University of Ottawa.

[165] This was not generally known, but was told to me later by a member of the Section executive who had participated in the "uprising."

[166] Betty Friedan, *The Feminine Mystique* (W.W. Norton Co., 1963).

[167] For a thoughtful discussion of the differences between the American and Canadian women's movements, see Naomi Black, "Ripples in the Second Wave: Comparing the Contemporary Women's Movement in Canada and the United States" in Constance Backhouse and David Flaherty, eds., *Challenging Times: The Women's Movement in Canada and the United States* (McGill-Queen's University Press, 1992), 94–109.

[168] The commission was appointed by the Pierre Trudeau Liberal government on July 27, 1983 (Lloyd Axworthy was then minister of employment and immigration), but her report was presented to the Progressive Conservatives under Brian Mulroney, then in office. She reported to Flora MacDonald, minister of employment and immigration.

[169] See larger discussion of employment equity in Chapter 16.

[170] See Ian Scott, *To Make A Difference* (Stoddart, 2001), 154–58.

[171] *Toronto Star*, March 1, 1984.

[172] Later she was an Ontario cabinet minister in the David Peterson government and, after that, policy advisor to the federal Liberal government of Jean Chrétien in and after 1993.

[173] In 2014, the newly created Alliance for Women's Rights, a coalition of about one hundred organizations, championed a leaders' debate for the 2015 federal election with a focus on women's concerns, but was not able to get agreement from the political leaders. See www.UpForDebate.ca.

[174] Kay Sigurjonsson and the Federation of Women Teachers' Associations of Ontario (FWTAO) arranged for the Women's Debate to use one of the rooms set aside for the FWTAO annual meeting at the Royal York Hotel in Toronto.

[175] *Globe and Mail*, May 26, 1984.

[176] *Toronto Star*, September 2, 1984.

[177] *Toronto Star*, September 2, 1984.

[178] September 3, 1985.

[179] *Globe and Mail,* April 2, 1987.

[180] *Toronto Star*, March 1, 1990.

[181] The source for this is an email to me from Deborah Coyne, October 1, 2016.

[182] For a discussion of the women's campaign against the Meech Lake and Charlottetown Accords, see Brandt et al., *Canadian Women*, 433 and 568–70.

[183] Cathy Dunphy reported on it for the *Toronto Star*, October 20, 1987. Participants included Beth Atcheson, Mary Eberts, Liz Simpson, Lillian Ma, Barbara Cameron, and Linda Nye.

[184] Clyde Wells became premier on May 5, 1989, smack in the middle of the efforts to ratify the Meech Lake Accord. He remained premier until January 26, 1996.

[185] As reported in the *Globe and Mail*, August 1, 1989, by Jeffrey Simpson.

[186] Reported in the *Globe and Mail* on February 16, 1989.

[187] *Toronto Star*, November 29, 2006.

[188] Report of the Royal Commission on the Status of Women (Ottawa: Minister of Supply and Services, 1970), chapter 2, paragraph 103.

[189] Freya Kodar, "Pensions and Unpaid Work: A Reflection on Four Decades of Feminist Debate," *Canadian Journal of Women and the Law*, vol. 24, no. 1, 2012, pp. 180–206.

[190] *Canada (Minister of National Health and Welfare)* v. *Preece*, 1983 C.E.B. & P.G.R. 8914, 1983 LNCPEN 1 (QL).

[191] Letter dated July 4, 1986.

[192] Letter dated October 7, 1986.

[193] See Brandt et al., *Canadian Women: A History*, 535–36; also listen to an excellent radio documentary made in 2010 with some of the women who had been on the Caravan forty years earlier at www.cbc.ca/player/play/1487832337.

[194] Among them were Doris Anderson, Maude Barlow, Pierre Berton, Martha Butterfield, Barbara Caplan, June Callwood, Catherine Charlton, Nancy Coldham, Myra Sable Davidson, Judith Finlayson, Mary Geatros, Doris Giller, Nancy Ruth Jackman, Maryon Kantaroff, Margo Lane, Penny Lipsett, Helen Lucas, Colleen Mathieu, Maureen McTeer, Ruth Miller, Lorraine Monk, Marion Powell, Erika Ritter, Kathy Robinson, Malka Rosenberg, and Laura Sabia.

[195] The chair was Jane Hill and the steering committee included among its members Isabel Bassett, Dr. Elaine Borins, Martha Butterfield, Selma Edelstone, Suzanne Grew Ellis, Judith Finlayson, Dr. Charles Gold, Chaviva Hošek, Nancy Ruth Jackman, Alan Leal, Myra Sable, Beverley Salmon, Ethel Teitelbaum. An earlier effort in 1978 to establish the Toronto Women's Health

Clinic was not successful when the minister of health refused to give the necessary permissions.

[196] *Toronto Star* editorial, November 13, 1987.

[197] *Toronto Star*, July 22, 1989. This elicited a grateful (and for me, gratifying) letter to the editor on August 1, 1989: "Thank you for printing Linda Silver Dranoff's comments (No male consent needed for abortion) in the July 22 issue. At last, a calm, unemotional, informed opinion from a superbly trained lawyer on a subject which seems to cause a sort of hysteria in both pro and anti factions."

[198] *Toronto Star*, October 16, 1989.

[199] *National Post*, March 2, 1999.

[200] See the excellent article on this by Constance Backhouse, "Edward Greenspan: A Feminist Reflection on the Eulogies Surrounding His Death" in the *Canadian Journal of Women and the Law*, vol. 27, no. 2, 2015: 157–83. The quote is from p. 171. Also see *R. v. Ewanchuk* [1999] 1 S.C.R. 330.

[201] From Ursula Franklin's address at the University of Toronto commemorative service for the fourteen women murdered at the École Polytechnique de Montréal (now Polytechnique Montréal), January 19, 1990, reprinted in *Canadian Woman Studies*, vol. 11, no. 4 (1991).

[202] *Van Bork v. Van Bork* [1993] O.J. No. 2668 (trial decision of Justice Ellen Macdonald). Supplementary reasons at [1994] O.J. No. 3906, [1994] O.J. No. 3408.

[203] The Canadian Association of Retired Persons

[204] *Moge v. Moge* [1992] 3 S.C.R. 813.

[205] *Magder v. Magder* [1993] O.J. No. 1674 (Ont. Gen Div.); [1994] O.J. No. 1334 (Ont. C.A.).

[206] *Santosuosso v. Santosuosso* [1997] O.J. No. 501, 27 R.F.L. (4th) 234.

[207] *Bailey v. Plaxton*, 6 R.F.L. (5th) 29; 47 O.R. (3d) 593; [2000] O.J. No. 1187.

[208] *Bailey v. Plaxton*, 15 R.F.L. (5th) 16.

[209] Justice Bertha Wilson gave the speech at Osgoode Hall Law School on February 8, 1990, and it was published as well in the *Osgoode Hall Law Journal* at (1990), 28 O.H.L.J. 507. See also Ellen Anderson, *Judging Bertha Wilson: Law as Large as Life* (University of Toronto Press, 2002); Kim Brooks, ed., *Justice Bertha Wilson: One Woman's Difference* (UBC Press, 2009).

[210] *Andrews v. Andrews* [1999] 45 O.R. (3d) 577; 50 R.F.L. (4th), 1 (Ont. C.A.).

[211] Of the Faculty of Law, University of Toronto.

[212] Of the Schulich School of Law, Dalhousie University.

[213] See the federal Department of Justice website at http://www.justice.gc.ca/eng/fl-df/spousal-epoux/ssag-ldfpae.html.

[214] I can no longer recall how I came to have a copy of that internal memo that showed that the government knew that what they were planning was financially ill-advised and against the public interest. I imagine a disaffected staff member must have passed it along, knowing how concerned I was about the rights of women. I took my obligation to that whistle-blower so seriously that I did not keep a record of who provided it, and now have no recollection of who it might have been.

[215] Masters were officers of the court below the level of judge. In family law, they mostly heard interim motions that could be brought before the court on any date the applicant chose, provided the applicant gave the respondent at least two days' notice of the hearing. The role of Family Law Master was eventually eliminated.

[216] *Toronto Star,* Life section, October 15, 1987.

[217] *Toronto Star* Life section, "Child access complicated by new bill," July 16, 1987.

[218] Lenore J. Weitzman, *The Divorce Revolution: The Unexpected Social and Economic Consequences for Women and Children in America* (The Free Press, 1985).

[219] *Thibaudeau* v. *M.N.R.* [1994] 2 F.C.R. 189 (Federal Court of Appeal).

[220] *Toronto Star*, May 19, 1994.

[221] *Thibaudeau* v. *Canada* [1995] 2 S.C.R. 627 (Supreme Court of Canada).

[222] *Report of the Federal/Provincial/Territorial Family Law Committee*, at p. 90, n. 52.

[223] http://www.esdc.gc.ca/en/esdc/programs/volunteer_awards/index.page?&_ga=1.15212982.186478362.1471478552.

[224] He was premier from 1995 to 2002.

[225] The Red Book had been written primarily by Liberal policy advisor Chaviva Hošek, who had been a president of the National Action Committee on the Status of Women and a cabinet minister in the Ontario Liberal government of David Peterson.

[226] She is now a justice of the Supreme Court of Canada.

[227] *Globe and Mail*, April 15, 2009.

[228] Among those I recall now are Bev Salmon, Ann Johnston, June Rowlands,

Barbara Hall, and Olivia Chow for municipal politics; Flora MacDonald when she ran for the leadership of the federal Progressive Conservatives; federal Liberal Carolyn Bennett and federal NDP Lynn MacDonald; and Ontario Liberals Elinor Caplan, Chaviva Hošek, Sylvia Watson, and Laurel Broten.

[229] Doris Anderson, *The Unfinished Revolution: The Status of Women in Twelve Countries* (Doubleday Canada, 1991).

[230] An earlier multi-partisan and non-partisan group, formed in 1984 and calling itself the Committee for '94, had the goal of electing women to half the seats in the federal House of Commons by 1994. Prime movers included Sylvia Bashevkin, Gloria Bishop, Libby Burnham, Donna Dasko, Frances Lankin, Christina McCall, Wanda O'Hagan, and Rosemary Speirs. The group developed a policy brief calling for public funding of nomination contests, elections, and party leadership campaigns; ran campaign schools; sponsored a legislative internship in Ontario; and more. Many of these women were part of the creation of Equal Voice too.

[231] *Globe and Mail*, October 16, 2008.

[232] See Dranoff, *Every Canadian's Guide to the Law*, 221–30. In 1997, when I wrote the first edition of *Every Canadian's Guide to the Law*, same-sex rights could be summarized in two pages; by 2011, in the fourth edition, it took ten pages to tell the story.

[233] This was called *Everyone's Guide to the Law: A Handbook for Canadians* in the first two editions, published in 1997 and in 2001.

[234] *Globe and Mail*, December 13, 1976.

[235] *Toronto Star,* May 13, 1987.

[236] *Globe and Mail*, September 14, 2007.

[237] Despite promises of support from an overwhelming majority of party members when she ran in 1976 as party leader, she lost by a wide margin. It was widely agreed that this was a result of sexism.

[238] *Globe and Mail*, October 25, 1986.

[239] *Globe and Mail*, August 4, 2008.

[240] *Globe and Mail*, April 28, 1975.

[241] *Toronto Star*, October 10, 2005.

[242] *Globe and Mail*, October 31, 2006.

[243] These are just a few: Doris Anderson, Sylvia Bashevkin, Laurel Broten, Mary Cornish, Brenda Cossman, Mary Eberts, Marlys Edwardh, Fay Faraday, Mary Lou Fassel, Ursula Franklin, Kathleen Lahey, Michele Landsberg, Laura Legge, Madam Justice Claire L'Heureux-Dubé, Barbara Jackman, Eva Ligeti, Dianne Martin, Carissima Mathen, Marilou McPhedran, Angela Miles, Mary

Jane Mossman, Helena Orton, Susan Rowland, Michelle Swenarchuk, Beth Symes, Lorraine Weinrib, and Julie White.

[244] www.oba.org/Sections/Women-Lawyers-Forum/A-Bit-of-History.

[245] See the book on the Ontario Committee on the Status of Women, forthcoming in 2017-2018, by Elizabeth Atcheson and Lorna Marsden, eds., to be published as part of the Feminist History Society series by Second Story Press. OCSW briefs and other archival materials may be found at http://yorkspace.library.yorku.ca/xmlui/handle/10315/2712.

[246] The Organizing Committee was Carolyn Bennett, Barbara Caplan, Joan Chalmers, Marilyn Churley, Kamala-Jean Gopie, Lyndsay Green, Barbara Hall, Marcia McClung, Marilou McPhedran, Jane Pepino, and Shelagh Wilkinson. Committee Members were Sally Armstrong, Moira Bacon, Sylvia Bashevkin, Libby Burnham, Sen. Catherine Callbeck, Sherrill Cheda, Kiki Delaney, Linda Silver Dranoff, Mary Eberts, Sylvia Fraser, Dina Graser, Lee Gold, Renata Hervey, Hon. Flora MacDonald, Rona Maynard, Maureen McTeer, Wanda O'Hagan, Virginia Rock, Beverley Rockett, Nancy Ruth Jackman, Kay Sigurjonsson, and Judy Steed.

INDEX

David, Rodica, 75, 190–191
Davidson, Myra Sable, 207, 225, 329
Davies, Christine, 63
Davis, Premier William G. (Bill), 117, 118, 137, 141, 142, 165, 183, 185
daycare (*See also* child care), 45-47, 58, 123, 206, 297–298, 308–309
DeGuire, Patricia, 314, 320
Dempsey, Lotta, 9
Demson, Sandra, 260, 320
Denis, Marilyn, 11, 200
Derrick, Anne, 317
Diamond, Robyn, 177–178
Dickens, Bernard, 225
Dickson, Brian, 155, 156
Dickson, Mary Louise, 128–129
Dion, Stéphane, 303
discrimination (*See also* women, discrimination in employment), 1, 7, 8, 11, 26-27, 34, 47-48, 52–55, 59, 66, 67, 109, 133
disinherited spouse, 125–129, 141, 164, 168, 170, 186, 193,
Dispute Resolution in Family Law: Protecting Choice, Promoting Inclusion (Boyd report), 258–259
divorce, 2, 6, 41, 52, 70, 71, 73, 79, 82–83, 85, 87–88, 99–102, 104, 107, 109, 115, 125, 127, 129, 141, 143–144, 146, 151, 161, 166, 170, 173, 174, 181, 193, 205, 206, 217–219, 256, 263–266, 269, 273–277, 286–289, 292, 294, 309, 310
Divorce Act (1968), 71, 73, 99, 100–101, 143, 173, 206
Divorce Act (1985), 265, 277
divorce, protection of children, 273–294
Dnieper, Robert, 59
domestic violence (*See* violence against women)
Don, Trudy, 130, 322
Doris Anderson Graduate Scholarship (York University), 323
Dranoff, Beth, 40-41, 45-47, 56-58, 75, 92, 116, 153-154, 233-234, 236-237, 243
Dranoff, Linda Silver, as a reader, 21
Dranoff, Linda Silver, as activist, 1, 13, 28–32, 48–49, 94, 95, 116-142, 151-179, 181-197, 199-227, 236, 257, 296, 325

Dranoff, Linda Silver, as advocate, 40–112
Dranoff, Linda Silver, as debater, 24, 32–34, 154
Dranoff, Linda Silver, as public speaker, 24, 27–28, 52, 64-66, 74, 110–111, 138-140, 141, 199–201, 233, 260,
Dranoff, Linda Silver, as single mother, 45–47, 58, 75, 234
Dranoff, Linda Silver, as writer, 1, 2, 12-13, 48-49, 52-55, 103–109, 116, 141, 166-167, 199, 201-202, 236, 295–296, 300-301, 307–313
Dranoff, Linda Silver, childhood, 17–22
Dranoff, Linda Silver, family life, 1, 9, 12, 92, 95, 103, 233–234, 237, 238, 243, 295, 327, 328
Dranoff, Linda Silver, father of, 19-21, 22, 26, 32-33, 45, 68–69, 78, 234, 238, 241–242, 243, 327
Dranoff, Linda Silver, high school life, 23–24
Dranoff, Linda Silver, interest in public policy, 12, 13, 27, 117, 123, 168, 199, 214, 233, 235–236, 287, 312
Dranoff, Linda Silver, law practice, 77-80, 81-89, 95-103, 148-158, 173-176, 218-220, 234-236, 245-257, 278-286
Dranoff, Linda Silver, mother of, 17, 19-20, 23-24, 25, 26, 40, 69, 78-80, 234, 237-238, 243
Dranoff, Linda Silver, personal life, 37-41, 92-94, 183-184, 236-238
Dranoff, Linda Silver, personal choices, 236–238
Dranoff, Linda Silver, professional choices, 234–236
Dranoff, Linda Silver, recognition of professional work, 241–244
Dranoff, Linda Silver, retirement, 296
Dranoff, Linda Silver, studying law, 45–57
Dranoff, Linda Silver, siblings of, 17-18, 25, 61, 68, 234, 243, 326
Dranoff, Linda Silver, university life, 25–35
Du Vernet, Carruthers, Beard, and Eastman, 56, 57–61, 89
Du Vernet, Ernest, 59–60
Duckworth, Muriel, 9

Mixed Member Proportional
(MMP), 305–307
Model Parliament (University of
Toronto), 27-28
Moge v. *Moge*, 262–263, 266
Moore, Christopher, 67
Morden, John W., 150
Morgentaler, Henry, 68, 105,
220–226
Morton, Desmond, 210
Mossman, Mary Jane, 11–12, 314
Mowat, Farley, 210
MPs salaries, 111, 312
Mulroney, Brian, 199, 206, 207–210,
215–216, 218, 224–225, 295, 299, 302,
324
Murdoch case, 71–74, 75, 144, 154,
155, 162, 179
Murphy, Emily, 7–8

National Action Committee on the
Status of Women (NAC), 51–52, 70,
112, 133, 161, 184–185, 190, 206, 217,
225, 227, 291, 321, 324, 329
National Ad Hoc Committee on the
Status of Women, 52
National Association of Women and
the Law, (NAWL), 49, 67–68, 112,
154, 190, 225, 227, 321, 324
National Council of Women
(NCW), 8
National Day of Remembrance and
Action on Violence against Women,
227
National Indian Brotherhood (now
the Assembly of First Nations), 70
National Post, 227
NDP (New Democratic Party), 161,
163, 170, 185, 186–189, 202, 204–207,
209, 258, 297, 301, 307
Nellie's, 328
Nelson, Clifford, 165
New Brunswick Council on the
Status of Women, 213
new reproductive technologies, 316
Newman, Elaine, 101
Niman, Harold, 265–266
Nixon, Richard, pardon of, 111
"no means no," 132–133
non-smokers' rights, 308
"notwithstanding clause, the" of the
Charter, 133–139,

O'Neil, Kathleen, 229
Oakwood Collegiate, 23–24
Obiter Dicta, 48–49
OCSW, *See* Ontario Council on the
Status of Women
Ontario Advisory Council on
Women's Issues, 186, 213
Ontario Arbitration Act (1991),
257–258
Ontario Bar Association (OBA;
formerly Canadian Bar Association–
Ontario), 128, 168, 189, 192, 195, 241,
257, 272, 288, 314-316, 318
Ontario Committee on the Status
of Women, 73–75, 110, 112, 146,
184–185, 321
Ontario Council on the Status
of Women (OCSW), 75–76, 110,
116–142, 124, 125, 128–129, 130, 133,
137, 140–142, 162, 164, 165, 168–170,
203, 204
Ontario Court of Appeal, 101,
149–152, 153, 169, 252, 254, 263
Ontario Courts Inquiry, 269
Ontario Government Standing
Committee reviewing sexual
harassment, 124
Ontario Human Rights Code 1981
amendments, 124, 141
Ontario Law Reform Commission
(OLRC) Report on Family Law,
73–75, 128, 143, 144, 145–146, 147,
159,171, 190, 192, 257
Ontario Liberal Women's
Perspective Advisory Committee,
165, 190, 193
Ontario Pension Benefits Act
(1987; *See also* Canada Pension Plan
and pension reform *and* pension
sharing), 255
Ontario Progressive Conservative
Women's Policy Conference, 110
Ontario Public School Men
Teachers Federation, 324
Ontario Women's Directorate
(OWD), 142, 193, 278
op-ed articles, 137-138, 169-170, 173,
204, 208, 211-212, 224, 233, 271, 288,
292, 297
Order of Canada, 243–244
Orton, Helena, 139, 262
Osgoode Hall Law Journal, 55

War Measures Act, 205
Waterman, Jay, 24, 60, 61, 77–79
Waye, Ashley, 315
Wednesday Women, 322
Weiers, Margaret, 10, 75–76, 104
Weiler, Karen, 74, 145–147
Weinrib, Lorraine, 260
Weitzman, Lenore, 286
Welch, Robert, 74, 142, 185–186
Wells, Clyde, 215
Wente, Margaret, 259–260
Westmoreland-Traoré, Juanita, 12
White, Julie, 322
widowed persons, rights of, 125–129, 181, 186, 193
Wieland, Joyce, 11
"Wife Battering in Canada: The Vicious Circle" 130
Wilkinson, Shelagh, 134, 228, 229, 322
"Will Women Judges Really Make a Difference" (Justice Bertha Wilson speech), 266
Wills and Trusts section of the CBA-O, 128-129
Wilson, Bertha, 131, 221, 266, 268, 316, 318–321, 328
Wilson, Cairine, 8
Wilson, Janet, 263, 266
Winter, Richard, 60
WLAO President's Award, 49
Women and the Constitution in Canada, 134
"Women as Lawyers in Toronto," published article, 55
Women in Canadian Life: Law, 89, 104–106, 310
Women in Educational Administration Ontario (WEAO), 1, 233, 321
Women in Canadian Life series, 104
"Women in the Law School, the Law Firm, and the Legal Profession" panel, 63-66
Women's Debate (1984), 205-207
"Women's Issues: Policy Suggestions and Analysis," Nov. 21, 1984, prepared for Roy McMurtry, 184
Women Lawyers' Forum (WLF; *See also* Feminist Legal Analysis Section/Committee), 318, 320

women, abuse of (*See* violence against women)
women, as judges, 12, 63, 64, 67, 74, 75, 88, 132, 227, 264, 265, 266, 291-292, 318, 328
women, defined as persons, 8
women, discrimination in employment, 6, 8, 10, 45, 52–54, 55–56, 65-66, 69, 115, 120–121, 129, 201, 204, 299-300, 327
women, in law, 7, 11–12, 316–317, 318–320
women, in politics, 6–7, 10–11, 199, 209, 304, 316, 326, 328–329
women, serving on juries, 8
Women's Bureau of the federal Department of Labour, 8
Women's Law Association of Ontario (WLAO), 49, 53, 66, 170–171
Women's Legal Education and Action Fund (LEAF), 139–140, 152, 202, 227, 241, 262, 291, 302, 321, 324, 327, 328
women's lib movement, 49–50
Women's Liberation Law (field of law), development of, 48–49
Women's Lobby Coalition, 184–185
Women's Movement for Suffrage, 9
women's movement, 2, 9, 63, 67, 68, 74, 115, 116, 121, 132, 133, 161, 199, 201, 202, 205–207, 209, 233, 241, 276–277, 296, 300, 302–303, 324, 325, 327, 329
Women's Place, 52, 104
women's studies, 10
Woods, Susan, 322
work-life balance, 92–94
Working Income Supplement, 293
working with clients, 95–103
Workmen's Circle, 22
World War II, 7
Wrye, Bill, 170
Wychwood Public Library, 21
Wyman, Ken, 31–32

York University, 10, 12, 46-49, 323
You're Beautiful, (City TV) 111
YWCA, 52, 184–185, 259, 322

ACKNOWLEDGMENTS

This story has taken me many years to write. Having lived it, I then relived it through the files and boxes of archival material I had retained and through the prism of memory and recollection.

During this long and tortuous path, I had enthusiastic assistance. My literary agent Beverley Slopen was once again a solicitous guide in the publishing process. My astute and respectful editors Linda Pruessen and Kathryn White helped to structure and focus the complex tale into a narrative that flows. The Feminist History Society gave knowledgeable and perceptive advice. I appreciate the encouragement and support of Second Story Press's inimitable publisher Margie Wolfe and her talented team, including Emma Rodgers, Allie Chenoweth, Melissa Kaita, and Carolyn Jackson.

My own readers provided discerning insights, constructive comments, and unique perspectives. Special thanks go to Beth Dranoff, Ursula Franklin, Susan Gibson, Judith Huddart, Jack Marmer, and Judy Silver for their willingness to read—and in some cases, to reread and reread—a manuscript that was continually being revised and polished. I am also grateful to Beth Dranoff for the intriguing title.

I appreciate the lawyers and staff who backed me up in my practice over the years, my sisters in the women's movement who shared my goals, and my loving family who have cheered me on.

My story is itself a *thank you* to those who influenced and supported and encouraged me and their contributions are present throughout the book.

ABOUT THE AUTHOR

LINDA SILVER DRANOFF, C.M., LSM is a lawyer, writer, and activist. As a lawyer she appeared at every level of court in a precedent-setting 38-year career, helping countless individuals to navigate the legal system. She had a 25-year stint as a columnist at *Chatelaine* and is the author of the books *Women in Canadian Life: Law*, *Every Woman's Guide to the Law* and *Every Canadian's Guide to the Law*. She successfully pressed for family law and other reforms, and was the founding chair of the Feminist Legal Analysis Section of the Ontario Bar Association (now the Women Lawyers Forum). Linda has been recognized many times for her legal work and activism by the women's community, the legal community, and beyond. In 2001 she received a Governor General's Award in Commemoration of the Persons Case, and in 2012 she was appointed to the Order of Canada. She lives in Toronto.

FEMINIST HISTORY SOCIETY

THE FEMINIST HISTORY SOCIETY is creating a lasting record of the women's movement in Canada and Quebec for the period between 1960 and the year of the Society's founding, 2010. We celebrate 50 years of activity and accomplishment by creating a written legacy, for ourselves, our families and friends, our communities, students, and scholars. The books we publish will be as spirited and diverse as the movement itself, meant to stand together and to encourage and challenge those who follow.

Feminism has a history that predates the 1960s and will continue long after 2010, but our series is intended to encompass events during these lively years. In 1960, the Voice of Women was founded. The decade of the 1960s also saw the appointment of the Royal Commission on the Status of Women and the creation of "women's liberation" groups across the country. That was just the beginning. Now is the time to take stock of what we did and how we did it.

Book topics will be as diverse as our wide-ranging campaigns for equality through transformative social, economic, civil, political, and cultural change. We make every effort to be inclusive of gender, race, class, geography, culture, dis/ability, language, sexual identity, and age. Individuals and organizations who participated in the movement are encouraged to contribute.

This is the eighth book in the Feminist History Society series.